TAX, SOCIAL POLICY
AND GENDER
RETHINKING EQUALITY AND EFFICIENCY

TAX, SOCIAL POLICY
AND GENDER
RETHINKING EQUALITY AND EFFICIENCY

EDITED BY MIRANDA STEWART

Australian
National
University

PRESS

ANU PRESS

Published by ANU Press
The Australian National University
Acton ACT 2601, Australia
Email: anupress@anu.edu.au
This title is also available online at press.anu.edu.au

National Library of Australia Cataloguing-in-Publication entry

Creator: Stewart, Miranda, 1968- editor.

Title: Tax, social policy and gender : rethinking equality and
           efficiency / Miranda Stewart.

ISBN: 9781760461478 (paperback) 9781760461485 (ebook)

Subjects: Taxation--Government policy--Australia.
           Income tax--Law and legislation--Australia.
           Equality before the law--Australia.
           Gender mainstreaming--Australia.
           Women--Taxation--Law and legislation--Australia.

Cover design and layout by ANU Press

Contents

Part III: Human capital, savings and retirement

Part IV: Towards gender equality in the tax-transfer system

List of figures

List of tables

List of acronyms

ABS	Australian Bureau of Statistics
ADR	age dependency ratio
ALP	Australian Labor Party
ANTS	A New Tax System
ANU	The Australian National University
ASFA	Association of Superannuation Funds of Australia
ASSA	Academy of the Social Sciences in Australia
ATO	Australian Taxation Office
ATR	average tax rate
CCB	child care benefit
CCR	child care rebate
CDR	child dependency ratio
CEDA	Committee for Economic Development for Australia
CEDAW	Convention on the Elimination of All Forms of Discrimination Against Women
CGE	computable general equilibrium
DPMC	Department of Prime Minister and Cabinet
DSS	Department of Social Services
EMTR	effective marginal tax rate
FTB-A	family tax benefit part A
FTB-B	family tax benefit part B
GDI	gender development index
GDP	gross domestic product
GFC	Global Financial Crisis

GST	goods and services tax
HECS	Higher Education Contribution Scheme
HECS-HELP	Higher Education Contribution Scheme-Higher Education Loan Program
HES	Household Expenditure Survey
HILDA	Household, Income and Labour Dynamics in Australia
ICESCR	International Covenant on Economic, Social and Cultural Rights
IGR	Intergenerational Report
IMF	International Monetary Fund
IZA	Institute of Labor Economics
LITO	low income tax offset
LNP	Liberal–National Coalition Party
LSAC	Longitudinal Study of Australian Children
MABEL	Medicine in Australia: Balancing Employment and Life
MTR	marginal tax rate
NATSEM	National Centre for Social and Economic Modelling
NFAW	National Foundation for Australian Women
OECD	Organisation for Economic Co-operation and Development
OLS	ordinary least squares
PAYG	pay-as-you-go
PIT	personal income tax
PPL	paid parental leave (Australian Government universal scheme 2011)
PTR	participation tax rate
SIH	Survey of Income and Housing
SG	Superannuation Guarantee
SNSF	Swiss National Science Foundation
TDR	total dependency ratio
TFR	total fertility rate

TTPI	Tax and Transfer Policy Institute
TUS	Time Use Survey
UN	United Nations
VAT	value added tax
WEL	Women's Electoral Lobby
WGEA	Workplace Gender Equality Agency
WHO	World Health Organization
WiSER	Women in Social and Economic Research (Curtin University)

Note: Throughout the book, dollar figures refer to Australian dollars, unless otherwise indicated.

Contributors

Patricia Apps, Professor of Public Economics, the University of Sydney Law School; Adjunct Professor, The Australian National University and the University of Technology, Sydney; Research Fellow of the Institute of Labor Economics (IZA), Germany.

Siobhan Austen, Professor of Economics, School of Economics and Finance, Curtin University; Director, Women in Social and Economic Reserach (WiSER).

Huong Dinh, Visiting Fellow, Research School of Population Health, The Australian National University.

Meredith Edwards, Emeritus Professor, Institute for Governance and Policy Analysis, University of Canberra.

Helen Hodgson, Associate Professor, Department of Taxation, Curtin Law School.

Guyonne Kalb, Professor and Director of Labour Economics and Social Policy Program, Melbourne Institute of Applied Economic and Social Research, University of Melbourne.

Kathleen Lahey, Professor and Queen's National Scholar, Faculty of Law, Queen's University, Canada.

Maria Racionero, Associate Professor, Research School of Economics, The Australian National University.

Kerrie Sadiq, Professor, School of Accountancy, Queensland University of Technology.

Rhonda Sharp AM, Adjunct Professor of Economics, University of South Australia.

Mathias Sinning, Associate Professor, Tax and Transfer Policy Institute, Crawford School of Public Policy, The Australian National University.

Julie Smith, Australian Research Council Future Fellow and Associate Professor, School of Regulation and Global Governance, The Australian National University.

Miranda Stewart, Professor and Director of the Tax and Transfer Policy Institute, Crawford School of Public Policy, The Australian National University; Professor, University of Melbourne School of Law.

Sarah Voitchovsky, Swiss National Science Foundation (SNSF) Research Fellow, Melbourne Institute of Applied Economic and Social Research, University of Melbourne.

Roger Wilkins, Professor and Deputy Director, Melbourne Institute of Applied Economics and Social Research, University of Melbourne; Deputy Director (Research), Household, Income and Labour Dynamics in Australia (HILDA) Survey.

Preface and acknowledgements

This volume arose out of an Academy of the Social Sciences in Australia (ASSA) workshop, 'Gender Equality in Australia's Tax and Transfer System', hosted by the Tax and Transfer Policy Institute (TTPI), Crawford School of Public Policy, The Australian National University (ANU). Grateful acknowledgements to the ASSA for funding the workshop; the ANU Gender Institute for supporting the visit by Professor Kathleen Lahey of Queen's University, Canada; and Women in Social and Economic Research (WiSER), Curtin University, for supporting travel of several participants.

The TTPI was established with an endowment from the Australian Treasury in 2013 and carries out policy-relevant research on taxes and transfers for public benefit. The research of TTPI focuses on key themes of economic prosperity, social equity and system resilience. Responding to the need to adapt Australia's tax and transfer system to meet contemporary challenges, TTPI seeks to inform public knowledge and debate on taxes and transfers in Australia, the region and the world. TTPI is committed to working with governments, other academic scholars and institutions, businesses and the community.

The ASSA Workshop Program aims to promote excellence in research in the social sciences, supporting collective intellectual work in the social sciences in Australia on issues of national concern. The workshop on 'Gender Equality in Australia's Tax and Transfer System' was co-convened by Professors Miranda Stewart, Peter Whiteford and Marian Sawer on 4–5 November 2015, bringing together 20 experienced and early-career researchers from the social science disciplines of economics, law, social policy and political science with representatives from government and community backgrounds to present new findings and debate this issue of contemporary importance to public policy. The workshop report is available on the ASSA website.

The aim of TTPI is to bring interdisciplinary perspectives to important research questions regarding the policy, design and operation of the tax-transfer system as a whole. The tax system and the transfer, or social security, system operate in combination to generate tax rates, income and asset tests and thresholds that differ, depending on the family structure, age and gender of individuals and families. Recognising gender inequality in the tax-transfer system and aiming to achieve gender equality is important for efficiency, equity and effectiveness of the tax-transfer system.

An understanding of the gender implications of the tax-transfer system is also critical to achieving government policy goals, such as increasing women's workforce participation, women's economic security in retirement or early childhood education and wellbeing. The tax-transfer system interacts with labour, housing and financial markets, affecting how individuals make work, saving and investment decisions in these markets. In turn, those decisions have consequences for individuals over the life course. These systematic interactions contribute to shaping women's family, social and working lives and economic wellbeing.

Both the ASSA workshop and this book have been a longstanding ambition of my own, and it is very exciting to present this volume in the Social Science series of ANU Press. I am grateful to the outstanding expert contributors to this volume who participated actively in the workshop and through various drafts, and have produced unique, novel contributions to the field.

Thanks also are due to Emily Millane and Lauren Murphy for excellent research assistance and to Diane Paul for her outstanding organisational skills. I am grateful to Professor Marian Sawer of the ANU College of Arts and Social Sciences and Professor Peter Whiteford of Crawford School for their support for the workshop and this project. I owe a debt to Professor Patricia Apps of the University of Sydney for her profound scholarship on gender in the tax system over the last few decades and to many outstanding scholars of tax and gender policy internationally, in particular the editors of the international collection *Challenging Gender Inequality in Tax Policy Making* (2011, Hart Publishing), Kim Brooks, Asa Gunnarson, Lisa Philipps and Maria Wersig, for inspiration.

Thanks to the Social Sciences Editorial Board of ANU Press, especially Professor Frank Bongiorno, for their speedy review and high standards for this volume. Acknowledgements to Beth Battrick for copy-editing and preparation of the index, Teresa Prowse for cover design and Emily Hazlewood and the team at ANU Press. All errors are, of course, my own.

Miranda Stewart
September 2017

Foreword

In '48 in one of my first classes in economics, I argued with my teacher (male) about the injustice of the female basic wage being less than that of a man. His response was that no one would employ women if they demanded equal pay.

Women's workforce participation has greatly expanded since then, we have seen successive challenges arguing for equal pay in the arbitration system—but, as the great Mary Gaudron said in 1979: 'We won equal pay for equal work in 1967. We won again in 1969 and again in 1972 and 1974. Yet we still do not have equal pay' (quoted in Burton 2010).

Those critical cases arguing for equal pay owed much to the work of women trade unionists including Edna Ryan (1984), who successfully presented the 1974 Women's Electoral Lobby (WEL) case for women to receive the adult minimum wage and was one of the 'founding mothers' of the National Foundation for Australian Women (NFAW).

Since the '70s, scholarly studies in economics, political science and other fields have greatly expanded our understanding of the extent of gender inequality built into the tax, health, education, retirement incomes, employment and social policies of our nation. Recently, the CEO of the Workplace Gender Equity Agency opined that at the current rate of change, it would take 50 years to get rid of the gender wage gap (Belot 2017).

On 6 July 2017, the Commonwealth Office for Women circulated *Towards 2025: An Australian Government strategy to boost women's workforce participation* (DPMC 2017). For all its shortcomings, the contrast between this strategy and the 'white picket fence' policies of the early Howard Government could not be greater.

That said, as this valuable book documents, inequality is built still into the very fabric of our policies. That must change.

In 2014, NFAW produced its first *Gender Lens* report on the Commonwealth 2014–15 Budget in response to the manifest unfairness of it. The report was produced by volunteers in a civil society organisation, after the fact and without access to government data or modelling capacity. Since then, our *Gender Lens* report has grown in coverage and sophistication. It has become an important contribution to public debate about the budget. But it cannot substitute for gender-aware policy formulation, for gender-aware budgeting by the government itself.

Australian women, and Australian society in general, need better gendered data, a reinstated Time Use Survey, policy that does not implicitly disadvantage women whatever their income, their social class, their disabilities or their ethnicities.

I commend the study of the entirety of this book to every politician hoping to obtain the votes of Australian women. And women—stand up for change.

Marie Coleman AO PSM DUniv.

References

Belot, Henry. 2017. 'Gender pay gap: Australian women could be paid less than men for another 50 years'. ABC News, 26 July. Available at: www.abc.net.au/news/2017-07-26/gender-pay-gap-women-could-be-paid-less-for-another-50-years/8745690

Burton, Pamela. 2010. *From Moree to Mabo: The Mary Gaudron Story*. Perth: UWA Publishing.

DPMC (Department of Prime Minister and Cabinet). 2017. *Towards 2025: An Australian Government Strategy to Boost Women's Workforce Participation*. Available at: womensworkforceparticipation.pmc.gov. au/

Ryan, Edna. 1984. *Two-thirds of a man*. Sydney: Hale & Iremonger.

Wright, Tony. 2016. 'In wanting what he'd been denied, John Howard picked two words and a fence to save career'. *Sydney Morning Herald*, 28 February. Available at: www.smh.com.au/federal-politics/political-news/in-wanting-what-hed-been-denied-john-howard-picked-two-words-and-a-fence-to-save-his-career-20160228-gn5k5r.html

1

Gender inequality in Australia's tax-transfer system

Miranda Stewart

During the 2016 Australian federal election, leaders on both sides of politics sought the 'women's vote'. Prime Minister-elect Malcolm Turnbull for the Liberal–National Coalition Party (LNP) declared himself a feminist, affirming equal opportunity for women and acknowledging that 'women hold up half the sky' (Grattan 2016). Opposition Leader Bill Shorten, of the Australian Labor Party (ALP), said on the eve of the election campaign that a Labor Government would champion 'the march of women to equality' (Shorten 2016).[1] Yet, in spite of these political commitments, there remain significant tensions and contradictions in core federal economic and fiscal policy affecting women and gender equality.

This volume focuses on gender inequality in two of Australia's main federal policy regimes: the tax system and the welfare or social security ('transfer') system, which together can be described as the tax-transfer system. The expert contributors to this volume from law, economics and social science backgrounds present novel theoretical and empirical research to deepen our understanding of the challenge of gender inequality in taxation, social security, child care, education, savings and retirement policy.

---

1   The politics and tensions on gender in the 2016 election are explored in more detail in Williams and Sawer (forthcoming).

The 2016 political commitments to gender equality by both sides of politics were not made in a vacuum. They built on some important, but incomplete, policy developments in the previous decade, which have been positive for gender equality. Many of these originated in the Rudd Labor Government of 2007, but have continued under subsequent LNP governments.

Financial support for child care in Australia has gradually expanded under governments of both stripes, and Australia has boosted the rate of four-year-olds in early childhood education to 85 per cent as a result of National Partnership Agreements commencing under the Rudd Labor Government in 2008 (Department of Education and Training 2017). In the 2017–18 Budget, the federal government extended this partnership funding for one year, to allow all four-year-old children to access 15 hours per week of kindergarten, but the future of this program remains uncertain. The Turnbull LNP Government enacted in 2016 a significantly expanded, although still means tested, child care subsidy to commence in 2018. The government acknowledges the need for improved child care as a necessary step in achieving increased women's workforce participation, which is an explicit government policy (DPMC 2017).

In 2011, the Rudd Labor Government introduced Australia's first paid parental leave (PPL) scheme. The subsequent LNP Government under Prime Minister Abbott appeared to support making this scheme more generous, although this was to be at the expense of other parts of the social security and welfare budget. After protracted and ultimately unsuccessful negotiations to cut social security expenditure following the 2014 budget (Leslie 2014), the PPL scheme has survived to date as enacted in 2011.

There is increased attention being paid to the gender pay gap since the Labor Government under Julia Gillard, Australia's first and only female prime minister, re-established the Workplace Gender Equality Agency (WGEA) in 2012 as a statutory federal agency charged with promoting and improving gender equality in Australian workplaces. WGEA had its origins in the Affirmative Action Agency, established under the *Affirmative Action (Equal Opportunity for Women) Act 1986* legislated by the Hawke Labor Government. WGEA has collected and published credible data over the past few years, demonstrating a persistent gender pay gap ranging from 15 per cent to more than 20 per cent (WGEA 2016).[2]

---

2   The reporting requirements of the Workplace Gender Equality Agency (WGEA) were reduced in 2015 as part of the government's 'red tape reduction strategy' (Harris Rimmer and Sawer 2016).

There is bipartisan support for gender equality in other areas. Prime Minister Gillard launched, with support from all state and territory governments, the National Plan to Reduce Violence against Women and their Children 2010–2022. The LNP Government has continued to implement it, developing the Third Action Plan 2016–2019.[3] In 2013, the Abbott LNP Government returned the Office for Women to the Department of Prime Minister and Cabinet, a move welcomed by women's groups. There has also been vocal support for increased representation of women in executive and leadership roles, although progress is slow and affirmative action and quotas have not been adopted. In the area of retirement and savings policy, there has been substantial public debate about women's disadvantage but little policy change. A recent bipartisan Senate report identified and criticised the significant imbalance in women's retirement savings in the superannuation system under the heading 'a husband is not a retirement plan' (Senate Economic References Committee 2016).

The growing policy work and political debate on gender inequality is heartening, but there remain significant gender gaps in work, care, education, employment and retirement in Australia. Some of these gender gaps are summarised in Table 1.1, and are discussed further below.

Table 1.1: Australian gender gaps at a glance, 2017

	Men	Women
Workforce participation	70%	59%
Employed part-time	17%	46%
Employed part-time with child <5	8%	62%
Average full-time weekly wage	100%	84%
Without paid leave entitlement and with dependant children	10%	20%
Average superannuation	100%	47%
Year 12 (by age 20–24)	86%	90%
Bachelor's degree (by age 25–29)	30%	40%
Unpaid care work	36%	64%
Unpaid housework	6.2 hours	18.7 hours
Representation in parliaments	68%	32%

Source: ABS (2016); Baird (2017).

---

3   See Department of Social Services, plan4womenssafety.dss.gov.au/ (accessed 3 June 2017).

Part 1 of this volume presents three theoretical and global frameworks for analysing gender inequality in the fiscal state: an international and comparative perspective; an economic analysis of fiscal sustainability; and a human rights framework for gender equality in fiscal policy. The focus turns in Part 2 to the central issue of women's economic security, work and care in market and household economies. Contributors address the intersection of tax, social security, child care and parental leave policies to support women's paid work; how Australia recognises and rewards unpaid care work for the wellbeing of women and children; and new empirical research on how women and men balance paid work and child care time. Part 3 turns to the development of human capital, investment and saving of women, including new research on the economic returns to higher education for women and men and Australia's higher education financing scheme; the position of women at the top of the income distribution; and retirement and age pension policy for adequacy of women's incomes in old age. In Part 4, the concluding chapter returns to the pathways and processes to achieve gender equality in the tax-transfer system.

Building on a feminist tradition of fiscal policy and research

Australian feminists as researchers, government officials, activists and (more recently) politicians, have engaged passionately in debating and changing tax and transfer systems for decades. The second wave of feminism in Australia was not just about sexism but also about the fiscal state. In the 1970s, women were significantly impoverished relative to men by a large gender pay gap and a sex-segregated labour market, more part-time than full-time work, unequal child care and heavy non-market work responsibilities. Despite improvements, many of these challenges continue today.

The 1970s saw the introduction of universal family allowances among other broad-based policies, but this faced a challenge of delivery in an increasingly fiscally constrained environment during the 1980s. Pioneering feminist researchers including Edwards (1981), Keens and Cass (1982), Baldock and Cass (1983), and Shaver (1989) showed that the structure of income tax rates, allowances, credits and concessions ('fiscal welfare'), the 'social welfare' system and 'occupational' welfare including work-related benefits such as superannuation, all produced significantly unequal gender and class effects in Australia, as in other countries. They also showed that assumptions of equal sharing of income inside the family and household were frequently wrong (Edwards 1981).

During the 1980s, means testing of family benefits was introduced based on couple income, as was already the case for other welfare payments. Proposals to extend the age pension to be universal (as it is in New Zealand) were not pursued. Feminist political and lobbying organisations, especially the Women's Electoral Lobby (WEL), were an active force engaging with federal policymakers about the budget, seeking to mitigate or counter these trends. They built on broader intersecting analyses of laws affecting gender inequality, including tax, welfare, labour, child support and family law, as explained by Graycar and Morgan (1990). Reforms on which feminist scholars and policymakers engaged, with some victories and some losses, included Jobs, Education and Training for sole parents, child support, the National Housing Strategy, Austudy and the Higher Education Contribution Scheme (HECS). In this active reform context, the 1980s saw senior policymakers such as Meredith Edwards undertake 'a femocrat's journey into attempting to ensure that policies on which I gave advice were consistent with these principles: taking account of work incentives, valuing unpaid work in the home and also the distribution of income within the family'.[4]

At this time, feminist scholarship on tax policy was just beginning to develop. The ground-breaking research of Patricia Apps (1981), was important in 'jostling and disturbing' the status quo of tax policy, which failed to recognise substantive unequal outcomes for women and men (Pugh 1983). Apps developed economic theories of optimal taxation and of the family to model and explain the care–work exchange in the household and the differential tax-transfer treatment of care inside and outside the family. This research demonstrated for femocrats working in government that it was both inefficient and inequitable for the tax system to subsidise spouse dependency given that the real income of the taxpaying spouse is augmented by the unpaid domestic activities of the other spouse. The teaching by Apps in public finance at the University of Sydney in the early 1990s informed this author and many others of the unequal economic effects of the tax-transfer system.

Another pioneering scholar on tax and gender was Judith Grbich who identified the role of the tax system in facilitating the accumulation of private wealth under the control of men, including through income splitting and the use of controlled entities such as discretionary trusts (Grbich 1987).

---

4   Presentation at ASSA Workshop on Gender Inequality in the Tax and Transfer System, 4–5 November 2015, The Australian National University.

In a different vein, a ground-breaking approach to tax-transfer modelling was led by Ann Harding, who brought this approach to Australia after working with Tony Atkinson at the London School of Economics. Harding worked with the Department of Social Security to establish the National Centre for Social and Economic Modelling (NATSEM) at the University of Canberra in 1993. This modelling enabled a detailed understanding of the distributional impact of the tax-transfer system and helped to demonstrate the effect on women and the fiscal cost of tax and welfare reform.

This scholarly and policy work brought a gender lens to major Australian reports on the tax system (Asprey 1975) and on poverty (Henderson 1975). Bettina Cass led the social security system review for the federal government (1985–88), producing numerous reports on the effects of the system. Also influential was substantial work on gender in the welfare state in the United Kingdom by, among others, Ruth Lister (1992). Across the Atlantic, during the late 1980s, Canadian feminist researchers, working through a series of governmental commissions of inquiry produced some of the first policy reports examining gender and tax policy. Reports included the first comprehensive gender analysis of a country's tax system by tax scholar, Kathleen Lahey (Lahey and Eaton 1988), the author of Chapter 2 in this volume.[5] Studies by the Canadian Advisory Council on the Status of Women (Maloney 1987), the Ontario Fair Tax Commission (1993) and Status of Women Canada (Young 2000) brought a new dimension by examining the role of tax concessions in reproducing gender inequality. The new research in this book builds on this strong tradition of research, policy analysis and reform on gender in the tax-transfer system.

Australia's tax-transfer system

This part briefly explains the tax and expenditure context of policy affecting women and the key concepts and structure of Australia's tax-transfer system. The tax-transfer system and the systems for funding child care and retirement policy are almost exclusively the responsibility of the federal government.[6]

---

5   This hefty and exciting type-written photocopied report was provided to Miranda Stewart in 1991 by tax professor Richard Vann, who had obtained it from the author, in a direct transfer of policy ideas across countries.

6   However, the detailed policy, design and delivery of many education, child care and other policies is carried out at the state and territory level or through intergovernmental processes in National Partnership Agreements and the Council of Australian Governments.

The federal tax system, illustrated in Figure 1.1, raises about 80 per cent of tax revenue in Australia. The federal income tax is by far the most important tax in Australia; the second largest tax is the goods and services tax (GST).

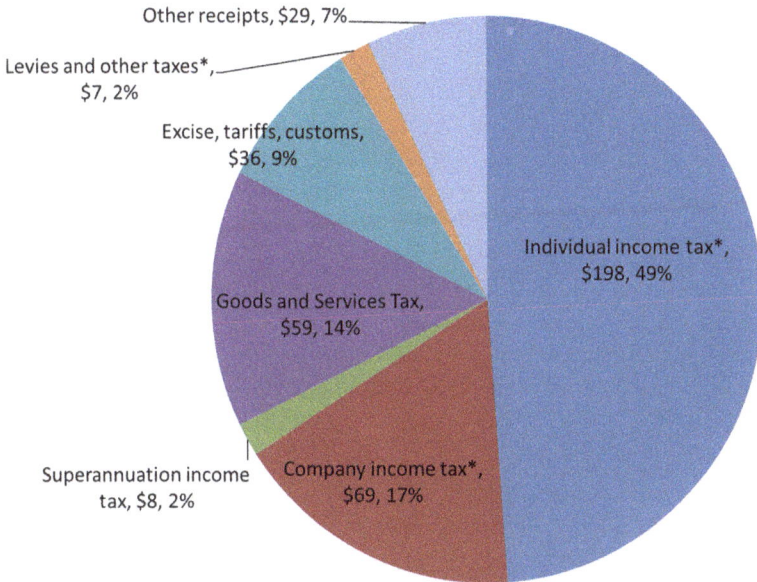

Figure 1.1: Commonwealth taxes, 2016–17 ($billion and percentage)

* Individual income tax includes the Medicare Levy and Fringe Benefits Tax; Company income tax includes Petroleum Resource Rent Tax; Levies and other taxes includes wine equalisation tax, luxury car tax, agricultural levies and other taxes.

Source: Australian Budget 2017–18, Budget Paper 1, Budget Statement 5, Table 9 (chart prepared by author).

The income tax

The federal income tax affects most people over the life course, directly as wage earners, business owners, homeowners, investors and retirees, or indirectly, in households as spouses or dependants. The individual income tax raised $198 billion in 2016–17, being 49 per cent of total federal revenues (including non-tax revenues). Individual income tax revenues include the Medicare Levy, currently 2 per cent, applied on taxable income of most taxpayers above a low threshold. The Turnbull Government proposes to increase the Medicare Levy to 2.5 per cent effective

1 July 2018, raising an additional $4 billion each year (Treasury 2017). As shown in Figure 1.1, the individual, company and superannuation income taxes combined raised three-quarters of federal revenues.

The institutional framework for individual income tax supports collection of income-contingent government tertiary education loans, provided under the Higher Education Contribution Scheme-Higher Education Loan Program (HECS-HELP). HECS-HELP loans are not counted as taxes but are an asset on the government's books, estimated at $44.7 billion at 30 June 2017 (Treasury 2017, Budget Paper 1, p. 7-20). These income-contingent loans are repaid by applying a surcharge on the income tax on a base of modified taxable income, so that they operate in effect as an increased tax rate for the individuals affected. This regime is discussed in Chapter 8.

Individual income tax is also a foundation of the retirement superannuation system because it is the vehicle for very substantial tax concessions for private retirement saving in superannuation funds. Tax concessions include a deduction for compulsory work-related contributions, the 'Super Guarantee' scheme, and for voluntary contributions to superannuation funds. These contributions and earnings are taxed at a low flat rate of 15 per cent (or sometimes lower) in the superannuation fund. Payouts on retirement, whether in a lump sum or pension stream, are tax-exempt. These concessions are among the largest tax expenditures reported by the Treasury, as discussed in Chapter 10 (and see Ingles and Stewart 2017a).

The transfer (social security) system

The largest and most important federal government function is social security and welfare, totalling $156 billion in 2016–17, and comprising more than one-third of federal expenditure, as shown in Figure 1.2. This function comprises mainly cash payments or 'transfers' by the government to individuals and families; it also includes expenditure on aged care and contributions to disability, veterans and child care services. Social security expenditure categories are summarised in Table 1.2 and the relative size of different payments is indicated in Figure 1.3. State and territory governments have primary responsibility for government spending on public goods such as child care centres, hospitals and schools, although the Commonwealth government contributes about half of the cost of those functions in direct spending and by grants to the states.

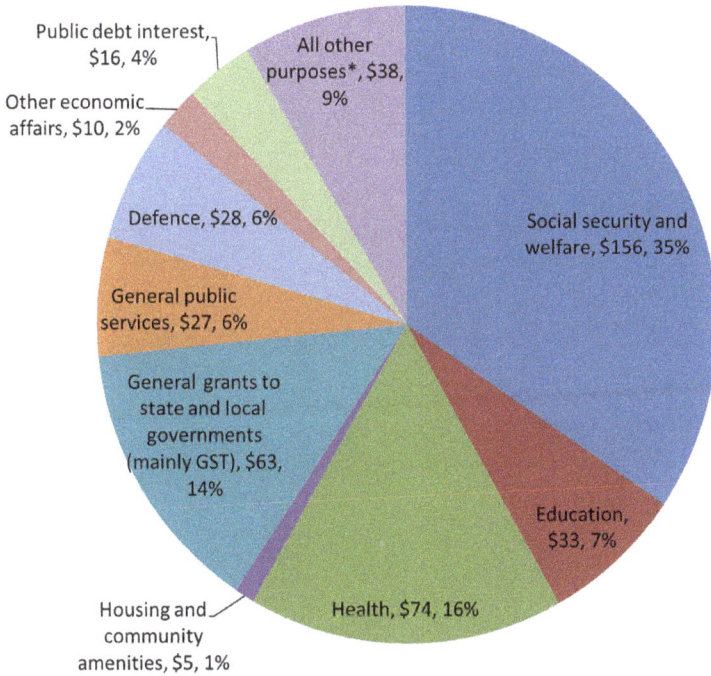

Figure 1.2: Commonwealth expenditures, 2016–17 ($billion and percentage)

* All other purposes includes expenditure categories of public order and safety; recreation and culture; fuel and energy; mining, manufacturing and construction; transport and communication; and other purposes excluding general intergovernmental revenue assistance and public debt interest.

Source: Australian Budget 2017–18, Budget Paper 1, Budget Statement 6, Table 3 and other relevant tables (chart prepared by author).

The transfer system is targeted by means tests and applies on the basis of need. Australia has the most tightly targeted transfer system in the Organisation for Economic Co-operation and Development (OECD); it also has relatively low spending on cash transfers compared to other OECD countries (Whiteford 2017). Nonetheless, it touches the majority of Australians at some point during the life course, through payment of child care and family benefits, unemployment benefits and youth allowance, rent assistance, bereavement allowances, veteran's, disability and age pensions and supported care facilities and services.

Table 1.2: Social security and welfare expenditure, 2016–17 ($billion)

Payment	$billion
Aged pension	$44.755
Aged care	$16.010
Family benefits	$24.495
Child care	$7.561
Paid parental leave	$2.169
Child support scheme	$2.041
Veterans pension and care	$6.575
Disability payments	$16.421
NDIS and other disability	$7.169
Carers	$8.132
Unemployed and sick	$10.994
Indigenous	$2.210
Other	$3.287
Administration	$3.879
TOTAL	$155.698

Source: Treasury (2017, Budget Paper 1, Statement 6, Table 9 and related tables, data extracted by author).

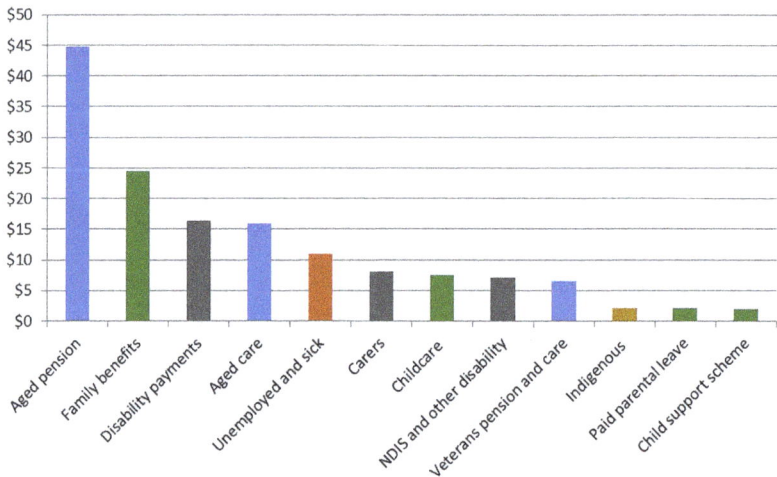

Figure 1.3: Main social security and welfare payments, 2016–17 ($billion)

Source: Treasury (2017, Budget Paper 1, Statement 6, Table 9 and related tables; chart prepared by author).

The tax-transfer unit, tax rates and means testing

Australian tax and social security laws today are drafted to be almost entirely 'gender-neutral'. Most formally discriminatory or gender-specific provisions have been eliminated from the statute books and administrative processes. Some of these changes have only just taken effect because of long policy transitions. For example, the eligibility age for the age pension used to be lower for women (60) than for men (65). Women born in 1949 and later will now qualify at age 65, as do men. The already-enacted policy to increase the eligibility age to 67 years is being phased in equally for women and men. Formal equality has also been achieved for same-sex couples, albeit not as married couples but instead as equal to de facto opposite-sex couples. Since 2009, all tax, superannuation and welfare laws recognise same-sex couples as 'domestic partners' (like opposite-sex de facto couples) and also recognise the children of those couples on an equal basis. In Australia, unlike some other countries including the US and Germany, formal status as 'married' is not required for equal treatment of couples in these laws.

However, some elements of the tax-transfer system affect individuals and families in a way that is, in substance and effect, discriminatory against women. On the other hand, important features of the tax-transfer system, such as the needs-based age pension, benefit many women who would otherwise live in poverty and who do not have sufficient retirement savings.

Key features of the tax-transfer system affecting gender include the unit of assessment, tax rates and means testing. The income tax applies to the individual as the tax unit, levying tax at progressive rates that rise as taxable income rises. However, most benefits in the transfer system are means tested on joint, or couple, income.

Tax rates for the 2016–17 tax year are in Table 1.3, and the basic structure of the marginal progressive tax rates and average tax rate is illustrated in Figure 1.4.

Table 1.3: Income tax rates and thresholds, 2016–17

Taxable income	Tax on this income
0–$18,200	Nil
$18,201–$37,000	19c for each $1 over $18,200
$37,001–$87,000	$3,572 plus 32.5c for each $1 over $37,000
$87,001–$180,000	$19,822 plus 37c for each $1 over $87,000
$180,001 and over	$54,232 plus 45c for each $1 over $180,000

Does not include Medicare Levy (2 per cent), temporary budget repair levy (2 per cent on top marginal tax rate) or HECS-HELP repayment schedule.

Source: ATO, www.ato.gov.au.

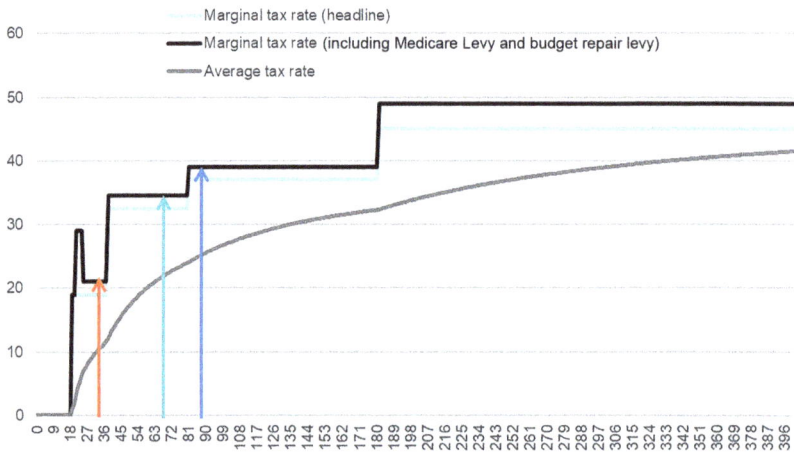

Figure 1.4: Progressive marginal and average income tax rates (%)

The 'bump' in the black line is the phase-in of the Medicare Levy.

Source: Author; ATO, 2014–15 tax rates.

The progressive individual tax rate structure is intended to reflect the ability to pay of the taxpayer, so as to deliver what is often called vertical equity. This is illustrated in Figure 1.4. The left-hand arrow on Figure 1.4 indicates a person on the minimum wage of about $35,000 per year, who faces a marginal tax rate (MTR) of 19 per cent plus the Medicare Levy and an average tax rate (ATR) of about 11 per cent, meaning that about 11 per cent of his or her taxable income is paid in tax. The middle arrow indicates a woman on average female full-time earnings of about $70,000, who faces an MTR of 34.5 per cent including the Medicare Levy and an

ATR of 22 per cent. The right-hand arrow indicates a man on average male full-time earnings of about $89,000, who faces a MTR of 37 per cent plus the Medicare Levy.

A person in the top 10 per cent of the income distribution earns about $94,000 (ignoring capital gains and before deductions and losses) and will face the 37 per cent MTR. A person in the top 1 per cent of the income distribution earns more than $237,341 in a year (ignoring capital gains and before deductions and losses) and will usually face the top MTR. In Budget 2017–18, the government proposes to increase the Medicare Levy to 2.5 per cent for all taxpayers. In contrast, the ALP proposes to limit that increase to the top two tax brackets and to retain the temporary budget repair levy of 2 per cent, bringing the top marginal income tax rate to 49.5 per cent. For more on top incomes, see Chapter 9.

The tax rate structure also aims to achieve horizontal equity between taxpayers in similar circumstances (with similar taxable income). However, significant differences between taxpayers, such as the cost of children or of disability support, are largely ignored in Australia's tax system. These characteristics are instead addressed through transfer payments to families in the social security (transfer) system.

Australia's transfer means tests determine eligibility, and amount of cash benefits payable, based on income and assets. Means testing produces an effect that is equivalent to a progressive tax rate scale in reverse: the higher the income or assets, the lower the payment or benefit, which is phased out or tapered over a range of income. Where the benefit recipient is a member of a couple, or dependant child of a family, the unit of assessment is a joint unit in which the means test is based on income or assets of both members of the couple and payment rates are set on a different, joint scale intended to reflect the cost of living of the family.

For example, one important benefit for families supporting children is family tax benefit part A (FTB-A). This benefit applies at a maximum rate of $5,493.25 per child under 12 per year (other rates apply for older children).[7] It is reduced for the family's adjusted taxable income over $51,904, at a taper rate of 20 cents per dollar of income over the threshold. This is equivalent to an MTR of 20 per cent at that threshold.

---

7   See Department of Social Services, www.dss.gov.au/families-and-children/benefits-payments/family-tax-benefit (accessed 3 June 2017).

The government proposes in Budget 2017–18 to increase this taper to 30 per cent once the family's adjusted taxable income reaches $94,316 (Treasury 2017). That is, approximately one average male wage and the wage for one day of part-time work at the average female wage. Child care and other family benefits, unemployment, age and disability pensions are also means tested on joint income although with different thresholds and taper rates.

Part 1: Frameworks for gender analysis

Part 1 presents three conceptual approaches to the analysis of gender inequality in the tax-transfer system. Gender inequality in fiscal and economic policy cannot be separated from the broad systemic challenges that Australia (like other countries) faces in financing government in the current era, as we enter a decade of fiscal deficits. Indeed, today, as in the 1990s, it can be argued that gender inequality remains central to discourses of fiscal austerity (Philipps 1996). Nor can we consider Australia's fiscal policy apart from broader international economic and policy trends.

In Chapter 2, Kathleen Lahey presents an international and comparative frame of analysis. She argues that the cumulative effects of tax and social expenditure cuts of the last few decades are part of a 'taxing for growth' agenda that has its origins in the neoliberal policies of the 1980s. Combined with pre– and post–Global Financial Crisis (GFC) fiscal austerity, these have contributed to Australia moving backwards on gender equality. Lahey observes that even as Australia's level of human development has risen to second place in the most recent UN Human Development Reports, its gender inequality index ranking has fallen.

Lahey then examines the specific effects of Australia's tax-transfer system for gender equality, including income taxation of capital, the company tax, the GST and the individual income tax-transfer unit on gender equality. She compares the status of women in Australia's tax-transfer system with Canada, the US and the UK, as well as with two Nordic countries, with a view to identifying its unique fiscal choices and reform options. While Australia did not implement fiscal austerity policies to the extent of some other countries after the GFC, Lahey argues that Australia has moved in the last decade towards a tax-transfer system aimed at reducing welfare payments, enforcing workforce participation and cutting tax rates especially on capital income, and has devoted little fiscal space to policies that can improve the economic status of women. There has been a failure to address the impact on women of high levels of unpaid work and workplace discrimination and low levels of earnings and child care resources. Lahey outlines policy alternatives capable of producing better outcomes for women over the life course.

Australia's fiscal base and national wellbeing also faces the broad demographic challenge of the ageing population, as projected in the *Intergenerational Report* (Treasury 2015a). Patricia Apps, in Chapter 3, explains how gender inequality in our tax-transfer system is undermining fiscal sustainability and economic growth, while changes in the tax-transfer system are contributing to increased income inequality. Australia's fertility rate has declined from 3.5 in the 1960s to 1.8 today. As the population ages, the ratio of working-age taxpayers to the dependant population in Australia is declining, as it is in many other developed countries. This will have a direct impact on the revenue that can be raised from all taxes, especially our most important tax, the income tax.

In contrast to the previous two years, the Turnbull Government in its 2017–18 budget has sought to raise taxes, rather than rely only on expenditure cuts to finance the deficit. However, broad-based tax reform has proved difficult in an era of contestation about the goals and distributional effects of tax reform; the government appears to have abandoned its *Re:Think* tax reform process initiated by its predecessor in 2014 (Treasury 2015b). Yet both the LNP and the ALP remain committed to a cap on federal tax at 23.9 per cent of gross domestic product (GDP) (once fiscal balance is reached), a tax level that will inevitably require austerity approaches to transfers and public spending more broadly. Apps shows that the tax burden is being pushed towards the middle and demonstrates how an optimal tax approach that takes the position of women seriously in tax policy regarding work and care would support a truly progressive income tax combined with public investment in child care. This would improve economic efficiency and fiscal sustainability by encouraging women to reallocate their time (as they have fewer children) from work in the home to work in the labour market.

It is important to remember that gender inequality in economic participation and outcomes breaches the human rights of women. In Chapter 4, Helen Hodgson and Kerrie Sadiq advocate a rights-based fiscal policy agenda. In 1975, Australia ratified the International Covenant on Economic, Social and Cultural Rights (ICESCR) and, in 1983, Australia ratified the

Convention on the Elimination of All Forms of Discrimination Against Women (CEDAW) (albeit with some reservations). Hodgson and Sadiq draw on an approach in a recent United Nations report, *Progress of the World's Women* (UN 2015) to apply a human rights gender lens to four important features of Australia's tax system: the individual income tax, GST, property taxes and taxes on retirement savings. In particular, they examine the impact of tax policy on the economic and social rights of women and argue for fiscal policy to be established in a framework that takes women's human rights seriously.

Part 2: Work and care

The Turnbull Government has stated a policy goal of increasing women's workforce participation, including signing up to the G20 target of increasing participation by 25 per cent by 2025 and the Minister for Women, Senator Michaelia Cash, released a Workforce Participation strategy in June 2017 (DPMC 2017).[8] Increased (market or paid) workforce participation by women has been framed as an issue of broad societal, political and budgetary concern for the nation, and is also important for women's equality, producing, as the G20 stated, a 'double dividend' for equality and the economy (Gurria 2015). However, tax-transfer policy remains conflicted on this policy goal, as discussed in several chapters in this volume.

Women's workforce participation has increased substantially since the 1970s, but is still significantly below men's. Trends in women's and men's employment are shown in Figure 1.5.

While the trend is positive, a closer examination of the data shows that we have entered an equilibrium in which women who have children work part-time, producing a family model of 1.5 earners. Indeed, the data show that the increase in women's workforce participation in Australia since the 1970s has been almost entirely in part-time work, as shown in Figure 1.6.

---

8   The G20 target of increasing participation by 25 per cent by 2025 may be achieved more by demographics than by policy in Australia.

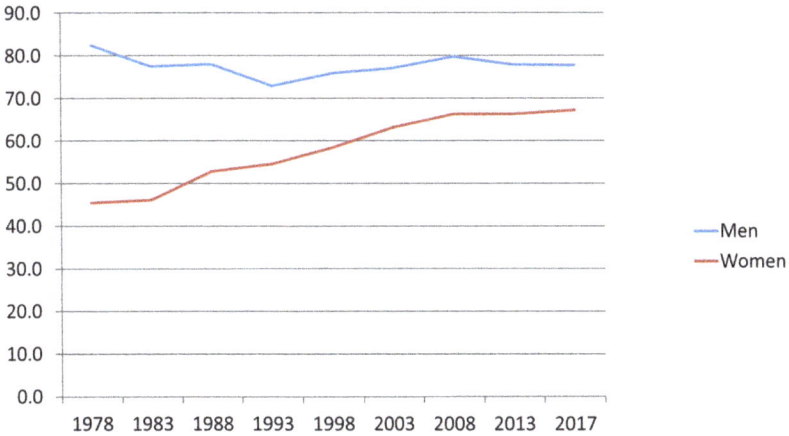

Figure 1.5: Women's and men's workforce participation, 1978–2017 (%)
Source: ABS (2017); Baird (2017).

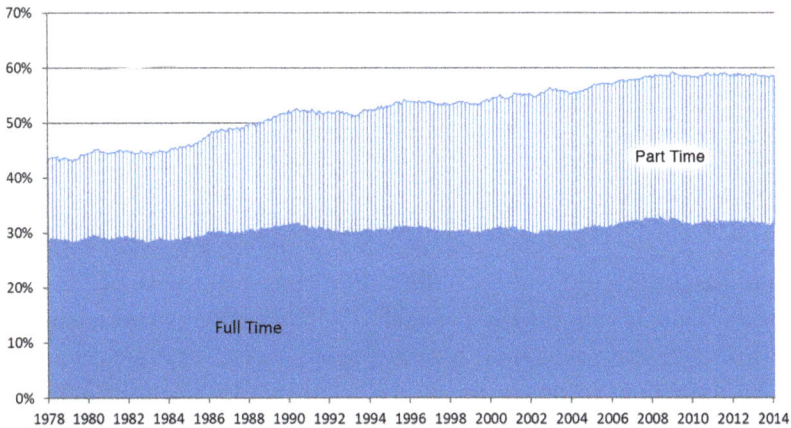

Figure 1.6: Part-time and full-time workforce participation of women, 1978–2014 (%)
Source: Stewart et al. (2015), Chart 2.4.

We can identify a key reason for the gender gap in full-time work if we examine the participation of mothers. Workforce participation drops dramatically once a women has a child and it never fully recovers, as shown in Figure 1.7.

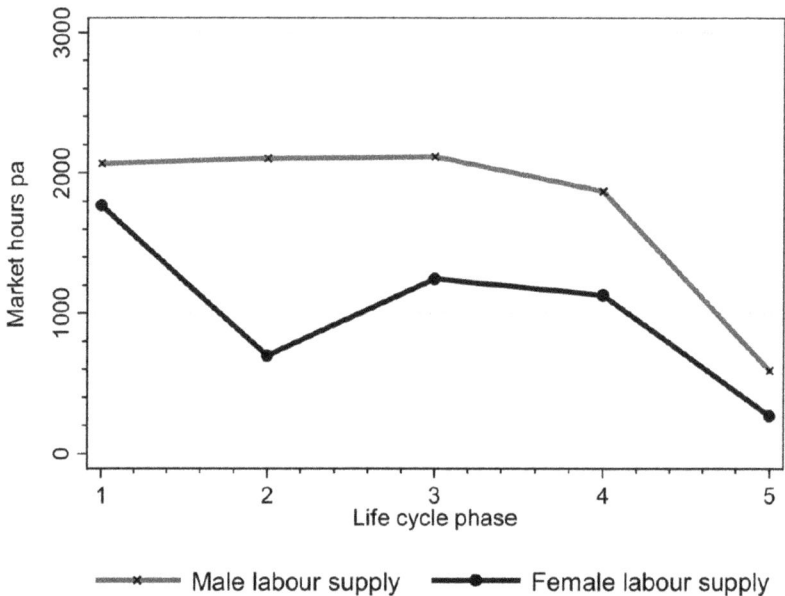

Figure 1.7: Gender labour supply gap (hours worked), 2015

(1) pre-children; (2) at least one child of preschool age is present; (3) children are of school age or older but still dependant; (4) parents are of working age but with no dependant children in the household; (5) retirement age (60+ years).

Source: Apps (2015).

Guyonne Kalb (Chapter 5) examines the combined influence of taxation and expenditure policies including child care, paid parental leave and education policy on the labour supply of women taking into account that many women at some point in their life are the primary carer of a child. Many studies focus on one aspect that affects female labour supply, while there are usually many interacting influences from taxes, transfers and family policies. In addition, through the dynamic relationship of labour supply over time, early influences can have long-term impacts on labour supply, and early decisions regarding labour supply are likely to have flow-on effects on later labour supply decisions. Kalb reviews the different influences and discusses the related literature, aiming to be illustrative rather than comprehensive and showing that it is the interaction of these policies that creates inconsistencies and perverse outcomes.

Kalb explains that we can do a better job in facilitating women's labour supply. It is clear from her analysis that Australian tax-transfer policy remains incoherent and proposals for reform face constraints of apparent (short-term) cost to government. Consistently with Apps, it is argued by Kalb that a societal investment in increasing female labour force participation would generate long-term returns both for individual women and collectively, including reduced fiscal cost of age pensions, increased taxation revenues, productivity yields and reduced loss of human capital.

Effective marginal tax rates

A key policy setting that contributes to this result is the high effective marginal tax rates (EMTRs) produced by tight means testing of benefits in Australia's tax-transfer and child care systems. The means test for withdrawal of benefits combines with the income tax rate structure on earnings to produce the effect, referred to in many chapters in this volume, of a high EMTR on earnings. The particular effect will depend on the circumstances of the individual, family structure, wages, hours of work and cost of child care.

An example recently examined by the Productivity Commission (2015), and modified by Ingles and Plunkett (2016) is illustrated in Figures 1.8a and 1.8b. Figure 1.8a presents the EMTR on the earnings of a second earner (P2, usually the woman) in a low-wage household where the primary earner (P1) is earning a full-time low wage and the family have two children aged two and three in child care. The second earner begins to earn income at a low wage. For example, the line shows EMTR for the second earner at $20,000 is about 70 per cent. This means that the family loses 70 per cent of earnings at that point in reduced benefits and increased net child care costs. Over the range from $20,000 to $25,000 of earnings, the EMTR on the second earner's wages exceeds 100 per cent. The coloured areas below the chart show the importance of lost benefits, net child care costs (after benefits) and tax in producing the EMTR. The ATR over the range from zero earnings to $25,000 is about 80 per cent.

In Figure 1.8b, the same data is presented on a per day basis. It shows that for the second earner to choose to increase her part-time work from two days to four days, the 'daily' effective tax rate is between 80 to 90 per cent. The effect of EMTRs, combined with the additional costs of working, mean that many mothers derive little, if any, financial return from a return to or increase in work hours.

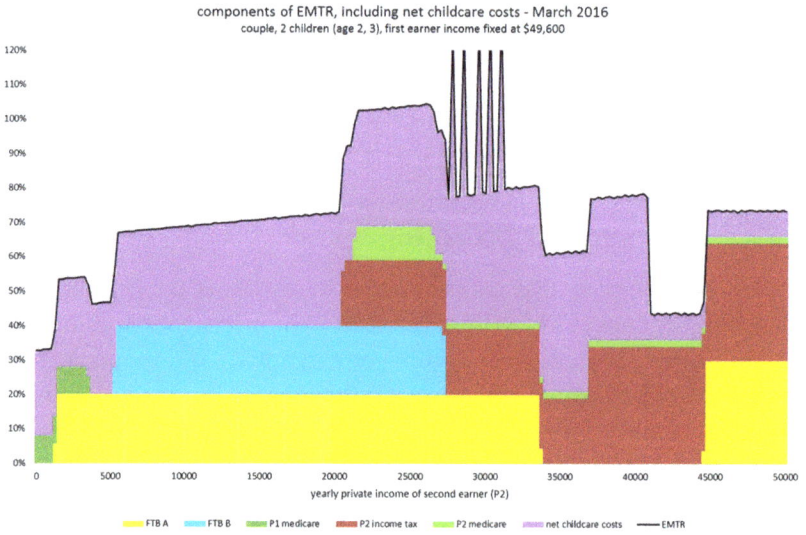

components of EMTR, including net childcare costs - March 2016
couple, 2 children (age 2, 3), first earner income fixed at $49,600

yearly private income of second earner (P2)

FTB A ▪ FTB B ▪ P1 medicare ▪ P2 income tax ▪ P2 medicare ▪ net childcare costs ▬ EMTR

Figure 1.8a: EMTRs per $1 of earnings, dual earner family with two children

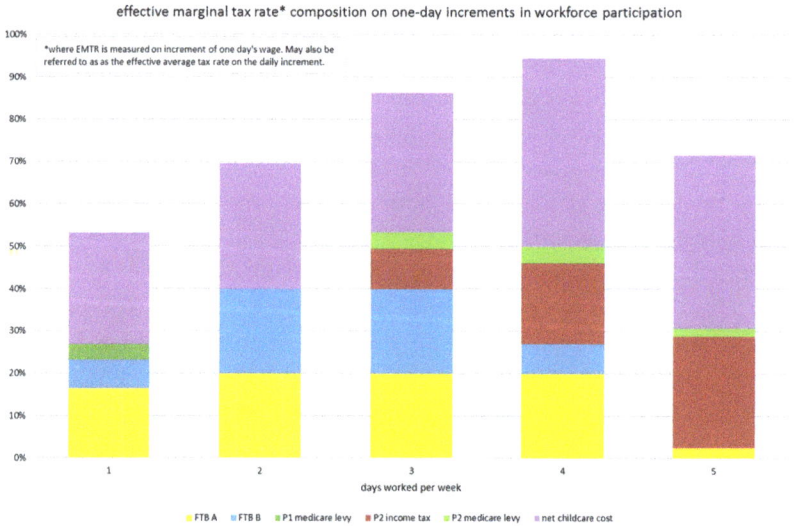

effective marginal tax rate* composition on one-day increments in workforce participation

*where EMTR is measured on increment of one day's wage. May also be referred to as as the effective average tax rate on the daily increment.

days worked per week

▪ FTB A ▪ FTB B ▪ P1 medicare levy ▪ P2 income tax ▪ P2 medicare levy ▪ net childcare cost

Figure 1.8b: EMTRs per day of work, dual earner family with two children

Income of the primary earner is fixed at the minimum wage plus 41 per cent, full year full-time ($49,600). Income of second earner is minimum wage plus 20 per cent—$20.75/hour (low-wage, full-time workers). This ratio is based on the ratio of men's to women's wages, full-time averages. Hours of care are 10/day at $8.50/hr. One aspect of long day care is that care is effectively charged for 10 hours in a full day, to a maximum of 50 hours per week. To mimic this, the assumption is that care hours grow faster than working hours, so that a 38-hour working week translates to 50 hours of care use.

Source: Ingles and Plunkett (2016).

The structural design of the tax-transfer system that produces the effect illustrated in Figure 1.8 is still not fully acknowledged by policymakers. Yet it is integral to women's economic disadvantage, as a result of the interaction with their position in discriminatory market and household economies. As Kalb shows, the decision not to work, or to work only a few hours per week, made on the basis of short-term financial impact because of high EMTRs, can have long-term consequences on the earning capacity of mothers over their lifetime. At the same time, it contributes to the social construction of gendered behaviour and reinforcement of gendered social norms. The Turnbull Government's new, expanded child care subsidy, to commence in 2018, will likely mitigate some of these effects, although it is still means tested and will not assist women in upper middle-income families.[9]

The value of care

It is important for women's and societal wellbeing that we do not focus exclusively on paid market work as the means to achieve gender equality. Julie Smith in Chapter 6 presents a 'bird's-eye view' of how gender equality in Australia has been helped or hindered in Australia's 'wage earner welfare state'. Smith focuses on the economic costs to women of their unpaid (home) reproductive and productive work, and the role of Australia's unique social protection and progressive tax regime in mitigating or exacerbating these costs. While acknowledging the importance of women's market work, Smith critiques policies aimed solely at boosting paid workforce participation. Household investments in children—such as breastfeeding and infant care—add enormously to women's and children's wellbeing and to social and economic wellbeing more broadly, as do other 'unpaid' care responsibilities (see, for example, AHRC 2013; Deloitte 2015).

Smith discusses the early financing of child endowment in Australia and the links between this policy aimed at supporting families and wage policy. Smith concludes that the evolution of Australia's social protection regime and its financing since the 1970s has been both an enemy and a friend of gender equality. A range of workforce policies that facilitate women doing caring work while not being disadvantaged in the labour market or over the life course, including in retirement, is required. Ultimately,

---

9   See Department of Education and Training, www.education.gov.au/child-care-subsidy-0.

contemporary policy is failing to respond to contemporary needs for resourcing care of dependant people at the cost of both gender equity, and economic efficiency.

The design of child care policies should also take account of how child care is organised within a household. There has been a lack of debate in Australia about sharing the burden and joys of care more equally between women and men, for example through mandating parental leave for men. Huong Dinh and Maria Racionero (Chapter 7) draw on the Australian Bureau of Statistics (ABS) Time Use Survey (TUS) of 2006 to present new findings about time use of parents in balancing child care and market work. Specifically, they focus on the question: do mothers and fathers in a couple differ in the way they trade off child care time for market time? They examine time spent by mothers and fathers at home in primary (development-oriented) child care, secondary (non-development-oriented) child care and market work. As a result of budget cuts, the ABS TUS has not been carried out since 2006, so this decade-old data is our only insight into Australian care and work time use at present.

Dinh and Racionero confirm previous findings that mothers prioritise child care time significantly more than fathers, who put more emphasis on work time. They find that mothers and fathers adjust their child care time differently based on which partner (father or mother) changes their time in market work, the type of child care and the age of the youngest child. When there is a preschool-aged youngest child, mothers prioritise primary (developmental) child care over secondary child care and over paid work. By contrast, in the same situation, fathers appear to prioritise secondary over primary child care. As time is a scarce resource and child care may have different qualities depending on the kind of care and age of children, parents cooperate to mitigate the loss in combined child care time in response to more market work time, but there are nuances in decisions that women and men make about care when they or their partners are choosing to increase market work.

Lone parents at the intersection of work and care

Several authors in this volume, including Lahey, Kalb and Smith, discuss the position of lone parents in the tax-transfer system. The tensions in Australia's tax-transfer policies for work and care are most evident in the case of lone parents, more than 85 per cent of whom are women. Families with a lone parent form about 20 per cent of families with a child under the age of 15 in Australia (Whiteford 2016). Even in today's era of blended families or 'shared care', it is common for children to be cared for by a primary carer in one household, while some parents are single by choice or necessity; moreover, violence against women and children is a key reason for sole parenthood.

In the 1970s, the introduction for the first time of sole parent pensions enabled a woman to look after children alone, by providing an income. Since the 1980s, the activation policy for workforce participation and increased conditionality and means testing of benefits began to push lone parents into the labour market. Increased benefits for families with children during the 1990s benefited lone parents.

Today, a more stringent work and study policy applies for lone parents. About half of lone parents receiving benefits do paid work or study at least part-time. Many lone parents are better off as a result of doing paid work and the system is designed to provide benefits while encouraging work. However, as illustrated in Ingles and Stewart (2017b), lone parents still face very high EMTRs if they seek to increase their work hours from part-time to full-time, taking account of net child care costs, except for the few who are able to obtain a high-wage full-time job. Those lone parents who are unable to work, and their children, have been made significantly worse off since 2014, when a policy shift moved lone parents off the pension payment scale onto the lower rate Newstart allowance once the youngest child in the household turns eight (Phillips and Joseph 2016). This policy has increased income inequality among lone parents, while those lone parent families who are dependant on benefits are among the poorest in the country (Whiteford 2016; Phillips and Gray 2017).

Part 3: Human capital, savings and retirement

In Chapters 8, 9 and 10, different aspects of investment in human capital, savings and retirement policy are discussed. Turning to the experience of women investing in higher education, Mathias Sinning (Chapter 8) uses the Household, Income and Labour Dynamics of Australia (HILDA) Survey for the period 2001 to 2014 to present a new analysis of the private returns to higher education for women and men. The human capital literature assumes that tertiary (post-school) education is an investment in human capital producing both private and public returns, and general results show that highly educated people earn more. The private return is calculated by Sinning to be the earnings of individuals calculated as a present value of lifetime earnings resulting from higher education.

Sinning confirms that both men and women have higher lifetime earnings from tertiary education compared to those without such education. However, consistent with other data about the gender wage gap, Sinning finds from the HILDA data that women consistently earn lower hourly wages than men at all levels of education. Once it is taken into account that women work part-time more than men, then women's weekly earnings may be significantly lower than those of men. Women with either a postgraduate or a Bachelor or Honours degree earn about 50 per cent more over their lifetime than women with Year 12 or below; there is no earnings benefit for women of postgraduate education. Men with postgraduate education earn about 83 per cent more than men with Year 12 or below, and also earn more than men with a Bachelor or Honours degree. Most strikingly, Sinning shows that women derive no earnings benefit from technical or vocational education, in stark contrast to men.

Sinning then discusses the costs and benefits of higher education funding through HECS-HELP. He shows how gender differences in earnings have considerable implications for the repayment of income-contingent HECS-HELP debts. The current threshold for repayment of the HECS-HELP debt is $54,869, at which point a repayment rate of 4 per cent of adjusted taxable income applies (on top of income tax).

The average outstanding debt of male university graduates converges to zero over a 30-year period, whereas the average outstanding debt of female university graduates remains positive. Many female university graduates never earn enough to repay their tertiary student loans in full, both because of the gender wage gap and because of part-time and interrupted work patterns. The government proposes in Budget 2017–18 to significantly lower the HECS-HELP repayment threshold to $42,000, and to introduce a sliding scale of repayment rate from 1 per cent of adjusted taxable income up to 4 per cent at the current threshold. As noted by the National Federation for Australian Women (NFAW 2017), this will cause many new graduates to repay loans sooner. For women who are working part-time while caring for children, or who are working on relatively low wages, it will push up both the EMTR and ATR that they pay, reducing further the after-tax return to work.

In Chapter 9, Miranda Stewart, Sarah Voitchovsky and Roger Wilkins present novel findings about women with top incomes. A gender analysis of the top income groups in Australia is possible because of the ability to obtain customised individual income tax statistics from the Australian Taxation Office (ATO). Building on the global movement of 'top incomes' research,[10] Chapter 9 presents the share of women in the top 10 per cent, 5 per cent, 1 per cent and 0.1 per cent in the income distribution. It compares patterns of top income women in Australia with other countries, as well as providing some possible explanations for the Australian trends.

As in other countries, Australia has experienced sustained increases in the income shares of top income groups since the early 1980s, and this is explained largely by reductions in top tax rates. Overall, the income share of the top 1 per cent has nearly doubled from just over 4 per cent in 1982–83 to just over 8 per cent in 2013–14. The income share of the top 5–10 per cent (91st to 95th percentiles) declined slightly to 2008–09, since when it has risen rapidly. Stewart, Voitchovsky and Wilkins find that in 2013–14, women account for one-quarter of the top 10 per cent. Higher up the income distribution, the proportion is lower, but women still comprise 17 per cent of the top 0.1 per cent. When compared to other countries including Spain, Denmark, Canada, New Zealand, Italy, the UK and Norway, Australia has a relatively low share of women in the top 10 per cent but a larger cohort of women in the top 1 per cent and 0.1 per cent. A significant proportion of women with top incomes derive income from savings and investment sources, rather than from high wages.

One possible explanation for the Australian results is the age profile of women with top incomes. Another possible explanation is tax planning by couples with top incomes. In all individual income tax systems that have a progressive rate structure, there is a structural incentive for related parties—especially family members—to split income so as to reduce the overall tax burden. In Australia, the legal structure and interpretation of the income tax has long facilitated certain kinds of income splitting. As explained by Apps (Chapter 4), the joint income-tested family benefits produce a 'quasi-joint tax unit' for many families with children. It is less well known—except to tax lawyers and the high-income individuals

---

10   See the World Wealth and Income database at: wid.world/.

and families who they advise—that a 'quasi-joint' tax unit can also be produced by splitting income among the 'professional and commercial classes'.[11] The trends presented in Chapter 9 are consistent with anecdotal evidence of family income splitting as a common practice among those with high incomes, enabling them to pay less tax, and undermines the overall tax base.

Gender and the retirement system

Many chapters in this volume, including Apps (Chapter 2) and Smith (Chapter 6) discuss the retirement savings system and the age pension, in relation to the impact for women who are economically disadvantaged over the life course. The age pension, which is not linked to savings accrued during paid work, operates as life course remuneration for many women who do unpaid care work or have interrupted working lives, as well as providing necessary income support where no private provision is available. The shift from the age pension, which was neutral between paid and unpaid work, to reliance on a second pillar of occupational superannuation has magnified gender inequalities in retirement income. Siobhan Austen and Rhonda Sharp in Chapter 10 present a detailed gender impact analysis to assess the sufficiency of the funding available for the retirement incomes of older Australian women. They do this by examining inputs (superannuation saving subject to tax concessions) and outputs from the retirement system (payments and incomes). They critique the supposed 'link' between the input tax concessions and the output retirement incomes as being weak in a number of respects. They conclude that current policies are producing especially poor outcomes for Australian women, with women experiencing higher levels of poverty and lower levels of wealth as they age.

Austen and Sharp argue for the importance of policy analysis at the individual level, so as to identify the gender impact of retirement and pension policy. Household analysis is often favoured in retirement incomes policy because of a view that wealth is distributed in family units. Austen and Sharp observe that maldistribution of the ownership and control of resources within households exposes individuals within the household (more often women than men) to the risks of poor decision-making and

---

11   As illustrated in judicial decisions such as *FCT v Everett* (1980) 143 CLR 440 at 457 per Murphy J.

inadequate resources. In any event, fully half of Australian women are single by age 75, meaning that the single unit analysis is appropriate. In the result, Austen and Sharp, as do several other contributors, argue for retaining the age pension as the first pillar of the retirement income system for women.

Part 4: Towards gender equality in the tax-transfer system

After decades of advocacy and policy change, gender equality remains unfinished business in Australian economic and fiscal policy. The tax-transfer system, intersecting with child care, parental leave, education, work and retirement policies, reproduces deeply gendered dynamics that disadvantage women in spite of political commitments to gender equality. Since the move of the Office for Women back into the Department of Prime Minister and Cabinet in 2013, there have been some developments in mainstreaming policy to achieve gender equality, although greater direction and leadership is needed. Government support for gender policy analysis has been lacking and both Labor and LNP governments, pursing governmental budget 'efficiencies', have dismantled policy and data capability for addressing gender inequality over the last few years.

In the final Chapter 11, Meredith Edwards and Miranda Stewart explore the policy and process of achieving gender equality in these core policy fields. They explore how to engage gender analysis, evaluation and research insights into policy processes to improve outcomes for women and Australian society as a whole. Australian tax-transfer policy seems to be in transition towards a new regime of care and work, in which women are increasingly engaged in the paid workforce. These issues are hotly debated but there is a real risk that the gender equality implications of new policies will not be fully acknowledged, in particular in an environment of fiscal constraint, so that new policies will continue to assume explicitly or implicitly that care work will continue to be done outside the market, or at a low market cost, mostly by women.

There is, today, a new global impetus to incorporate gender impact analysis into government budgeting (for example, see OECD 2016). Governments have a significant opportunity to reform policy in the tax-transfer system, child care and retirement fields as a lever to redress the disadvantages faced by women across the life course relative to men. Reforms to support gender equality can produce increased economic security and wellbeing for women and for the economy and population as a whole in the short and long term.

References

ABS (Australian Bureau of Statistics). 2016. *Gender Indicators—Australia—August 2016*. Publication 4125.0. Available at: www.abs.gov.au/ausstats/abs@.nsf/mf/4125.0 (accessed 2 March 2016).

ABS. 2017. *Labour Force, Australia, Detailed*—Electronic Deliver. Cat. no. 6291.0.55.001.

AHRC (Australian Human Rights Commission). 2013. *Investing in care: Recognising and valuing those who care*, Volume 1: Research Report. Sydney: Australian Human Rights Commission.

Apps, Patricia. 1981. *A Theory of Inequality and Taxation*. Cambridge: Cambridge University Press.

Apps, Patricia. 2015. 'The central role of a well-designed income tax in "the modern economy"'. *Australian Tax Forum* 30(4): 845–863. doi.org/10.2139/ssrn.2662280

Asprey, Ken (Chair). 1975. *Full Report 31 January 1975*. Taxation Review Committee (the 'Asprey Committee'). Canberra: Australian Government Publishing Service.

Baird, Marian. 2017. Presentation to International Association of Women Judges' Asia Pacific Regional Conference, 27–28 April 2017, Sydney. Available at: dcconferences.eventsair.com/QuickEventWebsitePortal/iawj2017/cs/Agenda

Baldock, Cora V. and Bettina Cass (eds). 1983. *Women, social welfare and the state in Australia*. Sydney: George Allen & Unwin.

Deloitte. 2015. *The economic value of informal care in Australia in 2015*. Report for Carers Australia. Deloitte Access Economics.

Department of Education and Training. 2017. Universal Access to Early Childhood Education: National Partnership Agreements. Available at: www.education.gov.au/national-partnership-agreements

DPMC (Department of Prime Minister and Cabinet). 2017. *Towards 2025: An Australian Government Strategy to Boost Women's Workforce Participation*. Available at: womensworkforceparticipation.pmc.gov.au/

Edwards, Meredith. 1981. *Financial Arrangements within Families*. Canberra: National Women's Advisory Council.

Grattan, Michelle. 2016. 'Turnbull finds it easy to declare himself a feminist'. *The Conversation*, 6 June. Available at: theconversation.com/turnbull-finds-it-easy-to-declare-himself-a-feminist-60574

Graycar, Regina and Jenny Morgan. 1990. *The Hidden Gender of Law*. Leichhardt: Federation Press.

Grbich, Judith. 1987. 'The Position of Women in Family Dealing: The Australian Case'. *International Journal of the Sociology of Law* 15(3): 309–316.

Gurria, Angel. 2015. 'Bringing gender equality to the core of the G20 agenda'. OECD.org. Available at: www.oecd.org/g20/topics/employment-and-social-policy/bringing-gender-equality-to-the-core-of-the-g20-agenda.htm

Harris Rimmer, Susan and Marian Sawer. 2016. 'Neoliberalism and gender equality policy in Australia'. *Australian Journal of Political Science* 51(4): 742–758. doi.org/10.1080/10361146.2016.1222602

Henderson, Ron. 1975. *Commission of Inquiry into Poverty*. Canberra: Australian Government Publishing Service.

Ingles, David and David Plunkett. 2016. *Effective Marginal Tax Rates*. TTPI Policy Brief 1/2016. Available at: taxpolicy.crawford.anu.edu.au/publication/9083/effective-marginal-tax-rates

Ingles, David and Miranda Stewart. 2017a. 'Reforming Australia's Superannuation Tax System and the Age Pension to Improve Work and Savings Incentives'. *Asia & the Pacific Policy Studies* 4(3): 417–436. DOI: 10.1002/app5.184

Ingles, David and Miranda Stewart. 2017b. 'Does It Pay To Work? The Case of a Single Parent with 4 Children'. *Austaxpolicy: Tax and Transfer Policy Blog*, 24 January. Available at: www.austaxpolicy.com/pay-work-case-single-parent-4-children/

Keens, Carol and Bettina Cass. 1982. *Welfare: Some Aspects of Australian tax policy: Class and Gender Considerations.* NSW: Social Policy Research Centre, University of NSW.

Lahey, Kathleen and M. Eaton. 1988. *The Taxation of Women in Canada: A Research Report.* Canada: Queen's University.

Leslie, Tim. 2014. 'Winners and Losers of the 2014 Budget'. *ABC News*, 13 May. Available at: www.abc.net.au/news/2014-05-13/budget-winners-and-losers/5433178

Lister, Ruth. 1992. *Women's Economic Dependency and Social Security.* Research Discussion Series no. 2. Manchester: Equal Opportunities Commission.

Maloney, Maureen. 1987. *Women and Income Tax Reform.* Background paper prepared for the Canadian Advisory Council on the Status of Women. Ottawa: Canadian Advisory Council on the Status of Women.

NFAW (National Foundation for Australian Women). 2017. *Gender Lens on the Budget 2017.* Available at: www.nfaw.org/gender-lens-on-the-budget/

OECD (Organisation for Economic Co-operation and Development). 2016. *Gender Budgeting in OECD Countries.* Public Governance and Territorial Development Directorate, 37th Annual Meeting of OECD Senior Budget Officials, Stockholm, 9–10 June.

Ontario Fair Tax Commission. 1993. *Fair Taxation in a Changing World: Report of the Ontario Fair Tax Commission.* Toronto, Canada: University of Toronto Press.

Philipps, Lisa. 1996. 'Discursive Deficits: A Feminist Perspective on the Power of Technical Knowledge in Fiscal Law and Policy'. *Canadian Journal of Law and Society* 11(1): 141–176.

Phillips, Ben and Matt Gray. 2017. *Distributional Modelling of the Australian Tax and Social Security System Changes: 2005–2015 and beyond.* Available at: csrm.cass.anu.edu.au/research/publications/distributional-modelling-australian-tax-and-social-security-system-changes

Phillips, Ben and Cukkoo Joseph. 2016. *Income Trends for Selected Single Parent Families*. ANU Centre for Social Research and Methods. Available at: rsss.anu.edu.au/sites/default/files/Cameo%20 analysis%20of%20single%20parents.pdf

Productivity Commission. 2015. *Childcare and Early Childhood Learning Final Report*. Available at: www.pc.gov.au/inquiries/completed/child care#report

Pugh, Cedric. 1983. 'Review of *A Theory of Inequality and Taxation*'. *Journal of Economic Issues* 17(3): 826–830. doi.org/10.1080/002136 24.1983.11504165

Senate Economic References Committee. 2016. *'A husband is not a retirement plan': Achieving economic security for women in retirement*. Report, 29 April. Commonwealth of Australia. Available at: www. aph.gov.au/Parliamentary_Business/Committees/Senate/Economics/ Economic_security_for_women_in_retirement/Report

Shaver, Sheila. 1989. 'Gender, Class and the Welfare State: The Case of Income Security in Australia'. *Feminist Review* 32(Summer): 90–110. doi.org/10.1057/fr.1989.21

Shorten, Bill. 2016. Budget Reply Speech. 3 May. Available at: www.alp. org.au/bill_shorten_budget_reply_2016

Stewart, Miranda, Moore Andre, Whiteford Peter and Grafton Quentin. 2015. *A Stocktake of the Tax System and Directions for Reform: Five years after the Henry review*. Report, Tax and Transfer Policy Institute. Available at: taxpolicy.crawford.anu.edu.au/files/uploads/taxstudies_ crawford_anu_edu_au/2015-03/stocktake_report_final_web_ version.pdf

Treasury. 2015a. *Intergenerational Report: Australia in 2055*. Canberra: Commonwealth of Australia. Available at: treasury.gov.au/ publication/2015-intergenerational-report/

Treasury. 2015b. *Re:Think Discussion Paper*. Australian Government. Available at: bettertax.gov.au/files/2015/03/TWP_combined-online. pdf

Treasury. 2017. *Budget 2017–18*. Available at: www.budget.gov.au

UN (United Nations). 2015. *Progress of the World's Women 2015–2016: Transforming Economics, Realizing Rights.* Available at: progress. unwomen.org

WGEA (Workplace Gender Equality Agency). 2016. *Gender Pay Equity Insights—2016 Report.* Available at: www.wgea.gov.au/sites/default/ files/BCEC_WGEA_Gender_Pay_Equity_Insights_2016_Report.pdf

Whiteford, Peter. 2016. 'Ideas for Australia: Welfare reform needs to be about improving well-being, not punishing the poor'. *The Conversation,* 21 April. Available at: theconversation.com/ideas-for-australia-welfare-reform-needs-to-be-about-improving-well-being-not-punishing-the-poor-56355

Whiteford, Peter. 2017. *Social security and welfare spending in Australia: Assessing long-term trends.* TTPI Policy Brief 1/2017. Available at: taxpolicy.crawford.anu.edu.au/publication/10880/social-security-and-welfare-spending-australia-assessing-long-term-trends

Williams, Blair and Marian Sawer. Forthcoming. 'Rainbow Labor and a purple policy launch: Gender and Sexuality Issues'. In Anika Gauja, Peter Chen, Jennifer Curtin and Juliet Pietsch (eds), *Double Disillusion' The 2016 Australian Federal Election.* Canberra: ANU Press.

Young, Claire. 2000. *Women, Tax and Social programs: The Gendered Impact of Funding Social Programs Through the Tax System.* Report for Status of Women Canada.

Part I: Frameworks for gender analysis

2

Australian tax-transfer policies and taxing for gender equality: Comparative perspectives and reform options

Kathleen Lahey

Australia was the world innovator of gender budget analysis in the 1980s; however, even as its levels of human development have risen to second place in the most recent United Nations (UN) Human Development Reports, its gender development rankings have fallen from year to year. This chapter places the Australian experience in the comparative and international context. It compares the status of women in Australia with other select Anglo-group and Nordic countries, and, with regard to child care policies, with South Korea, a leading country in the Asia-Pacific region. The chapter analyses the gender effects of the long-term focus in fiscal policy on taxing for economic growth that has led to falling tax ratios (tax revenues as a share of gross domestic product (GDP)) in the interests of incentivising business profits and capital accumulation. In this comparative context, the chapter examines how key tax policies, in combination with government expenditure programs, particularly as affected by fiscal austerity strategies after the Global Financial Crisis (GFC) of 2007–08, in turn affect the economic status of women and thus progress toward gender equality. This is discussed on the structural level and in relation to specific economic indicators such as women's high levels of unpaid work and workplace discrimination, and low levels of earnings and child care resources.

Taxing for economic growth vs taxing for equality

The history of contemporary taxation in Australia is, in many ways, the history of the search for capital accumulation and wealth by all available means—including through special treatment in taxation and spending laws. Debates over the use of households and corporations as tax units form part of that history, as they continue to be conceptualised as re/ productive associations that mediate the ownership and taxation of incomes and capital in private hands. It has long been agreed that taxes should increase with ability to pay (Smith 1904, Book V, Ch. II, pars 25– 28). However, even those advocating the use of tax systems to mitigate inequalities in incomes and wealth have agreed that the search for equality should not impair motivation to work and accumulate capital (Mill 1848, p. 510). Thus, efforts to bring capital gains into national tax bases failed until 1965 in the United Kingdom, 1972 in Canada and 1985 in Australia. Even after the introduction of capital gains taxation, these countries continue to provide generous exemptions for capital gains in their income and corporate tax systems.

During the 20th century, any balance that may have originally existed between principles of equality versus capital accumulation and productivity in the United Kingdom, Canada and Australia has discernibly shifted toward emphasis on 'taxing for growth'. The original concept of equality in taxation was displaced by appeals to equity (Parliament of Great Britain 1919, p. 2, par. 6), almost completely erasing the use of the term 'equality' in tax policy discourses. At the same time, treating corporations as separate legal persons for purposes of taxation, while eliminating what is called the double taxation of corporations and shareholders, has led to systems of corporate integration or imputation of corporate pre-tax profits to shareholder taxpayers. This effectively turns corporate income taxation into a temporary withholding tax on distributed or realised profits to shareholders. The shift is justified on the basis that it is a more equitable way to tax capital incomes and gains from corporate interests. In fact, it reduces effective tax rates on corporate capital incomes (see, for example, Ainsworth et al. 2015, p. 32, figure 10). Turning to individuals, even in Australia and Canada, both of which had from the outset treated married women as separate individuals for income tax purposes instead of jointly as in the UK, the concepts of equity and ability to pay were increasingly invoked to justify a growing number of joint (couple) income tested tax and benefit provisions. These provisions reinforce denial of women's separate fiscal personality, while reducing effective tax rates for high-income sole breadwinner spouses.

Three developments with their roots in the 1970s and 1980s have framed contemporary debates as taxing for economic growth vs taxing for equality. The first development concerns economic growth. The restructuring of the UK fiscal system by the Thatcher Government in the early 1980s, which reduced corporate and top personal income tax (PIT) rates, augmented revenues with higher flat-rated consumption taxes, and reduced income security spending through the use of means-tested benefits, was highly influential. These changes were justified as necessary to increase economic efficiency and growth. Largely due to the growing political popularity of tax cuts, they inspired the US Government under President Reagan and governments of other developed countries to implement variations on this overall theme.

By the mid-2000s, the Organisation for Economic Co-operation and Development (OECD) had begun regular annual structural surveillance of the GDP growth of its members (OECD 2005) and it had also identified a set of tax and expenditure policies calculated to contribute to increased economic growth. This 'taxing for growth' formula calls for the following changes, in descending order of priority: reduce high personal and corporate income tax rates, employer social security contributions, and tax benefits and expenditures; shift the revenue burden to other tax bases such as the value added tax (VAT) or goods and services tax (GST), or other consumption taxes; reduce social spending on health, income support, pensions, disability and unemployment benefits (in both quantum and duration); and increase women's paid work time with accessible child care and reduced second-earner tax barriers (OECD 2007, pp. 17–19). The OECD has applied this approach in every annual edition of *Going for Growth*. It has been applied in the EU and regionally, as well as by international development and financial institutions (e.g. Acosta-Ormaechea and Yoo 2010).

The second development relates to gender equality and originated in Australia. The 1970s saw support for women's equality including in governments, leading to the enactment of new anti-discrimination laws and active monitoring of legislation for its gender impact, which produced formalised gender budget analysis in the early 1980s (as explained further in Chapters 10 and 11). Gender budgeting practices first developed in Australia are now carried out in well over 100 countries and have opened the door to systemic examination of the gender impact of virtually all forms of government action (Sharp and Broomhill 2013; Budlender 2001).

The third development, also related to gender equality, was the ratification of the Convention on the Elimination of All Forms of Discrimination Against Women (CEDAW) (UN 1979) in the early 1980s, and then the adoption of the Beijing Platform for Action in 1995 (UN 1995). These both supported domestic constitutional and legal recognition of gender equality as a fundamental human right. CEDAW supported the enactment of statutory and constitutional sex equality provisions designed to require both formal and substantive equality in all laws, policies and practices (see, for example, Fredman and Goldblatt 2015). The Beijing Platform was important for the detailed guidance it provides on how all laws, policies and practices are to be evaluated for gender impact. The Beijing Platform expanded what is understood to fall within the scope of gender mainstreaming and gender budgeting in the context of periodic CEDAW reviews, including (from 2002) the adjudication of complaints brought against state parties under CEDAW optional protocols.

The call for 'taxing for gender equality' arose from the intersection of gender budget work and the growing recognition of women's equality in domestic and international law. However, the concept of gender equality in tax and welfare laws did not become concrete beyond domestic levels until well into the 2000s. Helen Hodgson and Kerrie Sadiq (in Chapter 4) describe how this human rights framework can be used in the development of fiscal policy.

By 2008, the combined effects of the GFC and resulting austerity policies brought increased urgency to demands for gender equality in both tax and expenditure policies. At this point, the OECD and the European Commission began to take note of the relationship between fiscal policies and economic inequality (see, for example, OECD 2008). The focus at these transnational policy levels remained on activating women's paid work, although growing concern about income inequalities did accelerate work on taxing for equality during this time. Beginning in 2010, the OECD and International Monetary Fund (IMF) began publishing reports on taxation and gender equality, searching for synergistic tax and fiscal policies to promote both equality and economic growth, and, as the Occupy movement protesting concentration of wealth in the hands of the rich grew, they also began publishing high-profile reports on income inequalities (OECD 2010a, 2011; Joumard et al. 2012). At the same time, CEDAW and the UN agencies began to include tax and fiscal issues in their critical gender work.

Strategies for 'taxing for equality' include reducing taxes on low incomes, particularly those of second earners and the self-employed, and increasing income security, pension and training supports for low-income and low-skill workers, single parents and middle-income workers. Funding such measures should come from increasing graduated personal and corporate income tax rates, and should be accompanied by increasing care resources to equalise unpaid workloads associated with low paid work levels, wealth and inheritance taxes and reduction in the use of tax expenditures and joint fiscal measures that have income and gender regressive effects. In Chapter 3, Patricia Apps provides a detailed discussion of the implications for women of a decline in PIT progressivity. Tackling inequalities also requires increased regulation of labour markets, a living wage, affordable education and increased taxation of capital incomes. Various studies have identified both tax and regulatory methods to reduce exclusive focus on growth, and have also pinpointed new tax and transfer policies that can counteract poverty and reduce overall income inequalities that are increasingly recognised as impediments to durable economic growth (Förster et al. 2014).

In 2016, taxing for gender equality became an acknowledged global policy priority as new transnational standards were adopted in relation to poverty, gender, economic and environmental development goals (UN 2016a; UN 2016c), and in relation to revenue issues and financing for development (UN 2015a). These documents contain express commitments to mainstreaming gender equality and poverty reduction outcomes on a systemic basis, including specifically in relation to all revenue issues (UN Economic and Social Council 2015). These commitments apply to global members in relation to all their domestic laws, policies and practices, as well as to all government acts involving transnational or international relations.

Two other important developments have deepened acknowledgement of the critical role of taxation in addressing gender equality and poverty issues. First, in 2014, the UN Special Rapporteur on Extreme Poverty and Human Rights produced a detailed analysis of how countless features of corporate and personal income taxation, value-added, excise, sales and property taxes, and various fees, charges and transfer laws systemically intensify women's economic disadvantages, perpetuate gender inequalities and poverty and thus violate international human rights laws (Carmona 2014, especially ss. I and II). The Special Rapporteur identified a lack of progressivity, lack of appropriate exemptions and failure to individualise tax laws as the most discriminatory features of income tax systems. In corporate income taxation, she found that the widespread use of low tax rates, special allowances and tax incentives largely benefits men because of their larger shares of private capital and their ability to form incorporated businesses under conditions that are not equally available to women.

With respect to consumption taxes, the most important of which are the VAT, sales and other flat-rated taxes, the Special Rapporteur expressed deep concern at the growing use of the VAT without careful design to protect those with low incomes. Consumption taxes can regressively reduce women's after-tax incomes to the point that they become unable to meet their own and their dependants' minimum nutrition and development needs. Not only does this pose serious risks to human development in the most fundamental sense, but it can also undo the beneficial impact of social protection or nutrition programs that may otherwise be provided by governments concerned with human wellbeing, particularly in the gestational and early years of life. To counter the many negative effects of existing tax and other fiscal policies on women, those living in poverty and other vulnerable groups, the Special Rapporteur made detailed recommendations on fiscal changes to support gender equality. In sum, these recommendations are conceptually simple—to use broad-based income tax systems with graduated rates built around actual ability to pay taxes to raise adequate and redistributive levels of revenues, and to make minimal use of flat-rated consumption taxes, particularly when they render basic necessities unaffordable to any members of society.

Second, two ground-breaking decisions were issued by the UN Committee on the Elimination of Discrimination Against Women that hold national governments accountable for failing their commitments to gender equality, poverty reduction and fiscal equality in tax/expenditure policies. In the 2014 *Blok* decision, the Netherlands was found to have violated women's maternity leave rights (UN 2014). In the 2015 *Canada Inquiry* decision, the UN Committee held all levels of Canadian governments accountable for a long and detailed list of violations of international poverty reduction and gender equality rights in its persistent failure to take effective steps to lift Indigenous women and communities from the depths of longstanding poverty (UN 2015b). In both decisions, the committee found that signing and ratifying CEDAW bound states to implement it, and ordered restorative payments and programs to be established by the governments in breach.

Taxing for gender equality matters

It can be seen from the above brief history that the set of policies aimed at 'taxing for growth' gathered momentum during roughly the same period of time in which gender equality has become increasingly accepted as a normative policy standard. When viewed in the aggregate and over time, the cumulative effects of the 'taxing for growth' cuts in taxation and social expenditure on the status of women are clear. Although the UK, Australia, Canada and the US each have distinctive fiscal profiles, important parallels are seen in the changes in the levels and composition of tax revenues in each of these four countries, especially when compared with two Nordic countries, Sweden and Norway.

The Anglo-group countries started out with relatively low tax ratios in the mid-1960s. Even then, however, there were substantial differences among them: Australia's tax ratio was the lowest at 19.9 per cent, the UK's was 29.3 per cent, the US's was 23.5 per cent and Canada's was 25.3 per cent. Swedish and Norwegian tax ratios are much higher (above 40 per cent of GDP) and have been higher throughout. Tax ratios have tended to increase in most countries since the 1960s, although the US tax ratio fell to 23 per cent in 2009, which reflected both the extreme tax cutting policies of the Bush Government and the effect of the GFC on revenues (OECD.Stat 2016a). These high and low tax ratios do not necessarily correlate with governmental political orientations: the highest tax ratios in Australia and the UK have been under conservative governments (under Howard during 2000 in Australia, and Thatcher in 1982 in the UK); and in the US and Canada, under liberal governments (Clinton during 2000 in the US, and Chrétien in 1997 in Canada).

Women's levels of human development as compared with men's appear to be vulnerable to the effects of falling tax ratios in developed countries. Using a time consistent (TC) recalculation of the United Nations new 2014 gender development index (GDI, TC), Table 2.1 demonstrates that having and maintaining high tax ratios appears to increase the chances of maintaining high levels of women's human development relative to men in some countries, and it does appear that countries with low tax ratios throughout appear to slow down women's rates of development. All the countries in Table 2.1 started out with high GDI, TC rankings in 1995. Twenty years later, every one of those countries had lost significant ground on that version of the GDI, and all but the UK had scaled down their tax ratios to varying degrees.

Table 2.1: UN GDI, TC version ranks, OECD tax ratios, selected countries, 1995 and 2013/2014

	Tax ratio 1995 (%)	Tax ratio 2014 (%)	Change in tax ratio (%)	GDI, TC 1995	GDI, TC 2013
Sweden	45.6	42.7	−2.9	2	4
Norway	40.9	39.1	−1.8	5	7
Canada	35.9	30.8	−4.1	7	15
UK	31.9	32.6	+0.5	16	25
Australia	28.2	27.5	−0.7	14	20
US	26.3	26	−0.3	3	8

Sources: Stotsky et al (2016), Appendix D, p. 57. These data were used to re-rank high-development countries for purposes of Table 2.1. Copy on file with author.

During the 20 years from 1995 to 2013, when the emphasis on tax cuts for economic growth intensified, all of these countries lost ground in terms of their GDI, TC rankings. Although the UK did not cut its tax ratio, it also lost considerable ground; tax ratios alone do not necessarily drive GDI, TC rankings.

Sweden and Norway, the two countries with the highest tax ratios in both 1995 and 2014, also fell in the GDI, TC rankings between 1995 and 2013, but they experienced the least downward movement of these six countries. It is notable that Canada, which made the deepest tax cuts overall, lost more ground on this index than either Australia or the US, even though the latter two countries started and ended with tax ratios significantly lower than that of Canada in 2014. The divergent taxation and transfer paths taken in the four Anglo-group countries have had considerable impact on the development status of women in those countries, while maintaining high tax ratios in the Nordic group countries at least correlates with crucial gender equalising steps taken in Sweden and Norway.

The dimensions of gender, income inequality, economic opportunities and economic outcomes are not static but are 'interactive' (Gonzales et al. 2015, pp. 5–6) and 'simultaneous' factors that all actively reshape gender status on an ongoing basis (Stotsky 2006, pp. 17–22). The overall health of public finances in a country is important in ensuring that country's ability to fund programs to improve the level of human development and gender equality. But explicitly taxing for gender equality also matters. The channels that connect macro-economic indicators like tax ratios with the gender impact of specific tax policies are themselves shaped by the status of women, defined at any point in time by existing 'norms, practices, and social institutions governing gender inequality' (Stotsky 2006, p. 18). Economic development engages all institutional arrangements—from access to education or transportation, to access to finance capital—that may affect women's opportunities and outcomes as levels of development change over time.

Gender economists have now confirmed the validity of the UN gender indices in measuring progress toward gender equality (Gonzales et al. 2015, pp. 5–6), and studies testing the sensitivity of the GDI, TC to changes in various indicators are now underway. While these gender equality indices do usefully present the generalised status of women over time, it is essential that they be used with individual country-specific indicators to evaluate how the gender impact of key policies on their own and in context contribute to understanding how changes in the 'broader picture' have come about (Stotsky et al. 2016, pp. 42–43; Gonzales et al. 2015).

Identifying what 'taxing for gender equality' might mean in relation to a specific country or region calls for multiple levels of analysis. On the macro-economic level, the composition of tax revenues can be extremely important in identifying factors that promote or undercut gender equality. Just as gender indicators represent in a single figure the combined effects of a wide range of socio-economic factors, so tax ratios represent total revenues collected by large composite revenue and expenditure systems that operate on all levels of government throughout each year in question. And just as changes in large institutions such as the education system or transportation can affect gender equalities, the types and amounts of taxes collected can affect total revenues collected and after-tax incomes, and consequently their gender incidence.

Thus, taxing for gender equality begins with large aggregates, but in turn depends on identifying fiscal gender effects at institutional levels like businesses, households and schools as well as at individual levels. At the same time, individual level gender effects are meaningful only to the extent that specific individual characteristics such as living conditions, earnings and assets, dependencies, education, geographic location, health and age can be examined in the context of population numbers and in the context of specific revenue and expenditure policies.

Indeed, full understanding of fiscal gender impact can only be gained by bringing all elements—debt, public capital, illicit financial flows and tax administrative capabilities—into the picture. But the complexities of fiscal gender impact analysis are such that great strides still need to be made in unpacking the complexities of specific tax and benefit systems, one country at a time.

Connecting national tax structures with gender equality

Breaking historical tax ratios down into their main revenue components helps illuminate how multiple layers of tax and expenditure policies interact to shape economic gender outcomes. Figure 2.1 compares the two Nordic countries Sweden and Norway, the UK, Canada, Australia and the US in terms of their overall tax ratios and main revenue categories. These are income and capital gains taxes on individuals and businesses, social security contributions, property taxes, payroll and workforce taxes, and taxes on goods, services, and other forms of consumption.

Public fiscal capacity is important to the status of women because, historically, women have more constrained access to money, and thus to economic power; public provision is essential to fill this gap. In every country, even now, women have lower incomes but longer workdays, more unpaid work hours and lower hourly wages than men because they are culturally expected to take more responsibility for social provisioning and care work than men. In a sense, the continued high levels of privatisation of all aspects of social reproduction and provisioning continue to place additional barriers in the paths of women's access to paid work and thus to economic equality (see, for example, UN Women 2015, pp. 70–104).

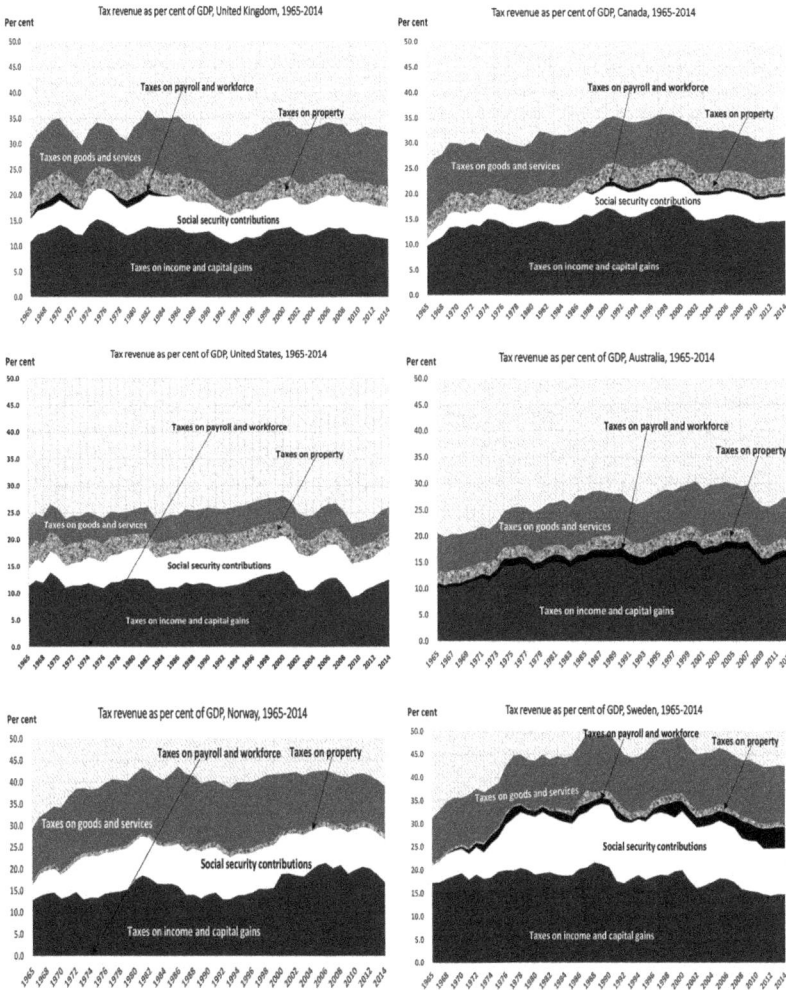

Figure 2.1: Composition of revenues, selected OECD countries, 1995–2013

Source: OECD.Stat (2016a).

The most striking difference among the countries in Figure 2.1 is the volume of total revenues collected by Norway and Sweden compared with the other countries: Sweden's total tax ratio is 16.7 per cent higher than the US ratio, and Norway's is 13.1 per cent higher. These two countries have greater fiscal capacity to invest in equality-promoting policies than the other four countries. One view of women's high levels of economic engagement and equality in Nordic countries is that they are the result of generations of investment in programs that support women's economic status (see, for example, Hernes 1987), although recent studies sharply differentiate 'maternalist' gender policies in Norway from longstanding recognition of women's individual workplace rights in Sweden (Sainsbury 2001, pp. 113–142, 133–137; Lundqvist and Fink 2016).

The composition of a country's tax revenues is relevant because tax systems not only raise revenues to fund government programs, but also withdraw cash from private hands, thus affecting the distribution of after-tax incomes by the types of tax laws that make up the overall revenue system. Finally, it is crucial to identify whether government spending and transfer programs are progressive or regressive in their impact on net after-tax incomes of women and men. At the macro-economic level, the degree of progressivity of the overall tax and transfer system affects the after-tax distribution of incomes overall and by gender.

In most countries, the main source of progressivity in the total tax/expenditure system comes from graduated tax rates applied to personal incomes and capital gains, together with the flatter rates applied to corporate incomes and capital gains. By that measure, Australia should produce the largest degree of redistribution of the six countries in Table 2.2, because its income taxes make up nearly 58 per cent of total revenues, followed by 48 per cent in the US and Canada. However, as the Gini coefficients in Table 2.2 demonstrate, the tax-transfer system in the UK is more redistributive than in any of the other countries in this set (167-point reduction), even though it raises just 34.9 per cent of its total revenue from income and capital gains taxes. In contrast, Norway raises 42.2 per cent of its revenue from income and capital gains taxes, but it starts out with a more equal distribution of market incomes, redistributes incomes almost as strongly as the UK through its tax-transfer system, and ends up with the highest level of income equality of the six countries. The US, which raises much more total revenue via income and capital gains taxes, redistributes the least in the tax-transfer process, and ends with the highest level of income inequality in terms of net disposable incomes after taxes paid and benefits received are all taken into consideration.

Table 2.2: Gini coefficients by income measures and revenue structures, selected countries, 2014

	Gini: Market income	Gini: Gross income	Gini: Disposable income	Change from market to disposable income Gini	% of all revenue from income, profits, and capital gains tax	PIT only as % of GDP
Norway	0.412	0.296	0.252	-0.16	42.5%	9.8%
Sweden	0.443	0.311	0.281	-0.162	34.9%	12.2%
Canada	0.44	0.361	0.322	-0.118	48.0%	11.3%
Australia	0.483	0.39	0.337	-0.146	57.9%	11.4%
UK	0.527	0.399	0.358	-0.167	34.9%	8.8%
US	0.508	0.433	0.394	-0.114	47.7%	10.2%

Gini: Scale 0 to 1, with 0 representing complete income equality and 1 representing the highest levels of income inequality; Gross income: before taxes; Disposable income: Net income after all transfers received and taxes paid; Revenue figures: All revenue from income, profits and capital gains tax includes taxes paid by both individuals and corporations; PIT (personal income tax): all revenue from taxes on personal income, profits and capital gains only.

Sources: OECD.Stat (2016a, 2016b).

Table 2.2 also demonstrates how important the progressive income tax components of overall fiscal systems are in these six countries—personal income, profits and capital gains taxes alone collected between 8.8 per cent and 12.2 per cent of GDP in revenues. The two Nordic countries have much larger overall revenue systems, and they have used those revenues to invest heavily over time in public infrastructure and services like education, health, housing, child care and transportation. Carefully designed public services and infrastructure can cut the costs of living for individuals, increase individual lifetime earnings and even enhance intergenerational transmission of economic status (Afonso et al. 2010, pp. 367–389). In such fiscal systems, higher levels of income equality and gender equality can be attained even without sharply progressive tax systems.

The longer view is also important in considering interactions among tax ratios, the overall tax mix and the degree of redistribution that may be generated by a specific tax-transfer system. As recently as one decade ago, each of the selected countries (except Norway) had higher levels of market income and disposable income equality than they do at present (OECD. Stat 2016a). Over time, the combined effects of tax cuts and reduced government public spending and transfers have produced higher after-tax/after-transfer Gini coefficients signalling increased levels of overall income inequalities for all of the six countries except Norway.

The gender impact of Australia's tax structure

Connecting the structure of tax systems with gender-specific incomes requires us to disaggregate the statistics for income of men and women. This enables us to get a picture of incomes over time. It shows that women's earnings at different ages are distinctively different from men's.

Figure 2.2 presents the average pre-tax and after-tax income, by age groups and disaggregated by gender, in tax statistics released by the Australian Taxation Office (ATO) for 2012–13. The gender income gap for men and women was at about 22 per cent at age 30 (and was lower than this up to age 24). However, during peak adult earning years (ages 45 through 49 for both women and men), Figure 2.2 shows that men's incomes soared while women's remained more or less flat. Women faced an average income gender gap of about 40 per cent during those years. At increased ages, the gender income gap again shrinks to about 22 per cent and then to 19 per cent over age 75, although the gap never closes (ATO 2015).

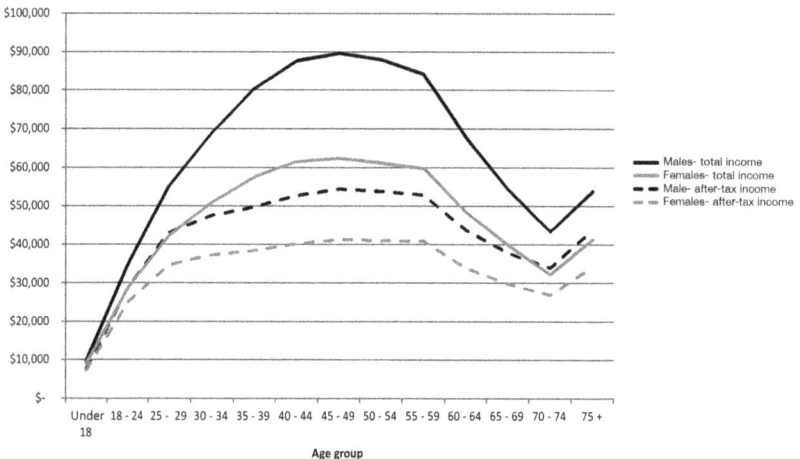

Figure 2.2: Average total and after-tax income, by age and gender, 2013
Source: Author's calculations and chart based on ATO (2015) data.

These gender income differences can also be expressed in terms of average individual incomes by age range. During peak earning years, men's average pre-tax income was $89,588, and women's average pre-tax income was $54,382. Note that taxable income includes some public transfers, such as the age pension, which are included in taxable income (although senior Australians and age pensioners get a higher tax threshold because of the Senior Australians and Pensioners Tax Offset); however, other transfers such as family benefits are not taxable. On an after-tax basis, men's average incomes were $62,358, and women's $41,247. This represented an average reduction in after-tax incomes of 30.4 per cent for men and 24.2 per cent for women, demonstrating that in that year, the Australian tax system was taxing women's average incomes more lightly than men's (ATO 2015).

The average redistribution from men to women will be different at every income level, but the gender impact of the tax system can be generalised by using gender shares of total after-tax incomes as an overall measure of gender redistribution. For example, in 2012–13, men started out with 62.1 per cent of all total incomes (defined as incomes from all sources plus public transfers). Women as a group started out with just 37.9 per cent of total incomes received in that year.

After taking account of various tax exemptions, deductions and tax rates in the PIT system, it can be seen that the combined impact of the income tax in 2012–13 slightly favoured women as a group. Men were left with about 1.8 per cent less after-tax income than they started out with at the beginning of the taxation process, for a total net after-tax/transfer share of 62.3 per cent. At the same time, women's total share was 1.8 per cent larger, bringing the combined share of all women's after-tax incomes to 39.7 per cent.

While this degree of gender redistribution may not seem like much, it represents a shift of substantial amounts of pre-tax incomes from men to women through the tax system. The 1.8 per cent increase in women's after-tax disposable income reduces the gender gap to 34 per cent for peak earning ages—6 per cent smaller than the pre-tax income gender gap. The gaps at other ages fell as well, from 22 per cent pre-tax to 19 per cent after-tax for early earning years and as low as 17 per cent after age 70. If detailed data on the distribution of market incomes, consumption taxes and all government transfers by gender were brought into the calculation, it is likely that the degree of gender redistribution through the entire transition from market to after-tax/transfer disposable income would be even more substantial. As a comparison, in Canada, the transition from total income to total after-tax/transfer disposable income shifted 2 per cent of income from men to women in 2011. Another 2 per cent shift in disposable income can be attributed to the transition from market to total incomes, and from after-tax/transfer incomes to consumable incomes, which also take consumption taxes into account (see Lahey 2015, p. 39, Table 9).

These single-digit adjustments cannot by themselves offset the effects of longstanding economic gender inequalities. However, they emphasise that the fundamental principle of ability to pay in taxation has important implications for the taxation of women. So long as women face multiple forms of gender discrimination in terms of higher levels of unpaid care and social provisioning work, unequal hiring, retention and promotion in paid work, lower wages, fewer working hours, less high-quality employment, less saving capacity and unequal access to finance capital, then, on average, women do indeed have less ability to pay taxes than men.

Thus the first step in taxing for gender equality is to ensure that the PIT system uses a wide range of rates and that personal income and capital gains tax systems are designed to raise significant amounts of total revenues overall. The gender regressivity or progressivity of the tax-transfer system depends on raising substantial shares of total revenues through the PIT because almost all other components of tax systems are regressive in impact and thus detract from progressivity.

Gender and company taxation, tax expenditures and the GST

As discussed above, the most progressive components of tax systems tend to be PIT rates. However, we should also consider the tax base and its regressive effects for gender equality. While personal and corporate income, profits and capital gains taxes are more progressive in impact than most other taxes, corporate income and capital gains tax rates are usually lower and flatter than personal wage tax rates in most countries. Figure 2.3 shows that this is the case in all but the Norwegian tax system, which until recent years essentially substituted increased company income tax revenues for PIT revenues. Reducing the overall amount of revenue raised through corporate taxation does not necessarily reduce the regressive impact of that component of the total tax system. This is because as corporate income tax rates are lowered, there is a larger benefit for high tax rate individuals to restructure their personal income and investment flows through corporations.

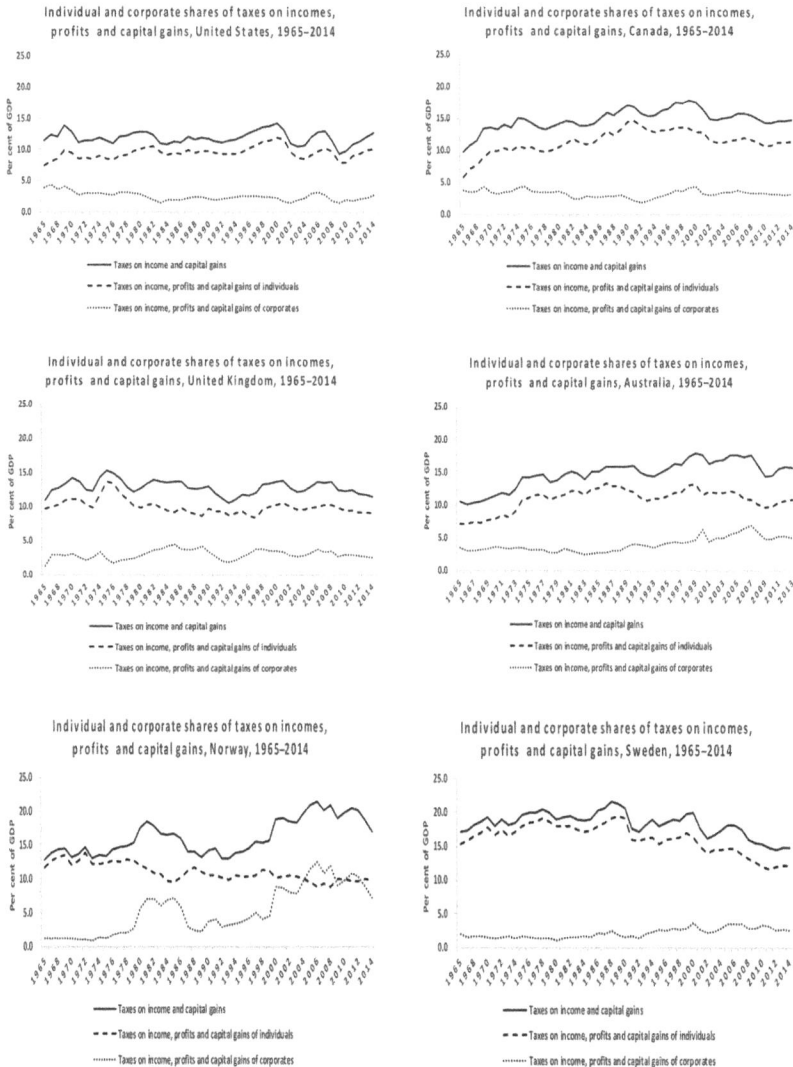

Figure 2.3: Individual and corporate shares of taxes on incomes, profits and capital gains, selected OECD countries, 2014

Source: OECD.Stat (2016a).

In general, the capital gains and dividends received by individual shareholders attract significant tax reductions, exemptions or other special treatment that reduce the overall progressivity of the personal tax-transfer system. This is true whether the role of the company income tax is reduced by lowering the company tax rate or by moving more fully toward 'integration' of corporate tax loads with individual taxation through mechanisms like Australia's dividend franking credit or Canada's partial corporate tax imputation system. Any measures that partially or fully merge corporate and personal tax burdens have this effect, because they eliminate permanently some component of either corporate or PIT bases from annual tax revenues, and thus can reduce the total tax collected on corporate-source incomes.

The use of tax systems to deliver tax expenditures in the form of exemptions, deductions, credits or deferrals also shrinks the tax base and thus its potential for progressivity. Finally, consumption taxes are based on consumption expenditure, not on income, exempt savings from taxation and, unless designed carefully, tax consumption by individuals of all ages, including those with little to no ability to pay. The gender impact of these systemic effects is affected by the socio-economic factors that shape women's lower average incomes and wealth. Women with high incomes benefit less from these lower taxes on capital income and gains because women have lower incomes than men at every point on the income scale. Only 23 per cent of those in the highest income decile are women, and the average incomes of women in each decile are lower than the average men's incomes in those deciles (ATO 2015, Table 3). This is explained further in Chapter 9 on the distribution of women with top incomes.

Gender, enterprise forms and the company tax

The gender effects of taxing corporations at flatter and lower rates than those applied to profits of unincorporated businesses produce a two-tiered income tax system that enables business owners and high wealth individuals to route income-producing activities through corporations at lower tax rates than will apply to unincorporated enterprises that are taxed within the PIT system.

In Australia, the 30 per cent corporate tax rate is high compared with that in many other countries. However, it is still 2.5 per cent lower than the 32.5 per cent PIT rate applied to incomes over $37,000, and is substantially lower than the 37 per cent and 45 per cent rates applied to incomes over $80,000 and $180,000, respectively (in 2016–17). The reduction of the company tax rate to 27.5 per cent for small businesses (under $10 million turnover) has produced a further 5 per cent rate advantage in incorporating a small business.[1] In sum, the tax benefits of incorporating a business enterprise are significant, increase in value as the size of business investments increases and also enable shareholder-owners to accumulate after-tax business profits in corporations with the possibility of realising the long-term increase in the form of capital gains, half of which are exempt from the income tax.

Just as there are significant income gaps in employment earnings in Australia and most other countries, so business profit gender gaps are also substantial. Women who are business owner/operators comprise 12.5 per cent of all women in Australia's paid labour force, but only a third of them incorporate their businesses. The average profit received by women unincorporated business owners in 2011 was $22,000, compared with $46,280 by men (ABS 2015).

In contrast with women in employment, who have average earnings of $52,000, self-employed women with no other employees had average incomes of $30,520, compared to self-employed men on $53,600. It seems likely that many women form their own businesses to adapt to lack of paid work opportunities and access to affordable child care. Almost half of women business operators surveyed had dependant children, and most were 55 or older, or in remote locations, or faced the additional barriers imposed on disabled, immigrant, Aboriginal or Torres Strait Islander women. Top detailed industrial occupations included hair/beauty, cleaning, child care, accommodation, food establishment, management and professional services. Most reported that retirement provisions were not a high priority (ABS 2015).

For women earning relatively low business incomes, incorporation produces little to no tax advantage, particularly if business profits are used immediately for living expenses instead of being retained in the company for business development. A similar picture emerges with respect to women-owned incorporated enterprises. Average incomes were $51,900 for women, $75,400 for men (ABS 2015). At the lower end of annual profits, incorporation could actually impose tax penalties on women.

---

1   The Australian Government has announced a further reduction of the company income tax rate in stages to 25 per cent, but this proposal has only partly been enacted to date.

The tax advantages of incorporation for women are relatively limited. Only the few who have sufficient start-up or finance capital and effective business plans will realise the potential tax advantages.

Women who own investment real estate or invest in shares can benefit from the capital gains tax reduced tax rate and the refundable dividend franking credit in the corporate-shareholder imputation system. However, in practice these tax provisions are not as valuable to women as to men. They operate to magnify women's existing income inequalities in two ways. First, women have lower annual incomes compared with men, less financial capacity for saving and investment, and they therefore receive smaller shares of such tax benefits. For example, women received just 29 per cent of the tax benefits of the dividend franking credit even though 42 per cent of those claiming the franking credit were women (ATO 2015, Table 3). Second, with lower incomes and facing lower tax rates, the proportion of saving from such tax provisions will be smaller than those realised by men, who have higher average incomes. This 'upside down' effect of tax concessions and other tax expenditures is a distinctive feature of income taxes with progressive rate structures. The higher the individual tax rate, the larger the total monetary value of a tax exclusion such as the capital gains tax 50 per cent discount.

Over time, the cumulative impact of men's larger shares of incomes and thus larger shares of concessionally taxed investment income and gains, larger shares of ownership in corporations and greater opportunities to accumulate wealth in corporations at lower marginal tax rates means that women lag behind men in accumulating wealth in Australia, both in terms of direct personal investments and in superannuation funds (Austen et al. 2014, pp. 25–52).

Gender and the GST

In the aftermath of the GFC, taxing for growth advocates have singled out increases in consumption tax rates (VAT, GST and carbon taxes) combined with cuts to both corporate and PIT rates as the best ways to increase government revenues while accelerating economic growth (OECD 2010b) in a 'tax mix' switch. Even though after-tax/transfer income inequalities have increased in most countries, including Australia, the UK and Canada, at least partly as the result of following these recommendations, Australian governments have pursued this path in recent years. Arguments against such a change because of the well-known regressive impact are made, for example, in Usui (2011).

The regressive impact of consumption taxation on low-income people and those in poverty is widely recognised, but the gender effects of this switch have been more difficult to examine. However, there is growing evidence that this tax shift—or any increase in GST or VAT rates on their own—will be gender regressive in two ways.[2]

First, women's average incomes are lower than men's, and are clustered more heavily in lower income ranges. Any increases in GST rates or elimination of GST exemptions will overtax women as compared with men. GST systems use flat tax rates and thus take a larger proportion of low incomes than from middle or high incomes (Apps and Rees 2013, pp. 679–693; Lahey 2015, Table 18). This means that women will bear a larger share of such GST changes as compared with men (Equality Rights Alliance 2016; Apps 2015, p. 18; Lahey 2015, pp. 77–79, Table 19; Apps and Rees 2013).

When proposals to increase GST rates are compared with the distribution of personal income and/or corporate income tax increases as an alternate route to increased revenues, it becomes clear that the choice is between obtaining additional revenues from the poorest or from the wealthiest. GST increases will impose new tax liabilities on those with the lowest incomes, while personal and/or corporate income tax increases will have no impact on those with the least ability to pay, and will concentrate tax increases on those with higher incomes (Phillips and Taylor 2015, pp. 17–27 and Appendix Tables; Lahey 2015, p. 78, Table 19; Apps 2015, p. 18; Apps and Rees 2013).

Second, attempts to ameliorate the income and gender regressivity of new or increased GST rates by distributing compensating welfare payments to those most likely to lose crucial purchasing power will also have negative gender effects. Such compensation payments are invariably based on household incomes and thus build in assumptions about shared consumption that may not be realistic. These compensatory payments would give women smaller shares of compensation than they would

---

2   This discussion refers to GST regressivity in terms of income as the welfare measure, not to expenditure or lifetime consumption as the welfare measures (OECD 2014).

receive if they were treated as separate individuals. As Patricia Apps has pointed out (see also Chapter 3), not only are these joint tax penalties, but these compensatory payments would not necessarily ameliorate the effect of overtaxation of women regardless of their own income levels or household incomes (Apps 2015, p. 18; Lahey 2005, pp. 30–31). They reduce women's access to such payments upon marriage, and violate the principle of independent taxation of individuals on the basis of their own ability to pay.

Taxes, transfers and making paid work pay

On average, women in Australia perform 65 per cent of all unpaid and 34 per cent of all paid work hours, but receive just 37.9 per cent of total incomes, including government transfer payments (UN 2006; ATO 2015, Table 3). Men work almost the same number of hours each day as women, but receive 62.1 per cent of total incomes because more of their time is devoted to paid work during their lives. These imbalances reflect the persistence of gendered sex roles in households and workplaces, government policy offices and cultural expectations that condition women to take most responsibility for physical and social reproduction, social provisioning and care work. It is left to individual women to figure out how to engage in whatever level of paid work they can manage as their lives unfold.

These traditional arrangements are culturally self-perpetuating; generation after generation of children and thus the whole of society are continually informed that this is what women should do, so that their mainly male partners can work full-time in full-year paid jobs. In this system, men begin earning higher incomes than women so early in life (as shown in Figure 2.1) that even if members of a couple decide to trade roles, it is not necessarily assured that they can step into each other's economic positions at will. Guyonne Kalb looks in more detail at how Australian tax and transfer settings discourage Australian women from engaging in paid work (Chapter 5), while the impact of 'market' work time on a male or female parent's choices about their time spent on child care is considered by Racionero and Dinh in Chapter 7.

Women's labour force participation rates have of course been increasing for well over a century. Although Australia has maintained a greater overall level of progressivity in its tax-transfer system than many other countries, despite having a smaller fiscal footprint (see, for example, Joumard et al. 2012, pp. 35–37), Australia's tax and social benefit programs have not provided the same quality of support for women's paid work as for men's. Australian government ambivalence about women's paid work is revealed through family tax and transfer policies focused on making the breadwinner's paid work pay. These tax and benefit policies help families live on what are essentially 1.5 salaries to stave off child poverty, but without redressing gendered time and earnings inequalities.

Canada, the UK and the US all share the same pattern. Even Norway, which has pursued a much broader Nordic revenue/social spending model, has come relatively late to confronting the same dilemmas. No country has managed to free everyone from longstanding sex-role stereotypes socially, economically or in fiscal policies.

Tax-transfer unit choice

Three structural problems still have to be addressed in Australian fiscal policy. First is the tendency to conceptualise women as part of marital, cohabitation or household units instead of seeing them as fully equal individuals in their own economic and legal right. Second is the reluctance to socialise (re)production fully enough to enable all women and men to participate on equal terms in economic production. Third is the concern that promoting the narrow policy objective of women's equality in paid work, without regard to women's unpaid caring and home production workloads and life course needs, risks instrumentalising women's paid work rather than promoting substantive gender equality as a matter of fundamental human economic rights (see, for example, European Commission 2010, pp. 17–19).

When the US, Canada and Australia enacted their first income tax laws, they all broke from the UK model of using the married couple as the basic tax unit and instead adopted the individual as the tax unit. The US, however, moved toward the married couple as a tax unit in the 1920s, as high-income individuals sought to legitimate income splitting for tax minimisation purposes, with the result that full spousal income splitting and joint filing was enacted right after World War II and remains undisturbed even today.

In spite of the individual tax unit, none of the Anglo-group countries seem to be able to let go of fiscal coverture even though married women's struggles to obtain equal property rights are over a century old. In the 1960s, Canada began suffering from US joint filing envy in the wake of the Carter Commission report (Government of Canada 1966). Australia followed suit in the Asprey Report in the 1970s (Asprey 1975, pars 10.1–10.33) but ultimately accepted the individual tax unit. In the 1990s, Prime Minister John Howard attempted to resuscitate a family unit proposal in Australia, using outmoded US arguments. Political controversy led to withdrawal of his proposal. However, the government instead enacted a modified income splitting proposal, limited to 'a family that has a mother staying home', through family payments tested on joint income. Evidence of the high costs of income splitting made it clear that other social programs might have to be cancelled to finance even this partial form of income splitting (Costello n.d.; Smith 1994, p. 5; Page Research Centre 2004, p. 2).

More recent Australian governments have pursued the same policy goals through an array of policies designed to support single-income couples, give cash payments to 'stay-at-home mums', compensate mothers' unpaid child care in the home and help mothers stay out of paid work. In its May 2015 Budget, the conservative Abbott Government finally acknowledged that these now-costly single-income couple benefits had become largely irrelevant in a labour market dominated by dual-earner couples and that lack of adequate paid child care services had become a substantial barrier to women's paid work. Thus, the Abbott Budget presented proposals to replace the array of tax benefits for single-income couples with enhanced funding for paid child care for both single- and dual-income families. As of mid-2016, this approach has been further amended to provide direct compensation for up to 85 per cent of child care costs, plus supplementary child care support for low-income parents.

Child care costs

As in the UK, the US and Canada, the Australian budgetary cost-cutting advantages of delivering direct spending and tax benefits on a joint means-tested basis are difficult to combat politically. But the unfortunate result of this conceptual view is that single parents, who continue to be mainly women, and coupled women who are conceptualised as 'secondary workers' continue to be expected to solve their own child care problems without sufficient public sharing of these high costs.

Cash transfers to families have some of the same negative fiscal effects as other joint or household-based benefits: even if they are included in taxable income, cash transfers provide net after-tax benefits to single-income couples, but couples that require paid child care to support a second income-earner will have to spend most such benefits on paid child care. The same effect is created for single parents, especially for those on social assistance but without accompanying child care funding. The greater the concentration of benefits on 'recognising' unpaid work contributions, the larger the divide between parents in paid work and those with an unpaid domestic worker. These are not trivial differences. In Canada, the total tax-transfer subsidy for unpaid care of various kinds came to C$24 billion in 2015, while only C$1.6 billion was made available as tax benefits for paid child care.

Table 2.3 quantifies net child care costs faced by second-earner and single parents from Anglo- and Nordic-group OECD countries in 2012, and includes South Korea for comparison. In Table 2.3, the left-hand column presents the net take-home pay for second-earner parents and shows this varies widely when the full costs of taxes payable on earnings (participation tax rates (PTRs) including income taxes and income supports), and net after-tax/transfer child care costs are taken into account. In the OECD, although only South Korea has made it financially possible for women who need paid child care to 'make paid work pay', to the same extent as for women with no paid care expenses, South Korea has not yet eliminated gender gaps in labour force participation rates and earnings as compared with men. This support for child care costs of parents in paid work is the case, even though South Korea still uses the family as the tax unit. Second-earner parents will take home as much as 89.6 per cent of their gross earnings in South Korea, but as little as 11.7 per cent in the UK.

Table 2.3: Participation tax rates and child care costs as percentage of earned income for second-earner and lone parents, selected OECD countries, 2012

	Second-earner PTR plus CCC	Second-earner PTR with no CCC	Second-parent CCC as % of pre-tax earnings	Lone parent PTR plus CCC	Lone parent PTR with no CCC	Lone parent CCC as % of pre-tax earnings
South Korea	10.4%	10.4%	–	60.0%	60.0%	–
Sweden	30.9%	22.2%	8.7%	61.7%	57.2%	4.2%
Norway	51.5%	29.3%	22.2%	66.0%	53.3%	12.7%
Australia	73.3%	42.2%	31.1%	69.2%	52.7%	16.5%
Canada	77.9%	31.4%	46.5%	94.1%	53.0%	41.1%
US	80.1%	27.4%	52.4%	91.0%	38.3%	53.5%
UK	88.3%	21.2%	67.1%	78.9%	70.4%	8.5%
OECD average	57.0%	31.5%	25.5%	73.4%	57.7%	15.7%

PTR: Participation tax rate for second earner, net of all taxes and income supports, as percentage of second earner's or lone parent's own new income, assumed to be 67 per cent of average country wage (first parent assumed to have income of 100 per cent average country wage); CCC: Child care costs, net of all tax and transfer effects, as percentage of second earner's or lone parent's own income; PTR plus CCC: Combined effect of both; all cases assume two children under five, full-time child care.

Source: OECD (2012).

These wide variations reflect differences in how tax-transfer systems affect second earners (here, with incomes at 67 per cent of average wages for the country) and in the market costs, tax implications and transfers associated with child care costs. The other two second-earner columns isolate the PTR from net after-tax/transfer child care costs, which also vary widely. In South Korea, the basic individual income tax rate and child care costs for second earners are only 10.4 per cent on the second earner's income, and zero for child care costs. Comparing the selected countries, child care costs net of taxes and transfers range from 8.7 per cent (Sweden) to 67.1 per cent (UK) of gross earnings.

So far as two-parent homes are concerned, the Nordic countries and South Korea appear to place high value on women's equal access to paid work. In contrast, the Anglo-group countries appear to place more value on homecare by a second parent, with the net costs of child care acting as a penalty that is designed to discourage paid work for second earners who cannot obtain high enough incomes to 'make paid work pay' despite high PTR plus child care costs ratios.

It may be that the same values shape the outcomes for sole parents in paid work as well. Net child care costs as a percentage of gross earnings (assuming second incomes at 67 per cent of average wages) appear to be lower for sole parents in all countries in Table 2.3 (except the US) by margins of 4.5 per cent (Sweden) to 58.6 per cent (UK). But when net after-tax/transfer child care rates are combined with PTRs, these margins disappear as single parent take-home pay falls to just 9 per cent of earnings (US) to 40 per cent (South Korea). When the high costs of paid child care and the realities of poverty levels are taken into consideration, it does not appear that paid work can pay at all for single parents who face typical gender income gaps on average women's wages. At these tax plus child care rates, and as low-income subsidies are tapered out, single mothers on average incomes face either living on income supports and foregoing paid work, or living below poverty levels unless they can gain access to comparatively highly paid work. Only Australia and the UK appear to have ensured (in 2012) that the combined tax and care costs of paid work for single parents are lower than for second-earner parents.

Recent changes to the tax-transfer rules in Australia suggest that even with heightened attention to the importance of affordable paid child care resources for single parents, paid work will barely 'pay' for single mothers who need to pay for child care while working for pay. This is because the combined effects of women's incomes and the costs of paid child care— even when the new government child care subsidy rates are taken into consideration—barely bring single-parent families above the poverty line (Ingles and Stewart 2017). The value expressed in these complex single-parent subsidy and tax systems appears to be that homecare for children whose parents have to rely on income supports or on whatever one of two parents can earn is better for children than paid child care.

The problem with these values, including in Australia, is that women are still marginalised in relation to paid work, whether they engage in only as much paid work as they can afford (given the total tax plus child care costs involved) or turn to self-employment. The benefits of self-employment as an alternative to third-party employment may include control over times when paid child care may be needed, working hours and location. But the downside includes lower incomes, less ability to save for retirement and greater economic vulnerability. It is clear from the ABS study on women in business that many women go into business not to accumulate capital assets, but to find sustainable sources of modest incomes (ABS 2015, Ch. 4). Similarly, women who take the income support route to solving this problem are also thereby excluded from income and retirement security benefits, and from the chances of becoming self-sustaining when their children are older.

As pressure to encourage more women into paid work to stimulate GDP growth increases, it may be that these implicit values will change. However, if the goal is not to optimise all human capital through the combination of early childhood education and higher and further education and workplace attainment for women as well as men, then merely increasing child care subsidies may not necessarily promote gender equality or human development.

Taxing for gender equality in Australia

Australian research and policy innovators began to work on adding the goal of economic security for women to the gender equality policy agenda, even as the Australian use of gender budget analysis to track the impact of fiscal policy analysis on women began to disappear. Supported by the Office of the Status of Women in the Prime Minister's Department and Cabinet in 2004, extensive work on documenting the dimensions of economic security throughout the life course was initiated. This long-term project defines economic security for women as including not just decent work that 'assures regular and continuous pay', 'delivers financial stability and independence' and provides 'basic essentials … at a reasonable standard of living', but also as calling for policies and programs that protect 'women from fear of social dislocation and isolation' while enabling them to 'support themselves across their lifecycle', 'support various family members still in their care', and save and invest at levels needed when facing 'unexpected changes in economic conditions as well as providing economic security in later life' (eS4W 2016, p. 9).

Australia's leadership in promoting women's economic security has begun to influence the framing of strategies for attaining women's equality in the current century. In 2016, the UN High-Level Panel on Women's Economic Empowerment drew heavily on the concept of economic security for women in its report on the policies and outcomes needed to fully empower and equalise women's economic status in all domains of women's work and lives. This report outlines promising policies to equalise adult unpaid work time, women's shares of assets, ownership and control of business enterprises and employment conditions and incomes, many of which include changes to tax policies and related government benefit systems (UN 2016b, pp. 52–96; Klugman and Melnikova 2016).

Australia has followed global trends in moving toward budgetary austerity, lower tax ratios, a focus on 'taxing for growth' and under-resourcing gender equality programs, as seen in the comparison with the UK, the US, Canada, Nordic states and South Korea in this chapter. Australia now appears to be taking some promising steps motivated by recognition that women deserve equal chances of sustainable and economically secure gender equal futures. But continued emphasis on 'taxing for growth' will preclude those futures until the steps called for here to achieve 'taxing for gender equality' become not just a goal but the reality.

References

ABS (Australian Bureau of Statistics). 2015. *Profile of Australian Women in Business*. Canberra: Office for Women.

Acosta-Ormaechea, Santiago and Jiae Yoo. 2010. *Tax Composition and Growth: A Broad Cross-Country Perspective*, IMF Working Papers. Washington DC: International Monetary Fund.

Afonso, Antonio, Ludger Schuknecht and Vito Tanzi. 2010. 'Income Distribution Determinants and Public Spending Efficiency'. *Journal of Economic Inequality* 8(3): 367–389. doi.org/10.1007/s10888-010-9138-z

Ainsworth, Andrew, Graham Partington and Geoffrey Warren. 2015. 'Do Franking Credits Matter? Exploring the Financial Implications of Dividend Imputation'. Centre for International Finance and Regulation, CIFR Paper 058, June.

Apps, Patricia. 2015. 'Gender Equity in the Tax System for Fiscal Sustainability'. University of Sydney Law School and IZA Workshop, 4–5 November. doi.org/10.2139/ssrn.2820856

Apps, Patricia and Ray Rees. 2013. 'Raise Top Tax Rates, Not the GST'. *Australian Tax Forum* 28(3): 679–693. dx.doi.org/10.2139/ssrn.2291299

Asprey, Ken (Chair). 1975. *Full Report 31 January 1975*. Taxation Review Committee (the 'Asprey Committee'). Canberra: Australian Government Publishing Service.

ATO (Australian Taxation Office). 2015. 'Individuals: Table 3, selected items, by taxable income, age, gender, and taxable status, 2012–13 income'. Taxation statistics 2012–13. Available at: data.gov.au/dataset/taxation-statistics-2012-13/resource/7ca3602e-4597-4e15-a30e-35580c93292d

Austen, Siobhan, Therese Jefferson and Rachel Ong. 2014. 'The Gender Gap in Financial Security: What we know and don't know about Australian Households'. *Feminist Economics* 20(3): 25–52. doi.org/10.1080/13545701.2014.911413

Budlender, Di. 2001. *Review of Gender Budget Initiatives*. London: Commonwealth Secretariat.

Carmona, Magdalena Sepulveda. 2014. *Report of the Special Rapporteur on Extreme Poverty and Human Rights. Mission to Mozambique*. 4 June. dx.doi.org/10.2139/ssrn.2502982

Costello, Peter. n.d. 'Webpage of the former Howard Treasurer'. www.treasurer.gov.au/DisplayDocs.aspx?pageID=&doc=transcripts/2006/168.htm&min=phc (site discontinued, last accessed 30 November 2006).

Equality Rights Alliance. 2016. *Pre-Budget Submission of the Equality Rights Alliance February 2016*. Sydney: Equality Rights Alliance.

eS4W (Economic Security 4 Women). 2016. *Lifelong Economic Wellbeing for Women in Australia: Research Report*. Melbourne: JERA International.

European Commission. 2010. *Europe 2020: A European Strategy for Smart, Sustainable, and Inclusive Growth*. Brussels.

Förster, Michael, Ana Llena-Nozal and Vahé Nafilyan. 2014. *Trends in Top Incomes and their Taxation in OECD Countries.* OECD SEM Working Paper No. 59. Paris: OECD Publishing. doi. org/10.1787/5jz43jhlz87f-en

Fredman, Sandra and Beth Goldblatt. 2015. *Gender Equality and Human Rights*, Discussion Paper No. 4, July. New York: UN Women. Available at: www.unwomen.org/-/media/headquarters/attachments/sections/library/publications/2015/goldblatt-fin.pdf?vs=1627

Gonzales, Christian, Sonali Jain-Chandra, Kalpana Kochhar, Monique Newiak and Tlek Zeinullayev. 2015. 'Catalyst for Change: Empowering Women and Tackling Income Inequality'. IMF Staff Discussion Note, October. IMF, Washington DC. Available at: www.imf.org/external/pubs/ft/sdn/2015/sdn1520.pdf

Government of Canada. 1966. *Report of the Royal Commission on Taxation.* Ottawa: Queen's Printer.

Hernes, Helga. 1987. *Welfare State and Women Power: Essays in State Feminism*, Oslo: Norwegian University Press.

Ingles, David and Miranda Stewart. 2017. 'Does It Pay To Work?— The Case of a Single Parent with 4 Children'. *Austaxpolicy: Tax and Transfer Policy Blog*, 24 January. Available at: www.austaxpolicy.com/pay-work-case-single-parent-4-children/

Joumard, Isabelle, Mauro Pisu and Debbie Bloch. 2012. *Less Income Inequality and more Growth—Are they Compatible? Part 3. Income Redistribution via Taxes and Transfers across OECD Countries.* OECD Economic Department Working Papers No. 926. Paris: OECD Publishing. dx.doi.org/10.1787/5k9h296b1zjf-en

Klugman, Jeni and Tatiana Melnikova. 2016. *Unpaid Work and Care: A Policy Brief.* For the UN Secretary-General's High-Level Panel on Women's Economic Empowerment. United Nations, New York.

Lahey, Kathleen. 2005. *Women and Employment: Removing Fiscal Barriers to Women's Labour Force Participation.* Ottawa, ON: Status of Women Canada.

Lahey, Kathleen. 2015. *The Alberta Disadvantage: Gender, Taxation, and Income Inequality.* Edmonton, AB: Parkland Institute.

Lundqvist, Asa and Janet Fink (eds). 2016. *Changing Relations of Welfare: Family, Gender and Migration in Britain and Scandinavia*. London: Routledge.

Mill, John Stuart. 1848. *Principles of Political Economy*. London: George Routledge.

OECD (Organisation for Economic Co-operation and Development). 2005. *Economic Policy Reforms 2005: Going for Growth*. Paris: OECD Publishing. Available at: www.oecd.org/eco/labour/economic policyreformsgoingforgrowth2005.htm

OECD. 2007. *Economic Policy Reforms 2007: Going for Growth*. Paris: OECD Publishing. Available at: www.oecd.org/eco/growth/ economicpolicyreformsgoingforgrowth2007.htm

OECD. 2008. *Growing Unequal? Income Distribution and Poverty in OECD Countries*. Paris: OECD Publishing.

OECD. 2010a. *Gender and Taxation: Why Care about Taxation and Gender Equality?* Paris: OECD Publishing.

OECD. 2010b. *Tax Policy Reform and Economic Growth*. Tax Policy Studies No. 20. Paris: OECD Publishing. dx.doi.org/ 10.1787/9789264091085-en

OECD. 2011. *Divided We Stand: Why Inequality Keeps Rising*. Paris: OECD Publishing.

OECD. 2012. 'Measures of child care costs and related work incentives, 2012'. OECD Tax-Benefit Models. Available at: www.oecd.org/els/ benefits-and-wages-statistics.htm

OECD. 2014. *The Distributional Effects of Consumption Taxes in OECD Countries*. Tax Policy Studies, No. 22. Paris: OECD Publishing. dx.doi.org/10.1787/9789264224520-en

OECD.Stat. 2016a. *Revenue Statistics: OECD Member Countries— Comparative tables*. Paris: OECD. Available at: stats.oecd.org/Index. aspx?DataSetCode=REV

OECD.Stat. 2016b. *Income Distribution and Poverty*. Paris: OECD. Available at: stats.oecd.org/Index.aspx?DataSetCode=IDD

Page Research Centre. 2004. 'An Evaluation of Income Splitting'. *Page Communication 2*. Charles Sturt University Page Research Centre, ACT.

Parliament of Great Britain. 1919. *Royal Commission on the Income Tax*. London: Her Majesty's Stationery Office.

Phillips, Ben and Matthew Taylor. 2015. *The Distributional Impact of the GST*. Canberra: National Centre for Social and Economic Modelling.

Sainsbury, Di. 2001. 'Gender and the Making of Welfare States: Norway and Sweden'. *Social Politics* 8(1): 65–112. doi.org/10.1093/sp/8.1.113

Sharp, Rhonda and Ray Broomhill. 2013. *A Case Study of Gender Responsive Budgeting in Australia*. London: Commonwealth Secretariat.

Smith, Adam. 1904 (1776). *The Wealth of Nations*. London: Methuen.

Smith, Julie. 1994. *Income Splitting*. Research Paper No. 10. Canberra: Government of Australia Parliamentary Research Service.

Stotsky, Janet. 2006. 'Gender and its Relevance to Macroeconomic Policy: A Survey'. IMF Working Papers. Washington DC: International Monetary Fund.

Stotsky, Janet, Sakina Shibuya, Lisa Kolovich and Suhaib Kebhaj. 2016. *Trends in Gender Equality and Women's Advancement*. IMF Working Paper WP/16/21. Washington DC: International Monetary Fund.

UN (United Nations). 1979. Convention on the Elimination of All Forms of Discrimination against Women. UN GA res. 34/10, 18 December 1979.

UN. 1995. *Report of the Fourth World Conference on Women*. New York: United Nations. Available at: www.un.org/womenwatch/confer/beijing/reports/plateng.htm

UN. 2006. *Time Use Data, Australia*. Time Use Survey, UN. Available at: unstats.un.org/unsd/gender/timeuse/

UN. 2014. *Blok v. Netherlands*, Communication No. 36/2012, UN Doc. CEDAW/C/57/D/36/2012.

UN. 2015a. Addis Ababa Action Agenda. Third International Conference on Financing for Development, endorsed by the United Nations General Assembly, Res. 69/313, 27 July, Addis Ababa, Ethiopia.

UN. 2015b. *Report of the inquiry concerning Canada*. CEDAW/C/OP.8/ CAN/1, 30 March.

UN. 2016a. Critical milestones toward coherent, efficient and inclusive follow-up and review at the global level. Seventieth sess., agenda items 15 and 16, A/70/684, 15 January.

UN. 2016b. *Leave No One Behind: A Call to Action for Gender Equality and Women's Economic Empowerment*. Report of the UN Secretary-General's High-Level Panel on Women's Economic Empowerment.

UN. 2016c. Paris Agreement. Twenty-first sess., Framework Convention on Climate Change, CN.63/2016; Treaties XXVII.7.d, open for signature 22 April.

UN Economic and Social Council. 2015. Review and appraisal of the implementation of the Beijing Declaration, Commission on the Status of Women, Fifty-ninth sess., E/CN.6/2015/3, 9–20 March.

UN Women. 2015. *Progress of the World's Women 2015–2016: Transforming Economies, Realizing Rights*. New York: United Nations.

Usui, Norio. 2011. *Tax Reforms toward Fiscal Consolidation*. Manila: Asian Development Bank.

3

Gender equity in the tax-transfer system for fiscal sustainability[1]

Patricia Apps

There has been a significant focus in recent years on the persistent gender pay gap in Australia. According to Australian Bureau of Statistics (ABS), data the gender pay gap, calculated as the difference between women's and men's average weekly full-time equivalent earnings and expressed as a percentage of men's earnings, is around 16 to 18 per cent (WGEA 2016; ABS 2016). A range of explanations have been offered. Among those frequently cited are gender differences in labour supply and career choices driven by a work environment that is insensitive to the needs of women with dependant children. The under-representation of women in leadership roles due to workplace practices is also a major concern. Less attention has been given to the contribution the Australian tax system makes towards widening the *pre-tax* gender pay gap by widening the *net-of-tax* gender wage gap, creating negative effects on the labour supply and therefore employment earnings of the vast majority of low- and average-wage women.

One of the most extraordinary aspects of the ongoing and longstanding tax reform debate in Australia is the almost complete absence of any reference to the impact on women. Instead, the focus of much of the discussion

1   The research was supported under the Australian Research Council's Discovery Project funding scheme (Project ID: DP120104115).

has been on lowering tax rates for top income earners, mostly men whose labour supply is known to be less responsive to tax rate changes. Many women, together with low- and average-wage earners generally, now face higher marginal and average tax rates under an income tax system that has become much less progressive. Many partnered mothers as second earners face effective marginal tax rates that are well above the top personal income tax (PIT) rate due to the withdrawal of family payments for dependant children on the basis of joint income. In this chapter, it is argued that the tax system now in place after three decades of incremental reforms is a major determinant of the persistent gender pay gap and that the reforms are ultimately unsustainable due to their negative impact on female labour supply, productivity and the tax base.

Part 2 begins with an outline of the changes to the PIT rate scale and low income tax offset (LITO) and the resulting shift in the tax burden towards those in the middle of the distribution of income. The LITO is characterised here as a tax policy instrument that serves the sole purpose of reducing the transparency of the distributional impact of the reforms in an economy with rising inequality. Treasury's view of bracket creep, the tendency for more wage earners to be drawn into the higher tax brackets purely as a result of inflation, is discussed as an illustration of the underlying long-term agenda of shifting the tax burden from the top towards the middle of the earnings distribution (see Treasury 2015a, 2015b).

In part 3, we turn to the taxation of the family. The analysis first identifies the gradual replacement of universal family allowances by joint income tested payments as a non-transparent strategy for raising tax rates on working partnered mothers. This was done during a period in which the government was simultaneously cutting taxes on top incomes. The section goes on to present data indicating a strong negative effect of this on female labour supply and household saving.

Finally, part 4 discusses the challenges presented by demographic change arising from the fall in the total fertility rate (TFR) from around 3.5 in the early 1960s to 1.8 today, and argues that the current tax, child care and retirement incomes policy settings are unsustainable. The analysis illustrates the misleading views on tax reform generated by the prevailing Treasury approach of modelling the economy as if we lived in a world in which women did not exist (see, for example, the computable general equilibrium (CGE) modelling in the Treasury Working Paper by Cao et al. (2015) and in KPMG (2010)).

Taxation of individual incomes

Income tax reform

The progressive rate scale of the PIT applies to individual incomes and therefore has the advantage that women on lower pay face lower marginal tax rates (MTRs) and, in turn, lower average tax rates (ATRs) than men on higher pay. The progressivity of the system reduces simultaneously the net-of-tax gender pay gap and the overall degree of inequality. In addition, a progressive individual-based system reduces distortions in the incentive to work outside the home, by applying lower taxes on women with lower earnings, who are known to be more responsive to changes in the net wage than higher-earning men. As discussed in Chapter 9 (Stewart, Voitchovsky and Wilkins), women make up only 23 per cent of top decile taxpayers and 17 per cent of those in the top 1 per cent of the income distribution.

These advantages of a progressive, individual income tax are well recognised. Yet recent decades have seen the transformation of the Australian income tax towards a far less progressive system, and one with an *effective* rate scale that is no longer *strictly* progressive. In 1985–86, the top rate was 60 cents in the dollar. By 1990–91, it had fallen to 47 cents, funded largely by accumulated revenue from bracket creep. The further accumulation of revenue from bracket creep over the next decade subsequently funded major changes that gave the greatest gains to those in the upper percentiles of income. From 2004–05 to 2008–09, the top bracket limit, the income level at which the top tax rate cuts in, rose from $70,000 to $180,000, providing large gains for those on high incomes. In 2007–08, the top marginal rate fell a further two percentage points, providing further gains for high-income earners. At the same time, individuals on very low incomes benefited from a rising zero rated threshold with the gradual expansion of the LITO from $243 in 2004–05 to $1,500 in 2010–11 and 2011–12. The withdrawal of the LITO at a fixed rate effectively raised MTRs across a new low income tax bracket to deny income earners above the upper threshold of the bracket the relatively small lump sum gains from a rising zero-rated threshold. The key role of the LITO was to make the higher effective MTRs across this bracket of low incomes, and the consequent loss of strict progressivity in the rate scale, non-transparent.

Table 3.1 illustrates the change in the MTRs when the LITO is combined with the PIT rate scale in the 2015–16 financial year. The Temporary Budget Repair Levy is excluded. Panel A of the table lists taxable income brackets and MTRs that apply to each under the PIT scale. Panel B reports the *true* rate scale when the LITO of $445 is included. The LITO increases the zero-rated threshold from $18,200 to $20,542 and its withdrawal at 1.5 cents in the dollar from $37,000 raises MTRs by this amount until it is fully withdrawn at the upper threshold of $66,666. The effect is to deny taxpayers above this threshold the lump sum gain of $445 from the higher zero-rated threshold.

Table 3.1: PIT + LITO marginal tax rate scales, 2015–16

Panel A: PIT		Panel B: PIT + LITO ($445)	
Taxable income bracket	MTR	Taxable income bracket	MTR
$0–$18,200	0.00	$0–$20,542	0.00
$18,201–$37,000	0.19	$20,543–$37,000	0.19
$37,001–$80,000	0.325	$37,001–$66,666	0.34
$80,001–$180,000	0.37	$66,667–$80,000	0.325
$180,001+	0.45	$80,001–$180,000	0.37
–	–	$180,001+	0.45

Source: Author's calculations.

A LITO of $445 is all that is required in the 2015–16 financial year to conceal the fact that the true rate scale is not strictly progressive. As noted above, in the 2010–11 and 2011–12 financial years the LITO was $1,500. In those years, the zero-rate threshold was not the $6,000 reported under the PIT scale, but $16,000. It is clear that the changes in the LITO since 2004–05 have been carefully crafted to conceal the rise in effective MTRs on incomes below average annual full-time earnings when, at the same time, the government was reducing tax burdens at much higher income levels by lowering top rates and raising the thresholds at which they applied. The changes can be shown to have resulted in a significant shift in the tax burden from the 'top' to the 'middle' during a period of increasing inequality.

Rising inequality

There is now an extensive literature on the rise in inequality of income and wealth in developed economies (see, for example, Atkinson 2015; Piketty et al. 2014; and Piketty and Saez 2003). Apps and Rees (2013) present an analysis of changes in the distribution of income in Australia drawing on data for matching samples of couples selected from the two most recent ABS Household Expenditure Surveys (HES), HES 2003–04 and HES 2009–10. The samples are selected on the criteria that both partners are aged from 20 to 60 years and the primary income partner is employed for at least 25 hours per week. The HES 2003–04 sample contains 2,447 couple income unit records and the HES 2009–10 sample, 2,408 records. The results are summarised below.

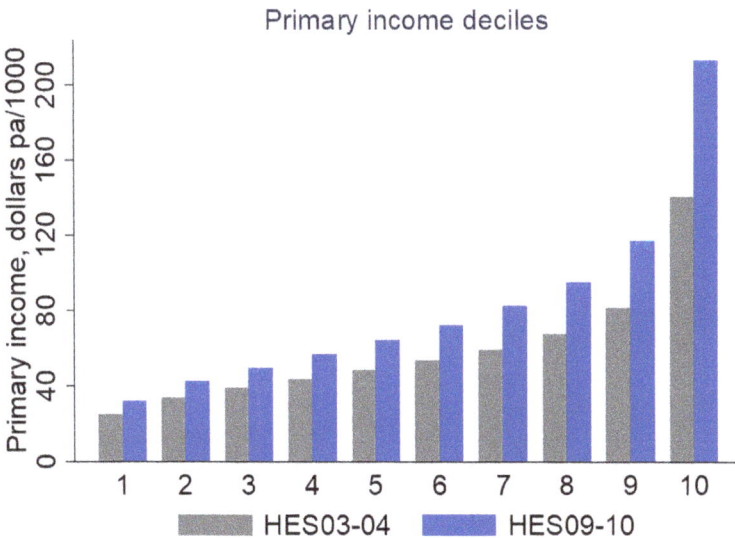

Figure 3.1: Rising inequality

Source: Author's calculations based on ABS HES data for 2003–04 and 2009–10.

The study finds a significant increase in inequality based on the change in the distribution of nominal primary private incomes over the six-year period. Figure 3.1 shows graphically the decile distribution of nominal primary private incomes in each of the two survey years.[2] In decile 1, there is a 28.6 per cent increase. This is followed by small increments up

---

2   Figure 3.1 expands the quintile distributions in Table 2 of Apps and Rees (2013) into decile distributions.

to decile 5, in which the rise is 32.7 per cent. The percentage gains are slightly larger in the next three deciles. Thereafter, the gains rise more steeply and quite dramatically towards the top decile. In decile 9, the nominal increase is 43.27 per cent and in decile 10 it is 52.17 per cent. The nominal rise in the top percentile is 71.02 per cent.

Figure 3.2 plots the decile distribution of nominal tax cuts over the period. The profile reflects the concentration of billions of dollars of tax cuts in the top percentiles and the shift in the tax burden towards the 'middle'. The lowest gain appears in decile 6, at less than $600. In decile 10 the gain is around $9,000 (40 per cent of total) and in the top percentile, close to $50,000.[3]

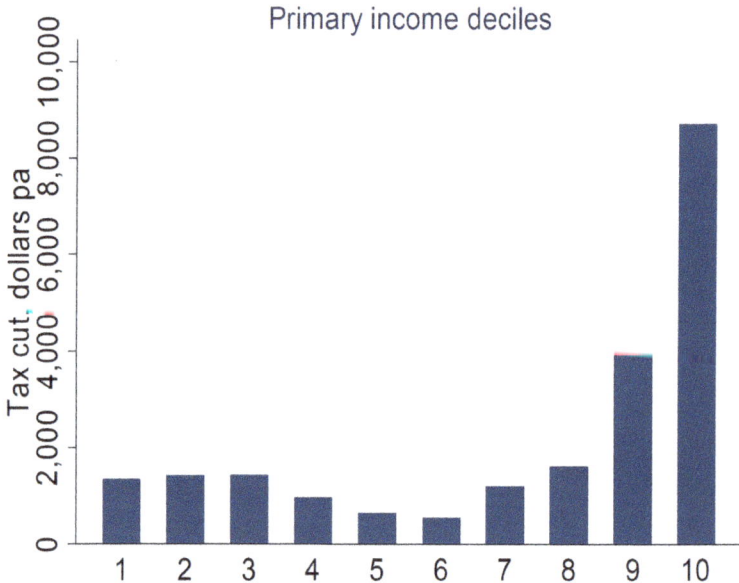

Figure 3.2: Shift in tax burden towards the 'middle'
Source: Author's calculations based on ABS HES data for 2003–04 and 2009–10.

The recent Treasury reports, *Re:Think* (Treasury 2015b) and the *Intergenerational Report* (Treasury 2015a), argue for lower income taxes to protect low- and middle-income earners from the adverse effects of bracket creep. Both documents claim to show that 'bracket creep affects lower and middle income earners proportionally more than higher income

---

3   This direction of personal income tax (PIT) reform with rising inequality it not unique to Australia. For an across-country survey see Peter et al. (2010).

earners' by comparing ATRs on three incomes in 2013–14 with the rates that will apply in 2023–24 if the incomes rise to expected levels and the PIT rate scale, LITO and Medicare Levy remain unchanged. The three incomes are $37,500, $75,000 and $150,000. The income of $75,000 is selected as representative of average annual ordinary full-time earnings in 2013–14, and so the lower and upper income figures represent half and twice average annual ordinary full-time earnings.

By 2023–24, the three incomes are projected to rise to $52,000, $104,000 and $208,000, respectively, as shown in Table 3.2a. The ATR is calculated to rise by 7.5, 4.7 and 3.8 percentage points from the lowest to the highest income. While the decline in the increments in the ATR as income rises does in fact demonstrate that lower- and middle-income earners are disadvantaged *proportionally* more than higher-income earners, in terms of absolute burdens (not reported in either document) the reverse is the case. As shown in the last row of Table 3.2a, the additional tax burden on the income of $208,000 is $7,904, which is over twice that of $3,900 on the income of $52,000 and over 60 per cent higher than the additional tax on the middle income. Thus, in absolute terms, high-income earners are the main beneficiaries of measures to reduce bracket creep.

Table 3.2a: Change in ATRs and tax burdens from 2013–14 to 2023–24

Income in 2013–14	$37,500	$75,000	$150,000
Income in 2023–24	$52,000	$104,000	$208,000
ATR in 2013–14	10.3	22.7	30.5
ATR in 2023–24	17.8	27.4	34.3
ATR increment	7.5	4.7	3.8
Tax increment	$3,900	$4,888	$7,904

Source: Author's calculations.

Table 3.2b: Change in ATRs and tax burdens from 2003–04 to 2013–14

Income in 2003–04	$24,500	$49,000	$98,000
ATR in 2003–04	15.4	23.7	35.1
ATR increment	−5.1	−1.0	−4.6
Tax increment	−$1,913	−$750	−$6,900

Source: Author's calculations.

In the light of Treasury's new concern for the 'middle', it is of interest to compare the results with changes in the previous decade. Table 3.2b repeats the calculation for 2003–04 to 2013–14. In 2003–04, average annual full-time earnings were around $49,000, and so the matching incomes are $24,500, $49,000 and $98,000. ATR increments over the decade are negative, with the lowest proportional gain for the middle income. In terms of absolute burdens, the gain for the middle income is $750, a small fraction of the $6,900 tax cut for the top income, which is in turn three times the gain for the lowest income. The ATR and tax increment profiles reflect a decade of rate changes that shifted the tax burden from top incomes toward the middle, as indicated in Figure 3.2. If we combine the two decades and repeat the calculation, we find that positive gains are limited to the top income.

Given this reform record, the rate scale changes enacted since the 2016–17 Budget can be viewed as consistent with a long-term policy agenda of lowering taxes across the top percentiles of income. Raising the current upper bracket limit of $80,000 to $87,000 for the 32.5 cent rate of the PIT provides a lump sum of $315 for individual taxpayers above $87,000 but no gain for taxpayers below the $80,000 threshold. Removing the Temporary Budget Repair Levy of 2 cents in the dollar will provide a rising absolute gain for those above $180,000, the threshold for the levy. Very few employed women gain from these rate changes, and less than half of employed men have incomes of over $80,000. As in preceding years, the rate scale changes will add to the budget deficit.

Labour supply incentives

It is frequently claimed that lower tax rates on top incomes under a less progressive rate scale will achieve efficiency gains from reduced labour supply disincentive effects. However, it is difficult to support this view because neither cross-section nor panel data show a sufficiently large increase in top earners' labour supply with rising top wage rates.[4] Some studies circumvent this evidence by directing attention towards the effects of tax policy on earnings, rather than labour supply. However, as Piketty et al. (2014) argue, a fall in earnings or taxable income in response to a higher tax rate is largely a reflection of an increase in tax avoidance and evasion as

---

4   See, for example, the profiles of earnings and hours of work based on the ABS HES data samples of couples in Apps and Rees (2013, Table 2.6). Studies for other countries report similar findings. See, for example, Moffitt and Wilhelm (2000).

income is under-reported or diverted to forms that are subject to lower tax rates, or to weakened bargaining power and consequently a lower share of profits, for example of senior executives in diverting the flow of profits from company shareholders to themselves. The authors recommend that tax avoidance and evasion, which essentially are a symptom of inadequate tax system design, should be dealt with directly and not through the tax rate scale. Based on low estimates of labour supply elasticities at the top, they propose a higher top tax rate in response to rising wage and income inequality.

This recommendation is consistent with the results for the structure of optimal tax rates reported in Andrienko et al. (2016) (see also Apps et al. 2014). Drawing on survey data for Australia, the UK and the US, the study constructs percentile distributions of primary wage rates and computes the profiles of labour supply elasticities across each wage distribution. Labour supply elasticities are found to be relatively high across the lower wage percentiles, to flatten across the middle and to approach zero towards the top. As a consequence, the optimal structure of MTRs is found to become more progressive as inequality rises in each of the three countries. Shifting towards a less progressive PIT rate scale to achieve a given degree of redistribution can therefore be expected to come at the cost of a worsening of work incentives where they really matter as well as in a reduction in fairness of the distribution of tax burdens.

The Andrienko et al. (2016) analysis highlights the importance of analysing the efficiency effects of a tax on individual earnings by drawing on a modelling approach that does not restrict the labour supply elasticity to a constant across the wage distribution and also does not represent the PIT by a simple flat-rate tax, as in the Treasury Working Paper by Cao et al. (2015) and in KPMG (2010, 2011). Based on a CGE model in which the total population of households is represented as a single person, Cao et al. assert that in general 'progressivity raises the marginal excess burden of a tax, which implies the marginal excess burden of the modelled personal income tax will understate the welfare cost of raising revenue via the actual personal income tax' (2015, p. 23). The authors appear not to recognise that when labour supply elasticities fall sharply with the wage and approach zero towards the top percentiles, as reported in Andrienko et al., an income tax with a progressive rate scale can be expected to dominate a flat-rate tax with respect to both efficiency (work incentives) and fairness.

In addition to, and largely because of, these limitations of their analysis, Cao et al. and KPMG claim to find that a consumption tax is less distortionary than an earnings tax. However, such an assessment is outside the scope of their model, based as it is on a single-person household. Most adults of working age live in couple households. When the tax system is based on *earnings*, these can be observed and taxed separately at marginal rates that minimise the disincentive effects on labour supply. On the other hand, individual *consumptions* within the household cannot be observed and therefore cannot be taxed on an individual basis. Consumption taxation is necessarily joint taxation. As a more limited policy instrument, a consumption tax cannot be superior to a well-designed earnings tax.

Taxation of family incomes

Family tax reform

The tax design problem for the two-parent family is more complicated than that for the single individual because of the need to consider the choice of tax unit in addition to the rate scale: should couples be taxed on the basis of their individual incomes or on their joint income? The two systems have very different outcomes for the distribution of the tax burden by gender, the net-of-tax gender pay gap and the overall distribution of the tax burden across households.

In choosing the optimal tax unit, we need first to recognise that the economics of the two-parent family differs fundamentally from that of the single-person household. The presence of a dependant child, and especially a preschool-aged child, creates an additional work choice. One partner can work at home providing child care and other domestic services as an alternative to working in the market and buying in care and related goods and services. In effect, the family is a small economy engaged to varying degrees in untaxed household production and exchange, where the latter creates an implicit wage within the household.[5] Consequently, we can expect the labour supply decision of the partner with the option of working at home to be more responsive to both average and marginal

---

5   It is a mistake to label home child care and domestic work in the two-parent family as 'unpaid', just because the exchange process within the household may be implicit. For a model of the household as a small economy with intra-household production and exchange/trade, see Apps (1982). There may also be lump sum transfers as in any small or large economy in which there is centralised decision-making and a concern for equity (see Apps and Rees 1988).

tax rates. Moreover, the hourly cost of child care has to be regarded as an additional tax on her wage, rather than on that of her partner, who would be going out to work in any case.

An important property of a system of family taxation based on the individual as the tax unit is that the marginal rates faced by each partner are independent. As noted in the preceding section, under a progressive rate scale a lower MTR typically applies to the income of the partner with the lower earnings and the labour supply that is more sensitive to the tax rate. In contrast, under joint taxation the MTRs faced by partners are interdependent; for example, if the male partner as primary earner is fully employed, the question of whether the female partner will take a job depends on the change in the household's total tax bill that results, including any effect on the male partner's MTR of her increase in income, that is, it depends on the incremental tax burden with respect to her work decision. The *effective* or *true* tax rate she faces can be well above that of her partner's rate.

The high efficiency cost of joint taxation due to the higher effective MTRs on the second earner has long been recognised in the literature (Boskin and Sheshinski 1983; for an overview see Apps and Rees 2009). Nevertheless, over recent decades Australia has shifted from the individual as the tax unit for the family to a system of 'quasi-joint' taxation by switching from universal to joint income–tested family payments. In the early 1980s, families received universal child payments and paid tax on the basis of individual incomes under the PIT scale. The first step towards joint income–tested child payments was the introduction of the 'Family Income Supplement' during the Hawke and Keating years in the late 1980s. Family cash benefits under this reform were initially paid together with universal family allowances, which had not been indexed for a number of years. In 2000, the Howard Government combined the two payments in family tax benefit part A (FTB-A), and in subsequent Budgets completely eliminated universality. This has had the effect of raising MTRs on the second income to well above the top rate of the PIT scale.

An argument frequently used in the Australian literature in support of this direction of reform appears in the Henry Review (Henry et al. 2009). The Review states:

The personal income tax structure should be the sole means of delivering progressivity in the tax system, supporting the more direct re-distributional role of the transfer system (Part 1, Overview, p. 29).

It goes on to argue for payments tested on family income:[6]

because family payments in Australia are paid at relatively high rates to achieve adequate levels of support for low-income families, it would be extremely costly to provide universal payments. Phasing out payments using a low withdrawal rate can provide some level of assistance to most families without the full cost of a universal payment (Part 2, pp. 556–557).

The argument fails to recognise that it is the disincentive effects of the structure of MTRs on labour supplies, and not simply the size of the transfer, that determine the real *economic cost* of a tax-transfer system.[7] Given the evidence on the second earner/female labour supply elasticities, a tax system that imposes effective rates on the incomes of second earners that are well above the top rate of the PIT scale applying to primary-earner incomes cannot be less costly, in terms of the real economic cost, than a well-designed, strictly progressive rate scale.

In the international literature, support for joint taxation draws on the view that horizontal equity, defined in the Mirrlees Review as taxing 'all families with the same joint income equally', requires joint taxation (Institute for Fiscal Studies and Mirrlees 2011). An implication of this 'principle' is that couples with the same total income are equally well off regardless of how much is earned by each partner—a high-wage single-earner household is no better off than one containing two low-wage earners working twice the hours for the same total income. The view implies that home production (e.g. parental child care) does not contribute to family welfare. While widely rejected, many (mostly male) economists continue to think of non-market time exclusively as the pure consumption of 'leisure' rather than production. The Mirrlees Review recommends retaining the individual as the tax unit for the formal income tax system but basing the withdrawal of family payments on joint income—in other words, implementing a quasi-joint family tax system as in Australia.

---

6   For a detailed analysis of the family tax recommendations of the Henry Review, see Apps (2010).

7   Similarly, the rhetoric of 'middle-class welfare' reflects a misunderstanding of 'cost' in economics.

In addition to home production, the horizontal equity principle ignores the tax design implications of a high degree of primary income inequality. Based on a model that takes account of the wage rates of second earners and variation in child care prices as determinants of across household heterogeneity in second-earner labour supply, Apps and Rees (2017) find that individual taxation strongly dominates a system of joint taxation, or of income splitting as in the US, on equity grounds. An important driver of the result is the sharp rise in wage rates in the top percentiles of the primary wage distribution. A system of full income splitting provides top-wage primary earners the opportunity for tax avoidance simply by having the second earner substitute untaxed household production for market work. Switching to individual taxation, by removing this opportunity, leads to a much fairer distribution of the tax burden at a lower efficiency cost—there are gains in both equity and efficiency.

A partial or quasi-joint family tax system can closely approximate the outcome of full income splitting when the additional revenue collected from the higher MTRs on second incomes contributes to the funding of tax cuts for the top percentiles of income. We now turn to numerical examples to illustrate the structure of marginal and ATRs under the Australian quasi-joint family tax system.

Marginal and average tax rates, 2015–16

The change in the structure of MTRs with the withdrawal of family payments on joint income is illustrated in Tables 3.3 and 3.4 for a family with two dependant children in the 2015–16 financial year. Table 3.3 reports the profile of MTRs and ATRs that apply under the PIT scale, LITO and FTB-A if the family is single income. Table 3.4 goes on to show the rates that apply to the second income in a family in which the primary income is $60,000. While the tax system also includes the Medicare Levy with exemptions and reductions based on joint income, and family tax benefit part B (FTB-B) withdrawn on the second income, these elements are omitted in order to focus on the impact of joint income–testing payments made in respect of each dependant child under FTB-A. The example assumes one child is under 13 years and the second is aged from 13–18 years.

The total 2015–16 Maximum Rate of FTB-A is $12,238, the sum of the Maximum Rate of $5,412.95 for a dependant child under 13 years and the Maximum Rate of $6,825.50 for a child aged 13–18 years. The total Maximum Rate is withdrawn at 20 cents in the dollar on a family income above $51,027 up to the Base Rate. The Base Rate is $2,230.15 per child, and is withdrawn at 30 cents in the dollar on a family income above $94,316.

Table 3.3: Tax rates 2015–16: Single income two-child family

Taxable income bracket	MTR	TAX* $	ATR*
$0–$20,542	0.00	−12,238	−0.60
$20,543–$37,000	0.19	−9,111	−0.25
$37,001–$51,027	0.34	−4,342	−0.09
$51,028–$66,666	0.54	4,103	0.06
$66,667–$80,000	0.525	11,103	0.14
$80,001–$89,918	0.57	16,757	0.19
$89,919–$94,316	0.37	18,383	0.19
$94,317–$109,183	0.67	28,344	0.26
$109,184–$180,000	0.37	54,547	0.30
$180,001+	0.45	–	–

* At upper-income threshold.
Source: Author's calculations.

Up to the threshold income of $51,027 for the Maximum Rate of FTB-A, MTRs are set by the PIT scale and LITO (see Table 3.1). Thereafter, with the withdrawal of the Maximum Rate at 20 cents in the dollar above this threshold the MTR rises to 54 cents in the dollar. At $66,666, the LITO is fully withdrawn and so the MTR falls to 52.5 cents in the dollar. At the threshold income for the Base Rate of FTB-A, the MTR rises to 67 cents in the dollar, the sum of the 37 cents PIT rate and 30 cents withdrawal rate of the Base Rate.

The key point to note is that the *true MTR* across each bracket in the second column of the table is the sum of the PIT rate and the withdrawal rates of the LITO and FTB-A. The third column reports the family's tax at the upper-income threshold calculated as the sum of tax payable under the MTR scale in the second column, net of $12,238 as a *universal payment*. Income testing the FTB-A payment does not remove its universality, it simply changes MTRs and lump sums—that is, the marginal rate structure of the tax system that funds the universal payment. The lump sum for each taxpayer is calculated as the difference between:

a. the amount of tax that would be payable if the MTR on the last dollar earned applied to the taxpayer's total income

b. the amount that is actually paid under the true rate scale plus FTB-A as a *universal payment*.

The importance of recognising that *effectively* every individual faces two tax parameters, a lump sum and a MTR, lies in the following: the lump sum has effects on total income only and so does not distort work decisions at the margin. It therefore has no efficiency cost. The MTR, on the other hand, gives rise to an efficiency loss due to the disincentive effect arising from the distortion it creates in the relative price of time spent in home vs market production. Thus, the true economic cost of the tax system depends only on the latter efficiency loss.

While leaving the universality of FTB-A in place, targeting on joint income has, in addition to a high efficiency cost, serious distributional consequences, as illustrated in Table 3.4. The table lists the true MTR scale and ATRs faced by the second partner contemplating going out to work in a household with a primary income of $60,000. She is denied a tax-free threshold, and instead pays 20 cents in the dollar up to the limit of the true zero-rated threshold of $20,542. She then pays 39 cents instead of 19 cents across the next bracket. At $34,317, her marginal rate goes to 49 cents in the dollar due to the withdrawal of the Base Rate of FTB-A at 30 cents in the dollar. At the $37,000 bracket point her MTR goes to 64 cents.

Table 3.4: Primary income = $60,000 pa: Tax rates on second income

Taxable income, $pa	MTR	ATR*
$0–$20,542	0.20	0.20
$20,543–$29,918	0.39	0.26
$29,919–$34,316	0.19	0.25
$34,317–$37,000	0.49	0.27
$37,001–$49,183	0.64	0.36
$49,184–$60,000	0.34	0.36

* ATR at upper-income threshold.
Source: Author's calculations.

The ATR profile in the third column of the table gives an indication of the extent to which withdrawing family payments on joint income, by shifting the tax burden towards two-earner households, shifts the burden towards partnered mothers as second earners. At $50,000, the effective tax on the second income is $17,991, which gives an ATR of 36 per cent, as shown in the table. If we include the Medicare Levy and the 2015–16 FTB-B payment of $3,139 for a family with two dependant children aged five to 18 years,[8] the tax on the second income rises to $22,130 and her ATR to 42.26 per cent.[9]

Even under an individual-based income tax, with both partners facing the same rate scale and receiving the same non-means-tested family payment, a two-earner family is disadvantaged relative to a single-earner family at any given primary income and wage pair because the former contributes more to the tax revenue that funds the family payment. For example, the contribution to tax revenue by a single-income family with a primary income of $60,000 under the PIT scale, LITO and Medicare Levy is $12,147. If the second partner switches from untaxed work at home to working in the market for an income of $50,000, she contributes an additional $8,547, which raises the two-earner family's total contribution to $20,694.

To gain an insight into the potential losses in terms of both fairness and tax revenues under the current family tax and child care subsidy system, we draw on data for a sample of 'in-work' two-parent families selected from the ABS Survey of Income and Housing (SIH) 2013–14 on the criteria that the primary income partner is employed for at least 25 hours per week and earns at least $10,000 per annum, both partners are aged from 20 to 60 years and a dependant child is present. The sample contains 2,436 records. The data on second hours indicate a very high degree of heterogeneity, with around a third of the sample (798 records) containing a second earner in full-time work, more than a third (931 records) with a second earner in part-time work, and the remainder (707) with only one partner in work. Relatively little of this heterogeneity can be explained by demographics or by the second wage. The average number of dependant children is 1.77 for the full-time group, 1.94 for the part-time group, and 1.95 for the non-participation group, while predicted gross wage rates tend to be marginally higher for the part-time group than for non-participants or for those employed full time.

---

8   Note that when FTB-B is included, the universal transfer for a primary earner on $60,000 rises by the FTB-B rate.
9   The withdrawal of FTB-B at 20 cents in the dollar raises the MTR on the second income by that amount from $5,402 to $21,097.

To indicate the potential revenue losses from labour supply disincentive effects, we compare taxes on the second income for low and high second hours at a given primary income. We first rank all households by quintiles of primary income and then split each quintile into two subsamples defined with respect to median second hours of work. Households with second hours below the median are labelled 'H1' and those with second hours at or above the median 'H2'.[10] Table 3.5a reports the data means of second annual hours and earnings and the annual income tax on the second income, labelled '2nd tax', for each household group across the distribution of primary income. The gap between the H1 and H2 '2nd tax' data means indicates the very significant losses to tax revenue associated with persistent zero or low second hours.

Table 3.5a: Second-earner income, taxes and hours by primary income (SIH 2013–14)

Primary income quintiles $pa		38,601	61,726	81,663	109,065	222,523
H1:	2nd hours pa	57	329	473	449	307
	2nd income $pa	3,297	6,867	16,357	17,499	21,902
	2nd tax $pa	114	699	1,360	1642	3,544
H2:	2nd hours pa	1,619	1,936	2,009	1,971	1,980
	2nd income $pa	26,527	40,891	52,208	62,141	80,170
	2nd tax $pa	2,101	5,283	8,579	11,487	17,654

Source: Author's calculations based on ABS HES data for 2013–14.

Table 3.5b: FTB-A payments by primary income: Two children aged 5 to 18 years

Primary income quintiles $pa		38,601	61,726	81,663	109,065	222,523
H1:	FTB-A	10,358	5,618	2,689	1,308	136
H2:	FTB-A	4,505	1,836	385	24	30

Source: Author's calculations based on ABS HES data for 2013–14.

Table 3.5b shows the impact of withdrawing FTB-A on joint income, holding demographics constant. The table reports the data means of family tax benefits for a subsample of families selected on the further criterion

---

10   This allows us to control for variation in the gross wage across employment status. Both groups are found to have close to the same predicted second wage within each quintile until towards the top percentiles. We can therefore conclude that the high degree of heterogeneity at a given primary income cannot be driven by the second wage alone. Apps and Rees (2017) show that the heterogeneity can, however, be explained by variation in the price of child care as a tax on the second wage.

that there are two, and only two, dependant children aged five to 18 years present. The additional burden for the second earner in each quintile is given by the gap between the FTB-A payments for H1 and H2. Those who lose the most are H2 households in the lower half of the distribution—in other words, low- and average-wage working mothers. This outcome is concealed by studies that report results for the distribution of family tax benefits by household income, a practice that reflects the assumption that the non-participating partner in the H1 household does not contribute to family welfare.

The child care benefit (CCB) and child care rebate (CCR) need to be included in the calculation of the tax on the second income. For the demographic group represented in Table 3.5b, the data means for both are relatively small, at $51 and $49 for the H1 household and $115 and $423 for the H2 household, for the CCB and CCR respectively. As we would expect, the CCB begins at a maximum in quintile 1 and falls to zero in quintile 5, while CCR has the reverse profile.

In contrast, the data means for CCB and CCR for 'in-work' families with a child aged zero to four are much larger for both household groups, at $1,166 and $1,177 per annum for the H1 household and $1,611 and $2,852 for the H2 household, respectively. The gap between data means across quintiles indicate that, on average, the higher claims for CCB and CCR by the H2 household contribute relatively little to reducing the far higher income tax burden on the second earner in two-earner households. Again, there is wide variation in the distribution of both CCB and CCR within each quintile. Given that the price of child care can exceed $100 per day this is not surprising. It is now widely recognised that the earnings of many partnered mothers, net of taxes *and* child care costs, can be negative. Thus, unless the family has access to informal care, such as a grandparent, working full time using formal care may not be financially viable. These conditions can be expected to contribute significantly to the high degree of heterogeneity in second-earner labour supply at a given primary income and second wage.

The preceding analysis highlights not only the loss of tax revenue due to labour supply outcomes under the current system of quasi-joint family taxation, but when viewed in the context of the income tax reforms outlined in Part 2, successive governments can be seen to have drawn heavily on the earnings of low- to average-wage working mothers as second earners for funding tax cuts across the top percentiles of income.

Participation rates and life-cycle labour supply

While female participation rates have risen since the 1970s, Australian rates have been lower than those of many comparable Organisation for Economic Co-operation and Development (OECD) countries. As reported in Treasury (2015b):

> while the participation rate of women between the ages of 15 to 64 in Australia has increased from 65.3 percent in 2000 to 70.5 per cent in 2013, Australia is ranked 13th of the 34 OECD countries for female participation (p. 44).

However, of greater concern is the far wider gap in labour supply. While the vast majority of males work full time, the majority of females in employment choose part-time work, a decision that can allow a larger share of FTB-A payments to be retained and high child care costs to be reduced. In the sample used to construct Table 3.5a, the participation rate of the second partner is 71 per cent and, on the basis of gender, 73.6 per cent. The gap in hours, however, is close to 50 per cent in both cases, and tends to persist in later years of the life cycle.

To assess more broadly the effects of high tax rates on partnered mothers as second earners, together with the high cost of child care in a largely privatised system, we need to organise the data according to a life cycle defined, not in terms of the age of 'head of household' as in the economics literature, but across phases that take account of the age and presence of dependant children. Using data for the sample of 'in-work' couples selected from the HES 2009–10 described previously, Table 3.6 presents average male and female hours of market work for four life-cycle phases as listed in the table. In the pre-child phase, which is represented by a relatively small subset of households in the sample, average female hours are over 85 per cent of average male hours. In the preschool phase, female hours fall to around a third of male hours, and then rise to 55 per cent in phase 3. In phase 4, when there are no longer dependant children present, female hours rise to just below 60 per cent of male hours, an outcome that is typically interpreted in the literature as evidence of persistence throughout the life cycle of decisions made in the earlier child rearing phases due to loss of human capital (see, for example, Shaw 1994).

Table 3.6: Life cycle labour supply by gender

Phase	Male hours	Female hours
1: Pre-children	2,213	1,882
2: At least one child of preschool age	2,127	764
3: Dependant child above preschool age	2,103	1,158
4: Pre-retirement—no dependant children	1,803	1,078

Source: Author's calculations based on ABS HES data for 2009–10.

In an analysis of time use data from the ABS Time Use Survey 2006 (Apps and Rees 2010), we find that while the market hours of partnered mothers are at their lowest average in phase 2, their average total working hours are at a maximum when calculated as the sum of market hours and time allocated to child care and domestic work (see also the analysis of time allocated to child care based on the same survey by Huong Dinh and Maria Racionero in Chapter 7, this volume). Male total hours of work, while below female total hours, are also at a maximum in phase 2. Thus each partner's 'pure leisure' is lower in phase 2 than at any other time in the family's life cycle. The data also show that market consumption expenditure is at its lowest point in phase 2. It is a phase in which the couple feels itself very short of both time and money. Economic models of the life cycle based on the assumption of a 'perfect' capital market, in which couples can borrow against future income at an interest rate as low as that paid on savings accounts, predict that they would do that to 'smooth' their consumption over time and ease the tightness of the constraints they face. In Apps and Rees (2010) the fact that they do not do so is taken as evidence that they face an 'imperfect' capital market in which borrowing, if it can be done at all, has to be at a rate well above the rate on savings, for example the credit card rate. Household expenditure data indicate that the problem is more acute when the ability of the family to offer collateral is lower.

These capital market conditions call for a program of public investment in child care to reduce the negative effects on female labour supply and to provide all children with equal access to early learning opportunities. A privatised system supported by price/cost subsidies is not a solution in this type of imperfect capital market, and in a child care market in which prices are driven by rising property values and profit seeking. Under the current policy approach, many parents will continue to have insufficient collateral to borrow at an affordable interest rate during the preschool years.

Household saving effects

When we turn to the data on household incomes and earnings we find, as we would expect, that median household income tracks median female earnings over the four life-cycle phases. We also find that median household saving, calculated as the difference between disposable income and consumption expenditure, tracks female earnings, as indicated in Table 3.7. The profiles provide strong evidence that tax policies with a negative effect on female labour supply have a flow-on negative effect on household saving.

Table 3.7: Life-cycle median household income, earnings and saving

Phase	Household income	Female earnings	Saving
1: Pre-children	$116,141	$47,502	$19,760
2: At least one child of preschool age	$83,824	$6,240	$5,824
3: Dependant child above preschool age	$110,244	$30,212	$9,776
4: Pre-retirement—no dependant children	$94,744	$26,208	$14,040

Source: Author's calculations based on ABS HES data for 2009–10.

The strong positive relationship between household saving and second earnings holds across the entire distribution of primary income. In Table 3.8, households are ranked by primary income quintiles and the subsample within each quintile is split into subsamples labelled H1 and H2 according to median second earnings. The table reports quintile data means of second earnings and regression estimates of household saving that control for the number and age of children.

Table 3.8: Second earnings and saving by primary income

Primary income quintiles $pa		34,265	54,701	71,982	96,648	201,855
H1:	2nd earnings $pa	330	9,745	9,494	16,794	12,835
	Saving $pa	-8,227	331	4,095	14,268	54,642
H2:	2nd earnings $pa	24,425	37,410	43,001	60,451	67,281
	Saving $pa	297	9,075	16,167	30,634	76,973

Source: Author's calculations based on ABS HES data for 2009–10.

The results reflect a second-earner saving rate that is significantly higher than that of the primary earner. The aggregate level of saving across quintiles 2 to 4 by H2 households exceeds that of the top quintile of H1 households. Reforms that raise effective tax rates on partnered mothers as second earners in order to fund lower top tax rates or a revenue shortfall from lower taxes on saving or capital income can therefore be expected to have the perverse effect of reducing the overall level of saving.

The analysis serves to highlight the importance of recognising the role of women in the economy, and the irrelevance of Treasury's CGE modelling approach that evaluates the economic cost of direct and indirect taxes on the basis of a model of the household as a single person with a single labour supply elasticity and marginal excess tax burden, and a single saving rate in a perfectly competitive capital market.

Demographic change and retirement incomes policy

Demographic change

Successive Intergenerational Reports (IGRs) have focused almost exclusively on the potential for budget deficits resulting from a rising aged dependency ratio (ADR), the ratio of people aged 65 and over to those aged 15–64. Dramatising the projected rise in the ADR in the coming decades is, however, misleading when a decline in the TFR is a major cause of population ageing. The focus of attention needs to be directed towards the total dependency ratio (TDR), the ratio of the *total* non-working to working-age population, and this includes the child dependency ratio (CDR), the ratio of those aged 0–14 to those aged 15–64. With the fall in TFR from 3.5 in the early 1960s to 1.8 today, the CDR is falling while the ADR is rising, due both to the fall in the TFR and increasing longevity. The historical graph of the overall TDR profile for Australia is U-shaped, with the rate in the early 1960s close to IGR projections for the middle of this century.

To assess the true effects of demographic change, the CDR and ADR need to be weighted by cost. It is straightforward to calculate that the resources required by a child are far greater than those required, on average, by a retiree. Every child requires at least a decade of parental and public investment in her/his education. Most importantly, every preschool child requires full-time care. Time use data reveal that a child is extremely costly in terms of parental time. The decline in the CDR since the 1960s therefore creates the potential for a significant 'social dividend'. Demographic change presents a *resource reallocation* problem, not a *saving* problem.

The key challenge is to put in place a set of reforms that allow the reallocation of parental time, primarily female labour time, from the home to the market. Under the required reforms, we would expect to see an expansion of the tax base that would provide additional revenue for productivity improving investments in child care, education, health care and the economy's infrastructure.

The preceding analysis of life-cycle profiles of female labour supply and the high degree of heterogeneity after the first child show the limited extent to which this outcome has been achieved. With the rise in female participation and the growth in the tax base since the 1960s, one of the major and most obvious policy mistakes has been the failure to invest incrementally in a publicly owned, early learning child care system. Instead, from 2004 to 2008, we saw much of the growth in tax revenues directed towards reducing the progressivity of the income tax and, over the last two decades, the gradual introduction of a system of quasi-joint taxation of families that shifts the tax burden from top incomes towards partnered mothers as second earners. This direction of reform, together with costly and limited access to child care, offers an explanation for Australia's poor performance in terms of female participation rates relative to comparable OECD countries and the persistent gender pay gap.

Superannuation vs the age pension

We now turn to retirement incomes policy (and see also Siobhan Austen and Rhonda Sharp in Chapter 10). Successive governments have focused on saving as the solution to the challenges presented by demographic change, and to this end have supported the expansion of Australia's tax-advantaged defined contribution superannuation system. The aim of the system is said to be that of replacing the public, pay-as-you-go (PAYG), non-contributory age pension with a mandatory fully funded private system over time. It is argued that because of the rising ADR, the age pension will become unaffordable. This argument is fundamentally flawed at several levels.

First, the argument fails to recognise that switching from a PAYG to a funded pension system cannot, *per se*, lead to an efficiency gain, as demonstrated by the famous Samuelson (1958) theorem for overlapping generation economies.[11] There is now a large body of research that draws on the Samuelson model to show that the switch to a fully funded scheme cannot be a solution to the problems raised by declining fertility and increasing ADRs (see, for example, Breyer 1989; Orszag and Stiglitz 1999). If it were true that the ratio of the dependant population to working-age population, weighted by cost, was necessarily rising, outcomes under a PAYG pension system and a fully funded system in a perfect capital market are identical. As shown by the Samuelson model, a negative interest rate in the latter case will achieve exactly the same outcome as the optimal changes to taxes and pension payments in the PAYG system. Moreover, a shift from PAYG to fully funding can make some members of the present working generation pay twice—they are forced to save for their own retirement while continuing to pay taxes that finance the pensions of the currently retired. Under Australia's tax-advantaged defined contribution superannuation system, women on relatively low pay face a high probability of this outcome. Their taxes support current pension payments while their relatively low super savings on retirement may exclude them from an approximately equivalent payment under the age pension.

Second, and more fundamentally, Australia's defined contribution superannuation system is not a retirement incomes policy. According to modern public economic theory, the key objective of a retirement incomes policy is the provision of insurance against longevity and aggregate (or social) risk in response to the inherent market failures and high transaction costs associated with the private provision of contracts to cover these risks. To deal with the issue of risk, we require a defined benefit system.

Australia's defined contribution superannuation system, with employer contributions and entity earnings taxed at 15 per cent, fails to provide insurance against longevity and aggregate risk. It is essentially a tax-advantaged saving scheme that provides the greatest gains for those with the most income to save. The benefits of the tax concessions go predominantly to primary earners, as shown in Figure 3.3, which is based on the HES 2009–10 sample of 'in-work' couples. The figure plots the distribution of primary- and second-earner superannuation balances by primary income.

---

11   Note that the theorem assumes a defined benefit system; that is, a true retirement income system.

Primary income deciles

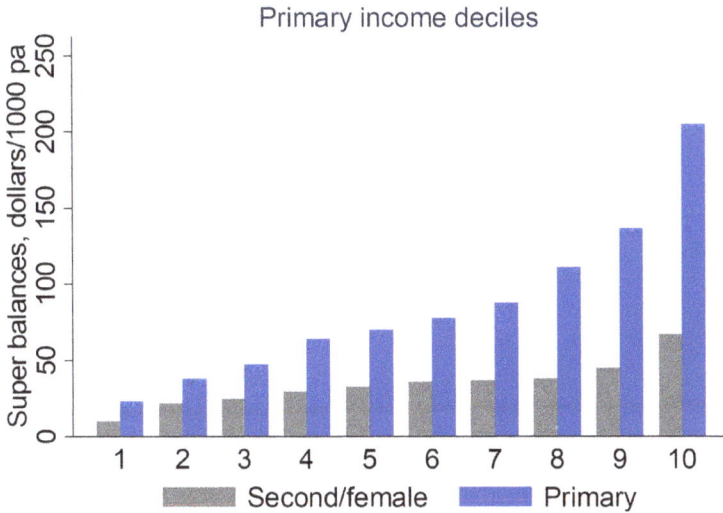

Figure 3.3: Primary/second-earner superannuation balances by primary income

Source: Author's calculations based on ABS HES data for 2009–10.

Given the gender gap in both pay and labour supply, women as a group cannot gain from tax-advantaged superannuation. The overall impact of the system is to widen the net-of-tax gender pay gap due to the preferential tax treatment of those on higher pay. It is therefore something of a puzzle that the Senate Economics Reference Committee Report, *Economic Security for Women in Retirement* (Commonwealth of Australia 2016), supports an increase in the Superannuation Guarantee to 12 per cent, and recommends that the planned gradual increase be implemented earlier than under the current timetable.

In addition to the limitations of the system with respect to equity, a significant loss is associated with privatisation due to high administrative costs (fees, commissions, advertising, excessive executive pay, etc.). It is recognised in the literature that administrative costs for public sector schemes are far lower. There is a clear trade-off: it is administratively less expensive to provide a uniform retirement program for all individuals than to have a large number of competing programs available, among which individuals can choose. It is generally accepted that the optimal policy is a universal public pension. The implementation of a universal pension is, however, likely to be strongly opposed by those who fail to understand the concept of *economic cost*, as discussed in the context of universal family payments in the preceding section.

As the limitations of the superannuation system become increasingly recognised, a frequent response is to shift the argument used to support much of its preferential tax treatment. Recent Budget estimates of the tax expenditure on superannuation concessions have exceeded $30 billion based on the comprehensive income tax benchmark. This figure is rejected by those who argue that the calculation should take account of opportunities for tax avoidance, for example through the use of trusts and negative gearing, to give a more reliable lower estimate.

It has also been argued that much of the tax expenditure can be justified in terms of reducing the double taxation of saving. Under a comprehensive income tax saving is said to be taxed twice and that the ideal tax system would exempt capital income (see, for example, Commonwealth of Australia 2008). The proposition that the optimal tax rate on capital is zero contradicts the central tenet of modern tax theory, that the optimal tax rate on a given source of income, whether labour or capital, can only be determined on the basis of empirical evidence on distributional outcomes and behavioural effects because we are in a 'second-best' setting. Even if capital were highly mobile, which is very much open to question in a number of important contexts, this does not imply an optimal rate of zero.

If we attempt to move towards a low capital income tax regime, for example, by increasing mandatory contributions to superannuation or cutting the company income tax rate, taxes elsewhere will have to rise. If the ongoing policy agenda persists, we can expect further shifts in the burden of taxation towards three groups—the 'middle', working married mothers and the next generation—with negative effects on the tax base, productivity and growth.

Conclusion

Reforms to the Australian tax-transfer system in recent decades have been directed towards shifting the tax burden from the top percentiles of the income distribution towards those on or below average earnings, in an economic environment of growing inequality in wages, incomes and wealth. This is clearly demonstrated through the survey data presented in this chapter. In addition, the simultaneous introduction of joint income–tested family payments has shifted the tax burden towards working partnered mothers, providing a further source of revenue for cutting top tax rates. Important consequences include a widening of the net-of-tax gender pay gap and a failure to promote the kinds of resource reallocations required for achieving fiscal sustainability in the face of demographic change.

Many of the policy views in recent Treasury reports suggest that there is little to no improvement in sight. All too frequently recommended reforms, such as lower top income tax rates, a tax-mix change through the expansion of the goods and services tax (GST) and lower capital income taxes, draw on economic models that are inconsistent with the evidence on behavioural effects, and which proceed as if we lived in a world in which women do not exist. Better economic models are readily available that would support a change in direction in the key policy areas considered in this paper: the restoration of a truly progressive, individual-based income tax system with effective constraints on evasion and avoidance; investment in the development of a high-quality, early learning public child care system; and recognition of the superiority of a publicly funded age pension system over a privatised and inequitably tax-advantaged defined contribution superannuation system. In short, this chapter advocates for the reversal of the policies introduced over the past three decades, often under cover of measures that disguise their real effects and supported by spurious and misleading arguments, the cumulative effects of which have been to construct an Australian tax system that is both less efficient and less fair, not least in the way that it treats working women.

References

ABS (Australian Bureau of Statistics). 2016. *Average Weekly Earnings, Australia*, Cat. no. 6302.0.

Andrienko, Yuri, Patricia Apps and Ray Rees. 2016. 'Optimal Taxation and Top Incomes'. *International Tax and Public Finance* 23(6): 981–1003. doi.org/10.1007/s10797-015-9391-y

Apps, Patricia. 1982. 'Institutional Inequality and Tax Incidence'. *Journal of Public Economics* 18(2): 217–242. doi.org/10.1016/0047-2727(82)90004-4

Apps, Patricia. 2010. 'Why the Henry Review Fails on Family Tax Reform'. In Chris Evans, Richard Krever and Peter Mellor (eds), *Australia's Future Tax System: The Prospects after Henry*, pp. 103–127. Australia: Thomson Reuter Australia Ltd.

Apps, Patricia, Ngo Long and Ray Rees. 2014. 'Optimal Piecewise Linear Income Taxation'. *Journal of Public Economic Theory* 16(4): 523–545. doi.org/10.1111/jpet.12070

Apps, Patricia and Ray Rees. 1988. 'Taxation and the Household'. *Journal of Public Economics* 35(3): 355–369. doi.org/10.1016/0047-2727(88)90037-0

Apps, Patricia and Ray Rees. 2009. *Public Economics and the Household*. Cambridge: Cambridge University Press. doi.org/10.1017/CBO9780511626548

Apps, Patricia and Ray Rees. 2010. 'Family Labour Supply, Taxation and Saving in an Imperfect Capital Market'. *Review of Economics of the Household* 8: 297–323. doi.org/10.1007/s11150-010-9094-1

Apps, Patricia and Ray Rees. 2013. 'Raise Top Tax Rates, Not the GST'. *Australian Tax Forum* 28(3): 679–693. doi.org/10.2139/ssrn.2291299

Apps, Patricia and Ray Rees. 2017. 'Optimal Family Taxation and Income Inequality'. Sydney Law School Research Paper No. 17/09. dx.doi.org/10.2139/ssrn.2910797

Atkinson, Antony. 2015. *Inequality: What can be done?* Harvard University Press. doi.org/10.4159/9780674287013

Boskin, Michael and Eytan Sheshinski. 1983. 'Optimal Tax Treatment of the Family: Married Couples'. *Journal of Public Economics* 20(3): 281–297. doi.org/10.1016/0047-2727(83)90027-0

Breyer, Friedrich. 1989. 'On the Intergenerational Pareto Efficiency of Pay-As-You-Go Pension Systems'. *Journal of Institutional and Theoretical Economics* 145(4): 643–658.

Cao, Liangyue, Amanda Hosking, Michael Kouparitsas, Damian Mullaly, Xavier Rimmer, Qun Shi, Wallace Stark and Sebastian Wende. 2015. 'Understanding the Economy-Wide Efficiency and Incidence of Major Australian Taxes'. Treasury Working Paper, WP 2015-01, Australian Government.

Commonwealth of Australia. 2008. *Australia's Future Tax System: Retirement Income Consultation Paper*. Canberra: Commonwealth of Australia.

Commonwealth of Australia. 2016. *Economic Security for Women in Retirement*. Report of the Senate Economics Reference Committee. Canberra: Commonwealth of Australia.

Henry, Ken et al. 2009. *Review of Australia's Future Tax System: Report to the Treasurer*. Australia's Future Tax System Review Panel (the 'Henry Review'). Available at: taxreview.treasury.gov.au

Institute for Fiscal Studies and James Mirrlees. 2011. *Tax by Design: The Mirrlees Review*. Oxford: Oxford University Press.

KPMG. 2010. *CGE Analysis of the Current Australian Tax System*. Canberra: Department of Treasury.

KPMG. 2011. 'Economic Analysis of the Impact of Using GST to Reform Taxes'. Report prepared for CPA Australia.

Moffitt, Robert and Mark Wilhelm. 2000. 'Taxation and the Labor Supply Decisions of the Affluent'. In Joel Slemrod (ed.), *Does Atlas shrug? The Economic Consequences of Taxing the Rich*, pp. 193–234. New York: Russell Sage Foundation; Cambridge and London: Harvard University Press.

Orszag, Peter and James Stiglitz. 1999. 'Rethinking Pensions Reform: Ten Myths about Social Security Systems'. In Robert Holzmann and Joseph Stiglitz (eds), *New Ideas about Old Age Security*, pp. 17–56. Washington: World Bank.

Peter, Klara Sabirianova, Steve Buttrick and Denvil Duncan. 2010. 'Global reform of personal income taxation, 1981–2005: Evidence from 189 countries'. *National Tax Journal* 63(3): 447–478. doi.org/10.17310/ntj.2010.3.03

Piketty, Thomas and Emmanuel Saez. 2003. 'Income Inequality in the United States, 1913-1998'. *Quarterly Journal of Economics* 118(1): 1–39. doi.org/10.1162/00335530360535135

Piketty, Thomas, Emmanuel Saez and Stefanie Stantcheva. 2014. 'Optimal Taxation of Top Labor Incomes: A Tale of Three Elasticities'. *American Economic Journal: Economic Policy* 6(1): 230–271. doi.org/10.1257/pol.6.1.230

Samuelson, Paul. 1958. 'An Exact Consumption-Loan Model of Interest with or without the Social Contrivance of Money'. *Journal of Political Economy* 66(6): 467–482. doi.org/10.1086/258100

Shaw, Kathryn. 1994. 'The Persistence of Female Labor Supply: Empirical Evidence and Implications'. *Journal of Human Resources* 29(2): 348–378. doi.org/10.2307/146102

Treasury. 2015a. *Intergenerational Report: Australia in 2055.* Canberra: Commonwealth of Australia. Available at: treasury.gov.au/publication/2015-intergenerational-report/

Treasury. 2015b. *Re:Think Tax Discussion Paper.* Australian Government. Available at: bettertax.gov.au/files/2015/03/TWP_combined-online.pdf

WGEA (Workplace Gender Equality Agency). 2016. *Gender Pay Gap Statistics*, March, Australian Government. Available at: www.wgea.gov.au

4

Gender equality and a rights-based approach to tax reform

Helen Hodgson and Kerrie Sadiq

This chapter applies a human rights framework to gender inequality in tax policy. Gender inequality in economic reform is a global issue. In its recent report, *Progress of the World's Women* (the UN Report), UN (United Nations) Women applies international human rights standards to assess laws and policies for substantive gender equality (UN Women 2015). The UN Report confirms that women's rights cannot and should not be separated from general principles of social and economic justice, and macro-economic and fiscal policy should not be designed in isolation from a human rights agenda; on the contrary, human rights should be one of the drivers of economic reform (UN Women 2015, p. 26).

UN Women is the UN entity responsible for promoting women's empowerment and gender equality. In the UN Report, UN Women advocates for a rights-based macro-economic agenda that will ensure that human rights, including the right to education and dignified employment, are protected, and are driving the process of macro-economic reform. In this chapter, we use this report as the starting point for demonstrating why a human rights framework should be used in the design of tax policy specifically. Our approach can be contrasted with approaches that focus more directly on redistributive measures. For instance, the International

Monetary Fund (IMF), in its recent report on fiscal policy and income inequality (IMF 2014), places a greater emphasis on targeting transfers rather than our broad-based, encompassing approach to tax policy.

We propose in this chapter the use of a framework for fiscal policy that incorporates human rights principles that address gender inequality. That is, human rights obligations need to be built into fiscal policy. In the next part, we discuss the relevant human rights treaties and set out and adopt the UN Women (2015) framework. We then apply this UN Women framework to the Australian tax system as a case study. We examine four common taxes (personal income tax (PIT), goods and services tax (GST), property taxes and taxes on retirement savings) to determine the extent of any inherent tax bias, then apply a human rights gendered lens to examine a range of tax reform proposals. In particular, we consider the impact that any reforms may have on the economic and social rights of women.

A rights-based approach

This chapter takes a human rights approach to gender inequality in tax systems, following Elson (2006) in this approach to budgets. The human rights implications of tax-transfer policy is a common thread throughout this book; see, for example, Kathleen Lahey's discussion of taxing for gender equality in Chapter 2 and Patricia Apps' discussion about the effects of gender discrimination in PIT policy in Chapter 3. Other authors have previously adopted an equality approach (Stotsky 1997) or a capabilities approach (Stewart 2011). Even in gender analysis, human rights obligations have not usually been embedded into fiscal policy, which is generally analysed separately for any gender impact on the basis of equity principles.

Gender impact analysis

Susan Himmelweit (2002, p. 50) argues that a gender impact analysis of fiscal policy allows an assessment of both the direct and indirect impact of budgetary proposals in deciding whether reforms should proceed. However, while this impact assessment can be applied at every stage of policy making, it is not fully incorporated into policy design. That is, such an analysis is separate and evaluative rather than embedded in the process of reform. In Himmelweit's approach (2002, pp. 64–65), a gender impact analysis of economic policy applies three principles. First, policies are assessed on both paid and unpaid economies. Second, there is an assessment of the distribution between men and women. Third, equity is evaluated both between and within households. Each of these assessments is valuable, but they provide a framework for assessing evidence of gender inequality and offer accountability solutions, rather than providing a framework for alleviating gender inequality within a macro-economic policy framework.

Equality in substance

As UN Women reminds us (UN Women 2015), equality in the law between men and women does not guarantee equality in practice. Formal equality is a separate concept from substantive equality or *genuine fiscal equality*. While equal rights embedded in the legal system provide a central reference point and reflect policy shifts, 'entrenched inequalities, discriminatory social norms, harmful customary practices, as well as dominant patterns of economic development can undermine their implementation and positive impact' (UN Women 2015, p. 12). Rather than the adoption of laws that treat men and women equally, substantive equality considers the application of these laws and the subsequent results and outcomes. As UN Women explains further:

> The concept of substantive equality arose out of the recognition that because of the legacy of historical inequalities, structural disadvantages, biological differences and biases in how laws and policies are implemented in practice, formal equality is not enough to ensure that women are able to enjoy the same rights as men. To achieve substantive equality, therefore, requires both direct and indirect discrimination to be addressed. It also requires specific measures to be adopted that redress women's disadvantages and, in the longer term, the transformation of the institutions and structures that reinforce and reproduce unequal power relations between women and men (UN Women 2015, p. 35).

Stotsky (1996) was among the first to recognise substantive difference in a global context and her framework of explicit and implicit bias is seen as a foundational tool for analysis. Explicit biases arise where the law specifically establishes rules that treat men and women differently. Implicit biases are more pervasive, and arise where the operation of the rules has a different effect on men and women, based on the interaction of the tax laws with social and economic norms. Consequently, explicit biases may be observed and addressed through formal equality measures, while implicit biases may be observed and addressed with substantive equality measures.

Subsequent research includes Barnett and Grown's (2004) hypothetical tax typology to develop recommendations for developed and emerging economies based on their level of development and the range of tax bases available. Also of significance is Grown and Valodia's (2010) comparative gender analysis across 10 countries with different levels of economic development and different tax systems.

While offering insight into explicit and implicit gender inequality issues, the above frameworks have been criticised as being based on the criteria of equal treatment for men and women (Elson 2006, p. 77; Young 1999). As such, they arguably fail to recognise and address differences between women and men, as required under various human rights treaties explained below. Hence, the identification of explicit or implicit bias is only the starting point. Explicit bias can be addressed through adopting an equality framework, but implicit bias needs more nuanced policy, and is best addressed through a human rights or capabilities framework.

Equality needs to be considered in the context of not only opportunities but also outcomes. Consequently, different treatment may be required to achieve substantive equality. The need for such an approach is well understood in a human rights context but is little understood in an economic policy context. UN Women explains:

> the concept of substantive equality has been advanced in key human rights treaties to capture this broader understanding: that inequality can be structural and discrimination indirect; that equality has to be understood in relation to outcomes as well as opportunities; and that 'different treatment' might be required to achieve equality in practice (UN Women 2015, p. 35).

A human rights approach allows policymakers to adopt differential treatment where it is necessary to address discrimination in macro-economic policy.

Fiscal equality

Kathleen Lahey argues that women's fiscal equality is fundamental to all human rights (see, for example, Chapter 2, this volume; and Lahey 2015, p. 10). Logically, macro-economic policy and its subset of fiscal policy should take into account the human rights principles to which governments have committed. UN Women proposes that action is required in three interrelated areas: redressing women's socio-economic disadvantage; addressing stereotyping, stigma and violence; and strengthening women's agency, voice and participation. Part of the progress towards substantive equality relates to women's rights to information about laws, government policy and budgetary details, including the right to scrutinise public budgets to 'ensure public services meet women's needs better; and having access to a range of high quality services can in turn support women's right to work, creating powerful synergies' (UN Women 2015, p. 13).

UN Women stresses that if substantive equality is to be achieved, economic and social policies must work in tandem, although traditionally economic policy is seen as promoting economic growth while social policy addresses its 'causalities', such as poverty and inequality. Economic policy can pursue the goal of gender equality and social justice, while social policies can contribute to economic growth. UN Women states:

> The specific policy package to achieve substantive equality will differ from context to context. Ultimately, the aim is to create a virtuous cycle through the generation of decent work, gender-responsive social protection and social services, alongside enabling macroeconomic policies that prioritize investment in human beings and the fulfilment of social objectives (UN Women 2015, p. 13).

While UN Women provides for targeted 'grass roots' action, it also recognises that broad-based priority areas within a policy-based framework must be prioritised. In addition to decent work for women and gender-responsive social policies, UN Women views rights-based macro-economic policies as a key priority area.

Applying human rights treaties

Human rights treaties have been signed by many nations, with two especially significant in the global context and specifically relevant in the Australian fiscal policy context: the International Covenant on Economic, Social and Cultural Rights (ICESCR) and the Convention on the

Elimination of All Forms of Discrimination Against Women (CEDAW). These treaties are recognised as important contributors to macro-economic policy, not only to guide that policy but especially in the context of the need for temporary special measures to correct for indirect discrimination. This is particularly relevant where there is a lack of substantive equality and applies where gender-neutral policies are actually modelled on male norm and lifestyles, and inherently incorporate stereotypical expectations, attitudes and behaviour (UN Women 2015, p. 36).

The ICESCR (1966) was ratified by Australia on 10 December 1975. In its Preamble, it recognises that:

> in accordance with the Universal Declaration of Human Rights, the ideal of free human beings enjoying freedom from fear and want can only be achieved if conditions are created whereby everyone may enjoy his economic, social and cultural rights, as well as his civil and political rights (ICESCR 1966, Preamble).

These socio-economic rights are understood to include the right to education, housing, health care and a certain standard of living. As part of those rights, there is a broad obligation of signatories to ensure the equal right of men and women to the enjoyment of all economic, social and cultural rights set forth in the present Covenant (ICESCR Article 3). Other significant Articles, discussed below, include the right to work (ICESCR Article 6), social security (ICESCR Article 9), protection and assistance to the family (ICESCR Article 10) and an adequate standard of living (ICESCR Article 11).

The treaty CEDAW (1979) was ratified by Australia on 28 July 1983. The CEDAW is generally understood to be a 'bill of rights' for women and contains 30 Articles defining key principles of equality 'based on the belief that basic human rights include the true equality of men and women' (HRC 2015). As a signatory, Australia has committed itself to ensuring the elimination of discrimination against women, defined in Article 1 as:

> any distinction, exclusion or restriction made on the basis of sex which has the effect or purpose of impairing or nullifying the recognition, enjoyment or exercise by women, irrespective of their marital status, on a basis of equality of men and women, of human rights and fundamental freedoms in the political, economic, social, cultural, civil or any other field (CEDAW 1979, Article 1).

Previous studies have adopted a CEDAW perspective as the basis for analysing public revenue, also drawing on the work of gender budgeting initiatives (e.g. Elson 2006). The uses and implications of gender budgeting are discussed further in Chapters 2, 10 and 11 of this book. These studies provide useful insights into current tax regimes. However, again, these studies tend to evaluate existing taxes rather than provide the foundation for reform with human rights obligations built into the fiscal policy framework. That is, rather than starting from a human rights perspective, these studies recognise the current criteria of tax reform design (efficiency, equity and ease of administration) as the design principles and reconceptualise current policy though a human rights lens. As an alternative, we propose that human rights obligations need to be built into fiscal policy.

The two treaties, when incorporated into fiscal policy, must work in tandem to achieve substantive gender equality. While the CEDAW provides an understanding of what is meant by gender equality and is specifically targeted at discrimination against women, the ICESCR addresses women's economic and social rights. These treaties set the obligations of signatory states and provide the basis for legislative change as well as obligations and guidance on appropriate means of addressing inequality. They require states to take a proactive role in ensuring equality in social and economic rights.

Once entrenched in domestic legislation:

> [these] laws that establish that women and men have equal rights provide the basis for demanding and achieving equality in practice. They are a touchstone for political and cultural struggles, set standards and incentives for changes in social norms and attitudes and influence shifts in policy (UN Women 2015, p. 28).

However, there are recognised limitations as legislative changes are only part of the story with such obligations providing 'the ethical basis and inspiration for collective action to change policies as well as social norms, attitudes and practices' (UN Women 2015, p. 16). As UN Women explains:

> human rights principles are also an important basis for the design of policies, for monitoring their implementation and outcomes and for holding all duty-bearers—States as well as global institutions and corporations—to account for the realization of substantive equality (UN Women 2015, p. 17).

Human rights principles and the ensuing legislative enactment of the required standards provide the basis for equality with 'power inequalities, structural constraints and discriminatory social norms and practices' needing to be addressed (UN Women 2015, p. 24). Despite the implementation of these treaties, women continue to experience economic inequality and it is suggested, therefore, that states 'have a proactive role as arbiters of social and economic rights' (UN Women 2015, p. 25) and human rights commitments must be incorporated into macro-economic policy if there is to be substantive gender equality.

Rights-based fiscal policies

To be effective, a global approach to human rights needs to be incorporated into state-based policies to support gender equality. The economic environment of a nation is created through its macro-economic policies, which, in turn, 'shape the overall economic environment for realising women's economic and social rights' (UN Women 2015, p. 194). Traditional macro-economic policy focuses on fiscal (tax and government expenditure) and monetary policy for the creation of jobs, wealth and improved living standards (Dolamore 2015). This policy has a significant effect on paid employment and fiscal resources needed to implement social policies and programs. Because of the emphasis on paid employment, macro-economic policies fail to adequately consider the importance of unpaid care and domestic work as well as non-market investments in people (UN Women 2015, p. 192) (see also the discussion by Julie Smith in Chapter 6).

Macro-economic policies provide the foundation for advancing substantive equality for women because they affect gender equality in four distinct ways: a direct impact on the quantity and quality of employment opportunities; the burden of unpaid care and domestic work; distributive consequences through taxation; and resources available to finance social policies (UN Women 2015, pp. 194–196). Macro-economic policy is traditionally regarded as gender-neutral. As such, it customarily fails to take into account substantive gender equality, instead focusing on the operation of the economy as a whole to provide a stable economic environment, which, in turn, fosters strong and sustainable economic growth. Kathleen Lahey explains that this has occurred because 'fiscal policies are constructed around one goal—taxing for growth—and largely ignore taxing for social needs' (2015, p. 8). However, distributive consequences are not gender-neutral. Nor are many gendered assumptions inherent in what appear to be gender-neutral tax regimes (Nelson 2015). This does not necessarily mean that taxing for growth and taxing for social policy are in opposition to each other. Rather, broad fiscal policy should include both, allowing the two to complement each other.

The current, narrowly focused, approaches to macro-economic policy, has an emphasis on growth of gross domestic product (GDP) that means structural disadvantages faced by women are not addressed (UN Women 2015, p. 196). GDP itself is measured according to goods and services produced, which means that non-market services (unpaid care and domestic work) are excluded, reinforcing the stereotype of the lack of value in such work. While the causal relationship between GDP growth and gender equality is mixed, within a human rights context, UN Women argues, first, that GDP growth is only successful if it leads to better social outcomes, which includes gender equality; second, that the lack of focus within macro-economic policy on employment creation limits the ability to address women's socio-economic advantage in the labour market; and third, that restrictive macro-economic policy choices affect the ability to fund gender equality social policy initiatives and ensure that the tax system has positive redistributive consequences (UN Women 2015, p. 19.).

These issues are seldom addressed through macro-economic policies. This is despite the recognition that:

> markets do not always function well; unregulated markets can result in financial crises, too little employment, an inadequate supply of public goods and services and environmental deterioration; distribution matters; and inequality affects economic stability and performance (UN Women 2015, p. 210).

In contrast, feminist macro-economists have developed frameworks that incorporate broader concepts such as unpaid labour and consider distributive outcomes. Building on this, a human rights–based approach to macro-economic policy requires a broader set of objectives to be considered, as well as the inclusion of social policies such as gender equality (UN Women 2015, p. 15). Such an approach can lead to, among other things, the democratisation of economic governance (UN Women 2015, p. 193).

UN Women suggests that the key principles and obligations for a human rights–based macro-economic policy are non-discrimination and equality; minimum essential levels of social and economic rights; progressive realisation and preventing policy reversals; maximum available resources; accountability, transparency and participation; and extraterritorial obligations (UN Women 2015, pp. 210–211). The Centre for Economic and Social Rights, a not-for-profit international human rights organisation, also highlights what it believes are the crucial functions of tax from a human rights perspective: resourcing, redistribution, representation and re-pricing (Donald 2015). UN Women summarises the value of a robust fiscal regime in the human rights context as follows:

> Human rights emphasize the dignity and freedom of the individual, but their realization depends heavily on solidarity and collective action. Putting in place policies for substantive equality requires collective financing, ideally through progressive taxation. The narrow targeting of social protection to the poorest households may seem to make it more affordable than building universal systems that benefit everyone. But universal systems can actually expand financing options by increasing the willingness of middle and higher income groups to pay taxes for well-functioning education, health or pension systems that they would also use (UN Women 2015, p. 17).

The UN Women framework

Within a fiscal policy context, there are numerous measures that can be adopted as part of the tax-transfer system. UN Women suggests four broad fiscal policy considerations (UN Women 2015, pp. 15–16) and associated tax strategies, which are adopted in this chapter. In Table 4.1, we suggest and adopt the UN Women framework for considering human rights obligations within fiscal policy.

Table 4.1: Fiscal policy strategies for a human rights framework

Fiscal policy	Tax strategies
Raise resources for gender-sensitive social protection and social services by enforcing existing tax obligations.	Improve the efficiency of tax collection through addressing institutional and capacity constraints, which can mobilise additional resources even if the tax mix and tax rates do not change.
Reprioritise expenditure (e.g. reducing expenditure on defence and increasing expenditure on social services).	Reprioritise expenditures towards areas that advance gender equality and support the realisation of rights. Design tax systems to redistribute income and to redress socio-economic disadvantage by ensuring that women and marginalised groups are not disproportionately burdened. Use gender-responsive budgeting to guide revenue mobilisation and spending decisions.

Fiscal policy	Tax strategies
Expand the overall tax base (minimising or removing tax exemptions and allowances that primarily benefit wealthier groups).	Increase tax revenues by introducing new taxes and tax policies that generate resources from under-taxed areas, such as the financial sector or natural resource exports.
Global policy coordination to minimise spill-overs and ensure governments can mobilise resources.	Global cooperation for the realisation of economic and social rights could be achieved through the universal acceptance of extraterritorial obligations of governments with regard to the realisation of rights beyond their own borders, as outlined in the Maastricht Principles, which include consideration of the roles of transnational corporations, non-governmental organisations and intergovernmental institutions.

Source: Adapted from UN Women (2015, pp. 15–16).

The strategies in Table 4.1 encompass accountability measures, both domestically and globally, as well as measures that address the adequacy and distribution of tax revenue. The end goal of a human rights–based macro-economic policy that incorporates gender equality issues is the recognition of economic and social rights for all (UN Women 2015, p. 209). However, the balance between social and economic policy must also be considered. Even when the divisions between social and economic policy are removed and the two are seen as one, there should not be an overemphasis on economic growth to the detriment of social justice. As Kathleen Lahey points out, this has not been the traditional approach:

> For more than a generation, the IMF and the World Bank have pushed governments to prioritise economic growth over social justice in their approach to fiscal policy. The results of this experiment are now in; sluggish growth, steepening inequality and the continued subjugation of women. It is time for a new vision of development, in which real needs take precedence over the fantastical desires that incubate in the global institutions (Lahey 2015, p. 8).

A rights-based approach to tax reform

There are numerous measures that a state can take to ensure that a rights-based approach to fiscal policy is adopted. Most obviously, it is the general tax system that funds investment in public services. Ensuring that enough revenue is raised can be achieved by enforcing the current tax regime as well as expanding the tax base. However, in doing so, a state needs to be mindful of the distributive effects, along with the progressivity of taxes.

States also need to be able to mobilise their resources without deterrence felt by the tax policies of other countries with preferential tax regimes. A global environment needs to be created to ensure that economic and social policies are seen as connected.

The effect of different taxes in the tax mix also needs to be considered within a human rights framework. The main issues to consider when human rights principles are applied to entire programs of tax reform are the balance between corporate and PIT, and the balance between direct and indirect tax (Elson 2006, p. 95). Previous analysis also suggests that when corporate taxes are lowered personal taxes are increased, and when income taxes are reduced sales taxes are increased, all with a greater incidence of tax falling on women (UN Women 2015, p. 76).

UN Women makes the case that progressive taxes are directly related to community solidarity (UN Women 2015, p. 207). It lists income tax as most progressive, followed by earmarked taxes, indirect taxes, public then private insurance schemes, user fees and self-provision as the most regressive forms of financing the provision of social services (UN Women 2015, p. 207). Barnett and Grown (2004) studied the effect that different tax bases have on the economic activities of women across a range of countries with different levels of development. The gender-tax typology developed in that study ranged from countries with a low level of economic development, where tax bias is more likely to be implicit, and the principal tax recommendations relate to targeted relief and exemptions; to countries where women's economic activities are fully integrated, and the primary recommendations are to remove explicit bias and to increase progressivity in the system through increased MTRs and targeted low-income relief.

Barnett and Grown (2004) make their first recommendation the removal of any explicit bias in the tax system. Any such bias would be clearly contrary to Article 2 of CEDAW, which requires that signatory states:

> Eradicate discrimination against women by introducing new laws or policy, changing existing discriminatory laws and providing sanctions for discrimination where it occurs (CEDAW 1979, Article 2).

We argue that a human rights framework requires that the governments address inequality by directing more resources to removing barriers to full economic participation by women. Specifically, the PIT, GST, taxes on capital, property taxes and retirement savings taxes should all be considered within a fiscal policy setting that incorporates human rights obligations. While explicit discrimination can be addressed through legislative reform, implicit bias is systemic and more difficult to address. Economic gender gaps tend to arise from societal norms and expectations, particularly labour market stereotypes about suitable occupations, social norms that assume women will take primary responsibility for domestic chores and the care of young children and the power of social norms so that women don't exercise their rights. CEDAW Article 5 specifically requires signatories to:

> Address and change social and cultural patterns that reinforce the stereotyping of women and traditional gender roles, or that promote the relative superiority or inferiority of either of the sexes (CEDAW 1979, Article 5).

In order to increase access to work, Article 10 of ICESCR requires signatories to provide protection to new mothers, including access to paid parental leave, and CEDAW requires signatories to address social and cultural patterns that reinforce gender stereotypical roles (Article 5), and ensure that women have the same training and employment opportunities as men (Article 10). This requires a greater fiscal investment in policies around paid parental leave and child care.

There is an increasing political awareness in Australia of the issues surrounding women's workforce participation as a means to improving the economic wellbeing of women (Senate Economics Reference Committee 2016). However, consistent with the austerity regimes adopted internationally, the Turnbull Government is seeking to fund any expansion of these programs to increase workforce participation through existing portfolio reallocations (e.g. proposing that funding for increased child care come from savings in existing programs). Notably, the UN Women framework classifies self-provision as the most regressive form of provision of social services, yet this is the norm for many women who are unable to access adequate or appropriate child or elder care. We argue that a human rights framework requires that the government direct more resources to removing barriers to full economic participation by women.

In the balance of this chapter, we examine four common taxes and social insurance systems against the human rights treaties ICESCR and CEDAW. This discussion draws on Australia as a case study of a developed nation that is a signatory to the treaties.

Personal income tax-transfer system

Progressivity of income tax

Although PIT is the most progressive tax, there has been a clear trend across the Organisation for Economic Co-operation and Development (OECD) countries since the 1980s to flatten PIT rate schedules. Among emerging nations, income tax tends to be less significant as a source of revenue than among developed nations (World Bank 2015).

There is a global trend to reduce the effective tax rates on investment income in order to counter the mobility of capital. Literature also suggests that lower tax rates on savings encourages increased savings among low-income earners, although higher income earners are more likely to redirect savings into tax-preferred models (OECD 2007). However, there is evidence that a reduction in the corporate tax rate leads to a greater reliance on other taxes to meet the fiscal requirements of government. Elson (2006, p. 95) documents examples where the burden is shifted either to PIT or, more usually, to indirect taxes to ensure fiscal adequacy. If that shift were to make PIT more progressive it would provide additional revenue to provide social services, but, historically, PIT reform measures have led to flatter PIT schedules.

Women are over-represented among lower income earners and pay less PIT as a result. However, tax reform that reduces PIT rates is not only regressive but reduces revenue available to governments to deliver social services. This creates a feedback loop: governments cannot afford to provide care services, pushing the burden back to women who may further reduce their hours in the paid workforce in order to provide unpaid care.

Studies of the gender wealth gap (e.g. Austen et al. 2014; Cobb-Clark and Hildebrand 2011) also show that the composition of the assets held by single women includes a higher proportion of wealth held in the primary home than in other asset classes, while men are more likely to hold wealth portfolios with a larger proportion of financial assets. As such, proposals that reduce the tax on investments are likely to deliver higher benefits to male investors.

Tax on income from investments, including tax on the gain from realisation of capital assets, is strongly progressive if included in a global definition of income and taxed at general progressive rates. This is because high-income earners derive a higher proportion of their income from investments than low-income earners. Conversely, many countries impose a schedular tax system under which capital income is taxed at a flat rate, or a final withholding tax (Harding 2013). Such systems disadvantage low-income earners who pay PIT rates below the statutory withholding rate on their earned income, including investors and retirees who are supporting themselves from the returns on those investments.

A significant element of the tax reform debate in Australia is the proposal to lower the company tax rate in order to encourage foreign investment in Australian companies. Australian Treasury modelling (Treasury 2015, p. 78) suggests that the economic benefits of a company tax rate cut would be shared among shareholders, customers and employees. However, a lower company tax rate also causes tax planning. In the Australian context, the gap between the top MTR of the PIT and the corporate rate (currently 19 per cent) drives decisions regarding business structures and encourages tax minimisation (Treasury 2015, p. 80). The caveat on this argument is that the dividend imputation system washes out the benefit of the reduction in corporate tax in respect of Australian shareholders when dividends are received (rather than profits being retained).

In Australia, capital gains are included in assessable income when gains are realised, but a discount reduces the taxable gain by 50 per cent. A review of Australian Tax Office (ATO) data shows that although taxpayers across all income ranges derive capital gains, about 3 per cent of taxpayers with a taxable income below $80,000 received capital gains, compared to 6.6 per cent of taxpayers with a total income between $100,000 and $150,000 and 19 per cent of taxpayers with a total income of more than $500,000 (ATO 2012, Table 9). Consequently, reducing the tax rate on capital gains tax is regressive and also likely to reduce revenue collections.

We argue that reform of taxation on capital assets must expand the tax base by removing exemptions, and make additional revenue available to redirect toward areas of social spending. Consequently, reductions in corporate taxes and other investment taxes are not consistent with a human rights approach to tax reform.

The tax and transfer unit

The relevant human rights treaties require that signatory states not only ensure equal economic rights to men and women (ICESCR Article 3; CEDAW Article 3) but specifically recognise the right to work (ICESCR Article 6; CEDAW Article 11). Barriers to workforce participation through joint tax systems and high effective marginal tax rates (EMTRs) are potentially in breach of these treaty obligations.

As discussed in several other chapters of this volume, the disincentive effects on women's work of a joint (couple) tax unit are well recognised in the economic literature. The secondary income earner in a household effectively bears a higher tax rate than the primary earner, reducing participation incentives on both efficiency and equity grounds.

Both treaties recognise the right of people to transfer payments:

> ICESCR Article 9: Recognise the right of everyone to social security, including social insurance … (ICESCR 1966, Article 9)

> CEDAW Article 13: Women have equal access to family benefits, forms of financial credit, including mortgages, and the same rights as men to participate in recreational activities and cultural life … (CEDAW 1979, Article 13)

The choice of the tax and/or transfer unit can also create a couple, or marriage, penalty or bonus where the joint tax payable differs from the tax payable by two individuals (see, for example, Adam and Brewer 2012, discussing the United Kingdom; Hodgson 2008).

The unit of assessment for the tax system may not be the same as for the transfer system. Under tax and benefit systems where the individual is the unit of assessment for tax purposes but the couple is the unit for transfer purposes, there is a mismatch that can result in the application of a couple penalty that may discourage participation in the labour market. When the tax unit operates in conjunction with a means-tested transfer system on a joint or household basis, the MTR compounds with the withdrawal of transfer payments, resulting in high EMTRs (Apps 2010).

Australia's personal income tax-transfer systems do not include any formal bias, with formal equality in tax-transfer legislation. Primary carers and spouses are recognised as gender-neutral, although the data reflect social norms, showing that primary carers are predominantly female and that male workforce participation rates are higher. Significantly, women still undertake more unpaid care than men, most while maintaining engagement with the paid economy, leading to one of the highest rates of part-time female workforce participation in the OECD (Craig 2007; Baird et al. 2017).

While Australia has adopted the individual as the tax unit, its transfer payments are determined on the basis of household income. Australia has paid payments in respect of dependants directly to the primary carer since the 1980s, apart from a short period in the late 1990s. However, as most family benefits are means tested on the basis of family income, a couple penalty arises when the primary carer assesses whether to increase paid work, as the EMTR on those earnings is considerably higher than the MTR if the primary earner takes on additional work (Apps 2010).

Although high EMTRs are recognised as a major deterrent to workforce participation rates, Australian measures to address the issue to date have been focused on the restructuring of transfer payments to withdraw eligibility for benefits from women when their children reach a certain age. This may have the desired effect of motivating women to increase their workforce participation. However, in the absence of other forms of support, it could merely reduce the income of that family, increasing disadvantage among single-income families, in contravention of ICESCR Article 11, which requires signatory states to ensure 'an adequate standard of living for himself and his family' (ICESCR 1966, Article 11).

Broad-based consumption tax

The second major tax base is a broad-based consumption tax, generally imposed as either a value added tax (VAT) or a GST, and levied in about 160 countries globally. Bias in consumption tax systems depends on the extent of any exemptions in the base on which the consumption tax is levied. Generally, the fewer exemptions in the consumption tax base, the less likelihood there is of explicit bias occurring in the system.

The ICESCR specifically recognises that states should protect the right to an adequate standard of living, including food, clothing, housing (Article 11) and health (Article 12). The CEDAW adds the protection of equal access to education and training (Article 10). Targeted exemptions and concessions in these areas would protect access to these basic rights.

The earning and allocation of household income is still gendered (Baxter et al. 2008; Himmelweit 2002; Stotsky 1996, p. 14), and studies of gendered spending patterns over the past 20 years have consistently shown that household finances should not be regarded as pooled funds (see, for example, Sonnenberg et al. 2011). A gender impact analysis of intra-household finances will examine not only who earns the money, but how financial resources are managed and controlled. Although researchers report that women are taking a more active role in household financial decisions, there is some evidence that this control is nominal rather than in substance, meaning that management does not equate to control (Bennett et al. 2010).

Gender bias in consumption taxes is most likely to result from different consumption patterns between men and women. Applying a human rights approach, a larger proportion of spending by women is on household necessities (Bennett et al. 2010). Gendered spending patterns within households result in a transfer of taxes and benefits from 'purse to wallet'. This has been explicitly recognised in relation to the delivery of benefits based on children and family, which are more effectively delivered directly to the primary carer than through tax concessions to the breadwinner in the family, as they are more likely to be applied for the benefit of those children (ANOP Market Research 1985; Goode et al. 1998), and is also recognised in Article 9 of ICESCR and Article 13 of CEDAW, which explicitly recognise the rights for everyone to receive social security.

Elson (2006, p. 88) goes further in applying the human rights framework, to note that spending patterns vary between higher and lower income families, and that tax policymakers should also take into account inequality between women, to ensure that assistance can be redistributed to women and families facing multiple disadvantages. Low-income households are more likely to be headed by women, and in both developed and emerging economies, single-parent households are over-represented among the lowest income households in the economy. The GST is acknowledged as a regressive tax; therefore, the burden will fall more heavily on those households.

Certain categories of expenditures are more significant in a household budget, and this may be reflected in the structure of the broad-based consumption tax adopted in a particular jurisdiction. The OECD (2014) notes that most OECD countries have reduced rates for a range of goods and services. There are four main categories of reduced rates:

- basic essentials (food, medical, energy and water)
- utilities that may have been publicly provided (public transport, postal services and telecommunications)
- activities that provide social benefits (charitable activities, culture, support or employment services)
- geographic locations that are considered to warrant special treatment.

Certain categories of spending merit special consideration under the relevant treaties, which protect the right to adequate food, clothing and housing for an individual and their family (ICESCR Article 11); education (CEDAW Article 10); and health care (ICESCR Article 12, CEDAW Article 12).

An example of an exemption with an implicit gender bias toward women is the zero rate applied to children's clothing and footwear in Ireland and the United Kingdom, which is not available on other clothing. As children's clothing is likely to be purchased by the primary carer, the lower VAT rate will reduce the cost to that parent, which will flow through to the family budget. In contrast, a broad-based consumption tax without exemptions, as in New Zealand, is likely to have a gender bias against women as women are responsible for more of the spending within the household. The OECD goes on to say:

> The OECD study confirms and provides evidence that most, if not all, of the reduced rates that are introduced to support the poor, such as reduced rates on food and on energy products, do have the desired progressive effect. Nevertheless, it clearly shows that despite this progressive effect, reduced VAT rates are a poor tool for targeting support to poor households. Alternative compensation methods usually proposed are direct compensation through transfer payments or reductions in other personal taxes, notably restructured income tax rate schedules. The report goes on to note that where alternative methods of delivery of benefits are not available, reduced rates may be the most appropriate tool. Thus, each system needs to be considered on a case by case basis (OECD 2014, p. 57).

Given that any increase in consumption taxes has an implicit adverse impact on women, any compensation should also be delivered symmetrically, to recompense women. Income tax cuts would result in a transfer from purse to wallet due to the lower workforce participation rate and lower income earned by women in both developed and emerging economies. However, compensation delivered through the transfer system is subject to politics, and is at risk of being scaled back if fiscal policy deteriorates, as was evident across the OECD following the Global Financial Crisis (GFC) (UN Women 2015, p. 195).

Australia has a single-rate GST with a range of exemptions including food, health, education and financial services. Reform proposals in relation to the GST are based around either increasing the rate and/or the base of the GST. Australia has comparatively strong public funding of both health and education. The Treasury has argued (2015, p. 136) that the GST exemptions on these items are regressive as private health and education services are accessed by higher income Australians. Phillips and Taylor (2015), in modelling for the National Centre for Social and Economic Modelling (NATSEM), support this in respect of education, finding that expanding the GST base to include private education would be neither progressive nor regressive, but in respect of food, health and water an expansion in the base would be regressive. The modelling included a breakdown between male- and female-headed households. The differences were most notable in respect of health and education, with more male-headed households adversely affected by the inclusion of health (79.9 per cent to 74 per cent) and education (32.7 per cent to 24.5 per cent). This could be a consequence of the over-representation of female-headed households in lower-income quintiles, with lower use of private health and education services.

The results of modelling an increase in the rate of the GST to 13 per cent or 15 per cent show that all quintiles would be worse off (Phillips and Taylor 2015, Tables 17 and 18), which would require compensation to be paid to low-income earners following any change in the base or rate of the GST. Phillips and Taylor went on to examine the outcome if changes to the GST were combined with lower PIT rates. Increases of 3 and 5 per cent in the tax rate were shown to be regressive overall, with female-headed households significantly worse off (2015, p. 57). This supports the proposition that compensation is better targeted through the transfer system.

Spending patterns also vary between higher- and lower-income families. As such, tax policymakers should also take into account inequality between women, to ensure that assistance can be redistributed to women and families facing multiple disadvantages.

Property taxes

One of the UN Women empowerment goals is to increase the level of land and other asset holdings by women, as this will provide a more secure economic base to build capabilities, and will provide more secure housing (UN Women 2015). There may be assumptions made about the ownership of property that are reflected in taxation systems; for example if property is assumed to be held by a male partner this may give rise to gender bias in a taxation system (Stotsky 1997). Housing is of particular concern to women who are likely to hold a higher proportion of their wealth in their primary residence (Austen et al. 2014; Cobb-Clark and Hildebrand 2011). Consequently, tax concessions relating to the principal residence are likely to favour women, and proposals to wind back such concessions will have an adverse gender impact.

A gender analysis of property taxes depends on the structure of the particular tax. A progressive wealth tax that is redistributive will increase the revenue available to provide services that benefit women and other economically disadvantaged groups. However, property and land taxes are often levied at a decentralised level and are related to the provision of local services. If these taxes are levied without reference to the taxpayer's ability to pay they are a form of user fee (Barnett and Grown 2004, p. 19), which UN Women identifies as one of the most regressive forms of financing the provision of services (UN Women 2015, p. 207).

The gender impact of property taxes will vary significantly between developed and emerging countries. In emerging countries, the challenge is to address legal barriers to women holding property and cultural norms that favour the transfer of family assets to males. For example, in India prior to 1956, the inheritance system under Hindu law created gender inequity in property ownership, which was reflected in the taxation system. This was addressed by the *Hindu Succession Act 1956*, which allowed a Hindu woman to inherit property. In developed economies, where the legal barriers have been removed, a human rights fiscal policy framework should focus less on the legal ownership of property and more on control over the property in question.

The ability to minimise tax through property transfers between spouses has a regressive impact that reduces the ability of the state to fund other necessary services. Income splitting strategies often depend on a change in ownership of assets as an element in tax planning strategies (Baron 2013;

Edwards 1986; Cullen and Dunne 2008; Hodgson 2008), so that the transfer of property between spouses erodes the tax base. Such transfers may be nominal only, with control of the asset remaining with the original owner of the asset, which may or may not result in improved bargaining power and economic empowerment (this is also discussed in Chapter 9 with regard to high-income women). Management of income and assets may be separated from control of that income or asset within a household, so that the person who manages the day-to-day operational decisions over income and spending may not be the person who controls the household income. This can be extrapolated to the management of financial assets: although legal ownership of the assets may be transferred, economic control of the asset may remain with the original owner, and property taxes are an appropriate way to maintain the progressivity of the taxation system.

Property rights are integral to economic rights, and UN Women recognises that women are disadvantaged where they do not have access to property. However, ownership of property may be separated from effective control, and property transfers may be a means of eroding fiscal adequacy through tax planning or income splitting strategies. These tax planning practices increase inequality between women as it reduces the fiscal resources the government needs to deliver social services. The application of transactional taxes on transfers and progressive wealth-based taxes on such assets is a tool that can be applied to address such tax planning practices.

Retirement income schemes (superannuation)

Retirement income insurance schemes, such as the superannuation system in Australia, which require contributions from wage income towards retirement saving, are classified by UN Women as among the more regressive social levies (UN Women 2015, p. 207). Although retirement income schemes are not taxes, to the extent that they are compulsory levies the principles of gender impact analysis should be applied, as explained in Sharp et al. (2015). These schemes are specifically recognised in human rights treaties as follows:

ICESCR Article 9: … recognise the right of everyone to social security, including social insurance … (ICESCR 1966, Article 9)

CEDAW Article 11: … Ensure that women have access to the same benefits, compensatory schemes and allowances as men, especially in relation to retirement and incapacity to work … (CEDAW 1979, Article 11)

In particular, women should have access to an income stream in retirement that is independent of other family members. If pensions are paid to the male head of the household, women are economically dependant on that person as they do not have control over their own finances. In systems where pensions are paid separately to each eligible member of the household, to the extent that pension levels are determined on family or household income, this principle may still be contravened as members of the household may not share income and assets. Retirement savings systems should be designed to encourage independent income streams following retirement.

The World Bank framework to provide a secure retirement income consists of a multi-tiered approach to funding retirement income (Holzmann et al. 2008). The zero-level tier consists of a universal state-funded pension entitlement; mandated contributory retirement income schemes make up the first and second tiers; and the third tier is made up of voluntary self-provision. The final, fourth tier consists of non-financial services including health provision and housing.

The basic or social pension is often the main source of income in retirement for women who have not participated in the paid economy (UN Women 2015, p. 155), and as such it is essential that social pension schemes be maintained at a level that ensures that the recipient can meet the basic living requirements. However, due to the fiscal cost of providing such pensions, governments will usually restrict eligibility through means tests or other limitations. Accordingly, social pensions are frequently provided as safety net measures rather than a universal entitlement. An adequate level of retirement income will generally require a combination of a universal base level pension and contributory pensions (UN Women 2015, p. 156). Contributory pensions or mandatory savings schemes provide further insurance against poverty in old age.

From a gender perspective, however, contributory schemes perpetuate the gender gaps that emerge earlier in life. Contributory schemes operate as a form of insurance by requiring that contributions are made on the basis of income earned while the contributor is working: they effectively spread the income earned while working across the contributor's life span. Women are at a disadvantage in systems of this type, as they are generally most effective where a contributor has a stable source of income over a lengthy working life. They do not generally address the typical female pattern of reduced participation in the paid labour market during child-rearing years

(Hodgson and Marriott 2013). This is exacerbated by the earlier retirement age provided under many schemes and the longer life expectancy. In this context, UN Women recommend that access to contributory schemes be equalised, and that female paid workforce patterns be considered in the design of such schemes. They also recommend that carer credits be made available to women who are not participating in the paid labour market due to care responsibilities (UN Women 2015, p. 155).

The third tier of the World Bank model includes self-provision schemes that encourage private savings to fund retirement. Such schemes are even more regressive than first- and second-tier schemes, as they are dependant on the participant having sufficient funds to save for retirement. For reasons discussed above, women are less likely than men to have funds available to invest in third-tier schemes. Phipps and Woolley (2008) examined the allocation of retirement savings within Canadian households. They found that even where women take control of the family finances, retirement savings are more likely to be held by men. This has important consequences for bargaining within older households: given the longer lives and earlier retirement ages of women, their retirement savings must be consumed at a slower rate than by their partner. This can lead to conflict over resource allocation where one party controls retirement savings.

The fourth tier of the retirement income system is important in developing a human rights approach to fiscal policy. Under the relevant treaties, participants are required to protect the right to adequate housing (ICESCR Article 11) and health care (ICESCR Article 12; CEDAW Article 12). Social housing and public health care should be available to ensure that the human rights of all persons, including pensioners, are protected. Fiscal policy must ensure the collection of adequate levels of revenue to fund these systems.

As discussed by Austen and Sharp in Chapter 10, in Australia the difference in workforce participation between men and women has generated a gender gap in superannuation contributions (Senate Economics Reference Committee 2016). This is exacerbated by tax on retirement savings, which is particularly regressive as tax concessions are available to both second- and third-tier retirement savings. Not only do higher-income earners contribute more through the mandated level of superannuation guarantee contributions based on payroll, they also have the ability to make higher levels of voluntary contributions.

The gender impact of the tax concession is twofold: women benefit less from the concessions that are available and the tax concessions on retirement savings redirect public money to retirement savings holders, generally men, away from pension recipients, who are more likely women. This imbalance can only be addressed by scaling back the extent of the tax concessions available on retirement savings, and redirecting the savings to social benefit programs.

The ICESCR specifically recognises that states should protect the right to an adequate standard of living, including food, clothing, housing (Article 11) and health (Article 12). The CEDAW adds the protection of equal access to education and training (Article 10). These treaties also require states recognise the right of everyone to social security, including social insurance (ICESCR Article 9), and that they have access to the same retirement and incapacity benefits as men (CEDAW Article 11). Consequently, policy considerations around retirement savings taxes need to take into account implicit bias. Retirement income schemes need to be redesigned to account for the different work and care responsibilities that women face, which impact on the ability of women to contribute consistently to contributory schemes.

Conclusion

Following the GFC, developed economies implemented austerity regimes in the tax-transfer systems that have had a significant impact on the economic security of women. Aggressive tax reform proposals, coupled with austerity measures, mean that women are further from substantive economic and social gender equality than they were 30 years ago (Nelson 2015). This result is arguably due to the neoliberal approach to macro-economic policy adopted by nations where the focus is on taxing for growth rather than a broader objective of taxing for social policy, which includes growth as part of the consideration. Such an approach is detrimental to gender equality. As Professor Kathleen Lahey explains, 'the negative effects of [just] taxing for growth on the status of women, poverty levels, and human development has been pervasive and profound' (Lahey 2015, p. 9; and see Chapter 2, this volume).

In the dominant fiscal policy approach, there is a traditional emphasis on the criteria of equity, efficiency and ease of administration as the primary relevant design criteria for tax reform (Elson 2006, p. 72). As we discuss in this chapter, the concepts of equity and efficiency have been critically assessed in the tax and feminist literature, in particular highlighting their limitations in analysing and addressing explicit and implicit gender inequality (see, for example, Hui 2013). Gender-responsive budgeting, including both gender impact analysis and political engagement components, has made significant inroads in some countries. However, much of this work focuses on an analysis of existing tax regimes, specific taxes and specific policies, rather than developing a holistic approach to tax system design that provides a macro-economic framework that takes into account gender inequality.

This chapter has argued that we should go beyond such analysis in proposing the application of a human rights framework to fiscal policy. It is recognised that human rights principles and the ensuing legislative enactment of the required standards only provide the basis for equality. As UN Women explains:

> Power inequalities, structural constraints and discriminatory social norms and practices also need to be addressed … Formal equality may result in unequal outcomes, and policies may need to treat women differently to men treatment to achieve equality … Despite the implementation of these human rights treaties, women continue to experience economic inequality. States, therefore, must adopt a proactive role as arbiters of social and economic rights (UN Women 2015, pp. 24–25).

While human rights principles and treaties may provide a basis for equality, the formal recognition and application of a human rights framework may go far in ensuring gender inequality is considered throughout the fiscal process, and not just as an ex–post analysis tool. This chapter explicitly applied the human rights treaties and the UN Women human rights framework for fiscal policy strategies to four areas of tax policy in Australia: PIT, GST, property taxes and taxes on retirement savings. In each case study, we demonstrated that a human rights–based framework would result in different considerations and different outcomes for gender equality.

References

Adam, Stuart and Mike Brewer. 2012. *Couple Penalties and Premiums in the UK Tax and Benefit System*. UK: Institute for Fiscal Studies.

ANOP Market Research. 1985. *What Women Think: A Survey of Mothers' Attitudes to Family Allowance, The Dependent Spouse Rebate and Family Finances.* Prepared for the Office of the Status of Women Department of the Prime Minister and Cabinet. Canberra: Australian Government Publishing Service.

Apps, Patricia. 2010. 'Why the Henry Review Fails on Family Tax Reform'. In Chris Evans, Richard Krever and Peter Mellor (eds), *Australia's Future Tax System: The Prospects After Henry. Essays in Honour of John W Freebairn*, pp. 103–127. Sydney: Thomson Reuters.

ATO (Australian Tax Office). 2012. *Tax Statistics 2012–13.* Table 9. Available at: data.gov.au/dataset/taxation-statistics-2012-13

Austen, Siobhan, Therese Jefferson and Rachel Ong. 2014. 'The Gender Gap in Financial Security: What We Know and Don't Know about Australian Households'. *Feminist Economics* 20(3): 25–52. doi. org/10.1080/13545701.2014.911413

Baird, Marian, Michele Ford and Elizabeth Hill (eds). 2017. *Women, Work and Care in the Asia Pacific.* ASAA Women in Asia series. Routledge.

Barnett, Kathleen and Caren Grown. 2004. *Gender Impacts of Government Revenue Collection: The Case of Taxation.* London: Commonwealth Secretariat. doi.org/10.14217/9781848590205-en

Baron, Gabriel. 2013. 'Selected Considerations in the Use of Professional Corporations'. *Canadian Tax Journal* 61(4): 1167–1192.

Baxter, Janeen, Belinda Hewitt and Michele Haynes. 2008. 'Life Course Transitions and Housework: Marriage, Parenthood, and Time on Housework'. *Journal of Marriage and Family* 70(2): 259–272. doi. org/10.1111/j.1741-3737.2008.00479.x

Bennett Fran, Jerome De Hanau and Sirin Sung. 2010. 'Within-household inequalities across classes? Management and control of money'. In Jacqueline Scott, Rosemary Crompton and Clare Lyonette (eds), *Gender Inequalities in the 21st Century*, pp. 215–241. Edward Elgar.

Cobb-Clark, Deborah A. and Vincent A. Hildebrand. 2011. 'Portfolio Allocation in the Face of a Means-Tested Public Pension'. *Review of Income & Wealth* 57(3): 536–560. doi.org/10.1111/j.1475-4991.2011.00437.x

Craig, Lyn. 2007. 'How Employed Mothers in Australia Find Time for Both Market Work and Childcare'. *Journal of Family and Economic Issues* 28(1): 69–87. doi.org/10.1007/s10834-006-9047-2

Cullen, Michael and Peter Dunne. 2008. *Income Splitting for Families with Children: A government tax policy discussion document.* Wellington: Policy Advice Division of Inland Revenue.

Dolamore, Robert. 2015. *The tools of macroeconomic policy—a short primer.* Parliament of Australia. Available at: www.aph.gov.au/About_Parliament/Parliamentary_Departments/Parliamentary_Library/pubs/BriefingBook44p/MacroeconomicPolicy

Donald, Kate. 2015. *Women's Rights and Revenues: Why We Can't Achieve Gender Equality Without Fiscal Justice.* 26 March, Centre for Economic and Social Rights, New York.

Edwards, Meredith. 1986. 'The Australian Tax Unit: An Evaluation'. In John G. Head (ed.), *Changing the Tax Mix: Papers Presented at a Conference Organised by the Centre of Policy Studies, Monash University.* Australian Tax Research Foundation Conference Series No. 6. Sydney: Australian Tax Research Foundation.

Elson, Diane. 2006. *Budgeting for Women's Rights: Monitoring Government Budgets for Compliance with CEDAW.* New York: United Nations Development Fund for Women. Available at: internationalbudget.org/wp-content/uploads/Budgeting-for-Women%E2%80%99s-Rights-Monitoring-Government-Budgets-for-Compliance-with-CEDAW.pdf

Elson, Diane. 2015. 'Gender Equality Requires More Tax Revenue'. *Tax Justice Focus* 10(1): 8.

Goode, Jackie, Claire Callender and Ruth Lister. 1998. *Purse or Wallet? Gender Inequalities and Income Distribution within Families on Benefits, Findings.* Joseph Rowntree Foundation.

Grown, Caren and Imraan Valodia. 2010. *Taxation and Gender Equity: A Comparative Analysis of Direct and Indirect Taxes.* Taylor and Francis.

Harding, Michelle. 2013. 'Taxation of Dividend, Interest and Capital Gain Income'. *OECD Taxation Working Papers.* OECD. dx.doi.org/10.1787/222

Himmelweit, Susan. 2002. 'Making Visible the Hidden Economy: The Case for Gender Impact Analysis of Economic Policy'. *Feminist Economics* 8(1): 49–70. doi.org/10.1080/13545700110104864

Hodgson, Helen. 2008. 'Taxing the Family—The Tax Unit: Should NZ Adopt a Family Based Income Tax?' *New Zealand Journal of Taxation Law and Policy* 14(3): 398–412.

Hodgson, Helen and Lisa Marriott. 2013. 'Retirement Savings and Gender: An Australasian Comparison'. *Australian Tax Forum* 28(4): 725–752.

Holzmann, Robert; Richard Paul Hinz and Mark Dorfman. 2008. *Pension Systems and Reform Conceptual Framework*. SP Discussion Paper No. 0824. World Bank. Available at: documents.worldbank.org/curated/en/716871468156888545/pdf/461750NWP0Box334081B01PUBLIC10SP00824.pdf

HRC (Human Rights Commission of Australia). 2015. *Woman of the World: What is CEDAW*. Available at: www.humanrights.gov.au/publications/woman-world-what-cedaw

Hui, Neha. 2013. *Gender Implications of Budget Policies*. New Delhi: Centre for Budget and Governance Accountability.

IMF (International Monetary Fund). 2014. *Fiscal Policy and Income Equality*. IMF Policy Paper. Washington DC: International Monetary Fund. Available at: www.imf.org/external/np/pp/eng/2014/012314.pdf

Lahey, Kathleen. 2015. 'Women and Taxation—From Taxing for Growth and Tax Competition to Taxing for Sex Equality'. *Tax Justice Focus* 10(1): 8–10.

Nelson, Liz. 2015. 'Gender and Tax Justice'. *Tax Justice Focus* 10(1): 4–5.

OECD (Organisation for Economic Co-operation and Development). 2007. *Encouraging Savings through Tax-Preferred Accounts*. OECD Tax Policy Studies No. 15. Paris: OECD Publishing.

OECD. 2014. *Consumption Tax Trends 2014: VAT/GST and excise rates, trends and policy issues*. Paris: OECD Publishing.

Phillips, Ben and Matt Taylor. 2015. *The Distributional Impact of the GST.* Canberra: National Centre for Social and Economic Modelling. Available at: www.natsem.canberra.edu.au/storage/ACOSS%20GST %20Report.pdf

Phipps, Shelley and Frances Woolley. 2008. 'Control over money and the savings decisions of Canadian households'. *The Journal of Socio-Economics: Special Issue on the Household Economy* 37(2): 592–611. doi.org/10.1016/j.socec.2006.12.042

Senate Economics Reference Committee. 2016. *Report of the Inquiry into Economic Security for Women in Retirement: A Husband is Not a Retirement Plan.* Australian Senate. Available at: www.aph.gov.au/ Parliamentary_Business/Committees/Senate/Economics/Economic_ security_for_women_in_retirement/Report

Sharp, Rhonda, Siobhan Austen and Helen Hodgson. 2015. 'Gender Impact Analysis and the Taxation of Retirement Income Savings in Australia'. *Australian Tax Forum* 60: 763–781.

Sonnenberg, Stefanie J, Carole B Burgoyne and David A Routh. 2011. 'Income Disparity and Norms Relating to Intra-Household Financial Organisation in the UK: A Dimensional Analysis'. *The Journal of Socio-economics* 40(5): 573–582. doi.org/10.1016/j.socec.2011.04.014

Stewart, Miranda. 2011. 'Gender Equity in Australia's Tax System: A Capabilities Approach'. In Kim Brooks, Asa Gunnarson, Lisa Philipps and Maria Wersig (eds), *Challenging Gender Inequality in Tax Policy Making*, pp. 53–74. Hart Publishing.

Stotsky, Janet. 1996. *Gender Bias in Tax Systems.* IMF Working Paper No. 96/99. International Monetary Fund. Available at: www.imf. org/en/Publications/WP/Issues/2016/12/30/Gender-Bias-in-Tax-Systems-2074

Stotsky, Janet. 1997. 'How Tax Systems treat Men and Women Differently'. *Finance and Development* March, pp. 30–33. Available at: www.imf. org/external/pubs/ft/fandd/1997/03/pdf/stotsky.pdf

Treasury. 2015. *Re: Think Tax Discussion Paper.* Australian Government. Available at: bettertax.gov.au/files/2015/03/TWP_combined-online.pdf

UN (United Nations) Women. 2015. *Progress of the World's Women 2015–16*. Available at: progress.unwomen.org/en/2015/

World Bank. 2015. *World Development Indicators*. Available at: data. worldbank.org/data-catalog/world-development-indicators

Young, Claire. 1999. 'Taxing Times for Women: Feminism Confronts Tax Policy'. *Sydney Law Review* 21(3): 487–499.

Treaties and other materials

Convention on the Elimination of All Forms of Discrimination Against Women (CEDAW). 1979. Available at: www.humanrights.gov.au/ convention-elimination-all-forms-discrimination-against-women-human-rights-your-fingertips-human

International Covenant on Economic, Social and Cultural Rights (ICESCR). 1966. Available at: www.humanrights.gov.au/international-covenant-economic-social-and-cultural-rights-human-rights-your-fingertips-human-rights

Part II: Work and care

5

Taxes, transfers, family policies and paid work over the female life cycle[1]

Guyonne Kalb

With female labour force participation having increased substantially over the past few decades, and continuing concerns about population ageing in the future, policies with positive labour supply incentives, aimed at increasing participation further for women, remain high on the agenda. Thus, an important question among policymakers should be: how well are the policies that are currently in place in Australia performing with regard to encouraging labour force participation? Rather than investigate the different policies in place in isolation, this chapter sets out to examine all social policies and tax and transfer policies together. An important question is whether policy goals and policy design are consistent, and whether these are consistent across the range of policies in the relevant policy area. To give an example, are family payment policies, child care subsidy policies and income tax policies working together to achieve the same aims, or are they encouraging families in different directions?

1   This chapter builds on research undertaken jointly with several colleagues. I am grateful for the insights I have gained over the years working with Barbara Broadway, Terence Cheng, Denise Doiron, Nicolas Hérault, Brendan Houng, Sung-Hee Jeon, Daniel Kuehnle, Bill Martin, Duncan McVicar, Wang Sheng Lee, Tony Scott, Domenico Tabasso, Thor Thoresen and Rezida Zakirova. I would also like to thank Claire Thibout for sharing her bibliography on the topic of 'doing gender' and time allocation within the household. Any errors and views expressed in this chapter are the sole responsibility of the author.

A person's work-related skills and knowledge (what economists call 'human capital') declines when s/he is not participating in paid work. Further, research on how people move into and out of participation in paid work (or 'labour market dynamics') has found that if a person is not participating in one year, s/he is also less likely to participate in the following year. Thus, leaving the labour force in one year, such as after childbirth, can have long-term implications for labour force participation. A temporary absence from the labour market could also result in lower wages upon return or in difficulties obtaining secure employment at the pre-leave level when wishing to return. This chapter takes a life course perspective, acknowledging the role of uncertainty when making important decisions.

To consider these issues, the remainder of this chapter is laid out as follows. In the next part, I discuss the range of government policies that influence female labour supply. The following part describes the dynamic process of labour force participation and how the impact of government policies can be amplified through the dynamics of labour supply. I then turn to the uncertainty associated with optimal decision-making and its importance in long-term outcomes and discuss the lifetime impacts of government policies (or lack of appropriate policy). Finally, I present some conclusions.

Government policies

There is a wide range of government policies that intentionally or unintentionally have an effect on female labour supply. These include the general tax-transfer system, the general social security system, family payments, child care subsidies, child care provision and unpaid and paid parental leave. Each is briefly discussed in the subsections below. All payment rates and income thresholds mentioned in this part relate to the March–June 2016 quarter.

Income tax and transfers

Australia's highly targeted social security, or transfer, system is based on household income (a couple, or joint, unit). The impact of this couple unit, with its reliance on a male breadwinner, is fundamental and it is discussed in a number of other chapters in this volume. The couple unit in the transfer system is in contrast to the income tax system, which is based on the individual unit. This is unlike tax systems in many other countries that allow for transfers of a tax-free range between married and de facto partners. The individual-based income tax system ensures each person pays no or little tax on the first dollars that are earned. However, since family benefits, allowances and pensions are withdrawn at varying rates with increasing household income, these may produce high effective marginal tax rates (EMTRs) especially for the, mostly female, secondary earners in households.

These medium to high effective tax rates occur from the first dollar earned by secondary earners. Besides a small 'free area' of $102 per fortnight, additional income at first reduces any income support at a rate of 50 per cent for allowances and then at a rate of 60 per cent (for fortnightly income over $252). Single principal carers are treated more generously; their allowance is withdrawn at just 40 per cent over a fortnightly income of $102. For pensions, which are mostly paid to individuals who are not expected to look for work, there is a higher withdrawal-free threshold of $162 per fortnight (or $288 for a couple family) after which the pension is reduced at a rate of 50 per cent. Single parents with a youngest child under eight receiving a parenting payment (at the pension rate) are again treated somewhat more generously with an additional free area of $24.60 per fortnight per child and a withdrawal rate of 40 per cent.

Although some effort has been made to reduce disincentives for low-income single-parent families and partnered principal carers, the above withdrawal rates, combined with child care costs, have a disincentive effect on female participation rates, particularly for low-income families with one or both adults depending on income support.

Family payments

Another type of payment that is based on household income is the family payment, thus potentially creating disincentives for the secondary earner. Although family payments in Australia are not universal, some payment continues to be made to families on high incomes, with the payment being withdrawn in two stages with increasing household income. The maximum rate of family tax benefit part A (FTB-A) varies between $5,412.95 and $6,825.50 per year per child (depending on the child's age) and is paid to families on annual household incomes under $51,027. Families on incomes over that amount receive 20 cents less in FTB-A per additional dollar earned, down to a base rate of $2,230.15 per child per year. This base rate can be received in full until annual household income surpasses $94,316, after which the base rate is reduced by 30 cents for every dollar over the threshold until no FTB-A is payable anymore. It is evident from these numbers that families on incomes well over $100,000 will still receive some family payment, and secondary earners in these families will face an EMTR of over 30 per cent. In low-income families the secondary earner is likely to face an EMTR of over 20 per cent from the first dollars they earn. The challenge for government is to balance government expenditure, EMTRs and the targeting of available resources to those most in need, with better outcomes on one aspect requiring a less favourable outcome on at least one of the other two aspects.

In addition to FTB-A there is family tax benefit part B (FTB-B), which is targeted at single parents and at families with children under 18 years of age with one partner earning under $100,000 per year. A payment of $3,139 per family if all children are at least of school age and $4,339.85 per family if there is at least one child under five years of age is provided to single parents having less than $100,000 in income per year and to families where the higher income earner has less than $100,000 per year, and the lower income earner has less than $5,402 per year. No FTB-B is paid to families with one person earning over $100,000 per year, while the benefit is reduced by 20 cents for every dollar earned over $5,402 by the secondary earner. As a consequence, a family with two earners on $30,000 per year each will not receive any FTB-B, while a one-earner family on $90,000 per year will. This is counterintuitive since the family with one stay-at-home parent has the benefit of more home production opportunities than the family with two earners who are likely to have little time for this (see, for example, Apps 2015, pp. 11–12; and Chapter 3, this volume).[2] That is, the FTB-B policy does not reflect that besides household income, the opportunity for home production (through the availability of additional non-market time) also determines a household's wellbeing.

---

2   Note that this is an improvement on the situation before July 2008 when there was only an income test on the secondary earner, and the payment was available to one-earner millionaires but not to low-paid dual-earner families. The income test on the primary income earner was first set at $150,000 and from July 2015 this was reduced to $100,000.

FTB-A and FTB-B combined are a major impediment to participate in the labour force for low- to medium-income mothers in medium-income households, potentially affecting a very large group of women. The current design clearly does not encourage female labour force participation; rather it is an impediment for a sizeable proportion of women.

What are the alternatives? In principle, family payments could be provided to all families with children as is done in some European countries. Although universal payments would provide the lowest disincentives to participate, this would be expensive if the payment rate is not to be lowered. Alternatively, family payments could be targeted more tightly, but this would shift the participation disincentive to low-income women in low- to medium-income households. The second-best (and more affordable) option in terms of encouraging labour force participation requires low withdrawal rates (i.e. loosely targeted payments). This ensures that the disincentive of high EMTRs does not occur for secondary earners in low-income households who are most likely to reduce labour supply, but it would still occur for secondary earners in medium- to high-income households.

Child care subsidies

When two parents are out at work at the same time, alternative care arrangements are required for preschool-aged children. If informal care (by grandparents, for example) is not available, then formal child care can make the cost of work prohibitively high. This is particularly the case for low-wage women, who may compare their hourly additional income with the hourly cost of child care, and find that they are working for limited or no additional household income. The provision of a child care subsidy can take away or at least reduce these costs to the family.

The government, until the reform enacted in 2017, provided two types of child care subsidies targeted at different groups. The first one was the child care benefit (CCB), which focuses on low-income families and is income tested on household income, but small amounts are also paid to high-income families. It provided partial (capped) reimbursement for expenditure on approved child care to facilitate study and/or work. Families are subsidised for up to 50 hours of care per week (or 24 hours of care per week if the primary carer is not in work and does not study). The subsidies paid depend on the household income and the actual fee paid (up to a maximum). The second subsidy was the child care rebate, which is available to everyone independent of income. It provides 50 per cent of out-of-pocket costs (i.e. net of the CCB) of approved care up to a maximum total amount, and only imposes a very light work or study requirement (i.e. any non-zero amount).

Although subsidies have helped to some extent, the cost of child care has remained a hurdle in Australia over the past two decades, particularly for single parents and for low-wage primary carers, as shown by the elasticity of hours worked with regard to cost or price of child care. An elasticity is defined as the percentage change in hours worked per 1 per cent change in cost or price. Table 5.1 presents elasticities as estimated by Doiron and Kalb (2005), Kalb and Lee (2008), Breunig et al. (2012), and Breunig et al. (2014). Compared to Kalb and Lee (2008), Breunig et al. (2012) find larger hours elasticities with regard to child care prices for partnered women of −0.64 on average, indicating a larger impact of the cost of child care on labour supply. Breunig et al. (2012, 2014) do not estimate elasticities for single parents, but Doiron and Kalb (2005) and Kalb and Lee (2008) find that single mothers, especially those with a preschool child and on a low wage, respond more strongly to child care price increases than partnered mothers.

Effective from 2018, these subsidies will be combined into a single child care subsidy, which will substantially increase the amount of subsidies available to families, and in particular to low-income families.[3] However, the work or study requirements are somewhat more stringent than for the current child care benefit and rebate. Once the new subsidy is in place, it will be interesting to see what the impact is on child care use and parental labour supply (particularly of the mother).

When considering the impact of cost on child care use and labour supply, a complicating factor is the potential impact of child care on child development. This will almost certainly play a role in the choices that parents make, but it is difficult to quantify or establish the importance of this. It is also likely that the characteristics of child care, such as the quality of its facilities or the qualifications of its carers (see, for example, Gregg et al. 2005), influence the impact of child care on child development and influence whether it is a positive or a negative impact. At the same time, quality is likely to influence the price of child care, and the quality of available child care is likely to affect usage by parents.

---

3   For further details see Department of Education and Training, 'Jobs for Families Child Care Package', www.education.gov.au/ChildCarePackage.

Table 5.1: Elasticity of hours worked estimates for households with children in 2002[a]

	with respect to net costs	with respect to gross price
Kalb and Lee (2008)/Doiron and Kalb (2005)		
Partnered women		
Total	−0.028/−0.034	−0.000/−0.021
Low wage (partner low wage)[b]	−0.026/−0.045	−0.013/−0.027
Low wage (partner high wage)	−0.036	−0.002
Preschool child	−0.078/−0.066	−0.019/−0.048
Preschool child and low wage	−0.075/−0.079	−0.030/−0.053
Single mothers		
Total	−0.137/−0.150	−0.164/−0.053
Low wages	−0.286/−0.263	−0.319/−0.062
Preschool child	−0.510/−0.280	−0.579/−0.175
Preschool child and low wages	−0.637/−0.054	−0.931/−0.216
Breunig et al. (2012)		
Average partnered woman with child under 13		−0.65
Breunig et al. (2014)		
Average partnered woman with preschool child	−0.099	−0.135

a) Elasticities are computed for each individual and then averaged across the individuals in the relevant group in Doiron and Kalb (2005) and Kalb and Lee (2008), while in Breunig et al. (2012, 2014) elasticities are computed for a woman with average characteristics.

b) A low wage is defined as a wage below the median wage. For partnered women, the Doiron and Kalb (2005) results considers the woman's wage and her partner's wage at the same time. That is, both need to be below the median value within their group.

Sources: Kalb and Lee (2008), Doiron and Kalb (2005), Breunig et al. (2012), and Breunig et al. (2014).

It is clear that in designing child care policies, the government needs to consider the impact on child outcomes as well as on female labour supply. Quality and time of parental child care also matters for mothers, as discussed by Dinh and Racionero (Chapter 9, this volume). Given that the quality of the home environment relative to the quality of child care affects whether usage of child care affects a child's development positively or negatively, the redistributional impact of child care policies on child care use is important. Gregg et al. (2005) show that there is some evidence that the negative impact of full-time child care in the first 18 months of a child's life is larger for children of higher educated women and smaller for children of single mothers. For part-time child care, no negative effects are found. In Australia, there is weak evidence (with the weakness possibly due to small sample numbers) that children from more disadvantaged backgrounds (e.g. from low-income families or from an Indigenous background) may benefit more from day care centre care than other children (Kalb et al. 2013). However, this study also shows that children from disadvantaged backgrounds are much less likely to attend child care centres. It therefore seems particularly important not to discourage child care use by these groups. An earlier study by Houng et al. (2011) found that the effects of day care were larger for disadvantaged groups such as single-parent families and to a lesser extent for families with primary carers who had not completed high school. The value of formal care relative to informal care is higher for these more disadvantaged families than for the average family, which makes access to formal care all the more important.

Besides the quality of child care, the intensity of child care use is also likely to play a role in the impact it has on child outcomes, as already indicated in the discussion of the research by Gregg et al. (2005) in the previous paragraph. For example, in research based on the Longitudinal Study of Australian Children (LSAC), Kalb et al. (2013) have found that an amount of between 15 and 29 hours per week has the largest beneficial impact on later learning outcomes (age four–five years). In an earlier study by Houng et al. (2011), also using LSAC data but focusing on children's care and outcomes at a slightly younger age (care at age zero–one and outcomes at age two–three), it was found that smaller amounts of day care were optimal than were found for the older group studied in the more recent report. However, note that compared to not using any formal care, any amount of formal care use is an improvement. The trade-offs that parents make between their 'market time' and home time is analysed by Dinh and Racionero in Chapter 7.

Child care provision

The previous subsection focused on the cost of child care, but an equally important consideration is whether there are any (local) shortages of child care places impeding parental labour force participation. These could be shortages in a general sense (i.e. any child care) or shortages in terms of child care that is of sufficiently high quality to be acceptable to parents, given that child care is more than just a means for parents to participate in the labour force. As mentioned in the previous subsection, the impact that child care has on a child's development and wellbeing is obviously going to be important to parents.

Despite the obvious importance of the availability of child care to parents' capacity to participate in the labour market or study, there does not seem to be central (public) information collected on the availability of child care places. Anecdotal evidence suggests that, for example, inner-city areas may have long waiting lists to obtain access to child care, but official systematic data on this across the nation is lacking. The level of unmet demand for child care could indicate a potential for growth of labour supply by parents, especially in a country like Australia with its high proportion of first-generation migrants. When insufficient child care services are available to enable labour force participation by both parents, families without the support of nearby family networks may struggle in particular.

As shown by Gustafsson and Stafford (1992), shortages may also mask the responsiveness of women to child care prices and EMTRs. If child care is rationed, then this restricts the parents' choices, taking out the combined employment and child care use option, or at least reducing the availability of this option. This is likely to lead to fewer women in the labour force than would occur if child care was readily available. Accounting for rationing of child care substantially increased the price elasticity of child care use and of labour supply. In Australia, we have not been able to incorporate child care availability in our modelling, so we may well be underestimating parents' responses to child care price changes.

Unpaid and paid parental leave

Parental leave is another key element in policy settings to support women's equality in paid workforce participation. Parental leave may be either paid or unpaid. All Australian employed mothers, who have been with their employer for at least 12 months prior to birth, have an entitlement to 12 months unpaid parental leave, after which they should be allowed to return to the position they held before the leave period, or if that position no longer exists, to a position comparable in status and pay. Effective 1 January 2011, the Australian Government introduced a universal paid parental leave (PPL) policy. At that time, 56.8 per cent of employed women aged 20 to 45 in Australia had some access to paid parental leave provided by their employer. However, this was not evenly distributed across all women.

Prior to 2011, there was no publicly funded paid parental leave scheme in Australia, although some employers offered their own employer-funded paid leave schemes. The PPL scheme introduced in 2011 aims to extend mothers' time away from paid work following a birth—among other things for maternal and child health reasons—while also promoting their attachment to their employer and increasing lifetime attachment to the labour force. PPL pays the primary carer of a newborn child—usually the mother—up to 18 weeks within the first 12 months following the birth at a flat rate corresponding to the Australian National Minimum Wage, which was equal to $656.90 per week at the time of writing. The payments can be received on top of any employer-funded parental leave payments and are taxable. Eligibility for this new scheme is almost universal: mothers are required to have worked for at least 330 hours and for at least 10 months over the 13-month period prior to the expected date of birth, with an individual adjusted taxable income of $150,000 or less in the financial year before the birth, and to be a permanent resident or citizen in Australia. Once a mother returns to work she becomes ineligible, although any remaining payment may be transferred to an eligible partner if they become the primary carer.

Although publicly funded, PPL is provided through employers in the majority of cases, and there are further associated measures designed to encourage mothers and employers to keep in touch during the leave period and to support activities that will facilitate the mother's return to work. For more detail on the PPL scheme see Martin et al. (2015). PPL was well received and is well used. By 30 June 2014, almost half a million families had received PPL payments, with the vast majority receiving the payment for the full 18 weeks (Martin et al. 2015). Women are well aware of this new payment; only a small proportion in a post-PPL survey had never heard of PPL (0.9 per cent) (see Martin et al. 2014).

The introduction of PPL follows several decades of rapid growth in women's participation in paid employment and education in Australia. The overall female labour force participation rate has increased from 34 per cent in 1961 to 59 per cent in 2011 (ABS 2011), primarily through increased employment of mothers. Between 1991 and 2011, the proportion of mothers in families with children under 18 who were employed rose from 55 per cent to 65 per cent (Baxter 2013).

Despite this growth, Australia still has among the lowest levels of labour force participation for mothers in the Organisation for Economic Co-operation and Development (OECD) countries. Figure 5.1 shows that in 2014, Australia is ranked below the average of the 31 OECD countries included in the graph, and is ranked about one third from the back. Compared to Sweden, which has the highest employment rate,

Australia's employment rate is just over 20 percentage points lower. In general, the countries with higher maternal participation rates tend to be those where parents have access to well-developed paid parental leave schemes complemented with extensive, affordable child care (see, for example, Jaumotte 2003). Kalb and Thoresen (2010) specifically compare Australia before paid parental leave was introduced with Norway, finding a 20 percentage-point gap in labour force participation of women with children aged one to four, but no gap for women without children. This is reflected in the labour force participation rate of women of prime childbearing age (25 to 34 years) in Australia, which compares favourably to other countries. In 2013, the OECD reports it was 74.4 per cent, similar to that of the US (73.5 per cent) and the UK (77.6 per cent), but well behind Canada (81.5 per cent), France (81.7 per cent), Germany (79.7 per cent), the Netherlands (85.2 per cent), Spain (86.0 per cent) and Sweden (84.0 per cent) (see stats.oecd.org).

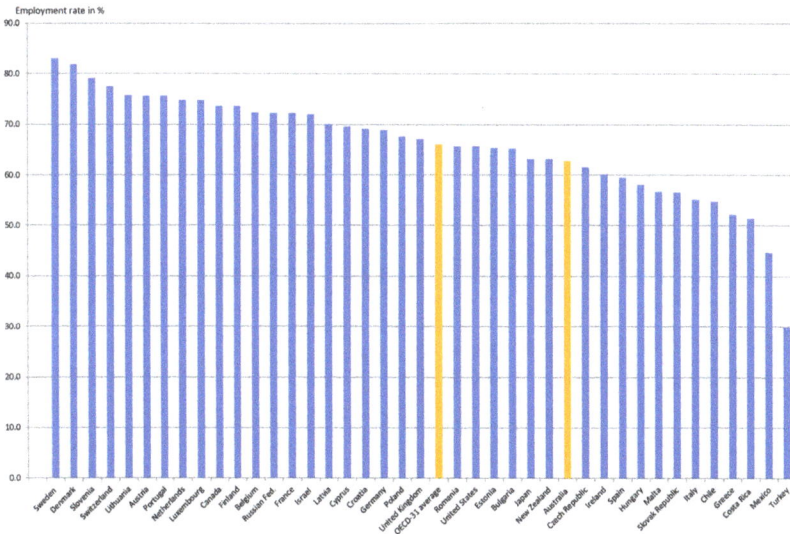

Figure 5.1: Maternal employment rates, 2014 or latest available year[a] (Employment rates for women (15–64-year-olds[b]) with at least one child aged 0–14[c])

a) Data for Denmark and Finland is from 2012, and for Chile, Germany and Turkey from 2013.

b) For Japan, all ages, and for Sweden women aged 15–74 are included.

c) For Canada children aged 0–15, for Sweden children aged 0–18, and for the US children aged 0–17 are included.

Source: OECD family database (see www.oecd.org/els/family/database.htm).

The distributional impact of the government-provided PPL is important. Wave 9 of the Household, Income and Labour Dynamics in Australia (HILDA) Survey data shows that at the time of introduction of PPL, 56.8 per cent of employed women aged 20 to 45 in Australia had access to paid parental leave provided by their employer. However, this was not distributed evenly across all women, but concentrated among those with fixed-term or permanent work (around 72 per cent compared to 19.1 per cent in casual work), those on above-median wages (71.3 per cent compared to 37.8 per cent for those on below-median wages), those in full-time employment (65.7 per cent compared to 41.2 per cent in part-time work), those with higher education (77.5 per cent for those with a university degree compared to 39.8 per cent for those with Year 11 or less) and those in professional occupations (76.5 per cent compared to 32.9 per cent for labourers). Overall, more advantaged women were more likely to have access to paid parental leave than less advantaged women. Thus, the newly introduced universal PPL addressed a need for this less advantaged group that was not being filled until the government policy in 2011.

Research shows that it is important to provide paid as well as unpaid leave. Unpaid leave allows women to hold on to their pre-birth job while enabling leave taking up to one year. That is, employers are required to provide mothers with the same or an equivalent-level job upon return after maternity leave. It keeps the woman's connection with employment. However, because the leave is unpaid, some groups of women may not be able to afford taking sufficient time off (Rossin-Slater et al. 2013; Broadway et al. 2016). Access to paid leave allows for longer leave taking after childbirth, especially in lower-income families. However, given that employer-provided paid parental leave is predominantly provided to women who are relatively advantaged, it is especially the low-wage and low-skill women who missed out on paid leave before the government introduced the universal PPL scheme in 2011. Broadway et al. (2016) show that the impact of this new scheme was particularly prominent among more disadvantaged groups of women and among women who have no access to employer-provided paid parental leave. The analyses showed that after a slowdown in return to work, women return more quickly and are more likely to return to the same job (i.e. they have a stronger attachment to their job and employer). One year after birth, 73 per cent of post-PPL women have returned to work versus 69 per cent of pre-PPL women. Although these effects are observed among all women, they are largest among relatively disadvantaged groups.

Since introducing the PPL scheme in 2011, there has been a debate about changing the current PPL scheme. This debate has ranged from providing 26 weeks of paid leave at wage replacement levels to reducing the current PPL entitlements dollar for dollar for women receiving payments from their employer as well. The latter would be a major change in the original intention of the PPL scheme. When PPL was first introduced, it was emphasised that the government scheme was to be complementary to payments already provided by the employer. At the time of introduction, employers were actually warned not to reduce or abolish their paid leave schemes in response to the government scheme.

This confused debate seems to be due to the lack of clarity regarding what type of payment paid parental leave is. In most European countries paid parental leave is seen and treated as a work entitlement, while in the recent Australian debate it was clearly seen by many as a welfare payment (even though it was introduced as a work entitlement). This distinction is important as a work entitlement implies no income testing, while a welfare payment usually implies strict income testing. The distinction also indicates different aims: income replacement in the case of a work entitlement and a safety net in case of a welfare payment. It should be noted that in order to be eligible for PPL a work history is needed, which makes PPL inconsistent with the safety net classification. It has been argued in the debate on paid leave provision that it is 'unfair' to provide paid leave to women with a recent labour market connection only. However, this is only the case if PPL is seen as welfare and not as a work entitlement earned through participation in the labour market. Treating PPL as a welfare payment versus a work entitlement is likely to result in different impacts on women's labour supply. A strong connection of PPL to employment (in terms of eligibility) is likely to encourage female labour supply.

Women tend to take on the lion's share of child care responsibilities in the household, so encouraging men to play a bigger role in the care for children could also facilitate women's labour force participation. Sweden replaced maternity leave with parental leave in 1974, and from that time the proportion of leave taken by fathers has increased from 0.5 per cent to 11.4 per cent in 1994, and 20 per cent in 2012 (Ekberg et al. 2013).

In 1995, Sweden introduced a reform that reserved one month of parental leave for the mother and one month for the father. In 2002, it added a month of paid paternity leave to the existing parental leave. Ekberg et al. (2013) find that it induced fathers to take more parental leave, but it did not seem to alter the fathers' shares in the subsequent provision of child care. The authors suggest that behavioural change is difficult to induce.

Finally, it is worth pointing out that effective parental leave policies cannot exist in isolation. They should be well coordinated with child care policies, since a successful transition back to the labour market crucially depends on the availability of affordable child care.

The dynamics of labour supply

Individuals who are jobless or unemployed in one year are much more likely to be jobless or unemployed in the following year than individuals who were in employment during the reference year, and vice versa: those who were employed in one year are more likely to be employed in the next year as well. That is, labour market participation exhibits a high degree of state dependence from one period to the next (e.g. Hyslop 1999; Haan 2010 with Heckman 1981 cited therein; Hérault et al. 2015).

This is partly due to an actual loss in human capital while being outside the labour force, especially in occupations that continuously evolve and experience substantial technological changes, but is also likely to be at least partly due to employers' perceptions. Employers may use current labour force status as a signal regarding the quality and suitability of an applicant. Former employees may experience habit formation and changed preferences as a result of temporarily moving out of the labour force, which reduces future labour force participation. Furthermore, building a career requires continuity in labour force participation. Becoming eligible for a promotion or being considered for a wage increase takes time on the job. These two features of the labour market can have major consequences for women's labour market outcomes. As a result of these, a temporary exit from the labour force and/or subsequent part-time participation can have long-term impacts, delaying or even stalling career progress.

Even among highly skilled women, different male and female working patterns are observed and are likely explained by the usually higher contribution to home production, especially child care, by women.

The availability of child care and the family-friendliness of workplace practices are therefore likely to be crucial in female labour supply decisions. Evidence from the broader female workforce suggests flexibility in working hours is an especially strong determinant of labour supply. Blau and Kahn (2013), for example, find that women in the US face a relatively binary decision between full-time work and non-participation, while in other OECD countries the working hour flexibility produced by family-friendly policies results in substantially higher female participation rates than in the US, with more women working part-time. Fochsen et al. (2005) find similar patterns within the Swedish nurse population, where the increased flexibility provided in work schedules since the mid-1990s has reduced exit from the profession for child rearing. Focusing on US women with a university qualification from Harvard, Herr and Wolfram (2012) find evidence that inflexible work environments lead to lower labour force participation once women have children. The research discussed in this paragraph points to a need for flexibility and family-friendliness of workplaces, if we are to keep new mothers in the labour force.

Keeping a strong connection to the labour market is important, but not always sufficient as is evident from tenure track outcomes for academics in the US, where it is shown that combining work and family after having children takes its toll on women's probability to be confirmed in their first postdoctoral position. Antecol et al. (2016) show that gender-neutral policies that provide extra time (often one year) in cases of ill-health or childbirth aimed at dealing with this disadvantage, faced mostly by women, appear ineffective at helping women (but do help men in obtaining tenure). This may be due to the fact that eligibility for the relevant policy does not require taking time off or showing that a substantial amount of time is spent in caring for children. Women may also be less likely to be promoted or be made partner (e.g. when working in a law firm), which may have major implications when the employer follows an up-or-out policy. The disadvantage faced by women may be due to no longer being able to work overtime or to perform specific aspects of the job, such as travel or dining with/entertaining clients. So even if a new mother remains in the labour market after childbirth, her caring role may affect her career development negatively.

The government policies discussed in the first section of this chapter and the dynamics of labour supply discussed in this section are likely to interact, leading to a reinforced impact of government policies, even if these policies only play a role in a person's life temporarily. Government policies that encourage women to exit the labour force have the potential to change the course of a person's life. This is due to the fact that once someone has moved out of the labour force, it may be difficult to re-enter, especially if the time out of the labour force has been prolonged. The latter is often the case for women who may take several years off after having children (e.g. until the youngest child starts school). After many years, re-entry may be at a lower level, leading to a further loss of human capital. This is a loss not only to the woman herself or her direct family, but also to society at large. It is not only leaving the labour market, but also a transition to part-time employment or to full-time work at lower intensity that could have a negative impact on career, human capital accumulation and lifetime earnings.

The uncertainty of optimal decision-making

The long-term impacts discussed in the previous section can be particularly serious when considering the uncertainty associated with one's life course. As a result, any decisions taken at one point in time that could be considered optimal under the circumstances may no longer be optimal at a later point in time, or under changed circumstances.

A decision that appears optimal under one set of circumstances may be detrimental in another set of circumstances. An obvious example is the choice many women make to temporarily withdraw from the labour market, or take up a less demanding job, after childbirth. When part of a couple, a stronger focus of one partner on providing care, while the other partner's focus is on maintaining a strong labour market position, may well be a rational choice. However, if the couple separates, then upon divorce the primary carer is likely to be disadvantaged in terms of their income-generating ability.

Despite the odds of divorce being quite high, (partial) specialisation with—in most cases—the woman focusing on the caring and home-making task remains very popular. This is evident from the low labour market participation rates of women with young children. Although most prevalent among relatively low-skill women, high-skill women also feel more responsible for the caring task than their (usually also high-skill) male partners. To give an example for a very high-skill profession (which requires many years of investment in training), female medical doctors are much more likely than male medical doctors to work part-time when young children aged zero–four are present: 79 per cent of female GPs and 65 per cent of female specialists work fewer than 35 hours per week compared with 16 and 8 per cent of their male counterparts, respectively. Female doctors are also much more likely (than male doctors) to indicate that they feel responsible for child care as reflected by a question on whether their employment is restricted by a lack of child care (see Figure 5.2).

Several papers report on a phenomenon sometimes called 'doing gender', where a woman's share of housework decreases with her relative earnings, but only up to the point where she earns the same as her husband (e.g. for Australia: Bittman et al. 2003; for Spain: Sevilla-Sanz et al. 2010). Beyond that point, her share of housework remains constant. This has been explained by hypothesising that when men earn less than their wives a gender-norm violation occurs, and thus either the wife, the husband or both move to more traditional behaviour in the realm of housework in order to neutralise this deviance. England (2011) and Sullivan (2011) point out that this relates to a small group of households only, and that the absolute level of income of the woman is important too, not just relative income (i.e. her housework does not decrease when both partners earn little). Such behaviour makes it much more difficult for women than for men to continue their high-level career after childbirth, and often it may be deemed impossible.

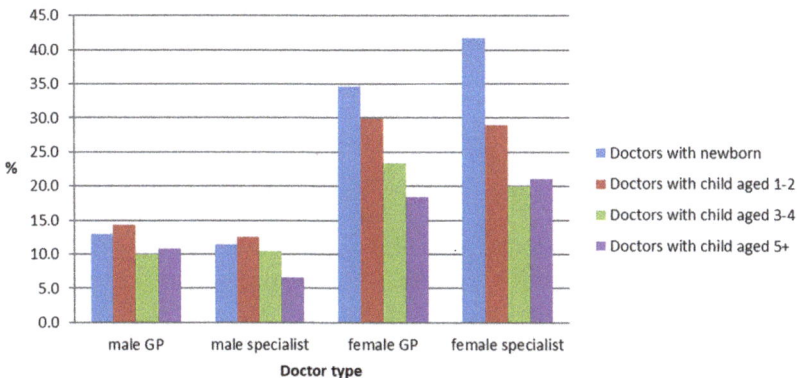

Figure 5.2: Proportion of doctors who agree with the statement that their employment is restricted due to lack of access to child care

Source: Own calculations from the Medicine in Australia: Balancing Employment and Life (MABEL) data.

With regard to a woman's share of child care time, the results on the impact of relative wages are quite mixed. The spouse's relative earnings seem to be irrelevant in Sevilla-Sanz et al. (2010). It appears that women wish to specialise in this type of caring activity, regardless of their relative productivity or bargaining power. A different result is found by Kalenkoski et al. (2009) who estimate that women whose partners have higher potential wages spend significantly more time on primary child care on all days, whereas men whose partners have higher potential wages spend significantly more time only on secondary child care and only during weekends. No associations are found for own wages for either men or women.

Among women who have relatively low education levels, or among women who have lower education levels than their partners, the proportion of women who are out of the labour force or who work part-time or who have 'downgraded' from a higher occupation status to a lower occupation status is likely to be much larger. These changes in labour force status or occupation status often occur after the first child is born; for example, childless women in Norway and Australia have similar labour force participation rates, while women with preschool children in Australia have much lower participation rates and much higher part-time rates (Kalb and Thoresen 2010).

There is also evidence that women make choices in anticipation of having children. Returning to the example of medical doctors, there is evidence that the increased feminisation of the workforce is not evenly spread over doctor types, but is particularly prevalent among the GP workforce. Modern GP practices arguably provide the most flexible working environment for a medical doctor (see Figure 1 in Kalb et al. (2017)). That is, women may pre-select into an occupation that is most likely to offer family-friendly work arrangements.

Although these choices may be optimal from a household perspective, they are almost certainly not optimal for women and are, at the least, a risky choice. If the household disintegrates for whatever reason, the woman may be left behind with limited financial resources as well as have few employment opportunities due to her reduced human capital and work experience.

Lifetime impacts

Over a woman's lifetime, the impacts described in the previous sections are likely to have substantial consequences. As women age, those who have children often build up less superannuation than their male partners. Although they can share in their partners' superannuation as long as they stay together, it is a different story after divorce since there is no designated part in her partner's superannuation that can be taken out and transferred to her. Similarly, when the primary breadwinner passes away, the primary carer left behind may need to survive on a relatively low pension, and may be expected to return to the labour market where finding a (high-quality) job may be difficult. These retirement income issues are covered in more detail by Austen and Sharp in Chapter 10.

Even if it were possible to transfer part of superannuation savings to the partner who specialised in home activities, there is the other issue of loss of skill. During the time spent out of the labour force (or even when working part time), women often lose part of their initial human capital, making it more and more difficult to catch up financially with every year out of the labour market.

Due to the above two issues, there is a relatively high proportion of women who have limited savings for retirement and, as a result, are mostly reliant on the age pension. At the same time, women tend to live longer than men, which compounds the effect of lower levels of savings. Therefore, as a group, older single women are on relatively low incomes, on average, and are more likely to be considered poor than other demographic groups (Wilkins 2015).

Specialising as the primary caregiver has a high personal economic cost to women, but it also has a large societal cost, in terms of foregone productivity and higher income support dependency rates, than is necessary in principle. By providing the wrong incentives at one stage of the life course, making it costly for young women to combine having a family and maintaining meaningful employment at a level they can manage, additional government expenditures are incurred at other points in the life course. These costs could be substantially reduced by investing in women's careers, and in children's care and development early in life.

Conclusion

There is economic and social value to be found in a more equitable approach to market work, household work and caring tasks. This is clear when taking a life course perspective that acknowledges the role of uncertainty when making important decisions. When highly capable women exit the labour force (even temporarily) or downgrade the occupation they choose because of familial pressures, there is an instantaneous loss to society. Women are now more likely to attain post-school qualifications than men, with 41 per cent of women aged 25 to 29 years having university degrees in 2011, compared to 30 per cent of men (ABS 2012). Further, in a time when separation or divorce of couples is relatively common, specialising in household work and caring at the cost of market work is not in women's best interests. There is also a price to pay for society when women with little labour market expertise and earning power become more reliant on the state.

Policy arrangements in Australia have counteractive effects, with some policies that are clearly intended to encourage labour supply being combined with policies that have the opposite effect. That is, government policy, despite talk about increasing female labour force participation, does little and often even seems to act counterproductively by maintaining policies that encourage women to become stay-at-home mums, such as FTB-B, which penalises the secondary earner on return to work.

Investments in increasing female labour force participation would have mid- to long-term fiscal returns in terms of a reduction of allowances and age pensions to be paid, increased productivity and tax revenue, as well as a reduced loss of human capital. Such investments can be compared to New Zealand's investment approach to social policy where current investments are justified by the prospect of future savings. Investments in female labour force participation are likely to have similar future pay-offs that should be kept in mind when deciding what we can and cannot afford. If future savings and returns are not kept in mind when making decisions, Australia will keep under-investing in achieving the goal of increased female labour force participation.

Care for children and home production are valuable activities. This chapter argues that strong female labour force participation can be compatible with these activities when the right support is provided. The support that government can provide includes maternity leave: during the first three to six months after childbirth, maternity leave is crucial for the health of mother and child, and for the development of the child. Following this period, it is crucial for the mother's return to the workforce and the child's continued healthy development to ensure that high-quality and affordable child care is available. Several studies have shown that part-time employment and employment after age one do not seem to hamper child development when the right child care is available (see, for example, Waldfogel 2004; Averett et al. 2005; Gregg et al. 2005; Berger et al. 2005; and Brooks-Gunn et al. 2010).

Women also need supportive partners who are willing to share the workload at home and in the labour market. However, to enable partners to be supportive, the government and employers need to put policies in place that do not penalise such behaviour, but facilitate men to take a larger share of parenting responsibilities. For example, family-friendly policies should be truly available to men and women, so men can stay at home with a sick child without being frowned upon. Neither should access to part-time hours be a hurdle. Both parents could work four days a week, reducing the number of child care days required to three days per week (which is around the optimal amount of formal care with regard to child development), while keeping both parents in the labour market for close to full-time hours.

Norway and other Scandinavian countries show that good child care and parental leave policies can work; mothers' labour force participation is substantially higher than in Australia. High-quality child care is widely available at much lower cost than in Australia. The role of men in caring is supported by policies around paid parental leave, with 10 weeks of 'mandatory' (use it or lose it) leave—about 20 per cent of total leave available—designated to the father. The new universal PPL scheme has had a positive impact in Australia, but current policy reviews may undermine its success, such as proposals to withdraw government leave payments dollar for dollar if the parent receives employer-paid parental leave, and stricter income tests.

Policies have to be thought through carefully and tested. As discussed in this chapter, some examples of family-friendly policies (such as stopping the tenure clock at universities in the US or designating part of the paid parental leave available to fathers) did not have the intended effect of strengthening mothers' links to employment. It could be that some policies take time before a behavioural change is achieved (e.g. paid paternity leave), or alternatively some adjustments to eligibility requirements may be needed to ensure the right group is targeted (e.g. stopping the tenure clock). Despite the difficulty in designing good policy, this is what is needed to encourage behavioural change, keeping in mind that change can be slow. In their 1994 publication (p. 124), Hersch and Stratton identified a crucial point: 'Thus allocation decisions that result in women doing more housework than men set up a vicious cycle, a cycle which is hard to break.' They then somewhat optimistically continued:

> Only the evidence indicating that younger women are spending less time on housework and more time in the labor market suggests that the gender difference in work histories and housework time may be diminishing. Such changes will further decrease the gender wage gap, leading to still greater equity in the allocation of house-work.

Unfortunately, 20 years later this does not yet seem to have fully materialised.

To conclude, government expenditures on paid parental leave and high-quality child care are clearly an investment in the country's future by ensuring economic growth, high productivity and a well-adjusted and educated next generation. That seems money well spent to benefit the whole population. The disincentive associated with the somewhat higher tax, to pay for these investments initially, can be spread across the whole tax-paying population, whereas in the alternative scenario the small group of parents of young children face extremely high taxes on their income through the accumulation of the usual taxes and the cost of child care should both parents wish to be employed. The impact of the former disincentive (spread out across the population) should be much less than the impact of disincentives for mothers of young children in the alternative scenario, where a few years of child rearing potentially produce a lifetime of relative disadvantage. In addition, society is likely to pay the price for saving now on support for families at a later stage, when women are likely to be more highly dependent on income support after divorce and in old age. In the alternative scenario, with an increased labour force (including a larger proportion of mothers) the cost to support families with children can be spread over this larger workforce now paying tax.

References

ABS (Australian Bureau of Statistics). 2011. *Australian Social Trends.* Dec 2011. Cat. no. 4102.0. Canberra: ABS.

ABS. 2012. *Gender Indicators, Australia.* July 2012. Cat. no. 4125.0. Canberra: ABS.

Antecol, Heather, Kelly Bedard and Jenna Stearns. 2016. *Equal but Inequitable: Who Benefits from Gender-Neutral Tenure Clock Stopping Policies?* IZA Discussion Paper No. 9904. Bonn, Germany.

Apps, Patricia. 2015. 'The central role of a well-designed income tax in "the modern economy"', paper at the Income tax conference: Looking forward at 100 Years: Where next for the Income Tax? Held on 27–28 April 2015 at the Tax and Transfer Policy Institute, Crawford School of Public Policy, The Australian National University.

Averett, Susan, Lisa A. Gennetian and H. Elizabeth Peters. 2005. 'Paternal child care and children's development'. *Journal of Population Economics*, 18(3): 391–414. doi.org/10.1007/s00148-004-0203-4

Baxter, Jennifer. 2013. *Parents Working Out Work. Australian Family Trends No. 1.* Melbourne: Australian Institute of Family Studies.

Berger, Lawrence, Jennifer Hill and Jane Waldfogel. 2005. 'Maternity leave, early maternal employment and child health and development in the US'. *Economic Journal* 115(501): F29–F47. doi.org/10.1111/j.0013-0133.2005.00971.x

Bittman, Michael, Paula England, Liana Sayer, Nancy Folbre and George Matheson. 2003. 'When Does Gender Trump Money? Bargaining and Time in Household Work'. *American Journal of Sociology* 109(1): 186–214. doi.org/10.1086/378341

Blau, Francine D. and Lawrence M. Kahn. 2013. 'Female Labor Supply: Why Is the United States Falling Behind?' *The American Economic Review* 103(3): 251–256. doi.org/10.1257/aer.103.3.251

Breunig, Robert, Xiaodong Gong and Anthony King. 2012. 'Partnered Women's Labour Supply and Child-Care Costs in Australia: Measurement Error and the Child-Care Price'. *Economic Record* 88(s1): 51–69. doi.org/10.1111/j.1475-4932.2012.00797.x

Breunig, Robert, Xiaodong Gong and Declan Trott. 2014. 'The New National Quality Framework: Quantifying Some of the Effects on Labour Supply, Child Care Demand and Household Finances for Two-Parent Households'. *Economic Record* 90(288): 1–16.

Broadway, Barbara, Guyonne Kalb, Duncan McVicar and Bill Martin. 2016. *The Impact of Paid Parental Leave on Labour Supply and Employment Outcomes*. Melbourne Institute Working Paper No. 9/16, University of Melbourne.

Brooks-Gunn, Jeanne, Wen-Jui Han and Jane Waldfogel. 2010. 'First-Year Maternal Employment and Child Development in the First 7 Years'. *Monographs of the Society for Research in Child Development* 75(2): i–148.

Doiron, Denise and Guyonne Kalb. 2005. 'Demands for Childcare and Household Labour Supply in Australia'. *Economic Record* 81(254): 215–236. doi.org/10.1111/j.1475-4932.2005.00257.x

Ekberg, John, Rickard Eriksson and Guido Friebel. 2013. 'Parental leave—A policy evaluation of the Swedish "daddy-month" reform'. *Journal of Public Economics* 97: 131–143. doi.org/10.1016/j.jpubeco.2012.09.001

England, Paula. 2011. 'Missing the big picture and making much ado about almost nothing: Recent scholarship on gender and household work'. *Journal of Family Theory & Review* 3(1): 23–26. doi.org/10.1111/j.1756-2589.2010.00077.x

Fochsen, Grethe, Katarina Sjögren, Malin Josephson and Monica Lagerström. 2005. 'Factors contributing to the decision to leave nursing care: a study among Swedish nursing personnel'. *Journal of Nursing Management* 13(4): 338–344. doi.org/10.1111/j.1365-2934.2005.00546.x

Gregg, Paul, Elizabeth Washbrook, Carol Propper and Simon Burgess. 2005. 'The effects of a mother's return to work decision on child development in the UK'. *Economic Journal* 115(501): F48–F80. doi.org/10.1111/j.0013-0133.2005.00972.x

Gustafsson, Siv and Frank Stafford. 1992. 'Child care subsidies and labor supply in Sweden'. *Journal of Human Resources* 27(1): 204–230. doi.org/10.2307/145917

Haan, Peter. 2010. 'A Multi-state model of state dependence in labor supply: Intertemporal labor supply effects of a shift from joint to individual taxation'. *Labour Economics* 17(2): 323–335. doi. org/10.1016/j.labeco.2009.05.004

Heckman, James. 1981. 'Heterogeneity and State Dependence'. In Sherwin Rosen (ed.), *Studies in Labor Markets*, pp. 91–139. Chicago: University of Chicago Press.

Hérault, Nicolas, Guyonne Kalb and Rezida Zakirova. 2015. 'A Study into the Persistence of Living in a Jobless Household'. *Economic Record* 91(293): 209–232. doi.org/10.1111/1475-4932.12178

Herr, Jane and Catherine Wolfram. 2012. 'Work environment and opt-out rates at motherhood across high-education career paths'. *Industrial & Labor Relations Review* 65: 928–950. doi.org/ 10.1177/001979391206500407

Hersch, Joni and Leslie S. Stratton. 1994. 'Housework, Wages, and the Division of Housework Time for Employed Spouses'. *American Economic Review* 84(2): 120–125.

Houng, Brendan, Sung-Hee Jeon and Guyonne Kalb. 2011. *The Effects of Childcare and Preschool on Child Development.* Final Report for Australian Government Department of Education, Employment and Workplace Relations. Available at: melbourneinstitute.unimelb.edu. au/assets/documents/sprs-reports/1-10_Final_Report.pdf

Hyslop, Dean. 1999. 'State dependence, serial correlation and heterogeneity in intertemporal labor force participation of married women'. *Econometrica* 67(6): 1255–1294. doi.org/10.1111/1468-0262.00080

Jaumotte, Florence. 2003. 'Labour force participation of women: empirical evidence on the role of policy and other determinants in OECD countries'. OECD Economic Studies, No. 37, 2003/2.

Kalb, Guyonne, Daniel Kuehnle, Anthony Scott, Terence Chai Cheng and Sung-Hee Jeon. 2017. 'What Factors Affect Doctors' Hours Decisions: Comparing Structural Discrete Choice and Reduced-Form Approaches'. Forthcoming in *Health Economics*.

Kalb, Guyonne and Wang-Sheng Lee. 2008. 'Childcare Use and Parents' Labour Supply in Australia'. *Australian Economic Papers* 47(3): 272–295.

Kalb, Guyonne, Domenico Tabasso and Rezida Zakirova. 2013. *Children's participation in early childhood education and care, and their developmental outcomes by Year 5: A comparison between disadvantaged and advantaged children.* Final Report for the Department of Education, Employment, and Workplace Relations. Available at: melbourneinstitute.unimelb. edu.au/assets/documents/sprs-reports/4-13_Final_Report.pdf

Kalb, Guyonne and Thor O. Thoresen. 2010. 'A comparison of family policy designs of Australia and Norway using microsimulation models'. *Review of Economies of the Household* 8(2): 255–287. doi.org/10.1007/ s11150-009-9076-3

Kalenkoski, Charlene, David Ribar and Leslie Stratton. 2009. 'The Influence of Wages on Parents' Allocations of Time to Child Care and Market Work in the United Kingdom'. *Journal of Population Economics* 22(2): 399–419. doi.org/10.1007/s00148-008-0192-9

Martin, Bill, Marian Baird, Michelle Brady, Barbara Broadway, Belinda Hewitt, Guyonne Kalb, Lyndall Strazdins, Wojtek Tomaszewski, Maria Zadorozny, Janeen Baxter, Rachael Chen, Meraiah Foley, Duncan McVicar, Gillian Whitehouse and Ning Xiang. 2015. *PPL Evaluation: Final Report.* Canberra: Australian Government Department of Social Security.

Martin, Bill, Belinda Hewitt, Mara A. Yerkes, Ning Xiang, Judith Rose and Laetitia Coles. 2014. *Paid Parental Leave Evaluation: Phase 3 Report.* Canberra: Australian Government Department of Social Security.

Rossin-Slater, Maya, Christopher Ruhm and Jane Waldfogel. 2013. 'The Effects of California's Paid Family Leave Program on Mothers' Leave-Taking and Subsequent Labor Market Outcomes'. *Journal of Policy Analysis and Management* 32(2): 224–245. doi.org/10.1002/ pam.21676

Sevilla-Sanz, Almudena, Jose Ignacio Gimenez-Nadal and Cristina Fernández. 2010. 'Gender Roles and the Division of Unpaid Work in Spanish Households'. *Feminist Economics* 16(4): 137–184. doi.org/ 10.1080/13545701.2010.531197

Sullivan, Oriel. 2011. 'An End to Gender Display Through the Performance of Housework? A Review and Reassessment of the Quantitative Literature Using Insights From the Qualitative Literature'. *Journal of Family Theory & Review* 3(1): 1–13. doi.org/10.1111/j.1756-2589.2010.00074.x

Waldfogel, Jane. 2004. *Social mobility, life chances, and the early years*. Centre for Analysis of Social Exclusion Paper No. 88, London School of Economics.

Wilkins, Roger. 2015. *The Household, Income and Labour Dynamics in Australia Survey: Selected Findings from Waves 1 to 12*. HILDA Statistical Report, Melbourne Institute of Applied Economic and Social Research, University of Melbourne.

6

Paying for care in Australia's 'wage earners' welfare state': The case of child endowment

Julie Smith

Australia's social protection regime, implemented during the 20th century through wage, taxation and social security systems, has been both an enemy and a friend of gender equality. Social protection in Australia was underpinned from 1907 by a 'wage earners' welfare state'—a wage regulatory system that mandated a basic wage for employed men, single or married (Castles 1985). State and federal wage tribunals set these wage standard at levels sufficient to support a family at a reasonable standard of living. However, these 'family wage' fixing arrangements allowed female employees to be paid just half the male rate. Gender wage inequality thus lowered employer costs and made the 'family wage' more economically feasible, but also institutionalised women's economic dependence on a male breadwinner, and reinforced gender roles in unpaid household work and care. The family wage system disempowered and created vulnerabilities for women, particularly those caring for young children, as their entitlement was indirect through a husband. Reinforcing this gender inequality, income taxation—based on the individual unit with progressive marginal rates—allowed deductions for (mostly high-income male) taxpayers with dependants. Even aside from debates on whether the legislated wage was indeed sufficient for a couple and at least one child, the 'family wage' system created an obvious need for alternative provision for females unsupported by a male breadwinner, including widows, deserted wives and single mothers.

An important counterbalance to the gender inequality of its 'family wage' was the Australian social security system, initiated in 1909 with the introduction of the federal aged pension. The aged pension, maternity allowances, child endowment and widow's pension—payments that particularly addressed the needs of women—were advocated and adopted in Australia during the next half century. Unlike other countries, in Australia these payments were financed from progressive taxation such as new land and income taxes, rather than social insurance levies on earnings, and payments were flat-rate rather than based on individual wage replacement. An individual's entitlement was not based on prior financial contributions. The design of Australia's 20th-century social security system thus acknowledged women as productive citizens who were contributing to building the country's capital (Lake 2012; Sawer 2012). As Marian Sawer observes (Sawer 2015, p. 25), there was at this time:

> clear recognition that old-age pensions needed to be non-contributory in order to give equal recognition to the paid and unpaid work performed by citizens. The advocates of old-age pensions insisted that the unpaid work performed by women in caring for others should not condemn them to the workhouse or to poverty in old age. A contributory basis for pensions would make a mockery of the work of married women.

Notably, in 1924, Australia's national statistician made calculations of the value of the nation's human capital, which encompassed women's non-market household production (Treadgold 2000). The report prepared by Commonwealth Statistician Wickens highlighted that the value of the country's human capital, at £6,211 million, was three times higher than its 'material capital' assets, such as factories, mines and railroads. Estimating that the cost of producing a 15-year-old child required 'capital outlay' of around £436, which was more than repaid by the future productivity of adults, Wickens' report concluded that:

> there can be no worse policy in any community than that under which the health of the citizens is sacrificed to the increase of material goods, particularly when that sacrifice occurs, as in the past it has frequently occurred, amongst the children (Wickens 1924, p. 554 cited in Treadgold 2000, p. 46).

Taxation and transfer systems may seem to treat men and women equally. However, men have higher wages, earnings and wealth than women, and spend less time meeting unpaid care responsibilities for children or adults. Men are less likely to experience poverty or financial deprivation, and their expenditure patterns are different (Grown and Valodia 2010). Fiscal systems that levy taxes on wages, incomes, consumption and wealth therefore affect men and women differently.

This chapter presents a gender analysis of the evolution of Australia's somewhat distinctive 'wage earners' welfare state' and its social protection 'twin', the tax-transfer system. It focuses on the origin and evolution of child endowment and later family payments, within a feminist economic framework that incorporates non-market household production, particularly care of children. Such a framework draws attention both to the contribution of the household economy to economic productivity and growth, and to the declining visibility of the unpaid care economy in Australian fiscal policy discussions. Though the contemporary loss of policy interest in gender equality has been linked to a diminished concern for redistribution issues (Sawer 2015), this paper emphasises the economic efficiency consequences. Connecting social science research on comparative welfare regimes with studies of women's time investments in young children, it draws on evidence from medical and health sciences to identify the health and labour productivity implications arising from fiscal and wage policies, which neglect the unpaid care economy and gender equity. Notwithstanding a shift from a male breadwinner model to a focus on 'women and work' and 'early childhood investment', it shows how gender biased perspectives on what counts as 'productive' presently stand in the way of fiscal and labour market strategies, which improve national productivity, as well as protect and encourage greater gender equality.

The chapter proposes that the erosion of the value and universality of child endowment illustrates one of two key ways that the goal of improving gender equality has been 'lost in translation' (Jenson 2009) during the 'incomplete transformation' of Australia's welfare state in response to women's changing roles (Esping-Andersen 2009).

First, and the focus of this chapter, is the dismantling of Australia's unique family wage system and the 'dual earner' model promoted as achieving gender equality, pursued without attention to the preconditions for wellbeing of women and children. This wellbeing is set by the limited resources of the unpaid care economy (Folbre 2002; Pocock 2006) and the interactions with gendered labour market institutions (Hakim 2000; Esping-Andersen and Billari 2015).

Second is the gradual marginalisation of the tax-financed public aged pension by policies that have since the 1990s compelled wage contributions to private superannuation, and provided substantial tax privileges to those making voluntary contributions (Smith 2004b). In this regime transition, the economic costs of taking time out to care for children during their lifetime has differentially adverse implications for women, especially low-wage earners throughout the life course. Parental time investments in children during the life course count for nothing in this publicly underwritten, market-focused system (Smith 2007).

During the 1990s, comparative political science scholarship on welfare state regimes identified three regime types describing how a country's social policies protect families from dependence on the vagaries of the labour market for survival: liberal-conservative, corporatist and social democratic (Esping-Andersen 1990). These 'three worlds of welfare capitalism', inhabited approximately by Anglo-Saxon, European and Nordic countries, tackled household income inequality and insecurity by 'decommodifying' labour—creating social entitlements which to varying degrees reduced workers' dependence on markets for subsistence.

More recently, responding to feminist critiques of 'the three worlds of welfare capitalism' and to concerns at declining birth rates and child development disadvantage, the extension of this welfare framework has highlighted its widening gaps and inequalities in societal support for social reproduction (Esping-Andersen 2005, 2008, 2011). Welfare regime scholars have identified that appropriate policy responses to the changing role of women are crucial for adapting and rebalancing the welfare state, but this is an 'incomplete revolution' (Esping-Andersen 1999). This new way of thinking about country's welfare regimes highlights that deep-seated gender bias in the design of 'welfare capitalism' threatens countries' capacity to compete in a global knowledge economy, which relies on high-quality human capital. Remedying this requires attention to the household economy.

Feminist scholars have challenged conventional conceptualisations of the welfare capitalism, arguing that its evolution during the 20th century was directed at 'decommodification' of wage labour. This crosses all three 'worlds of welfare capitalism' because of the design focus on a male breadwinner. It results in contemporary welfare regimes being poorly equipped to address gender inequality, and even recreating or entrenching it (O'Connor 1993; Orloff 1993, 1996). Because women are mainly held responsible for care work, their economic vulnerability lies particularly within the family and its care responsibilities.

The centrepiece of tax and welfare reform strategies and policies in Organisation for Economic Co-operation and Development (OECD) countries since the 1990s has been on boosting women's employment participation. Although recognising that women's economic independence may be supported through labour market participation, Orloff proposed that evaluation of welfare regimes also consider the contribution of benefits to women's empowerment vis-à-vis men within marriages and families (Orloff 1996). The implication is that female labour market integration has been overemphasised as the route to gender equality. Gender equitable regimes would enhance women's capacity to survive and support their children without having to marry to gain access to a breadwinner's income. As Lohmann and Zagel remind us, at the time of its emergence in the 1990s, the concept of 'defamilization' captured 'not only economic independence and the independence from care responsibility but also the freedom to choose who cares' (Lohmann and Zagel 2016, p. 3). This calls for greater attention to gender-specific aspects of 'defamilization'. This would involve evaluation of the extent to which countries' welfare regimes rely on women in families (not just the market and the state) to provide welfare, and scrutiny of how these regimes shape gender relations, including how women are enabled to achieve economic autonomy outside of marriage, and how unpaid and paid work is recognised and treated.

In Australia, the demise of the 'wage earners' welfare state' (Castles 2001) has been epitomised by the shift away from citizen entitlements, towards tightened eligibility, labour market participation requirements and means testing of social security benefits alongside policies of fiscal restraint and tax reform since the 1980s. Continuing policy blindness to the extent of household investments in children gives rise to concerns that the welfare regime reforms developed in the past decade—such as 'social investment' strategies focused on disadvantaged children—resulted in a 'loss in translation' of gender egalitarian strategies by displacing the equality claims of adult women (Jenson 2009; O'Connor 2013). The 'defamilization' of 'unpaid' care work to encourage women's 'paid' work participation (in some cases assisted by public funding of child care services), remains the main pathway by which 'welfare reform' addressed gender equality. However, improving gender equality requires an understanding of the crucial importance of unpaid care work as the foundation of a country's human capital. It also necessitates a model of productive work in which men become more like women, combining care with paid work, rather than replacing a 'family wage' system with wage and fiscal policies that result in women being burdened with both (Fraser 1994). In contrast with the contemporary characterisation of women receiving social security payments for their families as 'bludgers', 'leaners' or 'skivers' (Whiteford 2017), it can be argued that contemporary capitalist development is itself 'free riding' on women's unpaid care activities, whilst obscuring the importance and value of women's social reproductive work (Fraser 2016, p. 85):

> The real free riders in the current system are not single poor mothers who shirk employment. The real free riders are men of all classes who shirk care work and domestic labor, and the corporations who free ride on both the paid labor and the unpaid labor of working people.

A gender-equitable approach requires quality care services for children and the elderly and universal and adequate child/family allowances and tax benefits, paid and unpaid parental leave policies, and changes to the social and economic institutions for work and care to distribute the economic burdens of care of dependants more equally between men and women (Lohmann and Zagel 2016). Such policies require a strong public revenue base, and understanding of the gendered effects of fiscal and labour market policies, as well as how tax-transfer and labour market policies shape and constrain women's (and men's) paid and unpaid work. The tax-transfer system is an important institution that has been profoundly shaped by 20th-century values and norms, and continues to shape the organisation of Australian society in the 21st century.

Household production and Australia's social protection regime

The care economy

During the process of economic development, markets have come to account for a greater share of economic activity, and non-market household production has tended to decline. In part this is due to improved public infrastructure and household technology, and in part the rising opportunity costs of unpaid work as women's wages and job opportunities increased (Australia. Royal Commission into the Basic Wage 1920; Greenwood et al. 2005). However, social reproduction and its basis in the care economy may be drained of resources by competition with the market economy if societal arrangements recognising, protecting and rewarding it are inadequate (Folbre 2002). In 1985, Cass pointed out that the nature of transfers occurring in the non-market household sector was not from breadwinner to 'dependants', akin to welfare. Rather, it represents a system of hidden and unpaid welfare services provided by women (Cass 1985). Today, Australian families are finding it challenging to survive and reproduce amidst rising pressures from employment, while public services and related supports become less accessible and more costly (Pocock 2006). Market provision may fill gaps in provision but externalise its social costs such as those resulting from the minimising the costs of care, including diminishing care quality (Donath 2000) and relationships (Himmelweit 1995). Pocock (2006, p. 4) observes:

> While neoclassical economic theory treats labour as a commodity and happily embraces the market commodification of human effort, this denies a fundamental truth about workers: that they must reproduce themselves or the labour market cannot work. Such reproduction is a social function, which is undertaken by both individuals (when parents have a child) and society (when social fabric sustains households).

Focusing on market incentives and cost externalities highlights that children can be considered as 'public goods':

> Economic development tends to increase the costs [of children] to parents in general, and mothers in particular. Yet the growth of transfer payments and taxation of future generations 'socialise' many of the benefits of children … Parents who derive sufficiently high non-pecuniary benefits from their children may not care. Increases in the private costs of raising children, however, are exerting tremendous economic pressure on parents, particularly mothers … As children become increasingly public goods, parenting becomes an increasingly public service (Folbre 1994a, p. 86).

Early in the 20th century, as modern welfare capitalism emerged to decouple economic security from the vagaries of employment, an implied social contract for care was evolving to deal with parallel social dilemmas of providing care for dependant people such as children and the aged (Folbre 2001). Hence, institutional arrangements evolved during industrialisation that constrained women's choices so as to, in effect, coerce their low-cost availability for care work and diminish their bargaining power within the family. For example, until the 1880s in Australia women could not own property or hold a job after marriage, and wages for caring occupations have been low in part because of gender bias that views women's work as low skilled (England 2005). By the late 20th century, however, growing maternal labour market participation was increasingly in conflict with expectations regarding women's participation in the household economy (Folbre 2002). Incompatibilities and gender inequities facing the 'modern woman' underlie various forms of a 'baby strike' occurring in different countries (McDonald 2000, 2013).

The invisibility of women's economic contribution

Household production and care work is a substantial part of the economy, although not counted in measures of economic activity such as gross domestic product (GDP) (Miranda 2011; ABS 2014). Stiglitz et al. observe that as countries develop, the shift from home to market production may 'overstate increases in well-being' and 'policies that encourage market over non-market production distort the economy':

> We may be more confident about measuring … shifts from home production to market production that occur broadly within society—and it would be wrong not to make note of these changes. Failing to do so may seriously bias our estimates of improvements in societal well-being (Stiglitz et al. 2009, p. 39).

The standard international treatment of household production discounts the highly valuable role that families, especially mothers, play in human capital development (Abraham and Mackie 2005). This invisibility has been institutionalised since the 1940s by the United Nations' System of National Accounting (Waring 1988).[1] There are significant consequences of this invisibility of women's household production for policy advocacy, design, implementation and evaluation (Collas-Monsod 2011; Elson 2008; Himmelweit 2002). GDP also overstates taxable capacity where it is simply measuring a shift from household to market production, such as for child care services. Tax policy also routinely dismisses the importance of addressing tax disincentives facing secondary workers, despite women being disproportionately affected by fiscal drag (Grown and Valodia 2010).

---

1   Before this time, some countries counted non-market household production in their economic production or national income statistics.

In Australia, as women's workforce participation increased, some economic activities shifted from the household to the market. As a result of counting this shift as a growth in GDP (while not recognising household production), the rise in economic wellbeing during these decades was overstated (Smith 1982). This measurement distortion also meant the rise in tax burden was understated, perhaps contributing to rising 'resistance' to taxation during the 1970s (Smith 2001, 2004b).

China's recent rapid transition to a market economy provides recent evidence of the distorting focus of policy during market-based economic development. In that country, social services have failed to adapt to the shift of policy focus to market productivity. The time needed to care for children, and juggle paid workforce participation with their care, explains increasing gender discrepancies in wages and labour force participation, and is estimated to account for a third of the pay gap between men and women (Gustafsson and Li 2000; Cook and Dong 2011; Li et al. 2014; Dong and An 2015).

Unpaid care work and human capital: The example of infant and young child feeding

A particular example is the omission in valuation of home-produced goods especially breastmilk, which Stiglitz et al. explain is 'clearly within the System of National Accounts production boundary, is quantitatively non-trivial and also has important implications for public policy and child and maternal health' (2009, p. 39). Health authorities recommend exclusive breastfeeding to six months and continued breastfeeding to two years and beyond (WHO/UNICEF 2003). There is significant evidence that China's modernisation has been accompanied by a dramatic decline in optimal infant and young child feeding (Hou 2014), a boom in consumption of ultra-processed and fast food (Baker and Friel 2014) including milk formula (Baker et al. 2016) and an unprecedented epidemic of chronic disease and obesity and emerging health cost burdens (Popkin 2008).

The importance of early life care and nutrition, particularly breastfeeding (Lutter and Lutter 2012), for child development and their future productivity has long been recognised (Engle et al. 1999; Alderman et al. 2005) and has recently been confirmed in developed countries (Rollins et al. 2016; Victora et al. 2016). It is important for both women's and children's health (Grummer-Strawn and Rollins 2015). Avoidable maternal and child mortality and morbidity such as for maternal breast cancer or paediatric illness associated with short breastfeeding duration has also been shown to have large health treatment cost implications in the US, the UK and Australia (Smith et al. 2002; Bartick and Reinhold 2010; Bartick et al. 2013; Pokhrel et al. 2014). The early life experience of children contributes importantly to lifelong health, development and workforce earnings in a variety of country settings. For example, considerable evidence links full-time hours in formal care during infancy with poorer development and health outcomes (Waldfogel et al. 2002; Ruhm 2004) including in Australia (Harrison et al. 2009).

The quality of human capital underpins future productivity in the market economy, with a cumulative effect of early skill acquisition (Heckman and Masterov 2007). Effects of early nutrition on cognitive development translate into future earnings independent of family education or other parental factors (Victora et al. 2015). In the US, the labour productivity costs of low breastfeeding rates were recently estimated at US$40 billion a year (Hafstead and Lutter 2016). According to the World Health Organization (WHO) and partners, 'global economic losses associated with lower cognition from not breastfeeding reached more than $300 billion in 2012, equivalent to 0.49 per cent of the world's gross national income' (WHO et al. 2016).

However, caring for infants and young children is highly time intensive, especially where they are breastfed as recommended (Smith and Forrester 2013). Time costs of caring for young children are highly gendered in distribution (Craig and Powell 2013). Improved opportunities for maternal labour force participation may increase the opportunity costs to women and families of investing time in children, placing infants and young children in competition with the labour market for parental time (Smith 2004a; Pocock 2006).

The heightened competition between market and household economic activity at particular phases of the life course has important implications for the design and overall economic efficiency of contemporary social protection systems, including family and retirement income support (Smith 2007). Rather than integrating care work with market work, our social institutions, fiscal policies and labour market arrangements put women in a weak position for bargaining regarding pay and conditions given their continued propensity for involvement in unpaid care work. In many countries, such tensions between paid employment and household work or care responsibilities result in a 'motherhood penalty' in wages (Grimshaw and Rubery 2015). Comparative analyses of welfare regimes show that countries with social protection regimes that strongly integrate work and family, including through fiscal policies supporting access to paid maternity and parental leave and child care services, also have less gender inequality in pay and labour force attachment (Gornick and Meyers 2003; Budig et al. 2016).

In Australia, women's production of human milk is valued at $3.5 billion annually using national accounting methodology, yet is not counted as adding to GDP (though market breastmilk substitutes are) (Smith and Ingham 2005; Smith 2013). Despite global and national health recommendations, breastfeeding duration has barely improved in Australia since the 1980s (Amir and Donath 2008; AIHW 2011).

In the US, welfare reforms requiring labour force participation of sole parents have had detrimental effects on breastfeeding, despite increased breastfeeding being a goal of US nutrition policies for low-income women with children (Haider et al. 2003; Folbre 2006). This reinforces the observation by Cass three decades ago that the lack of visibility of hardships borne by women has contributed to ongoing life-cycle and class inequities that produce feminisation of poverty (Cass 1988a).

From 'family wage' to family payments: A case study of child endowment

This part examines the wage policy origins of child endowment schemes introduced in Australia from 1925, traces the evolution to its progressive income tax funding from the 1940s and canvasses gender aspects of its transition to tightly means-tested family payments by 2016. It identifies the links between this evolution of family payments through the tax-transfer system, and the move to equal pay for women in the 1970s. During the 1920s in Australia, social reformers and unions aimed to protect the living standards of wage earners with children from inflation and real wage erosion, while employers sought to cut wage costs and maintain cost competitiveness by making child support a public responsibility funded from general taxation. From before the time of introduction of the Commonwealth income tax in 1915, a 'bachelor tax' was debated in parliament on the grounds that the single wage earner was paid wages for a spouse and children he did not actually provide for, and so could fairly be taxed at a higher rate than the married man. The position taken by major interest groups during the Royal Commission on Child Endowment (1929) illustrates how child endowment and its financing was conceived and negotiated, and why child endowment came to be funded by Commonwealth income taxation.

Child endowment experiments: Context and contenders

Australian proposals for child endowment during the 1920s emerged from a complex background of employer, union and social activist challenges to the 'family wage' concept, which had been established in the previous decade (Jelly 1977; Cass 1983; Watts 1987). Some proponents of child endowment or family allowances saw them as a progressive social reform aimed at redistributing income to women and children, reducing family poverty and acknowledging the social and economic value of women's unpaid work in the home (Land 1975). High wartime inflation eroded competitiveness whilst creating considerable industrial unrest among workers who perceived the purchasing power of their wages to have been eroded by wartime price rises. Wage earners supporting families were worst affected, having relatively high expenditures compared to those without dependants. Employers, on the other hand, claimed the family wage was beyond the capacity of industry to pay and sought to dampen wage demands through introducing child endowment separate to arbitrated wages. The Piddington Royal Commission into the Basic Wage proposed replacing the 'child' element of the 'family' wage by introducing child endowment, financed by a levy on employers.

The 1927 NSW Family Endowment scheme

In 1919, the Holman Nationalist Government in NSW had proposed a Bill for child endowment of 5 shillings per child for adult male employees, funded by a contribution from employers. This was to be an alternative to a spectacular 28 per cent increase in the adult basic wage set by the wage fixing authority (Sawkins 1933). It involved redefining the basic wage unit as a couple, rather than a family of four (Commonwealth Bureau of Census and Statistics 1927). The proposal was also intended to protect NSW from increased costs that might force industries to close or move interstate (Evatt 1979). The Labor Party and unions saw the scheme as an attempt to 'filch' an expected basic wage increase. Employers in secondary and rural industries, on the other hand, were unconvinced that it would reduce their wage costs and uncompromisingly opposed the Bill. Conservatives also opposed it because it would undermine parental, especially paternal, responsibility to maintain children and thus also weaken work incentives (Cass 1983). The Bill scraped through the Assembly, but was blocked by the Legislative Council (Kewley 1973).

In 1927, child endowment was introduced in NSW by the Lang Labor Government, a year after Lang obtained office, funded by a payroll tax. The NSW Industrial Commission, chaired by Justice Piddington, had found that restoring the real value of the pre-war basic wage (£5/6/-) required a large increase in the basic wage. Commissioners ruled for a wage increase to £4/4/-, which would bring a man and wife with one child up to pre-war real basic wage levels. It strongly recommended the government introduce child endowment to protect the purchasing power of those with more than one child. It was expected that employers would benefit from lower wage costs, even if child endowment for the additional children was funded through introducing a payroll levy (NSW Industrial Commission 1926).

Women's organisations within the Labor Party were pressing for child endowment even before W.A. Holman's 1919 proposal (Cass 1983). They viewed child endowment as a prerequisite for women's equal pay, as well as an acknowledgement of women's economic contribution through non-market work and of the right of women and children to income separable from their husband/father's right to a living wage. Lang was lobbied to introduce such a measure immediately on attaining office in 1926 (Melville 1954).

The labour movement's conception of such a measure was that it should be financed through progressive taxation and paid for all children in a family, with an income ceiling high enough to make it available to most wage earners and as an addition to, not replacement for, the family component in the basic wage. Labour and social welfare groups were incensed when the *NSW Family Endowment Act 1927* only partially met the child component of the wage increase that had been foregone as a result of the 1926 Industrial Commission ruling (Cass 1983). The government's original Bill had proposed a 6 per cent payroll tax and a child endowment payment of 6 shillings. Incomes up to £364 per annum had been eligible. However, as passed, the Act provided only a 5 shilling per child payment and drastically limited eligibility to families on the basic wage or below, that is, on less than £221 per annum. Notably, the tax on payrolls was also to fund endowment for children of non-wage earners, such as 'farmers, dairymen, fruit-growers, self-employees, professional men and traders in a small way of business' (Charteris 1976). However, only around 28,000 of 712,000 children in 1927–28 would receive endowment.

Sustained pressure against the payroll tax by employers resulted in the levy being reduced to 3 per cent, and then suspended in 1927 (NSW Office of the Government Statistician 1933). It was further reduced to 1 per cent by January 1930 and from July 1932 revenues from the 'family allowance tax' were paid into consolidated revenue along with those from the unemployment relief tax (NSW Office of the Government Statistician 1933). From the end of 1933, child endowment in NSW was funded, along with unemployment relief and other social services, by special Depression taxes on wages (Bland 1976), and during World War II was part of the move to the Uniform Income Tax and National Welfare Fund.

The Commonwealth Royal Commission on Child Endowment

The Commonwealth Government appointed a Royal Commission on Child Endowment, tabling its report in March 1929 (Australia. Royal Commission on Child Endowment or Family Allowances 1929a). It arose from the failure to resolve state or federal financing of child endowment and problems created by overlapping wage arbitration.

The Hughes Government had not progressed Justice Piddington's 1920 proposal for child endowment (Australia. Royal Commission into the Basic Wage 1920) because of concerns about industry costs, but the Bruce–Page Government elected in 1923 viewed a national child endowment scheme as vital for its wages and industrial relations policies. Prime Minister Bruce committed to child endowment and wage arbitration reform during the 1925 election. However, he was unwilling to establish a national child endowment scheme while the states retained control over wage regulation. Bruce envisaged financing child endowment by a reduction in the basic wage, to follow from defining the wage unit as excluding children (Watts 1987). He opposed financing child endowment through general taxation, arguing that the necessary doubling of Commonwealth income tax would increase inflation and make mothers worse off (NSW Legislative Assembly 1927). The government's rural and business constituency was opposed to additional calls on general revenue. Bruce called a conference of state premiers in June 1927, but this failed to resolve the issue as Labor states were hostile to handing over wage arbitration to the Commonwealth

Government (Kewley 1973; Watts 1987). Premiers saw reducing state basic wages to fund a voluntary state scheme as politically unattractive, and believed the Commonwealth should pay for child endowment.[2]

The most vociferous critics of child endowment were the Retail Traders' Association of NSW, the Victorian Chamber of Manufactures, the Primary Producers/Pastoralists' Association of WA, the Employers' Federation of WA and the Victorian Taxpayers' Association (the last largely comprising commercial and professional interests). These objected to the proposal on both moral and economic grounds, fearing that raising the income of the family man would reduce his incentive to work or to better himself. They also argued that the financing of the scheme, whether from taxation or industry levies, would impose an unaffordable economic burden on industry and the national income. Primary producers joined urban industries and employers in opposing industry schemes financed by direct levies on payrolls, seeing these as increasing the cost of inputs to rural industry. Nevertheless, some industry groups, notably those employing married men on low wages and producing basic consumer goods, saw an economic advantage in child endowment, perceiving reduced wage costs and pressures. Rural industries and small business organisations sought to ensure the child endowment scheme was extended to include non-wage earners.

Overall, with only a remote potential reduction in wage costs, nearly all industry and employer groups favoured financing any scheme of child endowment from general taxation, not from a levy on industry or employers.

The Royal Commission explored the issue of child endowment with several economic experts, who differed on whether 'redistribution of wages' was essential, but favoured income taxation as the financing instrument, because of the inequity of payroll taxes in taxing only labour income, and because of the inflationary effects compared to income taxes. Increasing Commonwealth customs and excise revenues to finance child endowment was also criticised as self-defeating in its distributional effect because such indirect tax increases were regressive.

---

2   For more detail on the politics and discourse of the child endowment reform process, see Chapter 5 in Smith (2002).

Significantly, the beneficial effects of child endowment noted by the economic experts included increased future production capacity of labour from better care and nutrition in childhood. A leading conservative economist, Edward Shann, argued that 'the human capital of the country is as likely to respond to further investment as its fields and factories' (Australia. Royal Commission on Child Endowment or Family Allowances 1929b). Similarly, Gordon Wood gave evidence that spending would switch to essentials such as food, and as:

> the ordinary play of economic forces tends to limit investment in the persons and capacities of wage earners … the marginal returns to resources invested in the poor and their children would promise to be higher than the marginal return to resources invested in machinery and plant (Australia. Royal Commission on Child Endowment or Family Allowances 1929b, p. 106).

The Majority Report of the Royal Commission (Australia. Royal Commission on Child Endowment or Family Allowances 1929a) provided a comprehensive summary of the prevailing conservative arguments against child endowment. It argued that current wages provided adequately for children, and that public money would be used more beneficially in perfecting other social services. The Commissioners roundly condemned a national scheme of child endowment financed by an employer levy for the 'injurious result' it would have for industry (p. 9), and closed off the option of a scheme financed from general revenue by declaring the consequences from such an increase in taxation would be 'disastrous' (p. 9). A scheme that was additional to wages would boost 'extravagant' family spending and inflation (p. 100). The scheme was also eschewed for removing financial responsibility from parents and, thereby, their incentive to effort on behalf of their children (p. 71). The 'unity of interest' of parents was also threatened by paying endowment to mothers (p. 72), with the threat of increased numbers of deserting wives. Determining that a Commonwealth scheme was the only real option, the Majority Report then reported doubts about the Commonwealth's constitutional powers over endowment and wage fixing but concluded that industrial disputes would increase in number and intensity unless the Commonwealth controlled wage fixing as well as child endowment.

The Minority Report of John Curtin and Florence Muscio (Australia. Royal Commission on Child Endowment or Family Allowances 1929a) argued that a 'moderate' scheme financed from progressive taxation would be a good investment for the community. It noted that existing income tax deductions for dependant children recognised the value of the money and services expended in rearing and training children and were a form of family allowances. These, however, were only available to those whose income was high enough to attract Commonwealth income tax, which at that time excluded most wage earners. The Minority Report argued that the 'family wage' was 'a convenient fiction' regarding its adequacy for a family of five, and that wage fixing authorities were largely guided by market rates. They preferred income tax as the financing instrument, because it had recently been reduced and was less likely to be passed onto the cost of living than other proposed levies, including a luxuries tax or a poll tax. It would facilitate including non–wage earners and would, thereby, avoid creating incentives for preferring wage-work to self-employment. It would also redistribute income from those with the greatest capacity to pay tax to families in the greatest need, throughout the life cycle, and from those without dependant children to those with.

However, the Minority Commissioners rejected the transfer to the state of 'the whole financial responsibility for children', noting that 'the work of the father out of the home and of the mother within the home should pay the price of [their] enjoyment [of children]', but it was when 'the price exacted was too heavy and inflicted damage on the family' that child allowances should supplement that father's efforts. On this basis, child endowment was proposed only for families with more than the average number of two children. The basic wage was expected to meet the needs of the spouse and first child. The necessary revenue would be raised through lowering the Commonwealth income tax exemption for persons without dependants to £200 per annum, increasing tax on 'bachelors' who benefited from the 'excessive' basic wage—and by increasing the progressivity of tax rates on higher incomes. This was, as Watts points out, 'a prefiguration of the reality of the later welfare State' (Watts 1987).

The Bruce–Page Government accepted the Majority Report view that child endowment should not be separated from wage regulation. However, the states refused Bruce's request to relinquish their industrial powers to the Commonwealth to further such a scheme (NSW Legislative Assembly 1929); so, the Commonwealth Government would proceed no further with child endowment (Commonwealth Bureau of Census and Statistics 1929; Kewley 1973). By this time, Australian governments were increasingly preoccupied with the slide into depression. Action on national child endowment stalled until early in World War II.

Social insurance, the contributory principle and unwaged workers

In 1928, while considering the question of national endowment, the Bruce–Page Government had responded to the earlier Report of the Royal Commission on National Insurance (Australia. Royal Commission on National Insurance 1927) by tabling a Bill for a limited social insurance scheme to provide income support for the sick, disabled, widows and orphans (Kewley 1973). This Bill proposed financing a scheme of social insurance to be financed by an equal levy of 1 shilling per week on employees and employers for each male worker earning less than £416 per annum. The government would contribute only in the early years when the scheme was in deficit. The scheme was attacked on all fronts, including by friendly societies and insurance companies that feared the competition, and employers who were unwilling to accept responsibility for a share of the costs (Kewley 1969; Dickey 1980).

The debate on social insurance during the 1920s set the groundwork for taxation on a 'regressive, flat rate basis designed to ensure in practice that the poor paid for the needs of the poor' (Dickey 1980). During the Depression, Australian state governments had imposed various new flat or proportional levies on wages and income in order to provide unemployment relief and social services (Bland 1976). Between 1913 and 1939, several schemes for social insurance had been considered in detail in Australia, against the background of the spread of social insurance schemes overseas. The prospect of publicly funded social security appears to have been increasingly attractive to employers in the 1920s as such a scheme would relieve the wages system of the responsibility for family and other needs of employees at a time when the inherent conflict between 'needs' and 'capacity to pay' was becoming increasingly apparent.

By the late 1930s, the Labor Party had come to strongly oppose contributory insurance, its position represented by John Curtin seeing it as 'utterly unjust':

> The principle is bad from two aspects. One the one hand it imposes sectional taxation regardless of individual capacity to pay. On the other hand it confines eligibility for benefits to the insurance status of the contributors; and, as this status depends on contingencies which cannot be foreseen, either in point of time or in character the probability is that those most in need or equally deserving will not have rights assured them. They will have exhausted their ability to contribute and will be disqualified from the application of the scheme (Kewley 1969, p. 60).

In 1939, legislation for national social insurance had been passed and had received assent, but it was never implemented. Unlike previous proposals, it provided for a government contribution, making it into the 'tripartite' financing scheme common in Europe (Mouton 1984), the Treasury strongly objected to its cost (Watts 1987). The emerging international situation and political manoeuvring distracted political attention and disturbed the fragile political consensus that had been carrying the scheme forward. A fiscal debate triggered by Treasury's opposition renewed concerns from the Country Party and imposed severe strains on an already troubled Coalition Government. The scheme excluded unwaged workers caring for dependants, the self-employed and the unemployed. In June 1939, the Act was suspended and the scheme was abandoned (Watts 1987).

National child endowment and Commonwealth income taxation

The Uniform Income Tax Plan of 1942 finally laid the foundations for financing a system of 'contributory' social security in World War II, but without introducing contributory social insurance, which would have profoundly disrupted wage regulation. Ultimately, the contributory principle came to be applied in Australia through expanded income taxes on wage and salary earners.

A federal scheme of child endowment had been introduced by the Menzies–Fadden Government in 1941 amidst tense and complex negotiations to forestall a potentially inflationary increase in the basic wage. Its part-financing through payroll taxation was transitional. The Curtin Labor Government from late 1941 had a policy to fund child endowment through increased progressive taxation (Robertson 1974), because it was considered unfair that high-income taxpayers received a dependant child tax concession that was essentially a form of child endowment, but lower income earners received no such allowance. During 1942–44, Uniform Income Taxation extended taxation to low incomes (Australia. Committee on Uniform Taxation 1942), mainly reflecting the structure of the superseded state income taxes (Smith 2015). Mirroring states' income tax policies, the Commonwealth tax schedule introduced in 1942 included a dependant child rebate of £45 for the first child and £5 for each other child. A dependant spouse rebate had meanwhile been introduced as a response to economic conditions in 1936.

The lowered income tax threshold was made politically feasible by having child endowment in place and because uniform taxation permitted consistent heavier national taxation of higher incomes from 1942 (Mann 2015). Political acceptability of the income tax increase on lower wage earners was also increased by linking it to improvements in social services (Bailey 1980), including a new maternity benefit and widows pension, paid from a National Welfare Fund.

The Curtin Government sought to legitimise this approach by reference to the findings of the 1942 Report of the Joint Parliamentary Committee on Social Security, which had rejected social insurance and argued that 'the counterpart to the right of everyone in the community to protection against loss of income due to unemployment is the obligation of all the potential beneficiaries to contribute to the scheme' (Australia. Parliament Joint Parliamentary Committee on Social Security 1942). Because of the difficulties of covering non-employees under the conventional contributory arrangements, the committee had concluded that 'the simplest and most equitable plan in the present circumstances is to impose a general tax on every income earner in the community, with the exception of those on the lowest scale' (Australia. Parliament Joint Parliamentary Committee on Social Security 1942). It recommended a special social security tax on individuals or the earmarking of a portion of each individual's income tax for social security. In 1946, such informal earmarking of the higher wartime income taxes on low incomes and wage earners was formalised by the Menzies Government through introduction of a 'Social Security Contribution' to provide for the future funding of the National Welfare Fund (Kewley 1973; Butlin et al. 1982; Smith 2015).

An important reason for the resistance to social insurance in Australia was the failure of contributory schemes to address the needs of non–wage earners (including women providing child and household care). A similar debate took place in respect of the aged pension, leading to the abandonment of the 'contributory principle', in the early 1960s, in recognition of the fact that the extension of the income tax to lower income earners from the 1940s had made taxation 'a broadly contributory system'. In 1961, the Minister for Social Services admitted it was impractical to provide an equitable, secure and affordable contributory scheme for the aged pension. Study of contributory schemes in other parts of the world had shown that such a scheme could 'never be self-supporting':

There is no known way to free the Treasury—that is, the taxpayers of a country—from the responsibility of meeting the very substantial deficits which are inseparable from every publicly-controlled social security scheme. The inflationary pressures of modern society, no matter how they are restricted, sooner or later reduce the value of money: the demand for increased benefits and extended services appears to be insatiable; the rate of contribution can never be permanent or adequate to make the increasing commitment, and subventions from government sources approximate the proportions of a non-contributory scheme …

The end result is inevitably a stratum of social services. One at the private superannuation scheme level which, in various forms, is exclusive but rarely adequate; one at the public superannuation scheme level which has the same fault; one at the basic pension level with both pensions and contributions constantly under revision; one at the special assistance level which usually includes provision for rent, and one based on the poor law traditions of the old world or on public charity for the relief of extreme poverty (Commonwealth Parliamentary Debates, 5 September 1961, quoted in Kewley 1973, p. 103).

An 'incomplete revolution' or an invisible and shrinking care economy?

Today, Australia relies more heavily on income taxation than other OECD countries, in part because, as explained above, our social security system is not based on contributory social insurance. A key gender gap in Australia's welfare state—its formalised labour market discrimination against women—was partly addressed early in the 20th century by social security initiatives financed by expanding progressive taxes, including the aged pension and child endowment payments. These were specifically made available for women who were 'unpaid' and doing household economic production.

The redistributive role of the Commonwealth income tax changed substantially in the postwar decades as its revenue-raising role became predominant, rather than the progression of the tax scale (Smith 2001). Fiscal drag in the postwar years reduced progressivity. As in other countries (Grown and Valodia 2010), it is likely to have particularly affected women, as lower wage earners who were increasingly brought into higher income tax thresholds (Smith 2001). Base-broadening tax reforms in the 1980s aimed to replace income tax revenues with broad-based consumption taxation, purportedly to encompass the growth in the services sector, and improve work and savings incentives.

Indirect taxation (such as the goods and services tax, or GST) affects women and men differently, as discussed by Helen Hodgson and Kerrie Sadiq in Chapter 4 of this volume. The GST package of 2000 had important, though rarely discussed, implications for gender equality in the tax-transfer system and for financing social services (Smith 1998 (1992)). Experience with the earlier introduction of GST in New Zealand showed it was potentially a 'Trojan horse' for policy changes undermining gender equality (Smith 1998). On the other hand, GST exemptions such as for basic foods, child care services and medical care, increased excise taxation of commodities such as on tobacco and increased family payments as compensation for higher prices, helped limit the adverse impact of income tax cuts that shifted money from 'the purse to the pocket' (Smith 1999).

In the income tax base, there has been expanded use of concessions as an instrument of fiscal policy since the 1990s (Smith 2003). Income tax concessions were increasingly referred to as 'tax expenditures' from the 1980s, reflecting their comparable budgetary effects (Economic Planning Advisory Council 1986). The distributive consequences of tax concessions are often very regressive compared to direct spending programs (Surrey and McDaniel 1985). Tax expenditures tend to entrench the economic disadvantage and dependant status of women because they are commonly less accessible to women (Young 1999, 2000). The redistributive effects of these regressively distributive social policies are hidden from public view and reduce political transparency and accountability (Toder 1999, p. 5).

In particular, the major extension of superannuation tax concessions in Australia over the period 2003–09, along with rising compulsory superannuation levies on wage incomes, has significantly undermined gender equity in the fiscal system (Smith 2007). This is discussed further by Siobhan Austen and Rhonda Sharp in Chapter 10 of this volume. The growth of these tax expenditures has not only eroded income tax progressivity, but also contributed to ongoing fiscal 'crises' and cutbacks to public services and social security through weakening the revenue base (Smith 2004b, 2006). Ironically, the increased family payments introduced as compensation for the GST have been controversially treated as 'welfare' targeted for cutbacks, rather as a part of the benchmark tax system (Smith 2003). Meanwhile, women are now ineligible for the aged pension until aged 65 but generous superannuation is available to many men from 55 years. Labour market participation is increasingly an eligibility requirement for accessing pensions, but contribution to unpaid household work is not a condition of accessing superannuation. As a result, women are no longer available to provide child care to their young grandchildren, and the care economy shrinks further.

Tax-transfer policies since the 1990s have increasingly emphasised 'vertical equity' by tighter 'targeting' of outlays, involving expanded income tests and thresholds as well as freezing indexation or cutting payments. This produces higher effective marginal tax rates (EMTRs) on families supporting children and social security recipients, in particular on the second earner in the couple. Horizontal tax equity—focusing on comparable treatment of equals—has been given much lower priority.

What happened to Australia's social contract for care?

The history of child endowment during the postwar decades is briefly summarised below to illustrate a key aspect of how gender equality along with 'horizontal equity' has faded from the tax-transfer system (Table 6.1).

Table 6.1: 'Bird's-eye view' timeline of Australian wage-transfer tax system

Wages	Social security payments	Taxation
1908 first federal basic wage determination based on 1907 Harvester judgement	1909 aged pension for women with qualifying age of 60 years 1912 maternity allowance	1910 land tax 1915 income tax
1920 Royal Commission on the Basic Wage	1925 child endowment (NSW) 1927 Royal Commission on Child Endowment 1929 Royal Commission on Social Insurance	1925 payroll tax (NSW)
1932 basic wage cuts	State governments' unemployment relief and child endowment	1929–32 special wage and income taxes
1940 basic wage inquiry and 75% basic wage for women	1941 child endowment & 1942 widow's pension (Commonwealth) 1943 National Welfare Fund	1941 payroll tax (Commonwealth) 1942 Uniform Income Taxation including dependant child tax deductions 1945 Social Security Levy

Wages	Social security payments	Taxation
1966 basic wage and margins replaced by total wage and minimum wage for males 1972–75 minimum wage extended to adult females	1973 supporting mothers' benefit 1975 child endowment abolished 1976 family allowances replaced child endowment and dependant child tax rebates	1974 dependant child deductions replaced by tax rebate 1976 dependant child tax rebates abolished
	1983 means testing of family payments 1990 indexation of family payments 1994–95 dependant spouse rebate replaced 1997 family tax initiative	1985 Tax Summit and Women's Tax Summit
	1994 Women's eligibility for aged pension raised to 65 years	1992 Superannuation Guarantee Levy
1990 earnings indexation of family payments	1983 family income supplement (with payment to breadwinner then family allowance recipient, usually the mother, in 1984) 1987 family allowance supplement 1993 additional family payment	1985 Tax Summit, and Women's Tax Summit
	1994 home child care allowance 1995 parenting allowance 1998 parenting payment	1994 dependant spouse rebate abolished
	1997 family tax payment replaced additional family payment and basic family payment	1997 family tax initiative
1993–2009 Enterprise bargaining and Fair Work Act 2005 CPI indexation of family tax benefits 1993–2009	2000 family tax benefits replaced family allowances and family tax payment 2000 GST compensation package via family payments and income tax cuts	2000 A New Tax System (ANTS) including GST with a compensation package including increased family tax benefit and reduced personal income tax rates
	1994–2014 aged pension qualifying age increased to 65 years for women	1992 Superannuation Guarantee Charge 2002–03 superannuation tax concessions extended 2006–07 superannuation tax concessions extended

Wages	Social security payments	Taxation
	1998 child care assistance/ child care cash rebate 2000 child care benefit 2007 child care tax rebate converted to direct payment for 50% of out of pocket costs	2004 child care tax rebate for 30% of out of pocket costs replaced child care benefit
	2014 proposed budget measures on aged pension and family payments (means tests, eligibility, suspension of family tax benefit indexation)	2002–03 super tax concessions extended 2006–07 super tax concessions extended

Source: Author's research.

A decline in the real value of child endowment was the first crucial development in dismantling fiscal support for social reproduction and households' human capital formation. During the 1950s, child payments (measured as child endowment and tax allowances (at the top marginal tax rate of 67 per cent)) had been the equivalent of around 12 per cent of male average weekly earnings (Smith 1997). This declined drastically in the postwar decades. Most payment rates and coverage of the social welfare system were increased between 1941 and 1950, but child endowment remained unchanged until 1976, effectively halving its real value over time (Bray 2015). At the same time, income taxpayers were allowed a deduction for dependant children (Bray 2015). In 1974, reflecting the recommendation of the Asprey Taxation Review Committee (Asprey et al. 1975), dependant child rebates replaced deductions. As observed by Cass (1985, 1988b), tax deductions paid to fathers were, in effect, indexed for inflation over this time, but child endowment paid to mothers was not. The exclusion of the first child from child endowment until 1950 and the payment of lower rates for first children until 1989 implied that mother and child were maintained through a rising 'family wage', when in reality this increasingly required a second earner.

In 1976, dependant child tax deductions were merged with child endowment and restructured to form a universal family allowance. A tax rebate for sole parents was also introduced, acknowledging the economic significance of unpaid care work within families. Though initially seen as a sensible social reform reflecting feminist influences and supporting women's individual social rights (Edwards 1980), the value of the family allowance diminished as gender equity measure because, again, family allowance payments were not indexed for inflation. The non-indexation of tax rebates for families with children was a further factor reducing the disposable income of taxpayers supporting dependant children compared to single taxpayers (Cass 1988a). Unsurprisingly, child/family poverty became a significant issue within a decade.

Family payments were indexed from 1990, a move described as 'historic justice' for women (Cass and Brennan 2003). However, from the mid-1980s, means testing of social security payments was extended due to restrictive expenditure policies associated with a 'trilogy' of fiscal policy commitments adopted in response to current account deficits, population ageing and rising public health care costs (Gruen and Sayegh 2005). New payments were introduced targeted at low-income families and focused on poverty alleviation, and not on maintaining horizontal equity between those supporting children and those who were not (Mitchell et al. 1994). Although Australia's targeted child payments were comparable with other OECD countries in generosity, by the 1990s many fewer families were eligible as maximum payment levels were reached at a much lower income (Cass 1986; Harding and Social Security Review (Australia) 1986). This treatment of horizontal equity measures as 'welfare', needing targeting and wasteful has increasingly underpinned a shifting of the costs of children back onto families and particularly women.

The net result was that over the period 1964 to 1994, the situation of families earning less than average weekly earnings had improved compared to a single person without children, but families with incomes above average weekly earnings paid relatively more than they had in 1964 compared to childless taxpayers (Beer 1995). In effect, the transition away from the 'family wage' and unequal pay for women was paid for by increasing the net tax burden on parents with children, rather than on single taxpayers (Moore and Whiteford 1986).

The declining value of child endowment and family assistance has directly reduced women's incomes. Since its inception, child endowment was paid directly to primary carers, and was an important and highly valued income source to women (Edwards 1982). Alongside the reduced access and lower value of family payments, since the 1990s these payments have been increasingly incorporated into the tax system as 'family tax benefits', so that payments for children are not necessarily made directly to the carer. As Cass wrote in 1985:

> the undervaluation of women's caring work and physical labour in the household and the enduring tendency to regard these as non-work [allowed] the indexation of transfers for child support to remain a non-issue and policymakers to speak of community and family care as if women's work involved no costs (Cass 1985, p. 931).

Rather than defamilise the costs of children to reduce and redistribute the burden on women, there has been a coercive policy shift to 'recommodification', whereby women's workforce participation is a condition of eligibility for receipt of social security benefits (Cass and Brennan 2003). At the same time, the family tax benefit system increased EMTRs and considerably reduced financial returns to mothers participating in employment (Lambert et al. 1996). Such disincentive effects are particularly strong for those with infants and young children meeting high child care costs out of their earnings. Establishment of a quality regulated, subsidised child care system has been an important advance since the 1980s, but a comprehensive infrastructure to support dual responsibilities as carers and paid workers remains elusive.

There have been significant increases in female labour force participation over the past century and especially since the 1990s. However, as shown by Kalb in Chapter 5 of this volume, there has been much less growth in participation by mothers of infants and young children (Baxter 2013b). For example, in 2011, among all couple mothers with children aged less than 18 years, 38 per cent were in part-time employment while only 25 per cent were employed full-time. It appears that many Australian families prefer parental care for infants, with virtually no change in the use of non-parental child care between 1984 and 2011 for children below one year (Baxter 2013a).

A legacy of Australia's family wage–based approach to social protection is that other social institutions such as maternity leave and protection have been slow to develop (Smith 2007; McDonald 2013). Current policy focused on reducing the 'gender gap' in employment participation, rather than on gender inequalities in wages or inadequacies in employment entitlements such as maternity protection, has yet to address the way in which women's unequal care burden affects their equitable treatment in the labour market. Maternity leave paid for 14 weeks became available to working women in Australia only in 2011. This resulted improved maternal and child health including through longer breastfeeding duration and reduced maternal depression (Martin et al. 2014; Broadway et al. 2015). In contrast, in Norway, entitlement to paid parental or maternity leave up to around 12 months has supported stronger maternal labour force attachment and workforce participation, and near-universal breastfeeding of infants up to six months old (Helsing 2006).

Tax concessions and transfer payments are functionally equivalent, yet transfer payments such as family allowances paid primarily to women for the expenses of children have been regularly denigrated as middle-class welfare and creating dependency on welfare. Tax deductions, rebates and income splitting—which provide comparable or greater benefits to high-income or wealthy male taxpayers—are commonly characterised as 'tax equity measures'. A similar moral rhetoric surrounds access to the public aged pension, disproportionately by women, yet disregards the enormous fiscal burden and gender inequality of tax concessions for private superannuation based on a model rewarding market work over care work.

The invisibility of non-market household production also blinds policymakers to the economic necessity for policies that enable women's participation on equal terms with men in the labour market if we are to avoid continued low fertility and population ageing and ensure Australia participates in the global economy on the basis of its high quality of human capital and labour force productivity.

Conclusion

Australian governments remain content for society to 'free ride' on women's household and care work, and to its important contribution to human capital formation and productivity (Folbre 1994a, 1994b). Australia's 'wage earners' welfare state' institutionalised the 'male breadwinner model' in the social protection system from the start of the federation. However, early in the 20th century, important initiatives acknowledged women's vulnerabilities arising from their allocated role in the unpaid care economy. The gender analysis in this chapter, of how this system evolved, through a historical case study of child endowment, provides new insights into the causes, consequences and sustainability of tax and transfer policies since the 1980s. Tax policy reform since the 1980s has centred on reducing progressive income taxation, increasing indirect taxation, and curtailing the fiscal cost of Australia's tax-financed social security system. Although the tax-transfer system may seem neutral, taxes on income, consumption and wealth affect women and men differently, because of gender inequalities in wages, earnings, poverty and ownership of property and wealth, and differences in how men and women spend their money and their time (Grown and Valodia 2010).

Reflecting on Wickens' (1924) calculations on the value of Australia's human capital, it might be argued that social and economic institutions such as our tax-transfer system have made little progress in addressing the question of 'who pays for the kids?' (Folbre 1994b). Strong disincentives for unpaid care work in our system have been central to problems of falling birth rates in many countries since the 1990s (McDonald 2013) and contribute to the emerging 'crisis of care' for the sick, the elderly and children in the past decade (Fraser 2016). As the fiscal system has been weakened by unaffordable reductions in income taxation, a purported budget crisis has been used to justify tighter household means testing, reduced eligibility and weaker indexation of social security benefits, including family payments and aged pensions. Such fiscal strategies are both inequitable and economically inefficient because they create financial barriers and disincentives to women's employment participation and retirement saving. Australia seeks to position itself to compete in the global 'knowledge economy' and relies on the spectre of a rapidly ageing population and fiscal crisis to justify policies promoting 'participation, population and productivity'. Yet government policies have increased the financial and time penalties and undermined the rewards for child rearing (Smith 2007), and still fail to support full investment in children as the country's most valuable capital assets (Wei 2001).

Until the Hawke–Keating era, a universal family allowance paid directly to mothers represented an acknowledgement (albeit small and shrinking) of women's disproportionate contribution to the invisible care economy, but also of the social productivity of household time investments in children—human capital. Likewise, the widely available aged pension acknowledged that the cost of such investments fell particularly on women, by reducing their lifetime labour market earnings and limiting their capacity to save for the loss of the 'breadwinner' or for financial security in retirement. Aged pensions, child endowment and later widow's and sole parent's pensions had been financed by progressive taxation rather than contributory social insurance, because the unfairness and impracticality of excluding unwaged citizen workers from the social protection regime was recognised. Importantly, however, it was also because financing such measures from progressive taxation protected the competitiveness of Australian industry.

Feminist scholars have questioned whether contemporary welfare regimes reflect an 'incomplete revolution' in relation to women's roles, and whether social investment strategies focused on early childhood detract from gender egalitarian strategies. This chapter argues that changes in Australia's tax-transfer system during the dying decades of the Australian 'wage earners' welfare state' raise concerns about both aspects. Overall, Australia's tax-transfer system has 'refamilized' rather than 'defamilized' the costs of children during the transition from the 'wage earners' welfare state'. By neglecting consideration of the important 'unpaid care economy' to human capital formation during the first years of children's life, tax-transfer and labour market policies risk refertilising the seeds of the 'motherhood pay gap' (Grimshaw and Rubery 2015), while potentially undermining household investments in the care economy and future economic productivity.

Strengthening Australia's progressive income tax system including through curbing tax expenditures such as on private superannuation and investor housing, and tax relief for high-income earners, remains essential to funding the social services and benefit programs necessary for more equal female labour force participation, without sacrificing economically important household investments in human capital. Reducing the role of progressive income taxation, and winding back social protections directed at resourcing the care economy, such as child endowment/family allowances and the public aged pension, reinforces rather than redresses gender inequality, and undermines rather than promotes national economic, health and child development strategies directed at enhancing the productivity of Australia's human capital.

References

Abraham, Katherine G. and Christopher Mackie (eds). 2005. *Beyond the Market: Designing Nonmarket Accounts for the United States*. Washington, DC: National Research Council.

ABS (Australian Bureau of Statistics). 2014. *Spotlight on the national accounts: unpaid work and the Australian economy*. Available at: www.abs.gov.au/ausstats/abs@.nsf/mf/5202.0?OpenDocument

AIHW (Australian Institute of Health and Welfare). 2011. *2010 Australian National Infant Feeding Survey: Indicator results*. Canberra: AIHW.

Alderman, Harold, Jere R. Behrman and John Hoddinott. 2005. 'Nutrition, malnutrition and economic growth'. In Guillem López-Casasnovas, Berta Rivera and Luis Currais (eds), *Health and economic growth: Findings and policy implications*, pp. 169–194. Cambridge: MIT Press.

Amir, Lisa H. and Susan M. Donath. 2008. 'Socioeconomic status and rates of breastfeeding in Australia: evidence from three recent national health surveys'. *The Medical Journal of Australia* 189(5): 254–256.

Asprey, Ken (Chair). 1975. *Full Report 31 January 1975*. Taxation Review Committee (the 'Asprey Committee'). Canberra: Australian Government Publishing Service.

Australia. Committee on Uniform Taxation. 1942. *Report of the Committee on Uniform Taxation*. Committee chaired by Richard Charles Mills. Canberra: Government Printer.

Australia. Parliament Joint Parliamentary Committee on Social Security. 1942. *Second Interim Report from the Joint Parliamentary Committee on Social Security, dated 6th March 1942*. Canberra: Commonwealth Government Printer.

Australia. Royal Commission into the Basic Wage. 1920. *Royal Commission on the Basic Wage*. Committee chaired by A.B. Piddington. Canberra: Commonwealth Government Printer.

Australia. Royal Commission on Child Endowment or Family Allowances. 1929a. *Report of the Royal Commission on Child Endowment or Family Allowances*. Commission chaired by T.S. O'Halloran. Canberra: Government Printer.

Australia. Royal Commission on Child Endowment or Family Allowances. 1929b. *Minutes of Evidence: Royal Commission on Child Endowment or Family Allowances*. Canberra: Government Printer.

Australia. Royal Commission on National Insurance. 1927. *Fourth and Final Report of the Royal Commission on National Insurance: Membership, Finance and Administration*. Commission chaired by J.D. Millen. Melbourne: Government Printer.

Bailey, Kenneth Hamilton. 1980 (1944). 'The Uniform Income Tax Plan (1942)'. In Wilfred Prest and Russell Lloyd Mathews (eds), *The Development of Australian Fiscal Federalism: Selected Readings,* pp. 309–327. Canberra: Australian National University Press.

Baker, Phillip and Sharon Friel. 2014. 'Processed foods and the nutrition transition: evidence from Asia'. *Obesity Reviews* 15(7): 564–577. doi.org/10.1111/obr.12174

Baker, Phillip, Julie Smith, Libby Salmon, Sharon Friel, George Kent, Alessandro Iellamo, J.P. Dadhich and Mary J. Renfrew. 2016. 'Global trends and patterns of commercial milk-based formula sales: is an unprecedented infant and young child feeding transition underway?' *Public Health Nutrition* 19(14): 1–11. doi.org/10.1017/S1368980016001117

Bartick, Melissa and Arnold Reinhold. 2010. 'The burden of suboptimal breastfeeding in the United States: a pediatric cost analysis'. *Pediatrics* 125(5): e1048–e1056. doi.org/10.1542/peds.2009-1616

Bartick, Melissa, Alison M. Stuebe, Eleanor Bimla Schwarz, Christine Luongo, Arnold G. Reinhold and E. Michael Foster. 2013. 'Cost analysis of maternal disease associated with suboptimal breastfeeding'. *Obstetrics & Gynecology* 122(1): 111–119. doi.org/10.1097/AOG.0b013e318297a047

Baxter, Jennifer. 2013a. *Child care participation and maternal employment trends in Australia.* Melbourne: Australian Institute of Family Studies.

Baxter, Jennifer. 2013b. 'Parents working out work'. Australian Family Trends No. 1. Melbourne: Australian Institute of Family Studies.

Beer, Gillian. 1995. *Impact of Changes in the Personal Income Tax and Family Payment Systems on Australian Families: 1964 to 1994.* Discussion Paper No. 8. Canberra: National Centre for Social and Economic Modelling.

Bland, Francis Armand. 1976 (1934). 'Unemployment relief in Australia'. In Jill Roe (ed.), *Social Policy in Australia: some perspectives 1901–1975,* pp. 165–191. Melbourne: Griffin Press.

Bray, J. Rob. 2015. '100 years of the minimum wage and the Australian tax and transfer system: what has happened, what have we learnt and what are the challenges?' *Australian Tax Forum* 30(4): 819–844.

Broadway, Barbara, Guyonne Kalb, Daniel Kuehnle and Miriam Maeder. 2015. *The Effect of Paid Parental Leave on Child Health in Australia.* Melbourne Institute Working Paper Series No. 9/15. Melbourne: Melbourne Institute of Applied Economic and Social Research.

Budig, Michelle J., Joya Misra and Irene Boeckmann. 2016. 'Work–Family Policy Trade-Offs for Mothers? Unpacking the Cross-National Variation in Motherhood Earnings Penalties'. *Work and Occupations* 43(2): 119–177. doi.org/10.1177/0730888415615385

Butlin, Noel George, Alan Barnard and Jonathan James Pincus. 1982. *Government and Capitalism: Public and Private Choice in Australia.* Sydney: Allen & Unwin.

Cass, Bettina. 1983. 'Redistribution to children and mothers; a history of child endowment and family allowances'. In Cora Baldock and Bettina Cass (eds), *Women, Social Welfare and the State in Australia*, pp. 54–84. Sydney: Allen & Unwin.

Cass, Bettina. 1985. 'Rewards for women's work.' In Jacqueline Goodnow and Carole Pateman (eds), *Women, Social Science and Public Policy*, pp. 67–94. Sydney: Allen & Unwin.

Cass, Bettina. 1986. *Income support for families with children.* Social Security Review Issues Paper No. 1. Canberra: Australian Government Printing Service.

Cass, Bettina. 1988a. 'The feminisation of poverty'. In Barbara Caine, Elizabeth A. Grosz and Marie M. De Lepervanche (eds), *Crossing Boundaries*, pp. 110–128. Sydney: Allen & Unwin.

Cass, Bettina. 1988b. 'Women, welfare and the redistribution of income: the case of child endowment and family allowances'. In Cora V. Baldock and Bettina Cass (eds), *Women, Social Welfare and the State in Australia*, pp. xx, 330. Sydney: Allen & Unwin.

Cass, Bettina and Deborah Brennan. 2003. 'Taxing women: The politics of gender in the tax/transfer system'. *eJournal of Tax Research* 1(1): 37–64.

Castles, Francis G. 1985. *The working class and welfare: reflections on the political development of the welfare state in Australia and New Zealand, 1890–1980*. Taylor & Francis.

Castles, Francis. 2001. 'A farewell to the wage earner state'. *Eureka Street* 11(1): 29–31.

Charteris, A.H. 1976. 'Family endowment in NSW'. In Jill Roe (ed.), *Social Policy in Australia: Some Perspectives 1901–1975*, pp. 94–112. Sydney: Cassel.

Collas-Monsod, Solita. 2011. 'Removing the Cloak of Invisibility: Integrating Unpaid Household Services in the Philippines' Economic Accounts'. In Diane Elson (ed.), *Harvesting Feminist Knowledge for Public Policy: Rebuilding Progress*, p. 93. New Delhi: SAGE India.

Commonwealth Bureau of Census and Statistics. 1927. *Labour Report, 1926*. Melbourne: Government Printer.

Commonwealth Bureau of Census and Statistics. 1929. *Labour Report, 1928*. Melbourne: Government Printer.

Cook, Sarah and Xiao-Yuan Dong. 2011. 'Harsh Choices: Chinese Women's Paid Work and Unpaid Care Responsibilities under Economic Reform'. *Development and Change* 42(4): 947–966. doi.org/10.1111/j.1467-7660.2011.01721.x

Craig, Lyn and Abigail Powell. 2013. 'Non-parental child care, time pressure and the gendered division of paid work, domestic work and parental child care'. *Community, Work & Family* 16(1): 100–119. dx.doi.org/10.1080/13668803.2012.722013

Dickey, Brian. 1980. *No Charity There: A Short History of Social Welfare in Australia*. Melbourne: Nelson.

Donath, Susan. 2000. 'The other economy: A suggestion for a distinctively feminist economics'. *Feminist Economics* 6(1): 115–123. doi.org/10.1080/135457000337723

Dong, Xiao-yuan and Xinli An. 2015. 'Gender Patterns and Value of Unpaid Care Work: Findings From China's First Large-Scale Time Use Survey'. *Review of Income and Wealth* 61(3): 540–560. doi.org/10.1111/roiw.12119

Economic Planning Advisory Council. 1986. *Tax expenditures in Australia*. Council Paper No. 13.

Edwards, Meredith. 1980. 'Financial Support for Parenthood'. *Australian Journal of Early Childhood* 5(1): 36–38.

Edwards, Meredith. 1982. 'Financial arrangements made by husbands and wives: Findings of a survey'. *Journal of Sociology* 18(3): 320–338. doi.org/10.1177/144078338201800303

Elson, Diane. 2008. *The three R's of unpaid work: Recognition, reduction and redistribution*. Paper presented at the Expert Group Meeting on Unpaid work, Economic Development and Human Well-Being, New York, United Nations Development Program (UNDP), New York.

England, Paula. 2005. 'Emerging theories of care work'. *Annual Review of Sociology* 31: 381–399. doi.org/10.1146/annurev. soc.31.041304.122317

Engle, Patrice L., Purnima Menon and Lawrence Haddad. 1999. 'Care and nutrition: concepts and measurement'. *World Development* 27(8): 1309–1337. doi.org/10.1016/S0305-750X(99)00059-5

Esping-Andersen, Gøsta. 1990. *The Three Worlds of Welfare Capitalism*. Cambridge: Polity Press.

Esping-Andersen, Gøsta. 1999. *Social foundations of postindustrial economies*. New York: Oxford University Press. doi. org/10.1093/0198742002.001.0001

Esping-Andersen, Gøsta. 2005. *Children in the welfare state: A social investment approach*. DemoSec Working Paper 2005-10. Barcelona: Department of Political & Social Sciences, Universitat Pompeu Fabra.

Esping-Andersen, Gøsta. 2008. 'Childhood investments and skill formation'. *International Tax and Public Finance* 15(1): 19–44. doi. org/10.1007/s10797-007-9033-0

Esping-Andersen, Gøsta. 2009. *Incomplete revolution: Adapting welfare states to women's new roles*. Cambridge: Polity Press.

Esping-Andersen, Gøsta. 2011. 'The Importance of Children and Families in Welfare States'. In Gils Beets, Joop Schippers and Egbert R. te Velde (eds), *The Future of Motherhood in Western Societies: Late Fertility and its Consequences*, pp. 125–148. Dordrecht: Springer Netherlands. doi. org/10.1007/978-90-481-8969-4_9

Esping-Andersen, Gøsta and Francesco C. Billari. 2015. 'Re-theorizing Family Demographics'. *Population and Development Review* 41(1): 1–31. doi.org/10.1111/j.1728-4457.2015.00024.x.

Evatt, Herbert Vere. 1979. *William Holman: Australian Labour Leader*. Sydney: Angus & Robertson.

Folbre, Nancy. 1994a. 'Children as Public Goods'. *American Economic Review* 84(2): 86–90.

Folbre, Nancy. 1994b. *Who pays for the kids? Gender and the structures of constraint*. New York: Routledge. doi.org/10.4324/9780203168295

Folbre, Nancy. 2001. *The invisible heart: Economics and family values*. New York: The New Press.

Folbre, Nancy. 2002. 'The Revolt of the Magic Pudding; How to reshape a labour market that simply doesn't care'. *Australian Financial Review*, 5 April, pp. 4–5.

Folbre, Nancy. 2006. 'Measuring Care: Gender, Empowerment, and the Care Economy'. *Journal of Human Development* 7(2): 183–199. doi. org/10.1080/14649880600768512

Fraser, Nancy. 1994. 'After the Family Wage: What Do Women Want in Social Welfare?' *Social Justice* 21(1): 80–86.

Fraser, Nancy. 2016. 'Contradictions of Capital and Care'. *New Left Review* 100, July–August 2016.

Gornick, Janet C. and Marcia K. Meyers. 2003. *Families that Work: Policies for Reconciling Parenthood and Employment*. New York: Russell Sage.

Greenwood, Jeremy, Ananth Seshadri and Mehmet Yorukoglu. 2005. 'Engines of liberation'. *The Review of Economic Studies* 72(1): 109–133. doi.org/10.1111/0034-6527.00326

Grimshaw, Damian and Jill Rubery. 2015. *The motherhood pay gap: A review of the issues, theory and international evidence*. Conditions of Work and Employment Series No. 57. Geneva: International Labour Office.

Grown, Caren and Imraan Valodia. 2010. *Taxation and Gender Equity: A comparative analysis of direct and indirect taxes in developing and developed countries*. Routledge IDRC.

Gruen, David and Amanda Sayegh. 2005. *The evolution of fiscal policy in Australia*. Treasury Working Paper. Canberra: The Treasury.

Grummer-Strawn, Laurence M. and Nigel Rollins. 2015. 'Summarising the health effects of breastfeeding'. *Acta Paediatr* 104(467): 1–2. doi. org/10.1111/apa.13136

Gustafsson, Björn and Shi Li. 2000. 'Economic transformation and the gender earnings gap in urban China'. *Journal of Population Economics* 13(2): 305–329. doi.org/10.1007/s001480050140

Hafstead, Marc and Randall Lutter. 2016. *What Is the Economic Value of Improved Labor Market Outcomes from Infant Nutrition?* Resources for the Future Discussion Paper 16-29. Washington DC: Resources for the Future.

Haider, Steven J., Alison Jacknowitz and Robert F. Schoeni. 2003. 'Welfare Work Requirements and Child Well-Being: Evidence from the Effects on Breast-Feeding'. *Demography* 40(3): 479–497. doi. org/10.1353/dem.2003.0023

Hakim, Catherine. 2000. *Work-lifestyle choices in the 21st century: Preference theory*. Oxford: Oxford University Press.

Harding, A. and Social Security Review (Australia). 1986. *Assistance for families with children and the social security review*. Social Security Review. Woden, ACT: Department of Social Security.

Harrison, Linda J., Judy A. Ungerer, Grant J. Smith, Stephen R. Zubrick and Sarah Wise, with Frances Press, Manjula Waniganayake and The LSAC Research Consortium. 2009. *Child care and early education in Australia: The Longitudinal Study of Australian Children.* Department of Families, Housing, Community Services and Indigenous Affairs Social Policy Research Paper No. 40. Canberra: Department of Families, Housing, Community Services and Indigenous Affairs. dx.doi.org/10.2139/ssrn.1703234

Heckman, James J. and Dimitriy V. Masterov. 2007. *The Productivity Argument for Investing in Young Children.* Cambridge (USA): National Bureau of Economic Research. doi.org/10.3386/w13016

Helsing, E. 2006. 'Breastfeeding: baby's right and mother's duty?' In Wenche Barth Eide and Uwe Kracht (eds), *Food and Human Rights in Development,* pp. 323–355. Antwerp: Intersentia.

Himmelweit, Susan. 1995. 'The Discovery of "Unpaid Work": The Social Consequences of the Expansion of "Work"'. *Feminist Economics* 1(2): 1–19. doi.org/10.1080/714042229

Himmelweit, Susan. 2002. 'Making Visible the Hidden Economy: The Case for Gender-Impact Analysis of Economic Policy'. *Feminist Economics* 8(1): 49–70. doi.org/10.1080/13545700110104864

Hou, Arnold. 2014. 'Rate of exclusive breastfeeding declining in China'. *All-China Women's. Federation.* Available at: www.womenofchina.cn/womenofchina/html1/survey/17/3045-1.htm

Jelly, Fran. 1977. 'Child Endowment'. In Heather Radi and Peter Spearrit (eds), *Jack Lang.* Sydney: Hale & Iremonger.

Jenson, Jane. 2009. 'Lost in translation: The social investment perspective and gender equality'. *Social Politics: International Studies in Gender, State & Society* 16(4): 446–483. doi.org/10.1093/sp/jxp019

Kewley, Thomas Henry. 1969. *Australia's Welfare State.* Melbourne: Macmillan.

Kewley, Thomas Henry. 1973. *Social Security in Australia 1900–72.* Sydney: Sydney University Press.

Lake, Marilyn. 2012. 'State Socialism for Australian Mothers: Andrew Fisher's Radical Maternalism in its International and Local Contexts'. *Labour History* (102): 55–70. doi.org/10.5263/labourhistory.102.0055

Lambert, Simon, Gillian Beer and Julie Smith. 1996. *Taxing the individual or the couple: a distributional analysis.* NATSEM Discussion paper, No. 15. Canberra, ACT: University of Canberra.

Land, H. 1975. 'The introduction of family allowances: An act of historic justice?' In Phoebe Hall, Hilary Land, Roy Parker and Adrian Webb (eds), *Change, Choice and Conflict in Social Policy*, pp. 157–230. London: Heinemann.

Li, Haisheng, Qinyi Liu, Bo Li, Barbera Fraumeni and Xiaobei Zhang. 2014. 'Human capital estimates in China: New panel data 1985–2010'. *China Economic Review* 30: 397–418. doi.org/10.1016/j.chieco.2014.07.006

Lohmann, Henning and Hannah Zagel. 2016. 'Family policy in comparative perspective: The concepts and measurement of familization and defamilization'. *Journal of European Social Policy* 26(1): 48–65. doi.org/10.1177/0958928715621712

Lutter, Chessa K. and Randall Lutter. 2012. 'Fetal and early childhood undernutrition, mortality, and lifelong health'. *Science* 337(6101): 1495–1499. doi.org/10.1126/science.1224616

Mann, Evan. 2015. 'Resourcing War While Containing Inflation: Debate among Australia's Second World War Economists'. *Australian Economic History Review* 55(1): 20–41. doi.org/10.1111/aehr.12056

Martin, Bill, Marian Baird, Michelle Brady, Barbara Broadway, Belinda Hewitt, Guyonne Kalb, Lyndall Strazdins, Wojtek Tomaszewski, Maria Zadoroznyj, Janeen Baxter, Rachel Cehn, Meraiah Foley, Duncan McVicar, Gillian Whitehouse and Ning Ziang. 2014. *Paid Parental Leave Evaluation. Final Report.* Prepared for Australian Government Department of Social Services. Brisbane: University of Queensland Institute for Social Science Research.

McDonald, Peter. 2000. 'Gender equity, social institutions and the future of fertility'. *Journal of the Australian Population Association* 17(1): 1–16. doi.org/10.1007/BF03029445

McDonald, Peter. 2013. 'Societal foundations for explaining fertility: Gender equity'. *Demographic Research* 28: 981–994. doi.org/10.4054/DemRes.2013.28.34

Melville, G. 1954. *Fifty years of the LWCOC*. Golden jubilee souvenir of the Labor Women's Central Organising Committee 1904–54, Sydney.

Miranda, Veerle. 2011. *Cooking, caring and volunteering: Unpaid work around the world*. OECD Social, Employment and Migration Working Papers No. 116. Paris: OECD Publishing. doi.org/10.1787/5kghrjm8s142-en

Mitchell, Deborah, Ann Harding and Fred Gruen. 1994. 'Targeting welfare'. *Economic Record* 70: 292–340.

Moore, Jim and Peter Whiteford. 1986. *Trends in the Disposable Incomes of Australian Families, 1964/65 to 1985/86*. Research Paper No. 31. Canberra: Department of Social Security, Policy Review and Co-ordination Branch, Development Division.

Mouton, Pierre. 1984. 'Methods of financing social security in industrial countries: an international analysis'. In *Financial Social Security: The Options*, pp. 3–32. International Labour Office. Geneva: International Labour Organization.

NSW (New South Wales) Industrial Commission. 1926. *Interim Report and minutes of evidence*. Sydney: Industrial Commission.

NSW Legislative Assembly. 1927. *Report of Proceedings: Conference between the Commonwealth and State Ministers, Melbourne and Sydney, June–July 1927*. Sydney: Government Printer.

NSW Legislative Assembly. 1929. *Report of the Resolutions, Decisions and Proceedings of the Premiers' Conference*. Sydney, May.

NSW Office of the Government Statistician. 1933. *Official Year Book of New South Wales, 1931–32*. Sydney: Authority of the Government of New South Wales.

O'Connor, Julia S. 1993. 'Gender, Class and Citizenship in the Comparative Analysis of Welfare State Regimes: Theoretical and Methodological Issues'. *The British Journal of Sociology* 44(3): 501–518. doi.org/10.2307/591814

O'Connor, Julia S. 2013. 'Gender, citizenship and welfare state regimes in the early twenty-first century: "incomplete revolution" and/or gender equality "lost in translation"'. In Patricia Kennett (ed.), *A Handbook of Comparative Social Policy*, pp. 137–161. Cheltenham, UK: Edward Elgar. doi.org/10.4337/9781782546535.00017

Orloff, Ann. 1996. 'Gender in the welfare state'. *Annual review of sociology*, Vol. 22: 51–78. doi.org/10.1146/annurev.soc.22.1.51

Orloff, Ann Shola 1993. 'Gender and the social rights of citizenship: The comparative analysis of gender relations and welfare states'. *American Sociological Review*, 58(3): 303–328. doi.org/10.2307/2095903

Pocock, Barbara. 2006. *The labour market ate my babies: Work, children and a sustainable future*. Australia: Federation Press.

Pokhrel, Subhash, Maria A. Quigley, Julia Fox-Rushby, Felicia McCormick, A. Williams, Paul Trueman, R. Dodds and Mary Josephine Renfrew. 2014, 'Potential economic impacts from improving breastfeeding rates in the UK'. *Archives of Disease in Childhood*, 100(4): 334–340. doi.org/10.1136/archdischild-2014-306701

Popkin, Barry M. 2008. 'Will China's Nutrition Transition Overwhelm Its Health Care System And Slow Economic Growth?' *Health Affairs* 27(4): 1064–1076. doi.org/10.1377/hlthaff.27.4.1064

Robertson, John R. 1974. *J.H. Scullin, A Political Biography*. Nedlands, WA: University of Western Australia Press.

Rollins, Nigel C., Nita Bhandari, Nemat Hajeebhoy, Susan Horton, Chessa K. Lutter, Jose C. Martines, Ellen G. Piwoz, Linda M. Richter, and Cesar G. Victora. 2016. 'Why invest, and what will it take to improve breastfeeding practices?' *The Lancet* 387(10017): 491–504. doi.org/10.1016/S0140-6736(15)01044-

Ruhm, Christopher J. 2004. 'Parental Employment and Child Cognitive Development'. *Journal of Human Resources* 39(1): 155–192. doi.org/10.2307/3559009

Sawer, Marian. 2012. 'Andrew Fisher and the era of liberal reform'. *Labour History: A Journal of Labour and Social History* 102: 71–86.

Sawer, Marian. 2015. 'Does equality have a future? Feminism and social democracy in the era of neoliberalism.' In Anna Yeatman (ed.), *Feminism, Social Liberalism and Social Democracy in the Neo-Liberal Era*. Working Papers in the Human Rights and Public Life Program 1, pp. 24–35. Sydney: Whitlam Institute.

Sawkins, Dansie T. 1933. *The Living Wage in Australia*. Melbourne: Melbourne University Press.

Smith, Julie P. 1982. 'The value of household work in Australian national product'. Department of Economic History, The Australian National University. (Published in *Treasury Seminar Series, June 1987*. Australian Treasury: Canberra.)

Smith, Julie P. 1997. *Taxation reform and families with children*. Northcote, Victoria: Community Child Care Association.

Smith, Julie P. 1998 (1992). *Tax Reform, the GST and Women*. Australia Institute Background Paper 11. Canberra: Australia Institute.

Smith, Julie P. 1999. *Is the only good tax an old tax? An historical perspective on the GST debate*. Centre for Economic Policy Research Discussion Paper 398.

Smith, Julie P. 2001. 'Progressivity of the Commonwealth personal income tax, 1917–1997'. *Australian Economic Review* 34(3): 263–278. doi.org/10.1111/1467-8462.00195

Smith, Julie P. 2002. 'The changing redistributional role of taxation in Australia since Federation'. Economics Program, Research School of Social Sciences. Canberra, The Australian National University.

Smith, Julie P. 2003. 'Tax expenditures: The $30 billion twilight zone of government spending'. Department of the Parliamentary Library Research Papers No. 8. Available at: www.aph.gov.au/About_Parliament/Parliamentary_Departments/Parliamentary_Library/pubs/rp/rp0203/03rp08/

Smith, Julie P. 2004a. 'Mothers' milk and markets'. *Australian Feminist Studies* 19(45): 369–379. doi.org/10.1080/0816464042000278034

Smith, Julie P. 2004b (1993). *Taxing popularity: The story of taxation in Australia*. Sydney: Australian Tax Research Foundation.

Smith, Julie P. 2006. 'The challenge for more babies is a taxing one'. *The Age*. Available at: www.theage.com.au/small-business/the-challenge-to-have-more-babies-is-a-taxing-one-20090619-com1.html

Smith, Julie P. 2007. 'Time use among new mothers, the economic value of unpaid work and gender aspects of superannuation tax concessions'. *Australian Journal of Labour Economics* 10(2): 99–114.

Smith, Julie P. 2013. '"Lost Milk?": Counting the Economic Value of Breast Milk in Gross Domestic Product'. *Journal of Human Lactation* 29(4): 537–546. doi.org/10.1177/0890334413494827

Smith, Julie P. 2015. 'Australian State income taxation; a historical perspective'. *Australian Tax Forum* 30(4): 679–712. doi.org/10.2139/ssrn.2704627

Smith, Julie P. and Robert Forrester. 2013. 'Who pays for the health benefits of exclusive breastfeeding? An analysis of maternal time costs'. *Journal of Human Lactation* 29(4): 547–555. doi.org/10.1177/0890334413495450

Smith, Julie P. and Lindy H. Ingham. 2005. 'Mothers' milk and measures of economic output'. *Feminist Economics* 11(1): 43–64. doi.org/10.1080/1354570042000332605

Smith, Julie P., Jane F. Thompson and David A. Ellwood. 2002. 'Hospital system costs of artificial infant feeding: estimates for the Australian Capital Territory'. *Australian and New Zealand Journal of Public Health* 26(6): 543–551. doi.org/10.1111/j.1467-842X.2002.tb00364.x

Stiglitz, Joseph E., Amartya Sen and Jean-Paul Fitoussi. 2009. *The measurement of economic performance and social progress revisited; Reflections and overview*. Paris, French Observatory of Economic Conditions: Economics Research Center. Available at: spire.sciencespo.fr/hdl:/2441/5l6uh8ogmqildh09h4687h53k/resources/wp2009-33.pdf

Surrey, Stanley S. and Paul R. McDaniel. 1985. *Tax Expenditures*. Cambridge, MA: Harvard University Press. doi.org/10.4159/harvard.9780674436527

Toder, Eric J. 1999. 'Tax incentives for social policy: The only game in town'. *Leadership and Public Policy Series.* Paper No. 5. Maryland: The Burns Academy of Leadership, University of Maryland.

Treadgold, Malcolm. 2000. 'An Early Estimate of the Value of Australia's Stock of Human Capital'. *History of Economics Review* 32(1): 46–57. doi.org/10.1080/10370196.2000.11733340

Victora, Cesar G., Rajiv Bahl, Aluísio J.D. Barros, Giovanny V.A. França, Susan Horton, Julia Krasevec, Simon Murch, Mari Jeeva Sankar, Neff Walker and Nigel C. Rollins. 2016. 'Breastfeeding in the 21st century: epidemiology, mechanisms, and lifelong effect'. *The Lancet* 387(10017): 475–490.

Victora, Cesar G., Bernardo Lessa Horta, Christian Loret de Mola, Luciana Quevedo, Ricard Tavares Pinjeiro, Denise P. Gigante, Helen Gonçalves and Fernando C. Barros. 2015. 'Association between breastfeeding and intelligence, educational attainment, and income at 30 years of age: a prospective birth cohort study from Brazil.' *Lancet Global Health* April 3(4): e199–e205.

Waldfogel, Jane, Wen-Jui Han and Jeanne Brooks-Gunn. 2002. 'The effects of early maternal employment on child cognitive development'. *Demography* 39(2): 369–392. doi.org/10.1353/dem.2002.0021

Waring, Marilyn. 1988. *Counting for nothing: what men value & what women are worth.* Wellington: Allen & Unwin. doi. org/10.7810/9780868615714

Watts, Rob. 1987. *The Foundations of the National Welfare State.* Sydney: Allen & Unwin.

Wei, Hui. 2001. *Measuring the stock of human capital for Australia: A lifetime labour income approach.* Paper prepared for the Methodology Advisory Committee Meeting 16 November 2001. Canberra: Australian Bureau of Statistics.

Whiteford, Peter. 2017. '"Them" and "us": the enduring power of welfare myths'. *Inside Story*, 10 March. Available at: insidestory.org.au/them-and-us-the-enduring-power-of-welfare-myths

Wickens, C.H. 1924. 'Human Capital'. Report of the Sixteenth Meeting of the Australasian Association for the Advancement of Science, pp. 536–554. Wellington: Government Printer.

World Health Organization (WHO), UNICEF and IBFAN. 2016. *Marketing of Breast-milk Substitutes: National Implementation of the International Code. Status Report 2016*. Geneva: World Health Organization (WHO).

WHO/UNICEF. 2003. *Global strategy for infant and young child feeding*. Geneva: WHO and UNICEF.

Young, Claire. 1999. 'Taxing times for women: feminism confronts tax policy'. *Sydney Law Review* 21(3): 487–499.

Young, Claire F.L. 2000. *Women, tax and social programs: The gendered impact of funding social programs through the tax system*. Ottawa: Status of Women Canada.

7

Parents' primary and secondary child care time adjustment to market time: Evidence from Australian mothers and fathers

Huong Dinh and Maria Racionero

The increase in female labour force participation in recent decades has arguably contributed to improved outcomes for women, such as higher earnings, savings and retirement incomes. There are, however, concerns about the implications of this trend for children's development. The link between parental child care time and children's development has been extensively explored in the psychology and sociology literature, and also more recently in the economics literature (Del Boca et al. 2014). Time is a limited resource that parents need to allocate to work and child care, alongside other uses. While it has been extensively documented that employed parents spend less time with children than non-employed ones, there is less evidence on the nature and magnitude of the trade-offs between child care and market time. How much child care time do mothers and fathers sacrifice when they increase their market time? How do mothers and fathers adjust their child care time in response to an increase in their partner's market time? Does the trade-off differ for different types of child care time or according to the age of children?

The developmental psychology literature suggests that not just the total child care time but the type of child care time matters for children's development (Shaw and Bell 1993). A relatively common categorisation, which is easily implemented with time use survey data, distinguishes primary from secondary child care time. Primary child care is defined as being engaged in child care tasks (e.g. playing, reading or talking with children) as the main activity. Secondary child care is defined as being engaged in child care tasks while doing other activities (e.g. cooking, entertaining or gardening), rather than child care being the main activity. Primary child care requires more effort from parents and is thought to be more productive, in terms of children's development, than secondary child care (Zick and Bryant 1996; Gutiérrez-Domènech 2010). It has been shown that parents spend more of their total time providing secondary child care than primary child care regardless of employment status (Allard and Janes 2008). There is, however, less conclusive evidence on the way parents adjust their primary and secondary child care time, and in particular whether they prioritise one over the other, when they increase work time. Understanding how these adjustments are made is relevant when assessing the implications of increased labour force participation.

Previous studies have explored the relationship between parental child care time and market time. In this article, 'market time' stands for time spent in market work, as in Hallberg and Klevmarken (2003). Among these studies, a few have focused on the implications for primary and secondary child care (Nock and Kingston 1988; Gutiérrez-Domènech 2010; Craig et al. 2014; Bryant and Zick 1996). The available evidence is mixed. In the US, Nock and Kingston (1988) found a negative but very small relationship between parents' work time and some primary child care and secondary child care activities, with the magnitude larger for secondary child care. Bryant and Zick (1996) found a negative effect of parents' own work time on primary child care but a positive effect on secondary child care. In Spain, Gutiérrez-Domènech (2010) found that working mothers and fathers reduce primary child care time more than secondary child care when they increase their own work time. In Australia, Craig et al. (2014) found that full-time employed parents spend less time for both primary and secondary child care than non-employed parents. However, they found no evidence of significant differences in child care time between part-time and full-time employed parents. The available evidence on the effect of partners' work time is even patchier. Nock and Kingston (1988) found no significant effect of partners' work hours on either mothers' or fathers' primary child care time. However, they found effects of partners' work time on secondary child care time that differ by parent gender: fathers increase, while mothers decrease, secondary child care time when their partners increase work time.

The lack of conclusive evidence on the effects of market time on child care time may stem from the little attention paid to the prevalence of 'zero values' in time use data, the correlation between market time and child care time, or the role of the age of youngest child. In time use surveys, which are conducted on particular days, activities that household members do, but which do not happen to fall on those days, will be recorded as 'zero' in the survey; zero values of time use are common for child care and work-related activities. Individuals choose market time and child care time simultaneously. The time use decisions are therefore interdependent, making it important to properly account for the correlation between the time uses. While the age of children can affect how much child care time parents are willing to trade off for market time, only Bryant and Zick (1996) conduct the analysis separately by the age of the youngest child in the family.

Our study accordingly focuses on the trade-off of primary and secondary child care time for market time for Australian parents. Specifically, we examine the following questions: (1) Do parents trade off less primary than secondary child care time for their own increased market time? (2) Do parents spend more extra time in primary than in secondary child care time when their partners increase their market time?

We study mothers and fathers separately to identify whether there are gender patterns in the way they trade off primary and secondary child care time for market time. In many developed countries, including Australia, and despite the observed increase in women's workforce participation, fathers spend more time in paid work and less time in child care than mothers. Many mothers choose to reduce their hours at work, seek to access flexible working arrangements including self-employment, or work in lower status jobs or industries (Kaufman and Uhlenberg 2000; Sayer 2005; Craig and Sawrikar 2009). In Australia, both cross-sectional and longitudinal studies show that mothers choose to work part time in order to balance work and child care, an option less often taken by fathers (Charlesworth et al. 2011; Cooklin et al. 2016).

We also conduct our analysis separately by the age of the youngest child to explore whether there are child age-specific differences in how parents trade off primary and secondary child care for market time. There is a growing body of evidence on the importance of parental time investments in children's early years (Furedi 2001; Nadesan 2002; Quirke 2006; Wall 2010). The amount of time spent with children is particularly large when children are young and tends to decrease when they grow (Craig and Sawrikar 2009).

We use time-diary data on couples with children from the Australian Bureau of Statistics (ABS) 2006 Australian Time Use Survey (TUS), which provides the most up-to-date snapshot on how Australian parents allocate their time. We address the existing gaps in the literature and find relatively clear-cut evidence on how the trade-offs of child care time for market time differ for mothers and fathers, for primary and secondary child care time, and according to the age of youngest child. Our approach also enables us to explore the adjustments to primary and secondary child care time mothers and fathers make in response to increased market time by partners. These findings should help inform the design of policies to foster female labour force participation that take into account the effects of increased market time on child care time. The rest of the chapter is structured as follows. In Section 2, we describe the data source, data sample, key variables and covariates and main aspects of the econometric model used in the analysis. In Section 3, we outline the analysis results. In Section 4, we discuss the results and conclude.

Methodology

Data

The ABS TUS that we use contains two consecutive days worth of time-diary data on 6,902 people aged 15 and over in a random sample of 3,626 households. Respondents are asked to report detailed time use for main (primary) activities and any simultaneous (secondary) activities that they engage in—including who they are with and where they are throughout the day—with reference to over 226 defined activities, to a detail level of five-minute intervals. The survey also provides detailed information about personal characteristics such as education, employment status and earnings. More details on the TUS 2006 are available in ABS (2008).

Data selection

For our research purposes, we restrict our sample to working mothers and fathers in couple households, either married or cohabiting, aged 24–65 years with at least one child aged 0–14 (this is the range that the TUS collects child care data). This yields a sample of 544 working mothers and 700 working fathers.

Key variables

The key time variables are time in child care and market work. Following Craig et al. (2014), we classify parental child care time into primary and secondary. Primary child care time is the total sum of minutes during which a person reported being engaged in any of the following child care-related tasks as his or her primary activity: minding children, taking care of children, teaching/helping/reprimanding children, playing/reading/talking with children, performing physical or emotional care of children, travelling in association with child care or with children, and miscellaneous child care that includes child care not further defined or not elsewhere classified. Secondary child care time is the total amount of time that each parent spent for all mentioned child care-related tasks as a secondary activity. Our measure of child care time explicitly excludes any time that the reporting individual spent sleeping and napping with the child. Their 'default care' time is counted only if they were awake while the child slept. Ideally, the time with children should be recorded for each individual child but, in reality, it is hard to do so, especially for families with multiple children. Therefore, we use the time each parent recorded spending with all children present in the family. Time in market work is the total sum of minutes that the reporting individual devoted to work (including overtime and work brought home), travel and communication associated with employment-related activities, and any other employment-related activities. We use the actual market work time recorded in the diary rather than the contracted market work time as the former is more responsive to daily changes for reasons such as own sickness or a child's care need (Hallberg and Klevmarken 2003), therefore more accurately capturing the trade-off between market time and parental child care time.

Covariates

In exploring the relationship between child care and market time it is important to control for variables that may confound this association, known as covariates. The covariates that we include are person-level and household-level characteristics that are commonly used in time use studies (e.g. Hallberg and Klevmarken 2003; Kimmel and Connelly 2007; Craig et al. 2014). The person-level characteristics include age groups (25–34, 35–44 and 45–64), education level (completing Year 12 or higher versus Year 11 or lower), country of birth (Australian or primarily English-speaking country background versus otherwise), self-rated health (very good or excellent versus good, fair or poor), receiving non-labour income or not and the number of weekend days reported in the two-day diary. Household-level information includes number of children (1, 2–3, 4 and more), and household income group. The descriptive summary of covariates is provided in Table 7.A1 in the Appendix.

Econometric model

Following recent studies (Kimmel and Connelly 2007; Connelly and Kimmel 2009), we jointly estimate Tobit models of the trade-offs between (primary and secondary) child care time and market time, allowing for all three dimensions of time to be correlated, and controlling for relevant covariates. We do this to account for the 48-hour constraint faced by each respondent, which causes time spent in one activity to reduce the time available for another activity. This estimation approach also allows us to take into account zero time uses reported in time diaries. Additionally, it allows us to control for unobserved personal-specific characteristics that affect the individual's time allocation. The detailed econometric model is available in Dinh and Racionero (2016).

Results

Time use

Figure 7.1 presents the average time mothers and fathers report they spend on child care and work in the two diary days. On average, mothers spend 888 minutes for child care: 31 per cent of their time budget, nearly double the amount of time that fathers spend (472 minutes). Despite this substantial difference, both parents spend a third of total child care time in primary child care (301 minutes for mothers and 151 minutes for fathers), and two-thirds in secondary child care (588 minutes for mothers and 321 minutes for fathers). Mothers devote 360 minutes to work (about 40 per cent of their child care time) in contrast to 733 minutes for fathers (about 155 per cent of their child care time). The stark gender differences in child care time and work time suggest that on average mothers prioritise child care time while fathers prioritise work time, which is consistent with the findings in a number of previous studies (e.g. Acock and Demo 1994; Casper and Bianchi 2001; Baxter 2002; Craig and Bittman 2005).

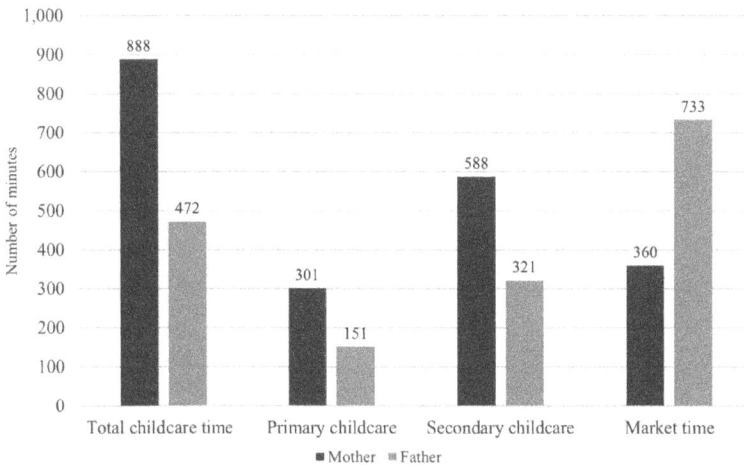

Figure 7.1: Unadjusted child care and market time by parent gender
Source: Authors' estimation based on ABS TUS 2006.

We also explore whether the child care–work time pattern changes with the age of children. This is shown in Figures 7.2 and 7.3. Both mothers and fathers with a preschool-aged youngest child report more than double time in child care (1,365 minutes for mothers and 641 minutes for fathers) compared with those with a school-aged youngest child (565 minutes for mothers and 329 minutes for fathers). This pattern holds for both primary and secondary child care: for example, mothers with a preschool-aged youngest child spend 468 minutes in primary child care and 897 minutes in secondary child care, while mothers with a school-aged youngest child spend 187 minutes in the former and 378 minutes in the latter. Both fathers and mothers spend more time in secondary child care than primary child care, regardless of the age of their youngest child, which is not surprising since primary child care requires more effort than secondary child care. The age of the youngest child seems to be a significant factor in the mother's decision of how much time to devote to work, but it does not seem to be the case for fathers. Mothers with a school-aged youngest child report 130 per cent of the amount of market time (400 minutes) compared with mothers with a preschool-aged youngest child (301 minutes). There is, however, no statistically significant difference for fathers, who devote 751 minutes to work when their youngest child is preschool-aged and 717 minutes when the youngest child is school-aged.

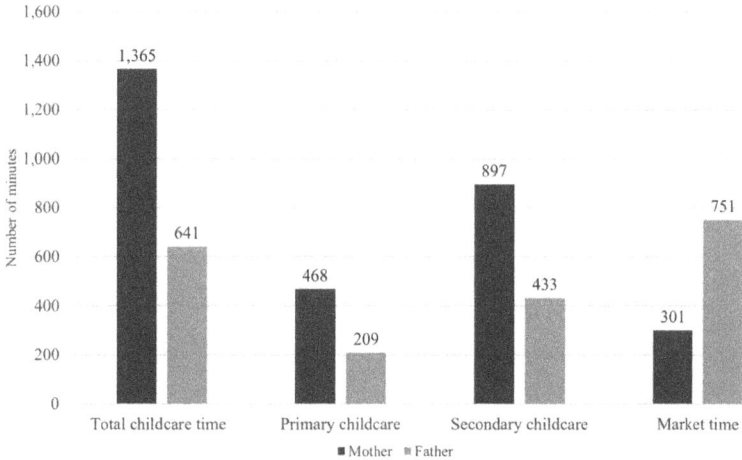

Figure 7.2: Unadjusted child care and market time by parent gender, youngest child at preschool age

Source: Authors' estimation based on ABS TUS 2006.

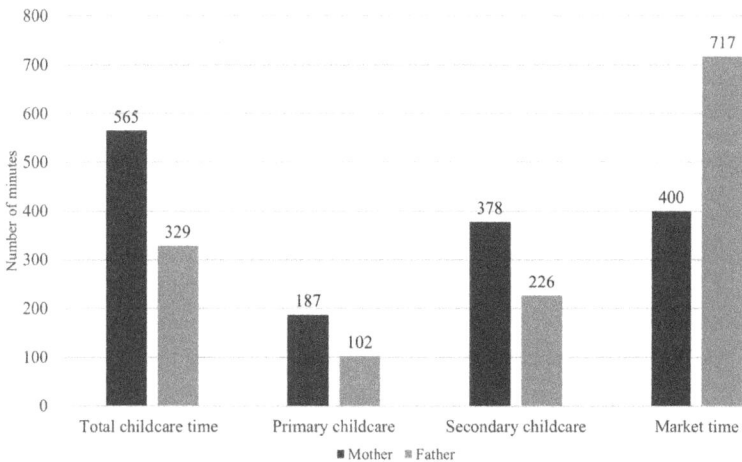

Figure 7.3: Unadjusted child care and market time by parent gender, youngest child at school age

Source: Authors' estimation based on ABS TUS 2006.

The stylised facts identified above warrant more rigorous analysis. The average patterns suggest that there are differences in primary child care time, secondary child care time and market time use by fathers and mothers, and by age of youngest child. However, in order to understand the precise relationship, we need to control for relevant covariates (i.e. other variables that affect these time uses and may confound the observed relationship) and to properly account for the correlation between time uses. We do so in our analysis and report the results in terms of the marginal effect of parental market time on parental child care time, measured by a change in the amount of minutes in child care time associated with an additional minute devoted to market work.

Tables 7.1 and 7.2 present the marginal effects of own and partners' market time on the amount of time mothers and fathers spend in primary and secondary child care for preschool-aged and school-aged youngest child, respectively. For convenience, the impact is interpreted below in terms of the change in minutes in each type of child care for an extra hour of work. The full regression results are available in Dinh and Racionero (2016).

Table 7.1: Trade-offs between market time and child care time, youngest child (0–4 years), adjusted

	Mother				Father			
	Primary child care		Secondary child care		Primary child care		Secondary child care	
	Coef.	SE	Coef.	SE	Coef.	SE	Coef.	SE
Own market time	0.13	(0.16)	-0.84*	(0.50)	-0.50***	(0.12)	0.85*	(0.48)
Partner's market time	0.11***	(0.03)	0.04	(0.09)	0.05*	(0.03)	0.22*	(0.13)

Robust standard errors in parentheses.
Significance level: *** p<0.01, ** p<0.05, * p<0.1.
Source: Authors' estimation based on ABS TUS 2006.

Table 7.2: Trade-offs between market time and child care time, youngest child (5–14 years), adjusted

	Mother				Father			
	Primary child care		Secondary child care		Primary child care		Secondary child care	
	Coef.	SE	Coef.	SE	Coef.	SE	Coef.	SE
Own market time	-0.25***	(0.08)	-0.28	(0.54)	-0.29***	(0.08)	-1.38***	(0.46)
Partner's market time	0.07***	(0.02)	-0.07	(0.08)	0.06***	(0.02)	0.33***	(0.12)

Robust standard errors in parentheses.
Significance level: *** p<0.01, ** p<0.05, * p<0.1.
Source: Authors' estimation based on ABS TUS 2006.

Do parents trade off less primary than secondary child care time for their own increased market time?

In families with a preschool-aged youngest child, mothers keep primary child care time unchanged but reduce secondary child care time by 50 minutes when they increase market time by one hour. By contrast, fathers reduce primary child care time by 30 minutes but increase secondary child care time by 51 minutes when they work an extra hour. In families with a school-aged youngest child, mothers reduce primary child care time by 15 minutes and there is no statistically significant change in secondary child care time when they increase market time by one hour. Fathers reduce both primary and secondary child care time, especially secondary child care by 84 minutes as opposed to 18 minutes in primary child care, when they work an extra hour.

The results indicate that parents' adjustments to primary and secondary child care time differ and depend on the parent gender and the age of the youngest child. When the youngest child is preschool-aged, mothers seem to prioritise primary child care over secondary child care: they keep primary child care time unchanged while reducing secondary child care time by a slightly lower amount than the increase in own market time. However, when the youngest child is school-aged, mothers seem to put more emphasis on secondary child care time: they maintain secondary child care time while reducing primary child care time, albeit at a lower rate than the increase in own market time. By contrast, when the youngest child is preschool-aged, fathers seem to prioritise secondary child care over primary child care; they increase secondary child care time but reduce primary child care time although at half the rate of the increase in own market time. When the youngest child is school-aged, fathers reduce time in both child care types but less so in primary child care than in secondary child care.

Do parents spend more extra time in primary than in secondary child care time when their partners increase their market time?

In families with a preschool-aged youngest child, mothers increase primary child care time by 7 minutes, but there is no evidence that they change secondary child care time when their partners' market time increases by one hour. Meanwhile, fathers increase primary child care time by 3 minutes and secondary child care time by 17 minutes when their partners' market time increases by one hour. In families with a school-aged youngest child, mothers increase primary child care time by 4 minutes with no evidence of changes in secondary child care time when their partners' market time increases by one hour. Fathers increase primary child care time by 4 minutes and secondary child care time by 23 minutes when their partners' market time increases by one hour.

The above results imply that the adjustments in child care time in response to an increase in partner's market time also depend on the type of child care time (primary or secondary), the parent gender and the age group of the youngest child. Regardless of the age of the youngest child, mothers seem to prioritise primary over secondary child care when their partners increase work time: mothers increase primary child care time and maintain secondary child care time. On the contrary, fathers seem to prioritise secondary child care compared with primary child care: regardless of the age of the youngest child, fathers increase both types of child care, but secondary child care significantly more than primary child care, in response to an increase in partner's work time.

Conclusions

Time is a scarce resource that parents need to allocate to work and child care, alongside other uses. In this study, we have explored the extent to which Australian mothers and fathers adjust their child care time in response to an increase in own and partner's market time. We focused on primary and secondary child care time. Primary child care is more interactive and is expected to have more productive effects on a child's development than secondary child care. While it had been previously documented that parents spend more of total child care time in secondary child care than primary child care, there was little conclusive evidence on how parents adjust their primary and secondary child care time, and in particular whether they prioritise one over the other, when they increase their work time. We have accordingly contributed to the literature by providing evidence on how mothers and fathers trade off both primary and secondary child care time for own and partner's increased market time. To do so, we used the most recent Australian TUS 2006.

We find that mothers and fathers adjust their child care time differently depending on which partner (father or mother) increases market time, which child care type (primary and secondary) is considered and the age group their youngest child belongs to (less than 5 years or 5–14 years old).

In families with a preschool-aged youngest child, and in response to an increase in own market time, mothers keep primary child care time unchanged but reduce secondary child care time significantly. By contrast, fathers reduce primary child care time moderately and increase secondary child care time significantly when their own market time increases. They may accomplish this by combining their primary activity (e.g. entertaining, gardening, etc.) with child care or reducing other time uses. In families with a school-aged youngest child, mothers decrease primary child care time and maintain secondary child care time, while fathers decrease both primary and secondary child care time, although more so the latter, in response to an increase in their own market time. Fathers and mothers also respond differently to the increase in partner's market time: mothers maintain secondary child care time and increase primary child care time, more so when the youngest child is preschool-aged, while fathers increase both primary and secondary child care time, with the increase in secondary child care time being larger, and more so when the youngest child is school-aged.

There is hence a gender pattern in the adjustments made by parents to primary and secondary child care time in response to an increase in both own and partner's market time. For families with a preschool-aged youngest child, mothers seem to prioritise primary child care time whereas fathers seem to prioritise secondary child care time. This holds both for responses to increases in own and partner's market time. The different choices that mothers and fathers make regarding the types of child care they engage in can have real implications for children's development and wellbeing: primary child care, where child care activities are recorded as the primary activity parents engage in, is likely to be more conducive to children's development and wellbeing.

The gender patterns are less obvious in the case of families with a school-aged youngest child. Both mothers and fathers decrease primary child care time, and fathers significantly decrease secondary child care time, in response to an increase in own market time. Both mothers and fathers increase primary child care time, and fathers significantly increase secondary child care time, in response to an increase in partner's market time.

Combining the parents' child care time adjustments to changes in own and partners' work time suggest that partners balance their child care time in order to minimise not only the loss in total child care time, but also the loss in each subcategory of primary and secondary child care time. In families with a preschool-aged youngest child, a reduction in mothers' secondary child care time due to her increased work time is partially outweighed by an increase in fathers' secondary child care time. Similarly, a reduction in fathers' primary child care time due to his increased work time is partially outweighed by an increase in mothers' primary child care time. In families with a school-aged youngest child, a reduction in mothers' primary and secondary child care time due to her increased work time is outweighed by an increase in fathers' primary and secondary child care time, largely so for secondary child care time. The decrease in fathers' primary and secondary child care time due to his increased work time is, however, associated with relatively small increases in mothers' primary child care time.

Our most compelling finding is that mothers prioritise primary child care, both in response to own or partner's increased market time, when the youngest child is preschool-aged. Their reluctance to trade off primary child care time suggests that they particularly value this type of productive but costly use of time. The mothers' avoidance of a one-for-one trade-off of primary child care for market time may mean that they allocate less time to other activities, including child care-free leisure, personal care and sleeping, that they reschedule activities from weekdays to weekends or to earlier in the day (Craig 2007) or that they increase the intensity of other activities in a reduced amount of time. Some of these adjustments are likely to negatively affect mothers' wellbeing.

More flexible work arrangements for both mothers and fathers, including flexible work schedules and work from home, could help couples, particularly those with young children, balance their child care time. Flexible work arrangements could mitigate existing problems of access to affordable, high-quality non-parental child care. Provision of high-quality non-parental child care, as discussed by Guyonne Kalb (Chapter 5, this volume) could also help relax the time constraints mothers face, particularly those with very young children, without compromising their health or their children's development.

In this study, we have focused on primary and secondary child care time, which is a relatively standard categorisation that is easily implemented using most time-diary data sets. Kalenkoski and Foster (2008) argue, however, that there are alternative ways of capturing the quality dimension of parental time inputs to child production. They propose alternative high- and low-quality time definitions that may be worth exploring in further research.

Appendix

Table 7.A1: Descriptive summary

	Whole sample	Mother	Father	t statistics[a]
Number of observations	1,244	544	700	
Personal characteristics				
Age group (%)				
(25–34)	23.1	26.5	20.5	2.4**
(35–44)	55.6	59.3	52.7	2.3**
45 and more	21.4	14.3	26.8	−5.4***
Education (%)				
Tertiary qualification	38.3	43.5	34.3	3.3***
Certificate or Year 12	40.0	32.3	46.0	−4.9***
Year 11 or below	21.7	24.2	19.7	1.9*
Australian or main English speaking (%)	86.1	87.1	85.4	0.4
English as the main home spoken language (%)	92.7	92.9	92.7	0.2
General health (%)				
Very good or excellent	30.2	27.4	32.4	−1.9*
Good, fair or poor	62.7	66.4	59.8	2.4**
Not stated	7.1	6.2	7.8	−1.1
Has disability or long–term health condition (%)	17.7	14.8	19.9	2.3**
Professional (%)	37.3	34.0	39.9	2.14**
Number of minutes worked in two days (%)				
<480	46.3	65.5	31.6	12.5***
480–839	19.2	17.8	20.3	−1.1
840–959	4.7	3.8	5.5	−1.4
960–1,199	16.4	9.8	21.5	−5.6***

	Whole sample	Mother	Father	t statistics[a]
1,200 or more	13.4	3.2	21.2	−9.5***
Work at weekend (%)	26.9	20.1	32.1	−4.8***
Receiving non-labour income (%)	43.4	41.8	44.5	−0.3
Household characteristics				
Number of children (%)				
One	36.6	37.9	35.6	0.8
Two	46.2	46.7	45.8	0.3
Three or more	17.2	15.4	18.6	−1.5
Youngest child group (%)				
(0–4)	43.8	40.9	46.0	−1.8*
(5–11)	41.0	42.8	39.6	1.1
(12–14)	15.2	16.3	14.4	0.9
Family with a disable child (%)	14.8	35.5	13.7	−0.3
Family with a disable person (%)	38.9	48.8	38.5	0.9
Having more than one women in the household (%)	10.8	31.0	11.8	1.1
Income quintile (%)				
Not stated	9.8	9.4	10.1	−0.4
Lowest	5.9	5.3	6.3	−0.8
2	16.3	14.3	17.9	−1.7*
3	25.6	25.7	25.5	0.1
4	23.1	24.8	21.8	1.2
Highest	19.4	20.6	18.4	1.0
Index of relative socioeconomic disadvantage (%)				
Lowest 20% – Most disadvantaged	12.6	11.4	13.5	−1.1
Second quintile	22.0	22.3	21.8	0.2
Third quintile	20.3	20.6	20.0	0.3
Highest quintile – Least disadvantaged	45.1	45.6	44.7	0.3

[a] t statistics for the mean difference between mother and father.

Significance level: *** $p<0.01$; ** $p<0.05$; * $p<0.1$.

Source: Author's summary based on TUS 2006.

References

ABS (Australian Bureau of Statistics). 2008. *Time Use Survey: User Guide, 2006*. Available at: www.abs.gov.au/ausstats/abs@.nsf/mf/4150.0

Acock, Alan C. and David H. Demo. 1994. *Family diversity and well-being*. Thousand Oaks, CA: Sage.

Allard, Mary D. and Marianne Janes. 2008. 'Time use of working parents: a visual essay'. *Monthly Labor Review* June: 3–14.

Baxter, Janeen. 2002. 'Patterns of change and stability in the gender division of household labour in Australia, 1986–1997'. *Journal of Sociology* 38(4): 399–424. doi.org/10.1177/144078302128756750

Bryant, W. Keith and Cathleen D. Zick. 1996. 'An Examination of Parent-Child Shared Time'. *Journal of Marriage and Family* 58(1): 227–237. doi.org/10.2307/353391

Casper, Lynne M. and Suzanne M. Bianchi. 2001. *Continuity and change in the American family*. Sage Publications.

Charlesworth, Sara, Lyndall Strazdins, Léan O'Brien and Sharryn Sims. 2011. 'Parents' jobs in Australia: Work hours polarisation and the consequences for job quality and gender equality'. *Australian Journal of Labour Economics* 14(1): 35.

Connelly, Rachel and Jean Kimmel. 2009. 'Spousal influences on parents' non-market time choices'. *Review of Economics of the Household* 7: 361–394. doi.org/10.1007/s11150-009-9060-y

Cooklin, Amanda, Huong Dinh, Lyndall Strazdins, Elizabeth Westrupp, Liana Leach and Jan Nicholson. 2016. 'Change and stability in work–family conflict and mothers' and fathers' mental health: Longitudinal evidence from an Australian cohort'. *Social Science and Medicine* 155: 24–34. doi.org/10.1016/j.socscimed.2016.02.036

Craig, Lyn. 2007. 'How employed mothers in Australia find time for both market work and child care'. *Journal of Family and Economic Issues* 28(1): 69–87. doi.org/10.1007/s10834-006-9047-2

Craig, Lyn and Michael Bittman. 2005. 'The effect of children on adults' time-use: analysis of the incremental time costs of children in Australia'. SPRC Discussion Paper. Sydney: Social Policy Research Centre.

Craig, Lyn, Abigail Powell and Ciara Smyth. 2014. 'Towards intensive parenting? Changes in the composition and determinants of mothers' and fathers' time with children 1992–2006'. *The British Journal of Sociology* 65(3): 555–579. doi.org/10.1111/1468-4446.12035

Craig, Lyn and Pooja Sawrikar. 2009. 'Work and Family: How Does the (Gender) Balance Change as Children Grow?' *Gender, Work and Organization* 16(6): 684–709. doi.org/10.1111/j.1468-0432.2009.00481.x

Del Boca, Daniela, Christopher Flinn and Matthew Wiswall. 2014. 'Household Choices and Child Development'. *The Review of Economic Studies* 81(1): 137–185. doi.org/10.1093/restud/rdt026

Dinh, Huong and Maria Racionero. 2016. *Parents' primary and secondary child care time adjustment to market time: Evidence from Australian mothers and fathers.* ANU Centre for Economic Policy Research Discussion Paper No. 695, Canberra.

Furedi, Frank. 2001. *Paranoid parenting: Abandon your anxieties and be a good parent.* London: Allen Lane.

Gutiérrez-Domènech, M. 2010. 'Parental employment and time with children in Spain'. *Review of Economics of the Household* 8(3): 371–391. doi.org/10.1007/s11150-010-9096-z

Hallberg, Daniel and Anders Klevmarken. 2003. 'Time for children: A study of parent's time allocation'. *Journal of Population Economics* 16(2): 205–226. doi.org/10.1007/s001480200133

Kalenkoski, Charlene and Gigi Foster. 2008. 'The quality of time spent with children in Australian households'. *Review of Economics of the Household* 6(3): 243–266. doi.org/10.1007/s11150-008-9036-3

Kaufman, Gayle and Peter Uhlenberg. 2000. 'The influence of parenthood on the work effort of married men and women'. *Social Forces* 78(3): 931–947. doi.org/10.2307/3005936

Kimmel, Jean and Rachel Connelly, 2007. 'Mothers' time choices caregiving, leisure, home production, and paid work'. *Journal of Human Resources* 42(3): 643–681. doi.org/10.3368/jhr.XLII.3.643

Nadesan, Majia. 2002. 'Engineering the entrepreneurial infant: Brain science, infant development toys, and governmentality'. *Cultural Studies* 16(3): 401–432. doi.org/10.1080/09502380210128315

Nock, Steven and Paul Kingston. 1988. 'Time With Children: The Impact of Couples' Work-Time Commitments'. *Social Forces* 67(1): 59–85. doi.org/10.2307/2579100

Quirke, L. 2006. '"Keeping Young Minds Sharp": Children's Cognitive Stimulation and the Rise of Parenting Magazines, 1959–2003'. *Canadian Review of Sociology/Revue canadienne de sociologie* 43(4): 387–406.

Sayer, Liane. 2005. 'Gender, time and inequality: Trends in women's and men's paid work, unpaid work and free time'. *Social Forces* 84(1): 285–303. doi.org/10.1353/sof.2005.0126

Shaw, Daniel S. and Richard Q. Bell. 1993. 'Developmental theories of parental contributors to antisocial behavior'. *Journal of Abnormal Child Psychology* 21(5): 493–518. doi.org/10.1007/BF00916316

Wall, Glenda. 2010. 'Mothers' experiences with intensive parenting and brain development discourse'. *Women's Studies International Forum* 33(3): 253–263. doi.org/10.1016/j.wsif.2010.02.019

Zick, Cathleen D. and Bryant, W. Keith. 1996. 'A New Look at Parents' Time Spent in Child Care: Primary and Secondary Time Use'. *Social Science Research* 25(3): 260–280. doi.org/10.1006/ssre.1996.0012

Part III: Human capital, savings and retirement

8

Gender differences in costs and returns to higher education

Mathias Sinning

This chapter contributes to the work on gender equality in Australia's tax-transfer system from a higher education perspective. Investments in education are associated with costs and returns. The costs of higher education are closely linked to the Australian tax system through the Higher Education Contribution Scheme (HECS), which is administered by the Australian Taxation Office and involves student loan repayments based on taxable income. The returns to higher education—the earnings resulting from investing in education—are immediately relevant from a personal income tax perspective and affect the likelihood of receiving transfer payments. Consequently, gender differences in costs and returns to higher education have important implications for the design of the tax-transfer system.

There are many reasons why people choose to pursue higher education in Australia. Some people want extra qualifications to help them advance in a specific career path. For many others—especially younger cohorts—higher education is very attractive because they are not ready to enter the 'real' world of full-time work. A decision to undertake further studies involves opportunity costs and trade-offs: we spend years at an education institution to get the desired qualification(s); we could have started to work and be earning money if we were not studying; we have to pay for those textbooks when we are studying. The list of costs associated with undertaking further education goes on, but these investments are expected to reap returns in the future. According to the Organisation for Economic Co-operation and Development (OECD) (2015), on average having a tertiary education qualification translates into 34 per cent higher relative earnings of 24–64-year-olds in Australia. People with higher levels of education are also more likely to be employed, remain employed and have more opportunities to advance in their career.

Knowledge about the private returns to education is not just relevant for the decision of individuals to invest in higher education but may also have important implications for the design of education policies. Studies that estimate the private returns to education in Australia focus exclusively on analysing a 'snapshot' of the population at one point in time: that is, they either use cross-sectional data (see, for example, Daly et al. 2010; Norton 2012) or employ longitudinal data to perform a cross-sectional analysis (e.g. Leigh and Ryan 2008; Marks 2008).

Unfortunately, cross-sectional models ignore the relevance of age and time effects. In particular, age-earnings profiles obtained from cross-sectional data implicitly assume that, for example, the earnings of a 35-year-old person in 20 years will be the same as those of a (comparable) 55-year-old person today. It appears likely that this assumption is unrealistic because people who were observed at one point in time do not retain their position in the earnings distribution for the rest of their working lives. Individual earnings may change considerably over time for various reasons. Empirical studies suggest that observed characteristics (such as education and labour market experience) explain a relatively small proportion of earnings variability (Higgins and Sinning 2013). Unobserved differences can result from temporary variation (due to illness, higher duties, bonuses, overtime, etc.) or permanent variation (such as ability, talent or motivation).

Against this background, this chapter generates new estimates of the private returns to higher education for women and men in Australia, using longitudinal data from the Household, Income and Labour Dynamics in Australia (HILDA) Survey, which follows a representative sample of the Australian population over the period 2001–14. The data allow us to compare the estimates obtained from a cross-sectional model to those of a longitudinal model that considers both age and time effects. The use of HILDA data limits our analysis to relatively small samples, and, in contrast to (cross-sectional) Census data, HILDA does not permit a disaggregated estimation of private returns to education by sub-group (such as field of study). However, the focus on HILDA data allows us to understand the relevance of longitudinal aspects when estimating private returns to education. Our analysis focuses on the calculation of average returns to education and therefore does not require a consideration of temporary and permanent variation in earnings. This is because dynamic panel data models typically assume that the model error terms are normally distributed with mean zero.

The chapter focuses on private *returns*—the private benefits from higher education. Specifically, we compare earnings of individuals with higher education and those with education at Year 12 and below to calculate the present value of lifetime earnings resulting from higher education. A complete analysis of the value of higher education would involve a comparison of the benefits to the *costs* associated with higher education. Although such a cost–benefit analysis is beyond the scope of this paper, we are able to study the implications of gender differences in earnings over the life course for the financial capacity of male and female university graduates to repay income contingent student loans. Guyonne Kalb, in Chapter 5, also takes a life course approach, looking at the effect of taxes and expenditure on labour supply. The Australian HECS, which was introduced in 1989 to finance tuition fees of Australian university students, constitutes an excellent example that allows us to illustrate the link between gender differences in earnings and gender differences in student loan repayments. Our discussion of student loan repayments relies on findings of Higgins and Sinning (2013) who pay particular attention to the importance of dynamic earnings modelling for the design of income-contingent student loans.

Our analysis of private returns to education reveals that lifetime earnings of men with a postgraduate degree (Master's or Doctorate) are about 83 per cent higher than those of men with Year 12 and below. Women with a postgraduate degree earn about 50 per cent more over their lifetime than women with Year 12 and below. Our findings also reveal that lifetime earnings of women with a Bachelor or Honours degree are about as high as those of women with a postgraduate degree. We further observe that women have no benefits from investing in vocational training. Gender differences in earnings have considerable implications for the repayment of income-contingent student loans. The average outstanding debt of male university graduates converges to zero over a 30-year period, whereas the average outstanding debt of female university graduates remains positive, indicating that many female university graduates in Australia do not have the financial capacity to repay their student loans in full.

The following section provides an overview of the literature on the estimation of private returns to education. The third section describes the data and provides some descriptive statistics. Our empirical strategy is explained in the fourth section. The main results are discussed in the fifth section. The sixth section illustrates the implications of gender differences in earnings for the repayment of income-contingent student loans. The seventh section provides a short discussion of the results. The final section concludes.

The literature on returns to education

The economic literature on the estimation of the returns to education is motivated by the human capital framework (Becker 1964), which considers education an investment in human capital. Extensive literature across many countries and time periods has shown that highly educated people generally earn more than less educated people (see Ashenfelter et al. (1999) and Psacharopoulos and Patrinos (2004) for surveys of the literature).

Most empirical studies use the human capital earnings function derived by Mincer (1974) to estimate the returns to education. The human capital earnings function relates the (logarithm of) earnings to the number of years of education and labour market experience. Education was typically measured in years, but many studies have adopted alternative model specifications that take into account that education is better represented by certain degrees rather than the number of years of education (see, for example, Jaeger and Page 1996).

The model includes labour market experience to isolate effects of on-the-job training on earnings from the effect of education on earnings. The original human capital earnings function includes a quadratic function of labour market experience to take into account that earnings typically increase at a declining rate and that increasing labour market experience may even reduce earnings at the end of the working life. It is unclear whether older workers suffer from declining productivity towards the end of their working life or whether the decline in earnings simply reflects different work–leisure preferences and, therefore, reduced hours of work (but at the same level of productivity). Our analysis focuses on the study of hourly wages to address this issue and to facilitate comparisons between male and female workers. Sections 3 and 4 provide a detailed discussion of earnings measures.

A large strand of the empirical literature on the returns to education has focused on a problem that is caused by unobservable variables that are correlated with education, such as individual ability or talent. The omission of these variables may lead to a bias in the estimated returns to education, and numerous studies have employed empirical strategies that allow them to identify the causal effect of education on earnings. These studies have typically employed instrumental variables strategies (Angrist and Krueger 1991; Card 1999) or made use of twin studies (Ashenfelter and Krueger 1994) to identify the causal effect of education on earnings. On balance, these studies show that the bias caused by unobservable variables is relatively small.

It is important to note that the human capital earnings function ignores the (monetary or non-monetary) costs of education. Monetary costs do not only include direct costs such as fees, books and equipment but also opportunity costs resulting from foregone earnings as a result of spending time in education. Heckman et al. (2005) conclude that non-monetary (psychic) costs of education are substantial, which may explain why many people do not invest in higher education, even if the returns to education are high.

An alternative approach to make inferences about the private returns to education is to calculate the net present value of an investment in education (Becker 1964; Schultz 1961). The net present value is the difference between the discounted present value of lifetime earnings and the discounted present value of the costs of investing in education. The calculation depends on a discount rate, which takes into account that the value of present earnings is higher than the value of future earnings.

The calculation of the net present value of an investment in education is typically based on the comparison of earnings of workers with Year 12 and below and workers who receive tertiary education and face direct costs. Opportunity costs can be obtained by assuming that if individuals with tertiary education had not made the investment, their earnings would be the same as those of individuals with Year 12 and below. The approach requires the collection of data on the direct costs of education and typically ignores potential biases resulting from unobserved factors.

Numerous studies have estimated the private returns to education in Australia and shown that an investment in higher education is highly profitable (see Daly et al. 2010). Leigh and Ryan (2008) employ a human capital earnings function to estimate the returns to education and compared different empirical strategies (instrumental variables and twin studies) to address potential biases caused by unobserved ability. They conclude that the rate of return to an additional year of education, corrected for ability bias, is around 10 per cent. Daly and Lewis (2010) study the net present value of investing in education and find that this approach produces higher returns to education than the preferred estimate reported by Leigh and Ryan (2008). Wei (2010) compares the returns to education obtained from a human capital earnings function to those of the net present value calculation and finds that the results obtained from the latter approach are higher.

Norton (2012) uses data from the 2006 Census and finds that at the median, lifetime earnings of men with a Bachelor degree are 65 per cent higher than those of men with Year 12 and below. The difference for women at the median is close to 80 per cent. Norton (2012) also studies the range of graduate earnings and concludes that the majority of graduates benefit from university education within each discipline with the exception of men studying performing arts.

The economic literature in Australia focuses exclusively on the cross-sectional analysis of private returns to education and ignores dynamic aspects of lifetime earnings. Unfortunately, age-earnings profiles based on cross-sectional models assume that, for example, the earnings of an average 35-year-old university graduate in 20 years will be as high as today's earnings of an average 55-year-old university graduate. This assumption may have severe consequences for the estimation of private returns to education.

Our analysis contributes to the empirical literature on the private returns to education in two important ways. First, we use hourly wages as an outcome measure to estimate private returns to education because they facilitate comparisons between men and women who exhibit very different levels of labour supply. Instead of using annual earnings (measured in dollars) to calculate lifetime earnings, we use annual averages of hourly wages to study wage differentials (measured in per cent) between different levels of education. The present value of these differentials may be used to calculate private returns to education (measured in per cent). Second, we use longitudinal data to consider both age and time effects (and the interaction between age and time) to predict future wages.

Data and descriptive statistics

Data

Our empirical analysis uses data from the HILDA panel for the period 2001–14. The first wave of the longitudinal survey consisted of 7,682 households and 19,194 individuals. The survey follows these households over time and all adult members of each household are interviewed annually. In 2011, a top-up sample was added to the survey to address sample attrition. The top-up sample will not be considered in our analysis to avoid potential inconsistencies resulting from the consideration of additional households.

The HILDA panel contains information about a range of topics, including individual earnings, educational attainment and labour market experience. In our cross-sectional analysis, we will compare three earnings measures, which produce slightly different results: hourly wages, weekly earnings and annual earnings. Our longitudinal analysis focuses on hourly wages, which facilitate comparisons between men and women who exhibit very different levels of labour supply.

To obtain representative results for Australia, we do not impose many restrictions on our analysis sample. Our analysis is based on an unbalanced panel: we include individuals who enter a survey household during the survey period. We restrict our analysis sample to 25–64-year-old persons who are either full- or part-time employed and who report positive annual earnings. We do not consider the top 0.1 per cent of the hourly wage and annual earnings distribution and we drop individuals who report (positive or negative) business income to avoid potential biases caused by outliers that are not necessarily representative.

Our analysis is performed separately for men and women because it appears likely that they will have different returns to education. After dropping individuals who do not report their education and labour market experience, our analysis sample includes 68,720 person-year observations (34,656 men and 34,064 women) over the period 2001–14. We employ person weights provided by HILDA throughout the entire analysis to obtain representative results.

Descriptive statistics

This section provides a description of the most important variables that we use to perform the empirical analysis. Table 8.1 includes average levels of education by gender in 2014. We observe that about 7.2 per cent of the male workers and 10.3 per cent of female workers in Australia have a postgraduate degree (Master's or Doctorate).

Female workers are also more likely to have a Bachelor or Honours degree or an Advanced Diploma/Diploma than male workers. The share of female workers with a Bachelor or Honours degree is 23.9 per cent, and the corresponding share of male workers is 19.0 per cent. Advanced Diploma/Diploma holders make up 13.3 per cent of female workers and 12.2 per cent of male workers.

In contrast, men are considerably more likely to have a Certificate I–IV then women. The share of male Certificate I–IV holders is 33.1 per cent, compared to 21.2 per cent of female Certificate I–IV holders. The fractions of male and female workers with Year 12 and below are 28.5 per cent and 31.4 per cent, respectively.

Table 8.1: Education by gender, 2014

	Men	Women
Postgraduate Degree (Masters or Doctorate)	0.072	0.103
	(0.259)	(0.303)
Bachelor or Honours	0.190	0.239
	(0.392)	(0.426)
Advanced Diploma or Diploma	0.122	0.133
	(0.327)	(0.339)
Certificate I–IV	0.331	0.212
	(0.471)	(0.409)

	Men	Women
Without non-school qualification	0.285	0.314
	(0.452)	(0.464)
Education in years	12.6	12.8
	(1.8)	(2.0)
Observations	2743	2691

Weighted numbers based on weights provided by HILDA. Standard deviations are reported in parentheses.
Source: Author's own calculations based on HILDA data.

When comparing the average total number of years of education of male and female workers, gender differences in educational attainment appear rather small. On average, male workers have 12.6 years of education, whereas the average number of years of education of female workers is 12.8 years. These numbers suggest that we cannot simply assume that educational attainment is sufficiently described by the number of years of education. For that reason, we will take into account different levels of education in our empirical analysis.

We may also study the association between educational attainment and earnings of male and female workers. In this section, we compare three types of earnings measures: hourly wages, weekly earnings and annual earnings. Figure 8.1 presents average hourly wages by gender and education in 2012. We find that the average hourly wage of men with a postgraduate degree is about $46. The average hourly wage of women with a postgraduate degree is only $39.

Figure 8.1 also reveals that workers with higher levels of education generally earn more than less educated workers. Male workers with a Bachelor or Honours degree earn about $44 per hour, those with an Advanced Diploma/Diploma earn about $37, while average hourly wages of Certificate I–IV holders are about $36, and male workers with Year 12 and below earn about $30 per hour.

A slightly different picture emerges when we look at the sample of female workers. Female workers with a Bachelor or Honours degree earn about $39 per hour, Advanced Diploma/Diploma holders earn about $29, and Certificate I–IV holders earn on average about $25, followed by female workers with Year 12 and below who earn about $27.

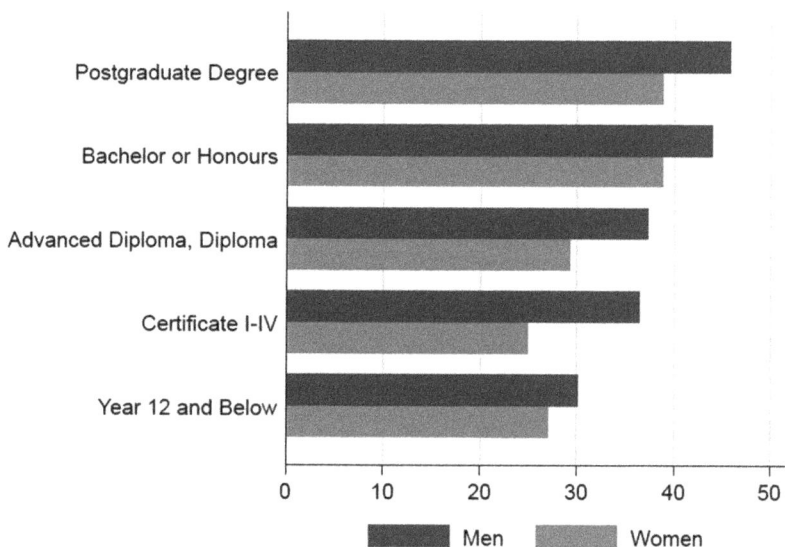

Figure 8.1: Hourly wages by gender and education, 2014
Weighted numbers based on weights provided by HILDA.
Source: Author's own calculations based on HILDA data.

The gender differences in average hourly wages presented in Figure 8.1 appear to be relatively small (only a few dollars), but they are in fact quite substantial. In particular, the earnings differentials between male and female workers become more obvious when we take into account that women are considerably less likely to be in full-time employment than men. For that reason, we also consider differences in weekly and annual earnings. Figure 8.2 presents average weekly earnings by gender and education in 2014.

We observe a considerable gender earnings gap along the entire educational distribution. Specifically, we find that men with a postgraduate degree earn on average about $2,037 per week, and that weekly earnings of women are only about $1,316.

The earnings gap between male and female workers with Bachelor or Honours degree is slightly smaller (men with a Bachelor or Honours degree earn about $1,867 and women earn about $1,289 per week) and we observe large gaps between male and female workers with Advanced Diploma/Diploma ($1,591 vs $1,021 per week) and Certificate I–IV ($1,526 vs $793 per week). The earnings gap between male and female workers with Year 12 and below is smaller in absolute terms (men earn about $1,255 and women earn about $830 per week) but still substantial in relative terms (women earn about 40 per cent less than men).

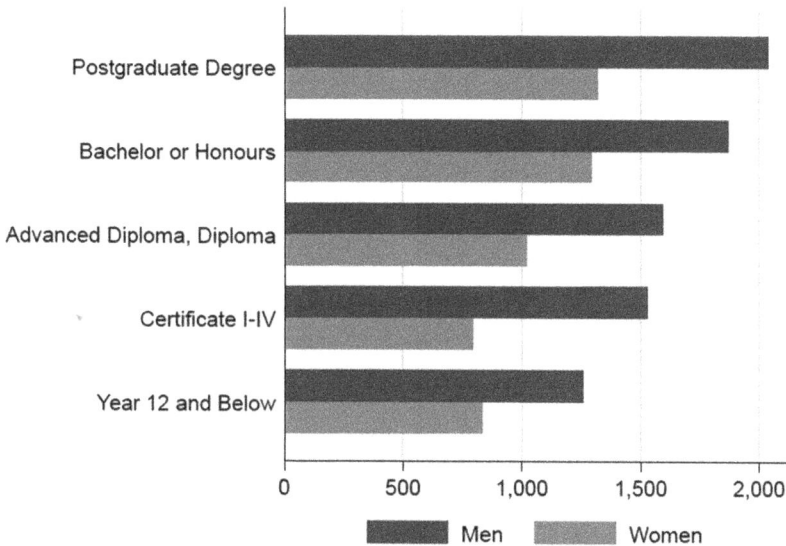

Figure 8.2: Weekly earnings by gender and education, 2014
Weighted numbers based on weights provided by HILDA.
Source: Author's own calculations based on HILDA data.

Figure 8.3 reveals how these differences translate into annual earnings differences. We find that average male workers with a postgraduate degree earn $107,908 in 2014. Average earnings of female workers with the same degree are $70,370, largely because female workers are more likely to be part-time employed.

Average annual earnings of male workers seem to increase by about $10,000–$15,000 for each level of education considered in our analysis: average male workers with Year 12 and below earn about $65,402, those with a Certificate I–IV earn about $77,662, average earnings of Advanced Diploma/Diploma holders are about $84,446, and male workers with a Bachelor or Honours degree earn on average about $99,455.

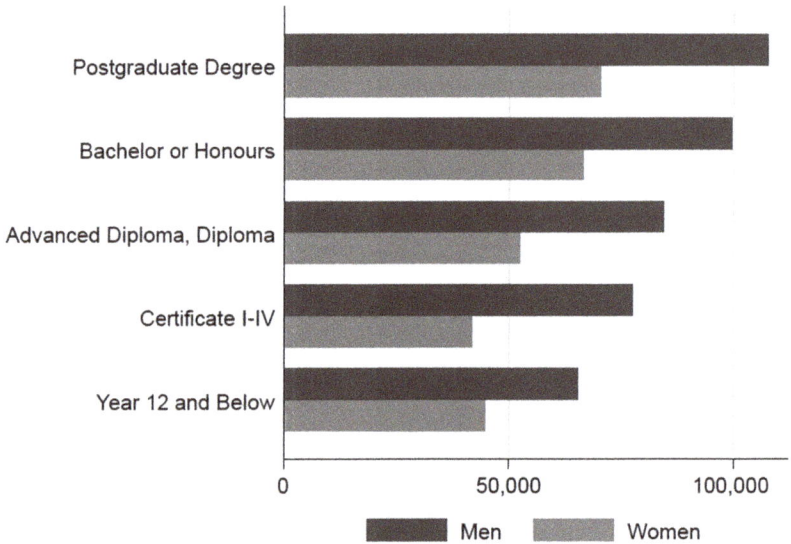

Figure 8.3: Annual earnings by gender and education, 2014
Weighted numbers based on weights provided by HILDA.
Source: Author's own calculations based on HILDA data.

In contrast, we do not find a linear increase in average annual earnings of female workers across the educational distribution. Female workers with Year 12 and below earn on average $44,760 per year, slightly more than average female workers with a Certificate I–IV, who earn about $41,799. Average annual earnings of female workers with Advanced Diploma/Diploma are $52,406, while workers with a Bachelor or Honours degree earn about $66,547.

Taken together, the results presented in Figures 8.1–8.3 highlight considerable earnings differentials both between male and female workers and across the educational distribution of male and female workers. Average annual earnings of women are strongly affected by labour supply. Although highly educated women earn higher hourly wages than less educated women, they do not necessarily have higher annual earnings because less educated women may work relatively long hours. In our empirical analysis, we will focus on hourly wages to take into account that labour supply patterns differ considerably between men and women.

Methodology

Cross-sectional analysis

The starting point of our empirical analysis is the conventional human capital earnings function (Mincer 1974), which relates individual earnings to education and labour market experience. The approach has served as the 'workhorse' of numerous cross-sectional studies over the last four decades. We use a linear regression model to estimate the rate of return to education. The human capital earnings function can be written as:

Equation 8.1

$$\log(y_i) = \beta_0 + \beta_1 educ_i + \beta_2 exp_i + \beta_3 exp_i^2 + X_i \beta_4 + u_i,$$

where y_i is one of the earnings measures (hourly wages, weekly earnings, annual earnings) used in our analysis, which refers to ith individual in a sample consisting of N observations ($i = 1, \ldots, N$). $educ_i$ denotes the number of years of education of individual i, exp_i is the number of years of labour market experience, and X_i is a set of additional control variables. We use a pooled sample over the time period 2001–14 in our analysis to estimate Equation 8.1 and therefore X_i includes indicator variables for each year, which capture year-specific effects, such as inflation. We adjust the standard errors of the model to take into account that we observe the same individuals repeatedly in our pooled sample. u_i is the model error term and $\beta_0, \beta_1, \ldots, \beta_4$ are the model parameters that have to be estimated. We are particularly interested in the parameter β_4, which measures the average effect of an additional year of education on earnings, given that all other factors remain unchanged. Our estimates of the human capital earnings function are presented in Tables 8.2 and 8.3.

We also estimate a modified version of the human capital earnings function, which takes into account that the returns to education are different across the educational distribution. Our model can be written as:

Equation 8.2

$$\log(y_i) = \gamma_0 + \gamma_1 postgrad_i + \gamma_2 bachelor_i + \gamma_3 diploma_i$$
$$+ \gamma_4 certificate_i + \gamma_5 exp_i + \gamma_6 exp_i^2 + X_i \gamma_7 + v_i,$$

where *postgrad*$_i$ is an indicator variable that takes on the value one if individual i has a postgraduate degree and is equal to zero otherwise. *bachelor*$_i$ is an indicator variable for individuals with a Bachelor or Honours degree, *diploma*$_i$ indicates an Advanced Diploma/Diploma, and *certificate*$_i$ indicates a Certificate I–IV. v_i is the model error term and γ_0, γ_1, ... , γ_7 are the model parameters. The estimated parameters of the indicator variables may be interpreted relative to the omitted reference category, which consists of individuals with Year 12 and below.

The two linear regression models described above do not take into account that unobserved characteristics (such as ability) may be correlated with educational attainment, which could bias our returns to education estimates. We ignore the potential bias caused by unobserved characteristics because the empirical literature on the returns to education shows that the bias is relatively small (see Leigh and Ryan 2008) and because our analysis focuses on understanding the difference between cross-sectional and longitudinal earnings models. It appears unlikely that the bias caused by unobserved characteristics is very different between these models.

Life-cycle analysis

We compare the results obtained from the cross-sectional models described above to those of a life-cycle model that considers age and time effects (and the interaction between age and time). The estimates obtained from the life-cycle model allow us to predict future wages of male and female workers by level of education.

We consider actual wages observed in 2001 as a starting point to predict wages over the time period 2002–40. Our wage regression includes age indicators, a time trend and interactions between age and time. The estimated parameters allow us to predict age–wage profiles over a 40-year time period. These profiles may be used to calculate the present value, *PV*, of wage differentials (measured in per cent) between workers with comparable levels of labour supply but different levels of education. The present value of the expected returns can be written as:

Equation 8.3

$$PV = \frac{B_1}{1+r} + \frac{B_2}{(1+r)^2} + \frac{B_3}{(1+r)^3} + \cdots + \frac{B_T}{(1+r)^T},$$

where B_t, $t = 1, \ldots, T$ is the benefit in period t and T is the total number of years. r denotes the interest rate.

The following section presents the results of the cross-sectional and the longitudinal analysis described above.

Results

Cross-sectional analysis

The estimates of the human capital earnings function for the sample of male workers are presented in Table 8.2. The estimates are based on the linear regression of a pooled sample covering the time period 2001–14. The coefficient measuring the relationship between the number of years of education and hourly wages indicates that an increase in education by one year (given all other factors remain the same) led to an average increase in hourly wages by 8.6 per cent. We also observe a rate of return to education of 9 per cent when we use weekly earnings as a dependent variable in our model. Average annual earnings increase by 10.3 per cent if education increases by one year (and all other factors remain the same).

The coefficients on the number of years of labour market experience and labour market experience squared show that the increase in earnings resulting from an increase in labour market experience is significant, but that earnings increase with labour market experience at a declining rate. The constant term is relevant for the construction of the regression model but its interpretation is not very useful because it captures average earnings of individuals without education and labour market experience.

The ordinary least squares (OLS) estimates presented in Table 8.2 are comparable to other cross-sectional studies that present estimates of the human capital earnings function for other countries and/or time periods.

Table 8.2: Returns to education of male workers: OLS estimates, 2001–14

	Hourly wages	Weekly earnings	Annual earnings
Years of education	0.086***	0.090***	0.103***
	(0.005)	(0.007)	(0.007)
Experience (years)	0.021***	0.042***	0.052***
	(0.002)	(0.003)	(0.004)
Experience squared/100	–0.030***	–0.073***	–0.088***
	(0.005)	(0.007)	(0.007)
Constant	1.937***	5.447***	9.067***
	(0.071)	(0.092)	(0.103)
R-squared	0.127	0.111	0.105
Number of observations	32775	32804	33613

Sample: Unbalanced panel. Weighted numbers based on weights provided by HILDA. All regressions include year indicators. Robust standard errors, which are reported in parentheses, were adjusted to take repeated observations into account.

Significance level: * $p<0.05$, ** $p<0.01$, *** $p<0.001$.

Source: Author's own calculations based on HILDA data.

Table 8.3 contains the estimates of the human capital earnings function for the sample of women. We find that an increase in education by one year (all else equal) increases hourly wages by 7.6 per cent. The corresponding relationship between education and weekly or annual earnings is 11.2 and 11.4 per cent, respectively. Empirical studies often find that the rate of return to education of female workers is higher than that of male workers. The smaller coefficient of education in the hourly wage regression stems from gender differences in full- and part-time employment.

Table 8.3: Returns to education of female workers: OLS estimates, 2001–14

	Hourly wages	Weekly earnings	Annual earnings
Years of education	0.076***	0.112***	0.114***
	(0.003)	(0.005)	(0.005)
Experience (years)	0.017***	0.026***	0.039***
	(0.002)	(0.004)	(0.004)
Experience squared/100	–0.027***	–0.037***	–0.055***
	(0.005)	(0.008)	(0.010)

	Hourly wages	Weekly earnings	Annual earnings
Constant	2.057***	4.836***	8.543***
	(0.041)	(0.071)	(0.081)
R-squared	0.135	0.135	0.114
Number of observations	32791	32820	32891

Sample: Unbalanced panel. Weighted numbers based on weights provided by HILDA. All regressions include year indicators. Robust standard errors, which are reported in parentheses, were adjusted to take repeated observations into account.

Significance level: * p<0.05, ** p<0.01, *** p<0.001.

Source: Author's own calculations based on HILDA data.

The estimates in Table 8.4 translate the returns to education into earnings differentials between groups with different levels of education. The coefficients on educational attainment presented in Table 8.4 compare average earnings of male workers with certain levels of tertiary education to male workers with Year 12 and below.

Given the same level of labour market experience, we find that hourly wages of male workers with a postgraduate degree are 41.6 per cent higher than those of male workers with Year 12 and below. The hourly wage gap between male workers with a Bachelor or Honours degree and male workers with Year 12 and below is 37.4 per cent. An Advanced Diploma/Diploma increases average hourly wages of male workers by 22.6 per cent if we compare them to those of male workers with Year 12 and below. Male workers with a Certificate I–IV earn on average 10.4 per cent more than male workers with Year 12 and below.

Table 8.4: Returns to education of male workers by level of education: OLS estimates, 2001–14

	Hourly wages	Weekly earnings	Annual earnings
Postgraduate Degree (Master's or Doctorate)	0.416***	0.436***	0.499***
	(0.034)	(0.043)	(0.047)
Bachelor or Honours	0.374***	0.396***	0.446***
	(0.025)	(0.030)	(0.033)
Advanced Diploma, Diploma	0.226***	0.249***	0.265***
	(0.025)	(0.030)	(0.036)
Certificate I–IV	0.104***	0.153***	0.178***
	(0.018)	(0.022)	(0.025)

	Hourly wages	Weekly earnings	Annual earnings
Experience (years)	0.021***	0.040***	0.051***
	(0.002)	(0.003)	(0.004)
Experience squared/100	−0.032***	−0.073***	−0.088***
	(0.005)	(0.007)	(0.007)
Constant	2.861***	6.408***	10.173***
	(0.028)	(0.039)	(0.046)
R-squared	0.116	0.102	0.095
Number of observations	32775	32804	33613

Sample: Unbalanced panel. Weighted numbers based on weights provided by HILDA. All regressions include year indicators. Robust standard errors, which are reported in parentheses, were adjusted to take repeated observations into account. Reference category: Year 12 and below.

Significance level: * $p<0.05$, ** $p<0.01$, *** $p<0.001$.

Source: Author's own calculations based on HILDA data.

We obtain similar earnings differentials when we use weekly or annual earnings instead of hourly wages as a dependent variable. The returns to labour market experience are slightly higher when we study weekly or annual earnings. Overall, the modified version of the human capital earnings function presented in Table 8.4 reveals that the returns to education are not necessarily constant across the educational distribution.

The picture changes somewhat when we consider earnings differentials between different levels of education within the group of female workers (Table 8.5). We find that hourly wages of female workers with a postgraduate degree are 38.4 per cent higher than those of female workers with Year 12 and below. The corresponding differences in weekly and annual earnings are 52.5 per cent and 51.2 per cent, respectively.

Table 8.5: Returns to education of female workers by level of education: OLS estimates, 2001–14

	Hourly wages	Weekly earnings	Annual earnings
Postgraduate Degree (Masters or Doctorate)'	0.384***	0.525***	0.512***
	(0.020)	(0.031)	(0.034)
Bachelor or Honours	0.347***	0.520***	0.523***
	(0.015)	(0.026)	(0.030)

	Hourly wages	Weekly earnings	Annual earnings
Advanced Diploma, Diploma	0.155***	0.271***	0.281***
	(0.018)	(0.031)	(0.034)
Certificate I–IV	–0.004	0.045	0.032
	(0.017)	(0.026)	(0.029)
Experience (years)	0.017***	0.027***	0.040***
	(0.002)	(0.004)	(0.004)
Experience squared/100	–0.030***	–0.041***	–0.060***
	(0.005)	(0.008)	(0.010)
Constant	2.871***	6.028***	9.749***
	(0.024)	(0.039)	(0.047)
R-squared	0.137	0.129	0.109
Number of observations	32791	32820	32891

Sample: Unbalanced panel. Weighted numbers based on weights provided by HILDA. All regressions include year indicators. Robust standard errors, which are reported in parentheses, were adjusted to take repeated observations into account. Reference category: Year 12 and below.

Significance level: * $p<0.05$, ** $p<0.01$, *** $p<0.001$.

Source: Author's own calculations based on HILDA data.

We also observe that hourly wages of female workers with a Bachelor or Honours degree are 34.7 per cent higher than those of female workers with Year 12 and below. The weekly and annual earnings differentials between female workers with a Bachelor or Honours degree and female workers with Year 12 and below are about 52 per cent. Interestingly, the parameters associated with having a Bachelor or Honours degree are not significantly different from the earnings differentials observed for female workers with a postgraduate degree. This result suggests that female workers with a postgraduate degree work less and therefore do not translate their hourly wage premium into higher weekly or annual earnings than female workers with a Bachelor or Honours degree.

We find that hourly wages of female workers with an Advanced Diploma/Diploma are 15.5 per cent higher than those of female workers with Year 12 and below. The weekly and annual earnings differentials between these two groups are about 27–28 per cent. Differences in earnings between female workers with a Certificate I–IV and female workers with Year 12 and below are not significantly different from zero, suggesting that the returns to vocational training of female workers are very low. The difference between the hourly wage regression and the earnings regressions presented in Table 8.5 may be attributed to the large share of part-time employed women.

Life-cycle analysis

Figure 8.4 presents the age–wage profiles of male workers based on the longitudinal model. We observe that the age–wage profiles of male workers are generally increasing at a relatively constant rate. Wages of male workers with a postgraduate degree grow much faster than those of male workers with a Bachelor or Honours degree after the age of 40.

Wages of male workers with an Advanced Diploma/Diploma are typically about equal or higher than those of Certificate I–IV holders. Beyond age 55, male workers with an Advanced Diploma/Diploma earn even more than male workers with a Bachelor or Honours degree. The age–wage profile of male workers with Year 12 and below is consistently below the remaining profiles, indicating that the returns to education in relation to this reference group are always positive.

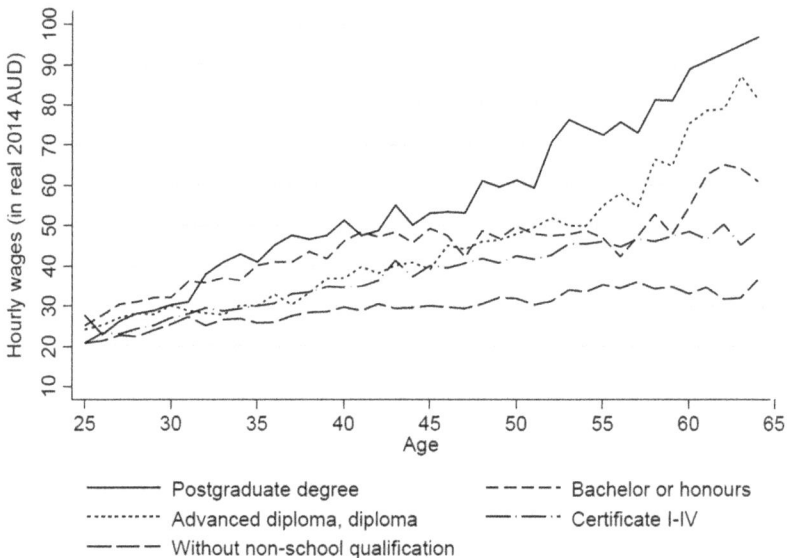

Figure 8.4: Age–wage profiles of male workers

Sample: Unbalanced panel. Weighted numbers based on weights provided by HILDA.

Source: Author's own calculations based on HILDA data.

Figure 8.5 depicts the age–wage profiles of female workers, which are much lower than those of male workers. We observe linear increases in average wages over the life cycle. The profiles reveal that average earnings of female workers with a postgraduate degree do not differ substantially from those of female workers with a Bachelor or Honours degree. We also observe that differences between the remaining groups (Advanced Diploma/Diploma, Certificate I–IV and with Year 12 and below) are rather small, suggesting that the returns to vocational education of female workers are very low.

We use the age–wage profiles presented in Figures 8.4 and 8.5 to calculate the returns to education of male and female workers based on the present value of lifetime earnings. The age–wage profiles of workers with Year 12 and below are used as a reference group to obtain results that are comparable to the estimated earnings differentials reported in Tables 8.4 and 8.5.

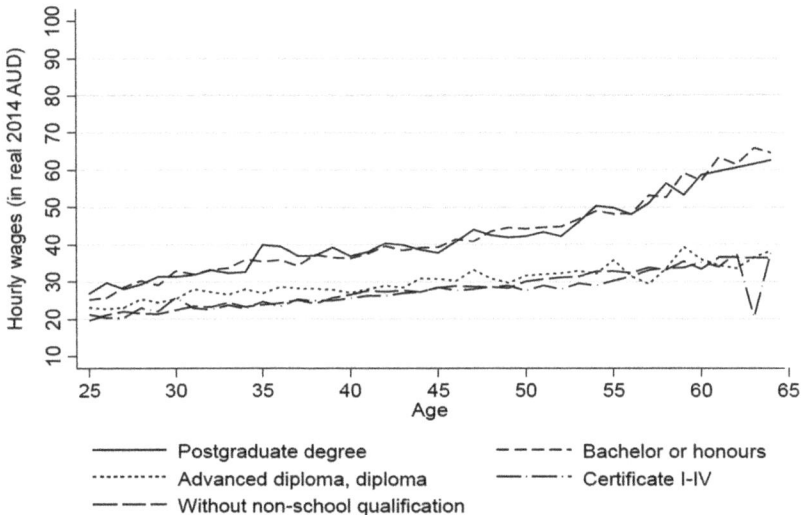

Figure 8.5: Age–wage profiles of female workers

Sample: Unbalanced panel. Weighted numbers based on weights provided by HILDA.
Source: Author's own calculations based on HILDA data.

Panel A of Table 8.6 summarises the cross-sectional returns to education of male and female workers presented in Tables 8.4 and 8.5. We compare these results to the dynamic returns to education (Panel B) that were derived from calculating the present value of lifetime earnings using the age–wage profiles presented in Figures 8.4 and 8.5. Panel C takes into account that individuals with different levels of education exhibit different employment probabilities and adjusts the numbers of the dynamic returns to education accordingly.

The numbers in Table 8.6 indicate that the returns to education derived from the longitudinal analysis are quite different from those of the cross-sectional analysis. We find that lifetime earnings of men with a postgraduate degree (Master's or Doctorate) are about 83 per cent higher than those of men with Year 12 and below (Panel C). Women with a postgraduate degree earn about 50 per cent more over their lifetime than women with Year 12 and below. The returns to education of both men and women with a Bachelor or Honours degree are about 50 per cent, indicating that women with a Bachelor or Honours degree earn about as much as women with a postgraduate degree. We also observe that women have no benefits from investing in vocational training. Overall, the empirical findings reveal considerable differences between cross-sectional and longitudinal models and between male and female workers.

Table 8.6: Returns to education of men and women (in per cent), cross-sectional vs life-cycle model

	Men	Women
A. Cross-sectional model		
Postgraduate Degree (Master's or Doctorate)	41.6	38.4
Bachelor or Honours	37.4	34.7
Advanced Diploma, Diploma	22.6	15.5
Certificate I–IV	10.4	-0.4
B. Life cycle model		
Postgraduate Degree (Master's or Doctorate)	77.1	47.1
Bachelor or Honours	48.2	46.4
Advanced Diploma, Diploma	41.8	8.2
Certificate I–IV	22.6	-2.1
C. Life cycle model, employment-adjusted		
Postgraduate Degree (Master's or Doctorate)	83.2	50.5
Bachelor or Honours	51.9	49.1
Advanced Diploma, Diploma	44.7	9.5
Certificate I–IV	24.6	-2.7

Sample based on unbalanced panel. Weighted numbers based on weights provided by HILDA.

Source: Author's own calculations based on HILDA data.

Implications for gender differences in costs of higher education

Although a detailed cost–benefit analysis is beyond the scope of this paper, we are able to study the implications of gender differences in earnings over the life course for the financial capacity of male and female university graduates to repay income-contingent student loans. Income-contingent student loans in Australia are characterised by two important features. First, they provide default insurance because individuals who do not earn money do not have to repay. Second, they provide consumption smoothing because repayments depend on current income.

Modelling the implications of gender differences in earnings for the financial capacity of male and female university graduates to repay student loans requires the consideration of income and labour market dynamics. Cross-sectional earnings models assume that variation in earnings observed between individuals at a certain point in time persists in the future. Cross-sectional models ignore considerable variation in earnings, which may have important implications for the prediction of future earnings.

Higgins and Sinning (2013) use longitudinal data to address the shortcomings of cross-sectional earnings models. They find that observed characteristics explain a relatively small proportion of earnings variability. Unobserved differences can result from temporary variation (due to illness, higher duties, bonuses, overtime, etc.) or permanent variation (such as ability, talent or motivation). Additionally, permanent unobserved shocks may be the result of job mobility and promotions or demotions (Meghir and Pistaferri 2004) and other incidents not accommodated by observed transitions in labour force or life states. Temporary and permanent differences and shocks constitute unobserved variation in earnings between individuals and over time for the same individuals.

Variance component models may be used to capture temporary and permanent variation in earnings. Based on the seminal work of Lillard and Willis (1978) and MaCurdy (1982), econometricians have applied variance component models to the context of earnings dynamics over the last three decades. Higgins and Sinning (2013) use HILDA data and decompose the residuals of an earnings regression into a permanent and a transitory component. The estimates obtained from their dynamic earnings model may be used to simulate the unobserved components of the earnings equation and to predict future earnings of male and female university graduates in Australia. Higgins and Sinning (2013) use these earnings predictions to calculate the remaining average debt of 2001 university graduates over the period 2002–30.

Figures 8.6 and 8.7 depict the average outstanding debt of male university graduates resulting from actual and predicted earnings models. Debt levels predicted by Model E3 are close to actual debt levels because this model uses both a temporary and a permanent component to model unobserved variation. In contrast, Models E1 and E2 produce less realistic predictions because they assume that all unobserved variation is either temporary or permanent, respectively. The average debt at the start of the simulation period is assumed to be $25,000 (in 2011 dollars). (See Higgins and Sinning (2013) for a detailed discussion of the underlying model assumptions.)

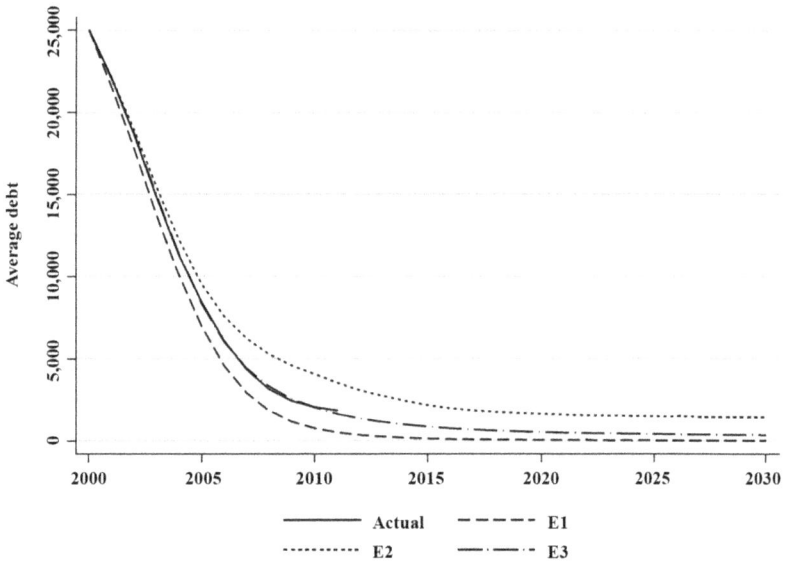

Figure 8.6: Average debt of male university graduates
Source: Higgins and Sinning (2013).

Figures 8.6 and 8.7 reveal considerable gender differences in actual and predicted outstanding debt levels. In particular, debt levels of male university graduates converge to zero over the projection period, while debt levels of female university graduates remain positive, indicating that many female university graduates do not have the financial capacity to repay their student loans in full. This result is remarkable because it implies that a considerable number of female university graduates rarely or never cross the minimum income threshold that would require them to repay their student loans.[1] This implies that the proposal to reduce the HECS repayment threshold announced in the 2017–18 Budget will have a gendered impact.

Taken together, these findings indicate that gender differences in earnings have considerable implications for the capacity of male and female university graduates to repay their student loans. A substantial part of the implicit subsidy of HECS may be attributed to female university graduates who are unable to repay their student loans in full. Australian taxpayers take over this part of the overall cost of higher education.

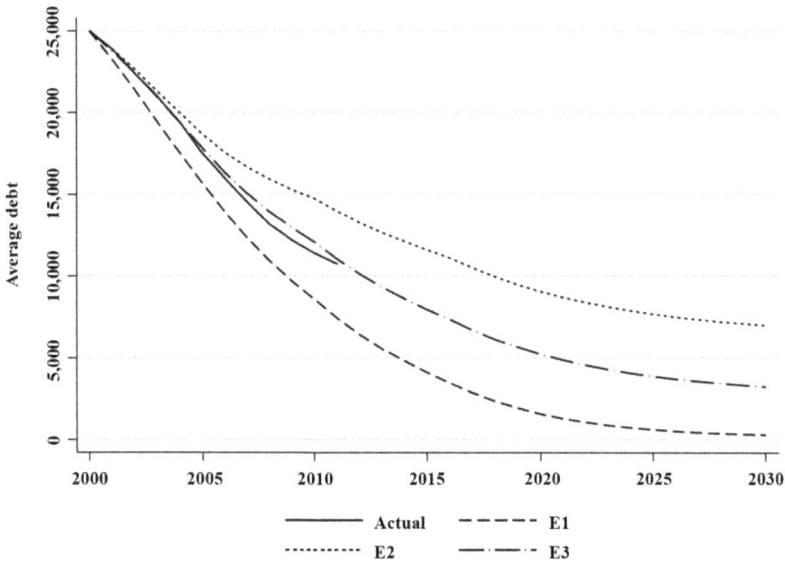

Figure 8.7: Average debt of female university graduates
Source: Higgins and Sinning (2013).

---

1   The model is based on the 2011 minimum income threshold of $44,912 (in 2011 dollars).

Conclusions

The results presented in this paper reveal a considerable earnings gap between men and women in Australia. Average earnings of male and female university graduates are about the same until about age 35. While average earnings of men rise from about $40,000 at age 35 to about $90,000 at age 60, average earnings of women increase only moderately from about $40,000 at age 35 to about $55,000 at age 60. Gender earnings gaps at any given level of education may be attributed to a range of factors, including gender differences in labour force participation, full-time and part-time employment, occupational choices, labour market discrimination, etc. The differences are also consistent with the view that Australia is lagging behind most other OECD countries in matters of gender equality in the labour market: data from the OECD employment database 2014 confirm that the gender wage gap in Australia is above OECD average and that the gap has remained remarkably stable since the early 2000s (see data.oecd. org/earnwage/gender-wage-gap.htm).

This chapter uses longitudinal data from the HILDA Survey to present new calculations of the private returns to education in Australia. The data allow us to compare the estimates obtained from a cross-sectional model to those of a life-cycle model, which uses longitudinal data to predict earnings over the life cycle.

We find that lifetime earnings of men with a postgraduate degree (Master's or Doctorate) are about 83 per cent higher than those of men with Year 12 and below. Women with a postgraduate degree earn about 50 per cent more over their lifetime than women with Year 12 and below. Our findings also reveal that women with a Bachelor or Honours degree earn almost as much as women with a postgraduate degree. We further observe that women have no benefits from investing in vocational training. Overall, the empirical findings reveal considerable differences between cross-sectional and longitudinal models and between male and female workers. Further research is needed to gain a better understanding of the factors that are responsible for the findings presented in this paper.

Our results for HECS debt calculations presented in the last section are a result of the considerable gender earnings gap. One could argue that HECS contributes to gender differences in earnings by subsidising female university graduates and thereby creating disincentives for women to work, but it appears likely that the effect of HECS on female labour force participation is rather small or insignificant. At the same time, HECS plays a critical role in the context of gender differences in earnings because the scheme provides default insurance and consumption smoothing to female university graduates and ensures that both men and women from low socio-economic backgrounds are able to obtain a university degree. The contributions of HECS to social mobility are likely to outweigh any potential negative side effects on work disincentives of female university graduates. HECS is particularly interesting from a public policy perspective because the scheme reduces economic inequality while potentially contributing to economic growth. Tax and transfer policies that aim to reduce economic inequality (such as social welfare payments) typically contribute to lower economic growth.

References

Angrist, Joshua and Alan Krueger. 1991. 'Does Compulsory Schooling Attendance Affect Schooling and Earnings?' *Quarterly Journal of Economics* 106(4): 979–1014. doi.org/10.2307/2937954

Ashenfelter, Orley, Colm Harmon and Hessel Oosterbeek. 1999. 'A Review of Estimates of the Schooling/Earnings Relationship, with Tests for Publication Bias'. *Labour Economics* 6(4): 453–470. doi. org/10.1016/S0927-5371(99)00041-X

Ashenfelter, Orley and Alan Krueger. 1994. 'Estimates of the Economic Return to Schooling from a New Sample of Twins'. *The American Economic Review* 84: 1157–1173.

Becker, Gary. 1964. *Human Capital: A Theoretical and Empirical Analysis with Special Reference to Education*. New York: Columbia University Press.

Card, David. 1999. 'The Causal Effect of Education on Earnings'. In Orley Ashenfelter and David Card (eds), *Handbook of Labor Economics*. Amsterdam: Elsevier. doi.org/10.1016/s1573-4463(99)03011-4

Daly, Anne and Philip Lewis. 2010. 'The Private Rate of Return to an Economics Degree in Australia: An Update'. *Economic Papers* 29(3): 353–364. doi.org/10.1111/j.1759-3441.2010.00072.x

Daly, Anne, Philip Lewis, Michael Corliss and Tiffany Heaslip. 2010. *The Private Rate of Return to a University Degree in Australia*. University of Canberra, Centre for Labour Market Research, Canberra.

Heckman, James, Lance Lochner and Petra Todd. 2005. 'Earnings Functions, Rates of Return, and Treatment Effects: The Mincer Equation and Beyond'. In Eric A. Hanushek and Finis Welch (eds), *Handbook of the Economics of Education*, Volume 1. Amsterdam: Elsevier. doi.org/10.3386/w11544

Higgins, Timothy and Mathias Sinning. 2013. 'Modeling Income Dynamics for Public Policy Design: An Application to Income Contingent Student Loans'. *Economics of Education Review* 37: 273–285. doi.org/10.1016/j.econedurev.2013.08.009

Jaeger, David and Marianne Page. 1996. 'Degrees Matter: New Evidence on Sheepskin Effects in the Returns to Education'. *Review of Economics and Statistics* 78(4): 733–740. doi.org/10.2307/2109960

Leigh, Andrew and Christopher Ryan. 2008. 'Estimating Returns to Education using Different Natural Experiment Techniques'. *Economics of Education Review* 27(2): 149–160. doi.org/10.1016/j.econedurev.2006.09.004

Lillard, Lee and Robert Willis. 1978. 'Dynamic Aspects of Earning Mobility'. *Econometrica* 46(5): 985–1012. doi.org/10.2307/1911432

MaCurdy, Thomas. 1982. 'The Use of Time Series Processes to Model the Error Structure of Earnings in a Longitudinal Data Analysis'. *Journal of Econometrics* 18(1): 83–114. doi.org/10.1016/0304-4076(82)90096-3

Marks, Gary. 2008. 'The Occupations and Earnings of Young Australians: The Role of Education and Training'. Longitudinal Study of Australian Youth (LSAY) Research Report No. 55. doi.org/10.1111/j.1468-0262.2004.00476.x

Meghir, Costas and Luigi Pistaferri. 2004. 'Income Variance Dynamics and Heterogeneity'. *Econometrica* 72(1): 1–32.

Mincer, Jacob. 1974. *Schooling, Experience and Earnings*. New York: National Bureau of Economic Research.

Norton, Andrew. 2012. *Graduate Winners—Assessing the Public and Private Benefits of Higher Education*. Melbourne: Grattan Institute.

OECD (Organisation for Economic Co-operation and Cultural Development). 2015. *Education at a Glance: OECD Indicators*. Paris: OECD Publishing.

Psacharopoulos, George and Harry Anthony Patrinos. 2004. 'Returns to Investment in Education: A Further Update'. *Education Economics* 12(2): 111–135. doi.org/10.1080/0964529042000239140

Schultz, Theodore. 1961. 'Investment in Human Capital'. *The American Economic Review* 51(1): 1–17.

Wei, Hui. 2010. *Measuring Economic Returns to Post-School Education in Australia*. Research Paper Cat. no. 1351.0.55.032, Canberra: Australian Bureau of Statistics.

9

Women and top incomes in Australia[1]

Miranda Stewart, Sarah Voitchovsky and Roger Wilkins

The study of top incomes has made great strides in recent years. The novel feature of this research is the use of tax records data, which have now been used to study top incomes over decades or even longer periods in a large number of countries (Atkinson and Piketty 2010; Atkinson and Piketty 2007).[2] Top incomes research has made a significant contribution to public and policy debates about income inequality and the role of the tax-transfer system; see, for example, the Organisation for Economic Co-operation and Development (OECD) study by Keeley (2015) and Australian Treasury study, Fletcher and Guttmann (2013).

For Australia, Atkinson and Leigh (2007) is the pioneering study on top incomes using individual tax return data. This was recently updated and refined by Burkhauser et al. (2015). Similar to a number of other countries, Australia has experienced sustained increases in the income shares of top income groups since the early 1980s. Top incomes research also provides

1   Sarah Voitchovsky acknowledges financial support from the Swiss National Science Foundation (SNSF). Roger Wilkins acknowledges financial support from the Australian Research Council (DP150102409).
2   The World Wealth and Incomes Database provides incomes and wealth data for 39 countries using tax returns and other sources. See: www.wid.world/#Home.

evidence of the sources of incomes of top cohorts. One general result is the increasingly important role of high wages relative to capital incomes over time for top income groups.

Existing top incomes research has paid relatively little attention to the demographic composition of those at the top of the income distribution, despite the fact that one particularly important demographic characteristic—gender—is observed in tax records data in nearly all countries with individual (as opposed to family) taxation. Seeking to address this gap for Australia, this chapter presents new evidence on the representation of women at the top of the income distribution and explores differences between men and women in the characteristics of those at the top of the distribution. We build on the international comparative research on women and top incomes by Atkinson et al. (2014, 2016) that has deepened and developed the broader body of research into the 'glass ceiling' for women's incomes in developed countries.[3]

Our results demonstrate that Australia shows some similarities but also deviates in some respects from the pattern of distribution and source of income in data for women in other OECD countries that have individual taxation. Once the results are presented, we seek to offer some initial explanations of the observed patterns for Australian top-income women. Our initial results demonstrate, not surprisingly, that there is significant gender inequality at the top of the income distribution, with women comprising only one-quarter of the top 10 per cent of individuals and just over 15 per cent of the top 0.1 per cent. Our results also show, however, that the numbers of women in top echelons are higher in Australia than other countries. This is not explained by higher wages, but may be explained by tax planning between spouses or within families in Australia's individual income tax system. In particular, income splitting may contribute to the trends observed for Australia.

In all individual income tax systems that have a progressive rate structure, there is a structural incentive for related parties—especially family members—to split or share income among themselves so as to reduce the overall tax burden of the family (see, for example, Head and Krever 1996). In Australia, the legal structure and interpretation of the income tax has long facilitated certain kinds of income splitting. Interactions between the

---

3   See a discussion of this research at www.weforum.org/agenda/2014/07/women-income-glass-ceiling.

income tax and cash transfer systems in Australia produce a 'quasi-joint tax unit' for many families with children (see Chapter 3, this volume; Henry et al. 2009). It is less well known—except to tax lawyers and the high-income individuals and families who they advise—that, for individuals deriving investment or business income, a 'quasi-joint' tax unit can also be produced through income splitting (Stewart 1999). The ability to split income among the 'professional and commercial classes'[4] is one issue highlighted in the recent Treasury *Re:Think Tax Discussion Paper* (Treasury 2015, p. 51).

Top incomes in Australia

The analysis presented in this chapter is based on customised tax tables supplied by the Australian Taxation Office (ATO) for the period 2000–01 to 2013–14. Identification of the gender composition of top income groups is possible using tax records data because personal income tax (PIT) data in Australia are reported at the individual level. This chapter presents the top income shares and income thresholds (the minimum income to be in top income group) for the income years ending 30 June 2001 to 30 June 2014, for women in the following four top income groups: 0.1 per cent, 1 per cent, 5 per cent and 10 per cent.

We then examine the income sources of these women, distinguishing wage income from non-wage income. The proportion of females and males in each group that is working age is identified and the wage share of the total income of working-age women in each of the top income groups, compared to the wage share of total income of working-age men in each of the top income groups, is analysed. We present international comparisons of the earnings share of women in top income groups. We then identify the most significant occupations for those top-income women who declare wage income and for the working age subset of these women (age 18 to 64).

The key descriptive statistics produced in the tax-based top incomes literature are income shares of top income groups such as the top 1 per cent. The focus on the top reflects both the strengths and weaknesses of tax records data. Tax data are well suited to the study of very high incomes. Household surveys of income (such as the Australian Bureau of Statistics' (ABS) Survey of Income and Housing) face problems of sampling error and potential

---

4   *FCT v Everett* (1980) 143 CLR 440 at 457 per Murphy J (in dissent).

non-response from the relatively small cohort with top incomes, which may make their results less reliable at the top of the income distribution than income tax data, which do not have these problems. However, many people in Australia and other countries are not required to file a tax return because their incomes are low and in many countries tax data do not contain government transfers, which are an important income source for low-income individuals.[5] Consequently, it is in general not possible to examine the full income distribution with tax records data. Indeed, the exclusion of some or all government transfers is part of a broader problem of imperfect capture of income by tax records data. For example, income not 'declared' to the tax authority is not captured. In addition, the legal definition of income is subject to change over time. For example, in many countries, realised capital gains were not included in taxable income until later in the 20th century.

A further challenge identified recently by Canadian researchers is the use of privately owned legal entities, such as companies and trusts, to hold income that arguably should be counted in determining the true incomes of individuals in top income cohorts. Wolfson et al. (2016) study the importance of controlled private companies in Canada in increasing the share of income of top income groups (held directly and indirectly) and in shifting the proportion of individuals in top income groups. To do this analysis, they link individual income tax data with business data. A similar effect might be obtained in Australia. The research presented in this chapter provides some intriguing indirect evidence of income splitting between spouses, which supports anecdotal evidence about the tax planning activities of top income individuals including through the use of privately owned trusts and companies in Australia.

Atkinson and Leigh (2007) produced the first estimates of top income shares for Australia based on tax records data, examining the period from 1921–22 to 2003–04. Drawing on tabulations of the number of tax filers in each range of total income, National Accounts data on household income and ABS population data, they produce estimates of the proportion of total income going to the top x per cent of individuals aged 15 years and over. Specifically, using the population data to ascertain the number of people in the top x per cent, they then use the tax tables

---

5   In Australia, some government transfers are in the tax records data (and included in 'earnings' as discussed below) but others (including the Disability Support Pension and Family Tax Benefit) are not.

to estimate the total income of the top x per cent. This is then divided by an estimate of aggregate income derived from the National Accounts to produce the estimated income share of the top income group.

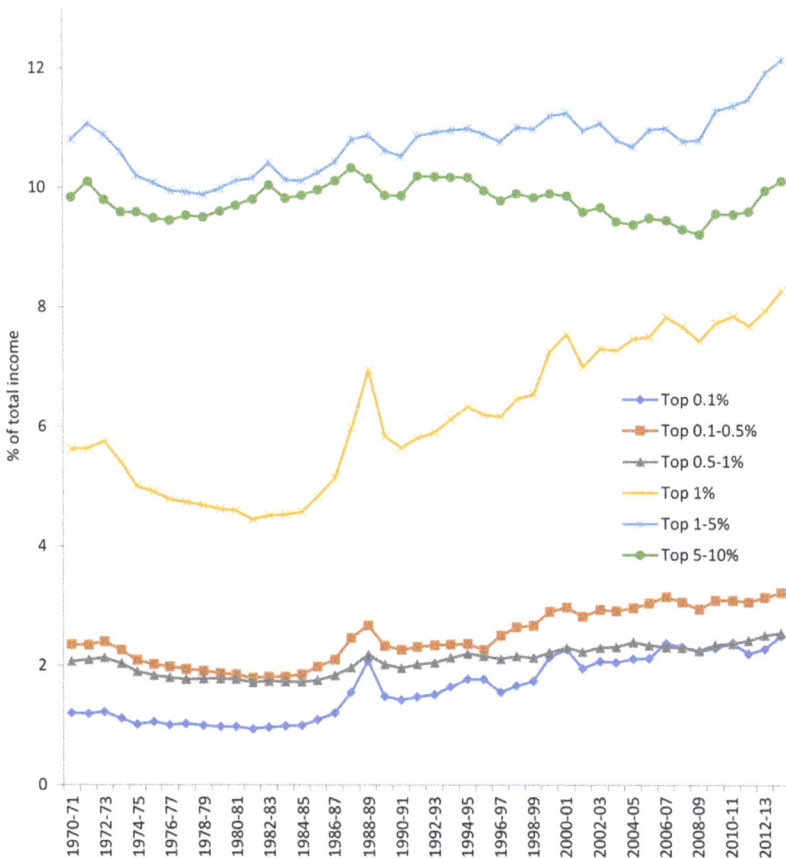

Figure 9.1: Income shares of top income groups in Australia, 1970–71 to 2013–14

Source: Burkhauser et al. (2015), updated; ATO Taxation Statistics including income from wages, businesses, investments, taxable government transfers and other sources as identified in the tax return.

Burkhauser et al. (2015) refined and updated Atkinson and Leigh's estimates, producing a more consistently measured series over the period 1970–71 to 2011–12 that excluded realised capital gains and dividend imputation credits.[6] The National Accounts measure of total income excludes both of these income components, which also only enter the tax data from the mid-1980s. Moreover, capital gains tax only applies to assets acquired after 1985, resulting in a growing proportion of all realised capital gains entering the PIT base from the mid-1980s on. We adopt the Burkhauser et al. (2015) series for our analysis in this chapter and therefore focus solely on income from wages, businesses, investments, taxable government transfers and other sources as identified in the tax return.

Figure 9.1 provides the broader context in which we examine women's representation at the top of the income distribution, presenting the Burkhauser et al. (2015) series updated to 2013–14 (the most recent tax year for which data are available). It shows that the income share of the top 5 per cent, and the income share of each top income group within the top 5 per cent, has increased in the last three decades. In particular, the income share of the top 1 per cent has doubled from just over 4 per cent in 1982–83 to just over 8 per cent in 2013–14. The income share of the top 5–10 per cent (91st to 95th percentiles) declined slightly to 2008–09, since when it has risen rapidly.

Women's representation in top income groups

As noted above, an important feature of the Australian PIT is that the tax unit is the individual, which means that all income of a tax unit can be attributed to one person. Moreover, the gender of tax filers is known by the ATO, making it possible to examine the representation of women in top income groups. This is also true for many other countries, but it is not the case in countries that allow (or require) joint tax returns to be filed by spouses, or indeed the family or household as a whole. Notably, this is the case in the US, Germany and France.

Figure 9.2 presents the proportion of women in Australia who are in the top 10 per cent, top 5 per cent, top 1 per cent and top 0.1 per cent by income. It shows that, in 2013–14, women made up about one-quarter (25.7 per cent) of the top 10 per cent, 22.3 per cent of the top 5 per cent, 20.3 per cent of the top 1 per cent and 17.2 per cent of the top 0.1 per cent.

---

6   Imputation credits are tax credits allowed to individuals for imputed company tax paid on dividends received by them (under Div. 207 of the *Income Tax Assessment Act 1997* (Cth)).

The period from 2000–01 to 2013–14 saw women's shares of top income groups rise slightly. The increase was greatest at the very top, with women's share of the top 0.1 per cent rising three percentage points, compared with a two percentage-point rise for the top 1 per cent and approximately one percentage-point rises for the top 5 per cent and top 10 per cent.

Figure 9.2 also shows a peak in women's share of top income groups, particularly the top 1 per cent and 0.1 per cent groups, in 2006–07. For example, the female share of the top 1 per cent rose from 18.3 per cent in 2000–01 to a peak of 21.4 per cent in 2006–07, before levelling off at approximately 20 per cent from 2008–09 onwards. As Figure 9.1 shows, while the 2008 Global Financial Crisis (GFC) had a fairly small negative effect on overall top incomes, there was nonetheless a small peak in overall top incomes in 2006–07. One potential explanation for the coincident peak in women's share of top incomes is that 2006–07 was a high point in economic returns to investments.[7]

Also potentially important is a tax policy change concerning superannuation that commenced at this time, being the major Howard–Costello 'Simplifying Superannuation' reforms. Effective from 1 July 2007, substantial deductible contributions could be made into superannuation funds (so-called concessional contributions) by self-employed people and employees. These deductible contributions were concessionally taxed at only 15 per cent in the superannuation fund (up to a cap of $50,000 per individual). Self-employed workers and employees could also make additional non-deductible contributions up to a cap of $150,000 per year or $450,000 over three years. Other changes lowered taxes on superannuation savings and payouts very substantially. In particular, earnings on so-called 'transition to retirement' pensions became tax-free. Superannuation payouts of pensions and lump sums were rendered completely tax-free once a recipient reached age 60. These highly generous superannuation tax concessions were reduced in reforms in recent years including in 2016 by the Turnbull Government.

An indirect effect of these superannuation tax reforms was that, instead of income being earned in, for example, a family trust and distributed to beneficiaries including women each year (appearing in their tax returns), it

---

7   Indicative of the high investment returns is that the ASX200 increased by 24 per cent over the 2006–07 fiscal year, its fastest fiscal-year rate of growth over the 2000–01 to 2013–14 period examined in this chapter.

would be more tax-effective for income to be earned in a superannuation fund that could be achieved by making deductible contributions into that fund. Superannuation fund earnings are not distributed until retirement and so these earnings no longer appear in individual tax returns (and in our data). This shift could imply a drop in the number of women in top income groups if women were previously disproportionally represented among the beneficiaries of trusts. Not all types of superannuation payments appear in the tax record data. Further research examining individual income tax returns, trust data and superannuation fund tax returns, in particular if they could be linked, would be productive in understanding the effect of the changes to the tax treatment of superannuation on characteristics of top income groups, including their gender composition.

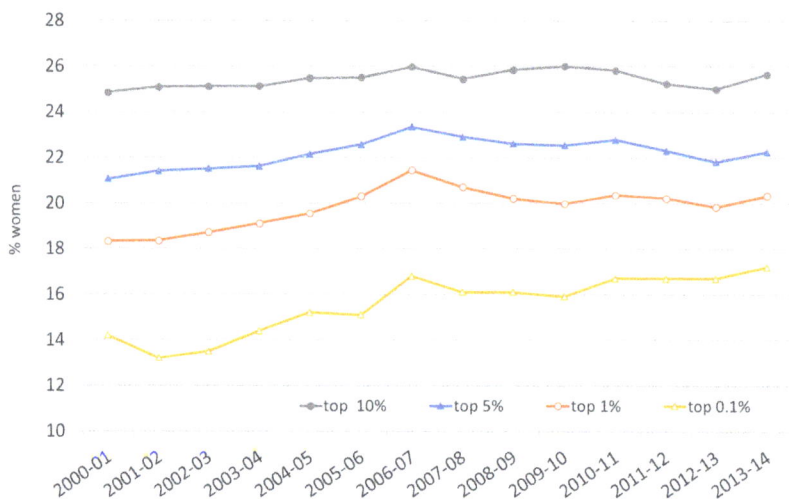

Figure 9.2: Share of women in top percentiles, Australia

Source: Authors' calculations using data provided by the ATO. Total income excludes imputation credits and capital gains.

How much are top incomes?

What puts a woman in the top 1 per cent of Australian incomes? Table 9.1 shows the income thresholds for the top 10 per cent, 5 per cent, 1 per cent and 0.1 per cent of the income distribution, from 2000–01 to 2013–14 (in current Australian dollars). In 2013–14, the total income (excluding capital gains and dividend imputation credits) required to be in the top 10 per cent was $94,236. The top 1 per cent total income threshold was $237,341 and top 0.1 per cent was about three times that, at $698,108.

Table 9.1: Minimum levels of total income, by year, in current $

	Top 10%	Top 5%	Top 1%	Top 0.1%
2000–01	54,335	68,946	128,671	373,260
2001–02	56,223	71,566	134,398	375,746
2002–03	58,265	74,119	139,272	399,391
2003–04	60,934	77,522	145,947	429,946
2004–05	64,410	82,021	155,695	468,675
2005–06	67,810	87,204	166,127	499,587
2006–07	72,331	93,214	178,963	570,083
2007–08	75,670	98,263	187,322	598,625
2008–09	79,250	102,854	194,295	582,172
2009–10	81,171	105,858	199,582	604,078
2010–11	86,074	113,417	213,689	648,214
2011–12	90,317	120,018	224,773	654,044
2012–13	93,231	124,975	232,994	665,531
2013–14	94,236	126,383	237,341	698,108

Source: Authors' calculations using data provided by the ATO. Total income excludes dividend imputation credits and capital gains.

Comparison with other countries

This paper compares Australian top incomes by gender with the results for several other countries with individual taxation, as shown in Atkinson et al. (2016). Other OECD countries with individual taxation that are examined are Spain, Canada, New Zealand, the UK, Denmark, Italy and Norway.

The comparisons across countries are carried out using the latest available tax data. The share of women in the top 10 per cent in Australia is similar to but somewhat lower than that in other countries in this comparison. Each of the UK, Italy, New Zealand, Canada, Denmark and Spain have a larger cohort of close to or above 30 per cent in the top 10 per cent, and Spain has the highest proportion of women in the top 10 per cent at 34.8 per cent. Only Norway has a significantly lower proportion.

Table 9.2: Proportion of women in top percentiles (comparative)

	Top 10%	Top 5%	Top 1%	Top 0.1%
Spain 2013	34.8	33.3	24.9	19.8
Denmark 2013	30.9	25.1	16.2	10.8
Canada 2014	29.7	25.2	21.7	15.3
New Zealand 2014	29.4	24.3	17.9	–
Italy 2014	29.0	25.9	19.6	12.7
UK 2013	28.0	24.6	18.0	10.8
Australia 2013	25.7	22.3	20.3	17.2
Norway 2013	21.5	17.8	13.7	13.6

Sources: Figures for Australia are authors' calculations based on data provided by the ATO, where total income excludes capital gains and dividend imputation credits. Figures for other countries come from Atkinson et al. (2016).

From the early 2000s, tax records indicate that the share of women at the top 10 per cent and top 5 per cent has generally been increasing in all countries (Figure 9.3). However, this trend is not so apparent in Australia. Figure 9.2 shows that the Australian trend of the proportion of women in the top 10 per cent is mostly flat between 2000–01 and 2013–14 with a total increase of 0.8 percentage points. This is the smallest increase in all the comparator countries over that period, as shown in Figure 9.3.

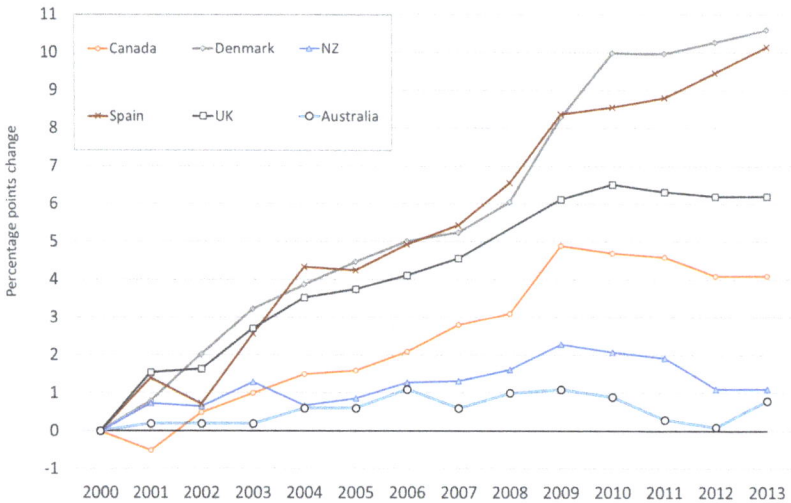

Figure 9.3: Change in proportion of women in top 10 per cent since 2000, various countries

Source: Data for Australia from authors' calculations based on data provided by the ATO; total income excluding capital gains and imputation credits. Data for other countries come from Atkinson et al. (2016). The curves for Italy and Norway are not shown for clarity. They reveal a total increase of 3.2 and 2.9 percentage points by 2013, respectively.

The pattern of women in the top 10 per cent and 1 per cent of the income distribution in Australia differs from that in the other countries examined, where the number of women tends to decline and become increasingly smaller as incomes increase. Table 9.2 indicates that women's share of the top 10 per cent is somewhat lower in Australia than in most countries shown in the table, but their share of the top 1 per cent and 0.1 per cent is higher than in six of these seven countries. Indeed, in 2013–14, the share of Australian women in the top 0.1 per cent, at approximately 17 per cent, is one-and-a-half times that of some other countries. As a result, of all the countries presented in Table 9.2, Australia has consistently had the highest ratio of the share of women in the top 0.1 per cent to the share of women in the top 10 per cent since the early 2000s.

The characteristics of women in the top 1 per cent

Tax records data contains relatively little information on the characteristics on tax filers. Nonetheless, in addition to gender, it is possible to identify several important characteristics, including age, income sources and, for those employed, occupation of employment. In this section, we describe the characteristics of women in the top 1 per cent of income earners, particularly focusing on the important ways in which they differ from men in the top 1 per cent.

Age

It is interesting to observe the differences in the age composition of women in the top 1 per cent compared with men. The age composition of women in the top 1 per cent is compared with that of men in Figure 9.4. The left panel of the figure presents the proportion of women in the top 1 per cent in each of five age groups over the 2000–01 to 2012–13 period.[8] The right panel presents corresponding information for men. For both men and women, the most common age range in the top 1 per cent is 35–54, followed by the 55–64 age range. However, the proportion of women in the top 1 per cent aged 45–64 (peak earnings age) is lower than the proportion of men in the top 1 per cent in this

---

8   The customised tables we obtained from the ATO do not contain data disaggregated by sex and age for 2013–14.

age range, which may reflect a generational change. On the other hand, the proportion of women in the top 1 per cent aged 65 and over is significantly larger than the proportion of men. Close to 15 per cent of women in the top 1 per cent were over 65 in 2012–13, compared to just over 5 per cent of men. This is consistent with the smaller role played by earnings for women in the top 1 per cent. Given women's greater life expectancy, older women may also inherit assets from husbands or other family members and derive non-wage income from these assets. Other research using estate tax return data for the US suggests that a higher share of women among the wealthy reflects a greater importance of inherited as opposed to self-made wealth (Elund and Kopczuk 2009).

Similar trends in the age composition between 2000–01 and 2012–13 are evident for women and men. The proportion in the 45–64 age range increased for both men and women, and decreased in all other age groups. A relatively high proportion of women in the top 1 per cent were under 35 years of age in 2000–01, but this age group experienced the greatest decline up to 2012–13, so that the proportion in the top 1 per cent aged under 35 was similar for men and women in 2012–13.

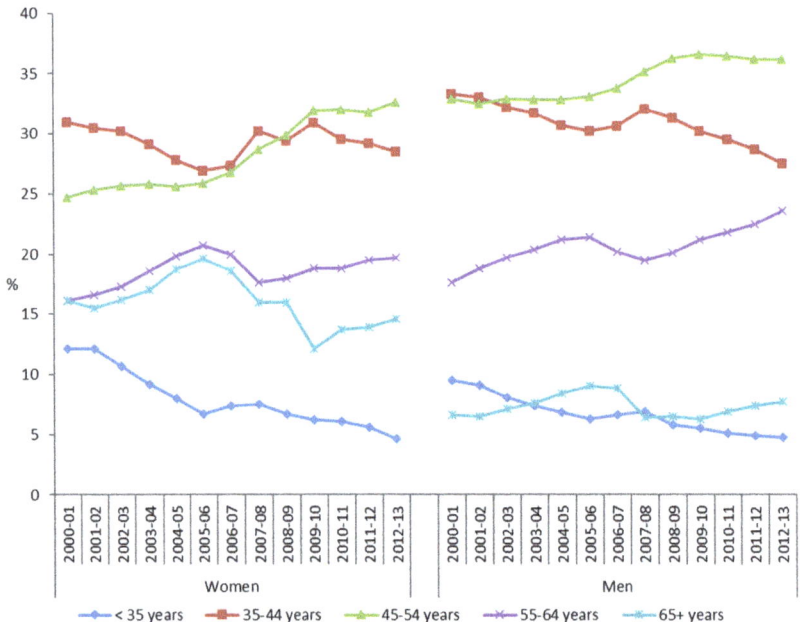

Figure 9.4: Age composition of men and women in the top 1 per cent, 2000–01 to 2012–13 (percentage of cohort)

Source: Authors' calculations using data provided by the ATO.

'Wage' shares of top income cohorts

Table 9.3 presents the shares of wages in total income of women and men in top income groups. 'Wages' comprise several components, namely: wages and salaries; employment allowances, earnings, tips and directors fees; employer lump sum and termination payments and exempt foreign employment income; and superannuation lump sum payments. However, 'wages' do not include Australian annuities and superannuation streams of various sorts. In general, the data show that women in the top 1 per cent tend to have less income from 'wages' as defined and more income from other sources than men. Further research using ATO data that disaggregates the superannuation payments is intended; this can provide more information about work and retirement savings income of men and women with top incomes.

Table 9.3: Share of total income from wages, all ages

	Women				Men			
	Top 10%	Top 5%	Top 1%	Top 5%–10%	Top 10%	Top 5%	Top 1%	Top 5%–10%
2000–01	70.4	60.9	41.3	83.4	82.5	78.7	66.6	90.7
2001–02	70.4	61.2	43.2	82.8	81.8	78.0	66.6	90.0
2002–03	70.3	61.2	42.3	82.9	81.4	77.4	64.9	90.0
2003–04	69.5	60.1	41.2	82.7	80.7	76.5	63.0	89.9
2004–05	68.5	59.0	39.8	82.1	80.1	75.6	61.7	89.9
2005–06	66.6	56.8	38.8	81.4	79.3	74.6	60.4	89.6
2006–07	62.2	52.3	34.1	78.1	76.9	71.9	57.2	88.3
2007–08	64.7	54.4	36.1	81.4	78.7	73.7	59.3	90.1
2008–09	65.7	55.6	37.5	81.1	79.5	74.9	60.5	90.2
2009–10	68.4	57.9	40.4	84.0	80.1	75.3	60.8	90.9
2010–11	66.0	55.4	39.1	82.4	79.4	74.4	60.2	90.6
2011–12	66.0	55.9	40.1	81.7	80.3	75.4	60.9	90.9
2012–13	66.9	56.8	40.9	82.1	81.0	76.3	61.6	91.4
2013–14	67.0	56.7	40.5	82.5	80.5	75.9	60.5	91.0

'Wages' comprise wages and salaries; employment allowances, earnings, tips and directors fees; employer lump sum and termination payments and exempt foreign employment income; and superannuation lump sum payments.

Source: Authors' calculations using data provided by the ATO.

Table 9.3 shows that in 2013–14, 67 per cent of total income for women in the top 10 per cent is derived from wages, broadly defined as explained above, compared to 80.5 per cent for men. For the top 1 per cent, the wage share falls to 40.5 per cent for women compared to 60.5 per cent for men. The high proportion of women with no occupation (and relatively low wage shares) who are in the top 10 per cent compared to men is explained to some extent by the age profile of women in top income cohorts, as discussed in the previous section. However, the inclusion of lump sum superannuation payments in the wage share data complicates this story. To understand better the importance of wages excluding superannuation lump sums, for women in the top 10 per cent, Table 9.4 presents the same information as Table 9.3, restricted to working-age (18–64) men and women. We observe that differences between men and women in the wage share are smaller when we restrict to working-age people, but nonetheless remain substantial.

Overall, the analysis of the income composition of women in the top 1 per cent compared with men indicates that employment plays a smaller role for top-income women than for top-income men.

Table 9.4: Share of total income from wages, working-age population only

	Women				Men			
	Top 10%	Top 5%	Top 1%	Top 5%–10%	Top 10%	Top 5%	Top 1%	Top 5%–10%
2001–02	75.7	67.4	49.3	86.2	84.2	80.6	69.0	92.0
2002–03	75.8	67.5	48.6	86.3	83.9	80.1	67.6	92.0
2003–04	75.4	67.0	47.9	86.3	83.4	79.4	65.8	92.0
2004–05	74.9	66.3	46.7	86.1	83.1	78.9	64.9	92.0
2005–06	73.4	64.3	46.0	85.8	82.5	78.0	63.9	91.9
2006–07	69.0	59.7	41.0	82.6	80.4	75.7	61.2	90.7
2007–08	70.5	60.8	42.6	84.9	81.3	76.6	62.6	91.7
2008–09	71.5	62.3	44.5	84.4	82.1	77.8	63.8	91.7
2009–10	73.0	63.2	46.1	86.7	82.3	77.8	63.7	92.3
2010–11	71.2	61.2	45.4	85.7	81.9	77.1	63.2	92.2
2011–12	71.4	61.9	46.9	85.0	82.8	78.2	64.2	92.5
2012–13	72.1	62.6	47.6	85.4	83.4	79.0	64.7	92.9
2013–14	72.3	62.9	48.0	85.7	83.2	78.8	64.1	92.6

'Wages' comprise wages and salaries; employment allowances, earnings, tips and directors fees; employer lump sum and termination payments and exempt foreign employment income; and superannuation lump sum payments.

Source: Authors' calculations using data provided by the ATO.

'Earnings' in the top 1 per cent compared to other countries

A broader category than wages is 'earnings', which we define as wages, pensions and government transfers. We utilise this composite category so as to enable cross-country comparisons, due to data constraints. The concept of 'earnings' reflects a broader notion of income earned through the labour market. Note that government transfers tend to be very small at the top of the income distribution. Atkinson et al. (2016) show that women in the top 1 per cent have a lower share of their income coming from this earnings measure than men in all the countries and years for which we have data. Atkinson et al. (2016), moreover, show that, since the mid-2000s, this difference has been largest in Australia.

In 2013–14, for example, the difference in the share of earnings between men and women in the top 1 per cent reached about 23 percentage points (the 'earnings' share for women is 43.7 per cent and for men is 66.5 per cent in that year). The share of earnings in total income has tended to increase for women in the top 1 per cent in most countries in recent years, making their income composition profile look more like that of men. This is again not the case in Australia where, if anything, the share of income from earnings for women in the top 1 per cent has tended to decline since 2000–01 (Figure 9.5). This is surprising given the overall context in which the share of income of the top 1 per cent has doubled, as illustrated in Figure 9.1. It indicates, at the least, that Australian women's earnings share at the top end has stagnated.

There are complexities in the subcategories of other sources of income reported for tax purposes in Australia and in other countries, so it may be difficult to clearly identify other types of income such as business and investment income. Difficulties may arise, for example, in determining the split between investment and self-employment or entrepreneurial income derived through partnerships and trusts. Nonetheless, in Australia, women in the top 1 per cent have one of the largest shares of income from non-earnings sources compared to women in the top 1 per cent in other countries, even when business and investment income are combined.

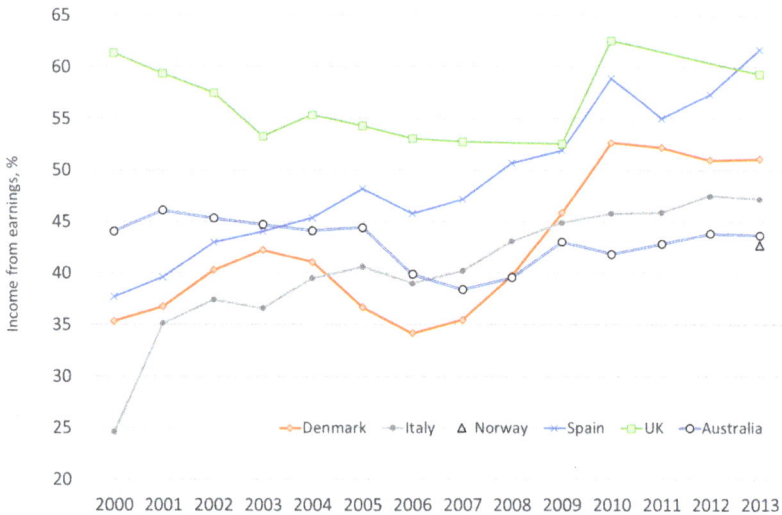

Figure 9.5: Share of income from earnings, women in top 1 per cent, various countries

Source: Data for Australia from authors' calculations based on data provided by the ATO. Total income excludes capital gains and imputation credits. Data for other countries from Atkinson et al. (2016). Data for Norway only available for 2013.

Occupations of women in top income groups

In contrast to many other countries, Australian tax records data include the occupations of employed tax filers, who are required to state their occupation on the tax return. We have done an initial analysis of the occupations data in Australian tax records and present some specific features in this section.

Analysing occupations in top income groups in Australia, we observe that a significant proportion of people (men and women) in this cohort do not report an occupation at all.[9] Table 9.5 presents the proportion of working-age women and men with no occupation in the top 10 per cent, 5 per cent and 1 per cent income groups. It shows that working-age women with top incomes are considerably more likely to have no occupation than working-age men. Women in the top 1 per cent are two-thirds more likely to report 'no occupation' (22.7 per cent) than men (14 per cent).[10]

---

9   Most of these people do not report any wage income at all or report a very low wage. We assume that most of these men and women do not work for wages or salary.

10   As shown in the Appendix, in all income groups, only a small proportion of individuals (between 1 and 2 per cent) report an occupation that cannot be classified. Consequently, this does not materially affect our results.

Table 9.5: Share of working-age men and women (age 18–64) with no occupation, by gender and income range, 2013–14

	Women				Men			
	Proportion with no occupation (%)	Share of total income from wages (%)	Average annual wage ($)	Average income ($)	Proportion with no occupation (%)	Share of total income from wages (%)	Average annual wage ($)	Average income ($)
Top 1%	22.7	2.2	10,493	478,737	14.0	3.1	16,057	513,777
Top 5%	15.1	3.0	7,477	245,814	7.7	3.9	11,406	289,833
Top 10%	10.4	3.2	6,229	193,290	6.3	4.1	9,141	223,546

Source: Authors' calculations using data provided by the ATO.

Focusing on working-age men and women who report an occupation, we investigated the top 30 occupational categories for women and men in the top 1 per cent income group. The full results are presented in Tables 9.A1 and 9.A2 in the Appendix. It is not surprising to find that a significant proportion of men and women in the top 1 per cent are in high-wage occupations. As noted in the introduction, one key finding from the general top incomes literature is that high wages are the main reason why people are in top-income cohorts and are a major cause of the increase in income share of the top 1 per cent.

However, when we disaggregate the data by gender, we observe that this finding applies more to men than to women, at least in Australia. Table 9.6 illustrates this. The upper panel of Table 9.6 classifies occupations into three groups based on the average wage of women in the top 1 per cent with that occupation—less than $200,000, $200,000 to $300,000, and more than $300,000. Table 9.6 presents the share of the top 1 per cent, the mean total income and the wage share of total income of the women in each of the three occupation groupings. Examples of the occupations in each occupation groupings are also presented. The lower panel of Table 9.6 presents analogous information for men.[11]

Table 9.6: Occupations in the top 1 per cent, working-age population, 2013–14

	Occupations with average wage below $ 200,000	Occupations with average wage between $ 200,000 and $ 300,000	Occupations with average wage above $ 300,000
Women			
Share in top 1%:	**17.9%**	**53.1%**	**29.0%**
Examples:	512 Office and Practice Managers	253 Medical Practitioners	111 Chief Executives
	531 General Clerks	271 Legal Professionals	132 Bus. Admin. Managers
	241 School Teachers	221 Accountants	149 Service Managers
Total income:	$ 400,000	$365,200	$ 444,400
% from wages:	34%	70%	72%
Men			
Share in top 1%:	**0.6%**	**30.8%**	**68.6%**
Examples:	142 Retail Managers	253 Medical Practitioners	111 Chief Executives
	334 Plumbers	271 Legal Professionals	233 Eng. Professionals
	121 Farmers & Farm Managers	231 Transport Professionals	133 Constr., Dist. & Prod. Managers
Total income	$ 365,700	$ 389,100	$ 452,000
% from wages:	42%	70%	78%

Source: Authors' calculations using data provided by the ATO; see detailed tables in Appendix.

Table 9.6 shows that nearly all working-age men in the top 1 per cent who declare wage income are in high-wage occupations (declaring wage income over $200,000) and these men derive 70 per cent or more of their total income from wages. We provide some examples of these occupations of top 1 per cent men in Table 9.6, including CEOs, engineering professionals and medical and legal professionals. As discussed above, only 14 per cent of men in the top 1 per cent declare no wage income.

Table 9.6 (columns 2 and 3) shows that for 82.1 per cent of women in the top 1 per cent, wages account for 70 per cent or more of their total income This group of women includes CEOs, medical practitioners—with anaesthetists being the highest earning—managers, legal professionals and accountants.[12] It is not surprising that medical practitioner is the most common occupation reported by women in the top 1 per cent in 2013–14,

11   Full results for women are presented in Appendix Table 9.A1, which shows, for each occupation group, its share of women in the top 1 per cent, the wage share of total income, the average wage and the average total income of those in the top 1 per cent, and the average wage of all women in the occupation group. Appendix Table 9.A2 presents the same information for men.

12   Line 1 of Table 9.A1 in the Appendix.

being 13.7 per cent of women in the top 1 per cent and 18 per cent of women in that income group who report an occupation. The average wage of female medical practitioners is $247,077 and their average income is $367,256. The next most common occupations for women in the top 1 per cent are CEOs, general managers and legislators (Members of Parliament); business administration managers; legal professionals; accountants, auditors and company secretaries; and advertising, public relations and sales managers. Taken together, these occupational categories comprise 39.8 per cent of women in the top 1 per cent reporting an occupation, and declare an average income above $350,000.

We also examine the level of wages for women in the top 1 per cent declaring an occupation. We find that women in the top 1 per cent tend to have wages that are three to four times higher than the average wage of all women in the same occupation (who file a tax return). The difference is smaller for men—that is, the difference between the wages of men in the top 1 per cent and the average wage of all men in the same occupation is somewhat smaller than is evident for women. It is interesting to consider why women with top incomes have wages so much higher than the average female wage in the same occupation across the population. This may be explained partly by the large share of women working part-time (who show up in lower income groups) compared to full-time. However, the tax data do not identify full-time/part-time status. We can conclude that women in top cohorts derive less of their income from wages than men, and there is a significant proportion of women in top cohorts who are in less highly remunerated occupations. These are also occupations where the gender wage gap tends to be lower (such as clerical and administrative workers).

We have a specific interest in the empirical results indicating that women tend to be more heavily represented at the very top of the income distribution in Australia than in other countries with individual taxation. One hypothesis is that the Australian system is unusually accommodative of income splitting among couples, whereby income of one member of the couple is, for taxation purposes, attributed to the other member of the couple. We explore this hypothesis by doing an analysis of occupations of women in the top-income cohorts. Among those women in the top 1 per cent who report an occupation, we can distinguish two main groups.

Table 9.6 shows that a significant proportion of women in the top 1 per cent report a (relatively) low-wage occupation and a low share of income from wages. Table 9.6 shows that only 0.6 per cent of men in the top 1 per cent (who report wage income) have wages of less than $200,000. However, 17.9 per cent of women in the top 1 per cent (who report wage income) declare wages of less than $200,000, and many of these women report occupations that are typically lower paid. Moreover, this cohort derives only 34 per cent of their declared income from wages. They are in the top 1 per cent because they have a high share of income from non-wage sources, such as investment or business income. This group includes women in occupations such as personal assistants, receptionists, general clerks, nurses and school teachers. The share of women in the top 1 per cent declaring occupations with an average wage below $200,000 is many times larger than the share of men who do this, as illustrated by the first column in Table 9.6. For example, the occupation general clerks is the eighth most likely occupation to be declared by women in the top 1 per cent, with a low average wage of $76,698.

Evidence of spousal income splitting in Australia

Why do we see a higher representation of women in Australia in the top 1 per cent, 0.5 per cent and 0.1 per cent income groups (but not in the top 10 per cent) relative to other countries, even with low occupational wages or no wage? The results are consistent with at least two possible explanations.

The first explanation is that top-income women in Australia, who record a substantial level of income from non-wage sources (such as business and investment income), do actually own and control the sources of income. It may be the case that women in the top 1 per cent in Australia have greater ownership and control of business, investment and capital assets than equivalent women in other comparable countries. However, it is not clear why this would be the case in Australia compared to other countries. One relevant fact may be the age profile of women with top incomes relative to men. Compared with men, women are relatively more likely to be in the top 1 per cent when they are older and earning non-wage income.

The second explanation is that the tax returns of top-income women in Australia record more income from business and investment (non-wage) sources because of tax planning. That is, the ability under Australian income tax law to record a 'split' income from business or investment sources between spouses may be greater than in other countries and this 'tax planning' or 'income splitting' effect may be contributing to the result. We do not have scope in this chapter to do a detailed comparison of the income tax law and ability to income split in Australia and other countries. However, we briefly explore here the ability to split income in Australia and the likelihood that in Australia the top incomes result arises in part because of income splitting.

The Australian federal income tax has, since its introduction in 1915, been imposed on the individual as the tax unit, applying a progressive marginal rate structure with several tax brackets. In 1975, the Asprey Committee stated that 'the right to be taxed as an individual has always been accorded in Australia' (Asprey 1975, p. 134; see discussion in Stewart 2011). However, in spite of the individual tax unit, from the earliest times, a quasi-joint spousal or family unit has been achieved by some taxpayers by income splitting between members of a couple and between parents and children in a family. Various approaches are used including deriving income through separate entities or arrangements (such as trusts, private companies and partnerships that hold businesses and investments) and using contractual arrangements or legal gifts to share or split ownership of interests in property that derives income (such as real property, shares or rights to royalty streams).

Income splitting generates tax advantages in a system with an individual tax unit and progressive marginal tax rates (MTRs). The Australian income tax rate scale is presented in Figure 9.6 for three of the years in the period under study—the first, middle and end years. MTRs and the income thresholds from which they apply have changed numerous times between 2000–01 and 2013–14, but the three years presented in the figure succinctly summarise their evolution between 2000–01 and 2013–14. The MTRs exclude the Medicare Levy, which applies to most taxpayers and was 1.5 per cent from 2000–01 and has been equal to 2 per cent since 2011–12. Consequently, for top earners, MTRs are 1.5 to 2 percentage points higher than presented in Figure 9.3.

Our top-incomes data do not take account of deductions and losses, so the top incomes analysis does not reflect the taxable income that would be subject to these tax rates. Nonetheless, in all years spanned by our data, most individuals in the top 1 per cent and top 0.1 per cent will face the top MTR on some taxable income. Only those with large current-year or past-year expenses or losses, or very substantial imputation credits on dividends to offset the tax, will not face the top MTR.

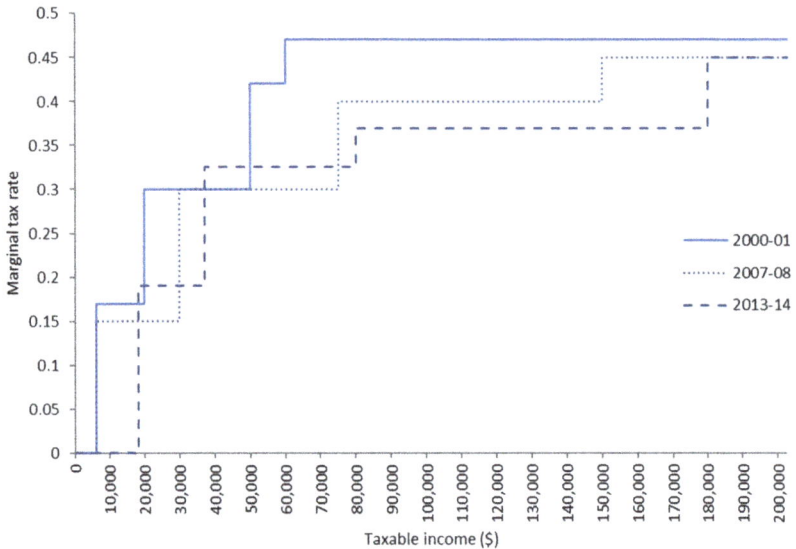

Figure 9.6: Marginal income tax rates in Australia

Source: Created by the authors using data provided by the ATO.

Income splitting involves the transfer of income from an individual taxpayer with a high MTR to another taxpayer with nil or low other income, so as to duplicate the benefit of the tax-free threshold and MTR structure across two or more individuals instead of one. It is necessary to consider the less visible court cases and administrative rulings to discover the production of a quasi-joint tax unit by judicial reasoning. Two examples, drawn from leading Australian tax cases, demonstrate the benefits. The first example is a 1921 case involving use of a trust to hold income-producing assets for a family, thereby splitting trust income among the family members. In *Purcell*, the High Court upheld an arrangement in which a taxpayer declared a trust of the beneficial interest in farming property for himself, his wife and his daughter equally.[13] This produced the result that the income of the farming property was distributed to each individual member of the family as a beneficiary of the trust so that each individual included that one-third share of farming income in their individual tax return. The terms of the trust deed ensured that the taxpayer retained control of disposition of all of the income and conduct of the business. The majority of the High Court upheld this arrangement, with only one judge considering that it was tax avoidance. Justice Isaacs

---

13   *Purcell v DFCT* (1920) 28 CLR 77; *DFCT v Purcell* (1921) 29 CLR 464.

(dissenting) concluded that the restructure was a 'device' for Mr Purcell to avoid taxation and remarked, presciently, that the case 'will afford a comfortable refuge to many an enterprising debtor or taxpayer desiring shelter from the financial obligations of the law'.[14]

The second example demonstrates how profits from a personal services business of one spouse in a partnership may be split between spouses. In the 1980 case of Everett, the taxpayer, a solicitor in partnership, assigned by gift six-thirteenths of his share in the partnership profits to his wife.[15] Mrs Everett could not become a member of the partnership, as was stated explicitly in the deed of assignment. The High Court upheld this division of the partnership rights between the (property) right to a share of the profits and the (personal) right to be a partner. The result was that when the partnership net profits were ascertained at the end of each fiscal year, Mr Everett included seven-thirteenths of the partnership net profits in his individual tax return and Mrs Everett included six-thirteenths of the net profits in her individual tax return. Mr and Mrs Everett would each benefit from the tax-free threshold and progressive individual MTRs on the income. One judge in lone dissent, Justice Murphy, would have held that the whole share of partnership net profit was personal exertion income attributable and taxable to Mr Everett.

Today, complex business and investment structures are widely used, especially in the small and medium enterprise sector comprising family or closely held businesses. These structures may incorporate separate legal entities including a discretionary trust for the family; a self-managed superannuation fund that faces a tax rate of 15 per cent or lower; and contracts for payment of deductible salaries to family members working in the business. In the 2014–15 year, there were more than 640,000 discretionary trusts in Australia with net profit in excess of $25 billion (ATO 2017, Table 4). There were more than 500,000 self-managed superannuation funds (SMSFs). An illustration of a tax-effective (compliant) small- and medium-enterprise business structure is provided in Figure 9.7 below.

---

14   *Purcell v DFCT* (1920) 28 CLR 77.
15   *Everett v FCT* (1980) 143 CLR 440.

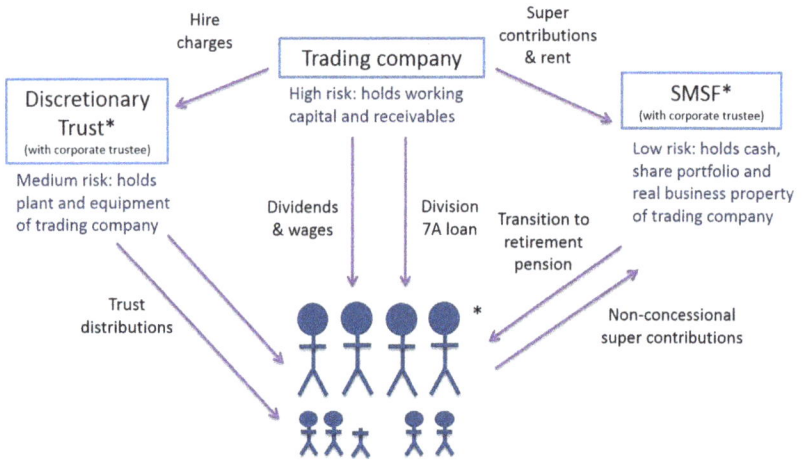

Figure 9.7: Small- and medium-enterprise business/investment structure illustration

* With corporate trustee controlled by business owners.

Source: Stewart et al. (2015, Chart 4.9).

A numerical example

To illustrate the tax benefit of income splitting, consider the *Everett* transaction assuming the 2013–14 income tax rates applied (ignoring all deductions and losses). Assume that Mr Everett was in the top 0.1 per cent of the income distribution in that year, with a share of partnership income of $700,000 and that Mrs Everett has no other income. As a result of a deed of assignment, Mrs Everett records six-thirteenths, or $323,077 of income, in her tax return and Mr Everett records seven-thirteenths, or $376,923, in his tax return.

At this level of income, both members of the couple remain in the top 1 per cent income group even after income splitting. The income and tax compared to the situation if Mr Everett were taxed on the whole partnership profit at 2013–14 MTRs (excluding the Medicare Levy) is shown in Table 9.7. This very simple example demonstrates the net gain in disposable income from income splitting in that year is $26,453.

This 'splitting effect' is equivalent to applying a married tax unit subject to the progressive income tax rate structure. This is illustrated by Wersig (2011, p. 214), who examines the financial benefit from the German married tax unit, which permits joint filing for married spouses, resulting in 'the greatest savings if only one partner earned the total household income'.

Table 9.7: Illustration of tax benefit from income splitting at top incomes

2013–14 tax rates	No income splitting		Income splitting	
	Mr Everett	Mrs Everett	Mr Everett (7/13)	Mrs Everett (6/13)
Income	$700,000	0	$376,923	$323,077
Tax payable	$288,547	0	$143,162	$118,931
Total tax (spouses)	$288,547		$262,094	
Net tax saving	$26,453			

Source: Authors' calculations applying 2013–14 tax rates. Medicare Levy of 2 per cent is not included.

Rules to prevent income splitting in Australia

Statutory rules and administrative practice set some limits on income splitting but do not prevent it. The *Everett* transaction was widely copied by other professional partnerships and was accepted by the ATO in administrative guidance. Meanwhile, other cases established that a right to income (such as a right to a royalty) could be assigned to a spouse so that the spouse would recognise the income from the asset for tax purposes, even without gifting the underlying asset to the spouse. Parliament has enacted some limits on income splitting and anti-avoidance rules may apply in some circumstances. Since 1981, assignments of a right to income of less than seven years are not respected for tax purposes (the income is taxed back to the assigning taxpayer).[16] Since that time, there is also no advantage from splitting income with minor children under the age of 18 as they must pay the top MTR on most income.[17] Some personal services income that is earned in entities (such as a company or trust) is taxed to the actual individual who earns the income (but this would not address the *Everett* scenario).[18] Since the introduction of capital gains tax in 1985, a capital gain may be taxable on assignment of an asset or rights

---

16 Div. 6A of the *Income Tax Assessment Act 1936* (Cth).
17 Div. 6AA of the *Income Tax Assessment Act 1936* (Cth).
18 Div. 85–87 of the *Income Tax Assessment Act 1997* (Cth).

to partnership income, deterring transactions of the *Everett* kind. Still, the capital gain will be low for new enterprises that have a low value, so income splitting is still attractive for new enterprises.

Apart from these limitations, it remains legal and attractive to split investment income with nil- or low-income spouses by holding assets in trusts and distributing income and capital gains on a 'flow through' basis through those entities. It is also attractive to employ family members in a business and pay a substantial salary to them, as long as this is within so-called 'reasonable' bounds. The ability to split income applies, in the words of Murphy J, mostly for the 'professional and commercial classes' and cannot be done by ordinary wage earners.

Conclusion

This chapter has presented novel research on the representation of women in top income groups in Australia and has explored differences between men and women in the characteristics of those at the top of the distribution. We also compared the Australian results to those in some other countries (building on Atkinson et al. (2016)).

The data shows that gender inequality is very substantial at the top end of the income distribution, even after decades of increased employment and savings by women. Women in Australia make up less than 25 per cent of the top 10 per cent and less than 21 per cent of the top 1 per cent. This low representation of women in top-income groups is similar across countries. In the representation of women in the top 10 per cent, Australia performs less well than comparable countries such as Canada, New Zealand, the UK, Denmark and Spain. Moreover, unlike most of our comparator countries, the trend in Australia is flat over time, not increasing.

As discussed by Patricia Apps (in Chapter 3), recent data show a persistent gender wage gap in Australia of around 17 per cent for average full-time equivalent weekly earnings (WGEA 2017).[19] The effect on weekly, annual and lifetime earnings of this, combined with part-time or broken work patterns, is presented by Sinning (in Chapter 8, this volume). It seems likely that the top incomes gap we observe in the tax data is substantially

---

19   The wage gap statistics rely on Australian Bureau of Statistics' (ABS) Full-Time Adult Average Weekly Ordinary Time Earnings (AWOTE) Trend data from the Average Weekly Earnings survey (Cat. no. 6302.0).

explained by the gender wage gap at the top of the wage distribution and by the relatively lower number of women working full-time in high-wage occupations (such as CEOs and surgeons) compared to men. Gender pay gaps are higher in the private sector, within some high-skilled occupations and for older women. For example, the gender pay gap for professionals is 19.7 per cent, for managers it is 28 per cent, and for chief executives and senior managers it ranges between 21 and 25 per cent (for total remuneration of full-time employees) (WGEA 2017, Figure 4).

We observe some interesting differences in levels and trends between Australia and other countries. In particular, in Australia, although the share of women in the top 10 per cent is lower, the share of women in the top 1 per cent and 0.1 per cent is higher compared with most other countries. One possible explanation is that there is greater opportunity to split income between members of a couple under Australia's income tax law than under the law of comparable countries. We test this hypothesis by exploring the data further, examining the age profile, wage and non-wage composition of income, and the occupations (and occupational wages) for women in top-income cohorts. We also explain how Australian income tax law facilitates income splitting for investment and business income in various ways. Our results on all these variables are consistent with the hypothesis that income splitting is a reason why we see more women in the top 1 per cent in Australia than in other countries.

A progressive individual income tax is important for gender equality, as reinforced by the discussion in a number of other chapters in this volume (including Chapter 3 and Chapter 4). However, the individual tax unit may be undermined by legal and illegal tax minimisation, exacerbating class inequalities and masking gender income disparities. As recently noted in the media, the use of family trusts appears to be growing and past attempts to tax trusts more consistently, for example like companies, have generally failed (e.g. Miller and Schneiders 2017). There is widespread anecdotal evidence of income splitting and our research provides further indication of it. Future research could explore the ability and limits on income splitting in comparable countries and could deepen our understanding of the Australian income tax law and its effects on women in top income groups. The results presented in this chapter combine with other evidence to suggest that reform of Australia's income tax system to reduce income splitting would make the system more equal on a number of metrics, as well as increasing integrity and revenues in the system.

Appendix

Table 9.A1: Working-age women in top 1 per cent, 30 most common occupations, 2013–14

Rank	Occupation label	Share of women in top 1% (%)		Share of income from wages (%)	Average wage ($)	Average income ($)	Average wage among all female taxpayers ($)
		Total	Of those with an occupation				
	No occupation	22.7	–	2.2	10,493	478,737	1,320
	Occupation not listed	1.2	–	78.0	299,993	384,813	35,295
1	Medical practitioners	13.7	18.0	67.3	247,077	367,256	108,534
2	Chief executives, general managers and legislators	12.4	16.3	60.8	306,652	504,663	69,968
3	Business administration managers	5.4	7.1	86.3	307,378	356,191	96,283
4	Legal professionals	4.7	6.1	73.7	276,294	374,743	91,822
5	Accountants, auditors and company secretaries	3.9	5.2	74.0	276,374	373,616	69,124
6	Advertising, public relations and sales managers	3.9	5.1	78.1	279,814	358,356	72,268
7	Office and practice managers	3.7	4.8	42.6	183,869	431,282	49,138
8	General clerks	2.1	2.8	18.1	76,698	423,124	38,493
9	Misc. hospitality, retail and service managers	1.3	1.7	78.0	302,948	388,631	53,842
10	Sales, marketing and public relations professionals	1.2	1.6	79.3	268,393	338,553	64,566
11	Tax, HR, management, marketing consultants (ATO code)	1.2	1.5	75.5	272,409	360,628	71,062
12	School teachers	1.1	1.5	36.8	127,787	347,000	58,583

Rank	Occupation label	Share of women in top 1% (%)		Share of income from wages (%)	Average wage ($)	Average income ($)	Average wage among all female taxpayers ($)
		Total	Of those with an occupation				
13	Tertiary education teachers	1.1	1.4	71.4	245,355	343,792	58,911
14	Financial brokers and dealers, and investment advisors	1.0	1.4	83.8	333,072	397,375	74,814
15	Information and organisation professionals	1.0	1.4	82.1	283,517	345,243	64,579
16	Real estate sales agents	1.0	1.3	75.0	258,687	344,939	54,485
17	ICT managers	1.0	1.3	87.5	302,503	345,864	97,004
18	Engineering professionals	1.0	1.3	86.4	282,524	327,179	83,267
19	Financial and insurance clerks	1.0	1.3	84.1	351,052	417,292	52,822
20	Construction, distribution and production managers	0.9	1.2	67.6	291,542	431,033	74,621
21	Natural and physical science professionals	0.9	1.2	73.9	248,302	336,016	63,742
22	Health therapy professionals	0.9	1.2	45.1	167,538	371,501	52,001
23	Human resource and training professionals	0.8	1.1	84.6	287,973	340,215	63,319
24	Accounting clerks and bookkeepers	0.8	1.0	36.3	153,769	423,063	42,480
25	Midwifery and nursing professionals	0.8	1.0	31.4	122,560	389,865	54,871
26	Personal assistants and secretaries	0.7	0.9	25.8	105,886	409,980	48,017
27	Education, health and welfare services managers	0.7	0.9	74.7	256,965	343,930	63,830
28	Health diagnostic and promotion professionals	0.6	0.8	41.1	140,937	342,825	61,041

Rank	Occupation label	Share of women in top 1% (%)		Share of income from wages (%)	Average wage ($)	Average income ($)	Average wage among all female taxpayers ($)
		Total	Of those with an occupation				
29	Contract, program and project administrators	0.6	0.8	68.8	236,700	344,168	63,885
30	Misc. clerical and administrative workers	0.5	0.6	41.9	172,353	411,258	44,059

Source: Authors' calculations using data provided by the ATO.

Table 9.A2: Working-age men in top 1 per cent, 30 most common occupations, 2013–14

Rank	Occupation label	Share of men in top 1% (%)		Share of income from wages (%)	Average wage ($)	Average income ($)	Average wage among all male taxpayers ($)
		Total	Of those with an occupation				
	No occupation	14.0		3.1	16,057	513,777	2,009
	Occupation not listed	1.4		84.4	360,440	426,942	52,608
1	Chief executives, general managers and legislators	18.2	21.4	69.3	393,735	568,540	111,719
2	Medical practitioners	10.4	12.2	59.2	274,395	463,642	168,748
3	Engineering professionals	6.1	7.2	89.0	304,868	342,521	111,733
4	Construction, distribution and production managers	5.1	6.1	85.5	312,780	365,962	105,495
5	Advertising, public relations and sales managers	4.0	4.7	85.7	320,603	374,006	103,234
6	Accountants, auditors and company secretaries	3.9	4.6	79.7	342,825	430,393	100,015
7	Business administration managers	3.4	4.0	87.5	363,070	414,955	133,542

Rank	Occupation label	Share of men in top 1% (%)		Share of income from wages (%)	Average wage ($)	Average income ($)	Average wage among all male taxpayers ($)
		Total	Of those with an occupation				
8	Financial brokers and dealers, and investment advisors	2.5	2.9	82.5	450,133	545,615	138,324
9	Office and practice managers	2.3	2.7	78.0	336,805	431,727	91,830
10	Legal professionals	2.2	2.5	67.9	283,629	417,436	121,509
11	ICT managers	1.8	2.1	89.1	304,344	341,527	119,834
12	Air and marine transport professionals	1.5	1.8	95.4	292,138	306,085	129,577
13	Building and engineering technicians	1.5	1.7	89.6	275,425	307,329	91,385
14	Misc. hospitality, retail and service managers	1.4	1.7	82.3	346,235	420,577	80,095
15	Natural and physical science professionals	1.4	1.6	84.8	306,722	361,660	90,412
16	Sales, marketing and public relations professionals	1.2	1.4	91.0	306,515	336,840	88,915
17	Financial and insurance clerks	1.1	1.3	82.5	424,689	514,839	89,220
18	Real estate sales agents	1.0	1.2	77.9	306,619	393,421	85,469
19	Tax, HR, management, marketing consultants (ATO code)	1.0	1.2	74.6	352,275	472,296	106,888
20	Information and organisation professionals	1.0	1.2	83.0	343,107	413,599	92,650
21	Business and systems analysts, and programmers	0.8	1.0	79.3	274,201	345,961	89,908
22	Stationary plant operators	0.8	0.9	87.6	267,320	305,214	110,015

Rank	Occupation label	Share of men in top 1% (%)		Share of income from wages (%)	Average wage ($)	Average income ($)	Average wage among all male taxpayers ($)
		Total	Of those with an occupation				
23	Construction and mining labourers	0.8	0.9	89.9	272,983	303,620	66,979
24	Tertiary education teachers	0.7	0.9	73.0	262,337	359,282	74,963
25	Electricians	0.7	0.8	87.0	253,911	291,942	89,605
26	Health therapy professionals	0.5	0.6	51.5	213,472	414,592	76,973
27	Insurance agents and sales representatives	0.5	0.6	82.9	293,579	354,056	60,695
28	Sports and fitness workers (incl. sportspersons)	0.5	0.6	89.2	374,814	420,225	43,762
29	Miscellaneous technicians and trades workers	0.4	0.5	92.0	272,285	295,959	74,230
30	Fabrication engineering trades workers	0.4	0.5	91.0	273,896	301,099	73,039

Source: Authors' calculations using data provided by the ATO.

Table 9.A3: Men and women in top 1 per cent with no reported occupation

	Women			Men		
	Share of women in top 1% (%)	Average share of income from wages (%)	Average income ($)	Share of men in top 1% (%)	Average share of income from wages (%)	Average income ($)
2009	25.3	2.8	411,089	15.5	4.4	450,443
2010	24.9	2.3	435,566	15.3	3.7	469,772
2011	24.6	2.6	436,048	14.9	3.9	478,314
2012	23.2	2.9	459,977	14.1	4.3	494,902
2013	22.7	2.2	478,737	14.0	3.1	513,777

Source: Authors' calculations using data provided by the ATO.

Table 9.A4: People in top 1 per cent with an occupation (incl. occupation not listed), by average wage in that occupation

		Women			Men		
		In occupations with average wage			In occupations with average wage		
		Below $200,000	$200,000 to $300,000	Above $300,000	Below $200,000	$200,000 to $300,000	Above $300,000
Share of people in occupations by average wage bands	2008	26.0	74.0		4.1	60.6	35.3
	2009	24.4	74.0	1.6	4.1	58.5	37.4
	2010	23.1	75.3	1.6	2.1	54.2	43.7
	2011	20.1	76.7	3.2	1.2	48.6	50.2
	2012	18.4	72.0	9.5	0.7	42.6	56.7
	2013	17.9	53.1	29.0	0.6	30.8	68.6
Share of income from wages	2008	40	72		56	79	78
	2009	40	72	83	56	78	78
	2010	36	71	82	49	76	77
	2011	35	71	84	44	76	78
	2012	34	69	86	41	74	78
	2013	34	72	70	42	70	78

Analysis conducted on occupations at the 3-digit level. The large jump in the share of women in occupations with average wage above $300,000 between 2012 and 2013 is due in part to the switch of '111 Chief executives' between the two categories in 2013. They represent more than 16 per cent of women in the top 1 per cent with an occupation in 2013. The story is similar but with a smaller jump when the analysis is conducted on occupations at the 4-digit level.

Source: Authors' calculations using data provided by the ATO.

References

Asprey, Ken (Chair). 1975. *Full Report 31 January 1975*. Taxation Review Committee (the 'Asprey Committee'). Canberra: Australian Government Publishing Service.

Atkinson, Anthony, Alessandra Casarico and Sarah Voitchovsky. 2014. 'How many women are in the 1%?' *World Economic Forum*. Available at: www.weforum.org/agenda/2014/07/women-income-glass-ceiling

Atkinson, Anthony, Alessandra Casarico and Sarah Voitchovsky. 2016. 'Top Incomes and the Gender Divide'. Melbourne Institute Working Paper No. 27/16.

Atkinson, Anthony, and Andrew Leigh. 2007. 'The Distribution of Top Incomes in Australia'. *Economic Record* 83(262): 247–261.

Atkinson, Anthony and Thomas Piketty. 2007. *Top Incomes over the Twentieth Century: A Contrast between Continental European and English Speaking Countries.* New York: Oxford University Press. doi.org/10.1111/j.1475-4932.2007.00412.x

Atkinson, Anthony and Thomas Piketty (eds). 2010. *Top Incomes: A Global Perspective.* Oxford and New York: Oxford University Press.

Atkinson, Anthony, Thomas Piketty and Emmanuel Saez. 2011. 'Top Incomes in the Long Run of History'. *Journal of Economic Literature*, 49(1): 3–71. doi.org/10.1257/jel.49.1.3

ATO (Australian Taxation Office). 2017. *Tax Statistics 2014–15.* Available at: data.gov.au/dataset/taxation-statistics-2014-15/resource/87e186d2-6b87-44c6-85de-4e8d17e1d2d3?inner_span=True

Burkhauser, Richard, Markus Hahn and Roger Wilkins. 2015. 'Measuring Top Incomes Using Tax Record Data: A Cautionary Tale from Australia'. *Journal of Economic Inequality* 13(2): 181–205. doi.org/10.1007/s10888-014-9281-z

Elund, Lena and Wojciech Kopczuk. 2009. 'Women, Wealth and Mobility'. *American Economic Review* 99(1): 146–178. doi.org/10.1257/aer.99.1.146

Fletcher, Michael and Ben Guttmann. 2013. 'Income inequality in Australia'. *Economic Roundup*, Issue 2. Available at: static.treasury.gov.au/uploads/sites/1/2017/06/3-Income-Inequality-Paper.pdf

Head, John and Rick Krever (eds). 1996. *Tax Units and the Tax Rate Scale.* Conference Series No. 16. Melbourne: Australian Tax Research Foundation.

Henry, Ken et al. 2009. *Review of Australia's Future Tax System: Report to the Treasurer.* Australia's Future Tax System Review Panel (the 'Henry Review'). Available at: taxreview.treasury.gov.au

Keeley, Brian. 2015. *Income Inequality: The Gap Between Rich and Poor.* OECD: Paris. dx.doi.org/10.1787/9789264246010-en

Millar, Royce and Ben Schneiders. 2017. 'The tax minimisation tool that nobody wants to talk about'. *The Age,* 6 April. Available at: www.theage.com.au/action/printArticle?id=1020217828

Stewart, Miranda. 1999. 'Domesticating Tax Reform: The Family in Australian Tax and Transfer Law'. *Sydney Law Review* 21(3): 453–486.

Stewart, Miranda. 2011. 'Gender and Tax Policy in Australia'. In Kim Brooks, Asa Gunnarson, Lisa Philipps and Maria Wersig (eds), *Challenging Gender Inequality in Tax Policy Making: Comparative Perspectives*, pp. 53–74. UK: Hart Publishing.

Stewart, Miranda, Andre Moore, Peter Whiteford and Quentin Grafton. 2015. *Stocktake Report.* The Australian National University, Tax and Transfer Policy Institute.

Treasury. 2015. *Re:Think Tax Discussion Paper.* Australian Government. Available at: bettertax.gov.au/publications/discussion-paper/.

Wersig, Maria. 2011. 'Joint Taxation and Income Splitting: The Case of Germany'. In Kim Brooks, Asa Gunnarson, Lisa Philipps and Maria Wersig (eds), *Challenging Gender Inequality in Tax Policy Making*, pp. 213–231. UK: Hart Publishing.

WGEA (Workplace Gender Equality Agency). 2017. *Gender Pay Gap Statistics.* Available at: www.wgea.gov.au/sites/default/files/gender-pay-gap-statistics.pdf

Wolfson, Michael, Mike Veall, Neil Brooks and Brian Murphy. 2016. 'Piercing the Veil: Private Corporations and the Income of the Affluent', *Canadian Tax Journal* 64(1): 1–30.

10

Budgeting for women's rights in retirement

Siobhan Austen and Rhonda Sharp

Key aspects of Australia's retirement incomes policy focus on needs rather than rights. Unlike most other countries, Australia has an age pension that is a means-tested payment, rather than a universal entitlement. The pension is set with reference to notions of an 'adequate' income, currently defined by the requirements of a 'modest' lifestyle. Private superannuation is earnings-based, and aimed at building improved lifestyles in retirement for individuals with a capacity to save. There are crucial gender implications associated with this policy approach, including aged women compared to men being disproportionately dependent on the age pension and more vulnerable to poverty. In contrast, the generous taxation concessions available for occupational and private superannuation tend to benefit men more than women, with high-income men on average benefiting the most. Whilst the gender inequality in superannuation has been widely noted (see, for example, Austen et al. 2015), few studies have an explicit focus on the gender issues associated with ensuring adequate retirement incomes.

This chapter argues that an analysis of how budget resources are raised and allocated and who benefits from them is a critical part of any evaluation of a retirement income system. Gender impact analysis of budgets, an essential step in the implementation of gender-responsive budgeting, seeks to make visible gender differentiated impacts of government budgets, which provide the basis for bringing about changes in budgetary decision-making processes and priorities (Elson and Sharp 2010, p. 522). An important task for a gender impact analysis of government spending and taxation policies is to assess whether sufficient funds are available to carry out all the measures that will promote gender equality.

Since the early 2000s, research and advocacy on gender-responsive budgeting has also applied a human rights framework for assessing the gender impacts of government spending and taxation policies (Elson 2002, 2006; Norton and Elson 2002; Pillay et al. 2002; Budlender 2004). A rights-based approach to gender impact analysis of budgets aims to identify gender inequalities in budget processes, allocations and outcomes, and to assess what governments are obliged to do to tackle these inequalities (Elson 2006, p. 3). As discussed by Helen Hodgson and Kerrie Sadiq (Chapter 4, this volume), Diane Elson's influential work (2002, 2006) demonstrated the potential of the approach utilising the Convention on the Elimination of All Forms of Discrimination Against Women (CEDAW), to which Australia is a signatory, as a standard for assessing government spending and taxation policies. This involves consideration both of whether expenditure is distributed equally and whether sufficient funds are available to carry out all the measures that are vital for the 'full development and advancement of women' (United Nations 1979, Article 4). Notably, it is necessary to go beyond the question of whether there is an equal distribution of expenditure, as it would be possible to have a distribution of funding that is non-discriminatory but insufficient to carry out all the measures important for the fulfilment of CEDAW (Elson 2006, p. 59). Similarly, revenue measures need to be designed to minimise any adverse effects on substantive gender equality. The goal of 'taxing for (gender) equality' and the crucial issue of the adequacy of public finance to achieve gender equality goals is discussed in detail by Kathleen Lahey (Chapter 2, this volume). A tax mix that has a high reliance on progressive income taxation is seen as generally favourable for the implementation of CEDAW (Elson 2006, p. 100). The use of tax concessions that can reduce the progressivity of the income tax system are therefore evaluated negatively in this approach.

CEDAW builds on the International Covenant on Economic, Social and Cultural Rights (ICESCR), which stipulates all parties take steps to achieve 'progressively' the full realisation of rights (Australian Human Rights Commission, n.d.). While this is a recognition that government resources are not unlimited in fulfilling economic, social and cultural rights, and implementation will take time, it does imply that core minimum standards should be met. For revenue measures, the ambition should be to create the 'maximum available resources for the progressive realization' of CEDAW (Elson 2006, p. 101). For expenditure, the ICESCR implies that expenditures are directed toward activities that protect and enhance agreed minimum standards.

Concern with the sufficiency of funds and their proper allocation requires a detailed analysis of the performance of budgets. Since the 1990s, a raft of budgetary reforms have been introduced across the world that facilitate the development of performance criteria and measures. Associated with this has been the adoption of budget formats that report on financial inputs and activities, outputs and outcomes to more closely link budgetary allocations with results. Sharp's (2003) research on utilising performance-oriented budgeting frameworks for gender-responsive budgeting shows there are both dangers and opportunities within these reforms. For example, gender inequality can be potentially reinforced by the typical performance criteria of economy, efficiency and effectiveness as these ignore women's unpaid contributions to public services and the quality of inputs. Still, opportunities include the use of gender-aware output and outcome indicators, and the use of gender equality as a performance criterion (Sharp 2003, pp. 77–78). Furthermore, performance-oriented budgeting offers a format for a gender impact analysis that incorporates a rights-based approach and consideration of the adequacy of funding.

An important part of the assessment of the sufficiency of funding for gender budgeting purposes is agreement on the outcomes to be achieved, including the 'core minimum standard' or 'adequate' outcome for women. This needs to be complemented by detailed analysis of the activities and outputs required to achieve the agreed outcomes and the costs of providing these activities and outputs. A range of factors that may potentially influence the linkages between funding and outcomes also need to be taken into account. For example, without proper management, funding may fail to reach activities; activities might be funded that do not effectively produce outputs; and outputs might fail to deliver outcomes that are judged to be 'adequate'. Analyses of this type are inevitably affected by the type of data that is available on, for example, the efficiency of program delivery. Assumptions will typically be required and should be tested for their influence on results. (See, for example, Pillay et al.'s 2002 study of the sufficiency of funding to meet the housing rights of poor women in South Africa.)

Using this approach, this chapter seeks to assess the sufficiency of the funding available for the retirement incomes of older Australian women and whether the policy contributes to gender equality. We start by briefly describing the *inputs* and *activities* of Australian retirement income and savings policy, focusing on the large and growing allocation of government resources to retirement incomes and how this is distributed between government pensions and occupational superannuation and private savings. We then proceed to an analysis of the *outputs* of this policy (realised levels of retirement income for women and men). We examine the outcomes of the current retirement income system and evaluate its performance, focusing in particular on the question of whether the retirement income available for Australian women is 'adequate', ensuring their 'full development and advancement'.

Inputs and activities of Australian retirement incomes and savings policy

Australia's retirement savings and income policy features a 'three pillars' model: the public age pension; a mandatory private superannuation system organised by a Superannuation Guarantee (SG) levy, currently set at 9.5 per cent of employee earnings; and private savings, some of which can occur through the superannuation system, in the form of voluntary contributions to superannuation accounts (Treasury 2006). Large inputs of government resources are associated with both the age pension and superannuation pillars of the current policy.

The distinctive features of the Australian retirement income system are: a targeted, rather than universal, age pension; superannuation accounts that are typically defined by contribution rather than benefit; and a generous level of tax concessions for superannuation. The Australian age pension entitlement is assessed on the basis of individual need, with reference to the person's level of income and assets. This approach contrasts with the one adopted in most Organisation for Economic Co-operation and Development (OECD) countries, where either a flat-rate age pension is afforded to all citizens (for example, Canada, Netherlands, New Zealand), or an earnings-related age pension is made available to labour force participants (for example, France, Germany). Countries such as Finland, Norway and Sweden combine flat-rate benefits with an earnings-related age pension. The superannuation pillar of the Australian retirement income system is also distinctive in that it features defined contribution accounts, which are not directly linked to an earnings-based pension. In contrast, defined benefit accounts, or a points system linked to earnings, feature in many other jurisdictions. However, in common with a number of other countries, the Australian retirement income and savings system incorporates significant tax concessions for savings in our superannuation system (OECD 2015).

In Australia, mandatory and most voluntary contributions to individual superannuation accounts, and the income earned on account balances, are taxed at a concessional 15 per cent rate, whilst most disbursements from superannuation funds are tax-exempt (members of untaxed funds, such as public sector schemes, are not tax-exempt but pay a concessional rate when they withdraw their superannuation). The 15 per cent rate on contributions compares favourably with the tax rate applied to wage income, which ranges up to 45 per cent, and creates significant opportunities for individuals to reduce their total tax bill by channelling income into superannuation (these opportunities were reduced in a minor way in reforms enacted in 2016). The 15 per cent tax rate that is levied on income earned during the accumulation phase of a superannuation fund compares favourably with marginal tax rates (MTRs) on other forms of income from savings. Pensions and lump sums withdrawn from a taxed superannuation fund are tax-exempt where the member is aged over 60 years, and income within superannuation funds is tax-exempt to the extent that assets are used to pay a pension. Overall, individuals who are able to make contributions to their superannuation accounts save tax on their wage income and savings, and are able to access their accumulated funds tax-free in retirement.

The generous tax treatment of retirement savings is costly, with the Treasury's own estimates putting this figure in 2015–16 at $16.3 billion for the concessional taxation of employer contributions and $13.6 billion for the superannuation entity concessions relative to an income tax benchmark (Treasury 2016). The combined cost of the tax concessions is rapidly becoming similar to the cost of the system's other key pillar, the age pension, which had an estimated cost of $43.2 billion in 2015–16 (Australian Government 2016b). Together, these two cost elements were equivalent to 16.2 per cent of the total forecast expenses of the Australian Government in 2016–17 (Australian Government 2016a).

The links between the various activities associated with retirement income and savings policy and the retirement incomes are critical to system efficiency. Despite its targeted design, expenditure on the age pension contributes in a direct and substantial manner to the incomes of older Australians. In 2011–12, the median fortnightly income from all sources was close to $800 for men aged 65 years and older and $740 for women (ABS 2012). Government pensions and other payments typically made up 70 per cent of the income received by men in this age group and 81 per cent of the income received by women. The full age pension for a single person in 2013 was $827.10 each fortnight, indexed to 25 per cent of male average weekly ordinary time earnings (Treasury 2009). Individuals in couple households on the full age pension received a fortnightly payment of $623.40 (Department of Social Services 2014). At this time, 794,316 women (approximately 34 per cent of all women over 65) and 595,836 men (approximately 28.6 per cent of all men over 65) received the full age pension; a further 511,851 women and 447,924 men received a part pension (Department of Social Services 2014; ABS 2015).

A range of factors complicates the relationship between current tax expenditures on superannuation and the incomes of older Australians. First, a large proportion of the current tax expenditures flow to individuals who are currently still in paid work. As such, even in a mature superannuation system there will not necessarily be a close proportional relationship between current expenditure and retirement incomes. As the SG scheme was only introduced in the 1980s, the relationship between current tax expenditures and the current retirement incomes of older Australians is weaker still. More critically relevant to the relationship between tax expenditures on superannuation and the higher retirement incomes in a mature system is the concentration of benefits within the group of individuals who are able to make contributions to their superannuation accounts. The expenditures deliver no direct benefits for individuals who have not participated in paid work and only limited benefits to those with part-time working hours, low wages and/or interrupted paid work careers. The fees charged by superannuation funds, variations in rates of return on investments and the degree to which money accumulated into superannuation accounts is annuitised also affects the relationship between tax expenditures on superannuation and retirement income.

Reflecting the influence of these factors, in 2013–14 the median superannuation balance for women aged over 65 was $5,586, as compared to $37,032 for men. Reflecting the large degree of inequality in superannuation account balances, average superannuation balances were much higher: $280,183 for men aged over 65, and $215,467 for women in this age group. Fully 45.9 per cent of women and 37.8 per cent of men aged over 65 had zero superannuation assets in 2013–14. These statistics show that retirement income is yet another dimension of the question of whether work pays for women—a question considered by Guyonne Kalb in Chapter 5, while the much lower earnings of women relative to men are illustrated by Mathias Sinning in Chapter 8.

Outcomes and evaluative criteria for Australian retirement income and savings policy

The sufficiency of funding available to support retirement income would ideally be assessed with reference to an agreed set of outcomes for retirement income and savings policy, including the 'core minimum standard' or 'adequate' level of retirement income. Whilst this is seemingly commonsensical, especially given the large volume of public resources devoted to retirement incomes and savings, the objectives of Australia's retirement income and savings system as a whole were only recently enshrined in legislation.

The Turnbull Liberal–National Coalition Government introduced the Superannuation (Objective) Bill and it was enacted by parliament in late 2016. The objective of superannuation is now stated in the law as being to 'provide income in retirement to substitute or supplement the Age Pension' (Section 5, *Superannuation (Objective) Act 2016*; see Parliament of Australia, House of Representatives 2016, p. 3115). This objective was criticised by a large number of key policy players, including the Association of Superannuation Funds Australia (ASFA), the Australian Council of Social Services, the Australian Labor Party and the Tax Institute (Swoboda 2017), in particular for failing to provide criteria for judging the system and the failure to incorporate a concept of adequacy into the policy objectives.

The government's enacted objective for superannuation is a marked departure from the founding vision of the 'three pillar' policy, which although not legislated was articulated on a number of occasions, including a 1991 address by Paul Keating, following his resignation as Treasurer in the Hawke government. These statements provide a richer sense of the planned objectives of the Australian retirement income system, and we utilise them to evaluate the system's subsequent performance. In his 1991 address, Keating emphasised goals relating to higher retirement incomes, dignity and increased independence for older Australians:

> A system of more adequate private provision of retirement income sympathetically interfaced with the public pensions system will not only better provide for the aged, but is more likely to preserve the dignity and independence each have enjoyed in their pre-retirement years (Keating 1991, p. 7).

The retirement income scheme also aimed for increased equality amongst older Australians, with the ultimate goal of improved social cohesion and happiness: 'It will make Australia a more equal place, a more egalitarian place and, hence, a more cohesive and happy place' (Keating 1991, p. 7). Gender equality was an implied goal, with Keating claiming that the SG scheme incorporated, 'particular concessions to women, long disadvantaged as part time or temporary employees' (Keating 1991, pp. 3–4).

To achieve these objectives, the retirement income system incorporated a number of design elements. The age pension was maintained 'as the foundation of equity and adequacy in retirement income arrangements', with the income of private superannuation playing a 'complementary' role (Keating 1991). To achieve meaningful improvements in retirement incomes on the age pension, superannuation contributions were mandated for all employees, and the SG rate was planned to reach 12 per cent by 2000. The intention was for superannuation contributions to be used to fund annuities and surviving spouse benefits, and lump sum withdrawals were discouraged:

> [The 12 per cent rate] will provide a level of benefit exceeding even the most optimistic expectation of the future level of the age pension. For those workers who stay on to age 65 the level of benefit will reach towards 50 per cent of pre-retirement income on an annuity basis, with full indexation to inflation, and 70 per cent reversion to the surviving spouse (Keating 1991, p. 9).

Many of these design elements were altered in subsequent years. For example, the SG rate has thus far only reached 9.5 per cent and, whilst lump sum payments were taxed at the individual's MTRs under the original Keating legislation, all income received by people aged over 60 was made tax-exempt under changes introduced by the Howard–Costello Government in 2007. More recently, and perhaps more fundamentally, the role ascribed to the first pillar of the Australian retirement system has been shifted. Rather than the age pension being the 'foundation for equity and adequacy', it is increasingly being recast as a residual element of the system, and as a form of welfare:

> We need, in superannuation, to have a system that ensures that when people get to retirement age they won't be dependent on a welfare payment, [they won't be dependent] on a pension (Australian Treasurer, Scott Morrison: Morrison 2015).

The various changes that have been made to the retirement income and savings system over recent decades undoubtedly affect its current performance. However, Keating's statements on the aims and objectives of the retirement income system remain relevant to its evaluation. The first evaluative criteria implied in the statements is *adequacy*: does the funding and delivery of retirement incomes and savings policy, in its current form, achieve the 'provision of needs and dignity' for older Australians through all the years of their retirement? The second criterion is *equality*: does the system promote income equality amongst older Australians? The criterion of *gender equity* cuts across these broad criteria: does Australia's retirement income and savings system produce adequate retirement incomes for both men and women, and are its benefits equally distributed between men and women?

Adequacy: Needs and dignity for all the years of retirement

The available evidence on whether the Australian retirement income system protects older people from the risks of poverty is mixed. On the one hand, key measures show that Australia records a very high rate of old age poverty, with the retirement income of one in three older Australians falling below the poverty threshold. Australia has the second-highest level of poverty for persons 65 and over, with only Korea being higher among the 34 OECD countries (see Table 10.1). Against this, a number of influential commentators emphasise the high rate of home ownership amongst older Australians, and how this increases their disposable income relative to other groups (see Bradbury and Gubhaju 2010). Furthermore, the *depth* of old age poverty in Australia—that is, the proportion of older Australians with incomes *substantially* below the poverty line—is relatively small.

Table 10.1: Old age poverty rate: Australia in an international perspective

	Old age poverty rate of all persons 65+ (calculated as % with income < 50% below median income)
Australia	33.5
France	3.8
Germany	9.4
Canada	6.7
Netherlands	2.0
New Zealand	8.2
Finland	7.8
Japan	19.4
Korea	49.6
Norway	4.1
Sweden	9.3

Source: Author's table using information from OECD (2015).

A key driver of old age poverty in Australia is the level of the full age pension. Currently set at around 47 per cent of median income, the full single age pension (including Pension Supplement and Clean Energy Supplement) is slightly below the standard that ASFA sets for a 'modest' lifestyle for a person who owns his or her own home outright and is in 'reasonably good' health. As ASFA acknowledges, this standard, which equates to around $22,365 per year (an amount close to the annual single age pension), makes 'only fairly basic activities' affordable. It allows $74.23 per week for food expenditures and $38.06 per week for health (ASFA 2013). In contrast, ASFA's standard for a comfortable lifestyle specifies a minimum income of $42,158 annually for single people who own their own home (Clare 2014). This standard enables what ASFA defines as a 'good standard of living'. According to ASFA, it provides the means for the older person 'to be involved in a broad range of leisure and recreational activities, ... purchase household goods, private health insurance, a reasonable car, good clothes, a range of electronic equipment, and holiday travel' (ASFA 2013).

A key question is whether the superannuation pillar of the retirement income system will deliver improved outcomes by affording all older Australians a 'modest' or 'comfortable' lifestyle. Recent modelling of the superannuation accumulations of Australian men and women entering paid work in 2015 by Phil Gallagher (2016) provides some important insights. Gallagher explored a number of 'cameos' relating to men's and women's earnings and how these interact with retirement income policy settings to affect the system's outputs. The cameos relate to men and women at different points in the male earnings distribution (those with wages at the 10th percentile, median, average, and with earnings 1.5 and 2.5 times the male average wage, respectively). Gallagher's modelling encompassed an assumption that men work full-time for all years between age 22 and 65. However, reflecting common patterns of female workforce participation, the stereotypical woman in Gallagher's analysis works full-time between age 22 and 30; is absent from paid work between age 30 and 35; works part-time between age 36 and 45; and returns to full-time work between age 46 and 65. The modelling assumed that wage rates will grow in nominal terms by 3.78 per cent per year and that women's wage rates will remain lower than men's across most of the earnings distribution by an amount equal to the current gender wage gap (of about 17 per cent). The SG rate was set at 12.5 per cent and superannuation funds were assumed to generate positive but conservative rates of return. In the pension phase, all superannuants were assumed to draw down their accounts (set at the age-based minimum plus 7 per cent and a 12 per cent drawdown at age 67) such that the accounts are exhausted at life expectancy (91 for women and 89 for men).

Gallagher's modelling identifies a number of outcomes of the current retirement income system. First, *under the above assumptions*, the second pillar of the system enables higher levels of spending (and, thus, improved lifestyles) for all older Australians. As is shown in Table 10.2, in the baseline scenario, the retirement income achieved by each cameo exceeds the OECD poverty line (50 per cent of median earnings), which is an improvement on current outcomes. However, only single men and couples with earnings 2.5 times the average wage achieve a level of retirement income that exceeds the ASFA-defined comfortable living standard (as described earlier). Furthermore, the improvements in retirement income for women on low earnings are relatively small.

Table 10.2: Gallagher's modelled outcomes of Australia's retirement income system

Earnings 'cameo'	Measure: % of OECD poverty line					Measure: % of comfortable standard				
	10%	median	mean	1.5* mean	2.5* mean	10 %	median	mean	1.5* mean	2.5* mean
Scenario 1: Base (Age-based minimum plus 7% drawdown; retire at 65; 12.5% SG)										
Female	104.0	112.8	117.5	130.9	155	60.4	65.5	68.2	76.0	90.0
Male	117.7	135.7	142.3	167.5	218.9	68.3	78.8	82.6	97.3	127.1
Scenario 2: Minimum drawdown (Minimum drawdown; retire at 65; 12.5% SG)										
Female	101.1	107.2	109.1	109.6	110.5	58.7	62.3	63.3	63.7	64.2
Male	108.9	108.6	106.7	112.1	149	63.2	63.1	62.0	65.1	86.6
Scenario 3: Retire at 60 (Minimum plus 7% drawdown; retire at 60; 12.5% SG)										
Female	98.5	104.6	108.3	118.4	134.1	57.2	60.8	62.9	68.8	77.9
Male	107.1	120.5	125.1	139.7	172.6	62.2	70.0	72.6	81.1	100.2
Scenario 4: 9.5% SG (Minimum plus 7% drawdown; retire at 60; 9.5% SG)										
Female	99.6	107.1	111.5	123.8	143.1	57.9	62.2	64.8	71.9	83.1
Male	111.1	127.6	133.4	152.0	198.5	64.5	74.1	77.5	88.3	115.3

Source: Author's table using information provided by Gallagher (2016).

Importantly, Gallagher also shows that the predicted outcomes from the retirement income system are sensitive to key modelling parameters. For example, if superannuation pensions are only drawn down at a minimum rate, none of the 'cameos' (relating to men and women with particular earnings characteristics) will achieve a 'comfortable' living standard. Furthermore, as the data in Table 10.2 for Scenario 2 shows, none of the 'female cameos' will achieve a retirement income significantly above the OECD poverty line. Describing this scenario as a 'disaster', Gallagher also notes that it is a distinct possibility, given that 'minimum drawdowns are substantially preferred by Australian pensioners' for reasons that include precautionary motives relating to provisioning for possible health and care costs late in life.

The predicted outcomes of the current retirement income system are also dependent on the length of individuals' paid work careers and the superannuation contribution rate. Gallagher's initial projections were based on scenarios where both men and women retire at 65 and the SG rate is 12.5 per cent. However, currently the majority of Australians are not working at age 64 and the SG rate is only 9.5 per cent. Furthermore, as data presented below show, the rate of full-time employment amongst women falls below the level assumed by Gallagher in several age groups. The modelled outcomes with a retirement age of 60 (Scenario 3 in the Table 10.2) and a 9.5 per cent SG rate (Scenario 4 in Table 10.2) are much lower than in the baseline setting. Reducing the retirement age to 60 causes one of the 'female cameos' to fall below the OECD poverty line. Holding the SG rate at 9.5 per cent has similar negative impacts on retirement incomes. Lower rates of full-time work will also reduce retirement incomes.

Overall, then, the Australian retirement income system currently appears to pass the *basic* test of 'adequacy', with the age pension playing a key role in ensuring that the living standards of older Australian homeowners do not fall substantially below the poverty line. The superannuation pillar should, in a mature system, help to further reduce the incidence of poverty amongst older Australian homeowners.

However, even amongst homeowners, the majority of Australians—other than men on high earnings—will not achieve a comfortable lifestyle with the means 'to be involved in a broad range of leisure and recreational activities … purchase household goods, private health insurance, a reasonable car, good clothes, a range of electronic equipment, and holiday travel' (ASFA 2013). Furthermore, older Australians remain vulnerable to policy change. Any erosion in government-funded health and aged care services will, at best, force many retirees to hold onto their superannuation assets—to provision for possible late-life needs—and this will limit their ability to use their financial assets to support their living standards in retirement. Similarly, many older Australians are highly vulnerable to policy moves that could further limit the pension to a narrow, safety net role.

The Committee for Economic Development for Australia (CEDA 2015, pp. 76–78) notes that in the immediate period, because policy settings are based on an assumption of homeownership, many non-homeowner older Australians will continue to experience financial stress. Fully 42.9 per cent of female non-homeowners aged 65 and over (and 36.2 per cent of men) rate their financial situation as uncomfortable (Productivity Commission 2015). These proportions, which fall to 12.8 per cent and 11.3 per cent respectively in the group of homeowners, highlight a critical gap in the design of the current retirement and income system. Going forward, this deficiency in the system will become more significant, due to falling rates of homeownership, especially among low-income individuals. Divorcees are a further vulnerable group. Almost one-third of male divorcees (and 27.3 per cent of their female counterparts) rate their financial situation as uncomfortable. These rates fall to 19.4 per cent and 18.8 per cent respectively in the group of married individuals aged 65 and over (Productivity Commission 2015), suggesting that the current retirement income and savings system is also poorly equipped to respond to changing household circumstances.

Equality

As noted earlier, the current retirement income scheme was designed to achieve increased equality amongst older Australians (Keating 1991, p. 7). However, as the above discussion implies, and as shown in the tables throughout, the shift toward the superannuation pillar has not been successful on this score. Little change in the level of income inequality has been achieved since 1986. In 1986, the older household at the 90th percentile of the income distribution had equivalised incomes three times those achieved by households at the 10th percentile. In 2012, this ratio was largely unchanged—at 2.9.

Table 10.3: Inequality among older Australian households—ratios of the 90th to the 10th percentile equivalised incomes of Australians aged 65 and over

	1986	1990	1995–96	2012
Single women	2.5	2.6	2.4	2.2
Single men	3.0	2.8	3.1	2.8
Couples	2.0	2.9	3.1	3.3
All households[1]	3.0	2.8	2.6	2.9

[1] The data for 1986, 1990 and 1995–96 relate to pensioner households aged 60 and over.

Source: Estimates from unit record files, ABS (2012) and Whiteford and Bond (2000, p. 35).

The distribution of wealth continues to be extremely unequal and, given the rising significance of superannuation, this is making Australia less, rather than more, egalitarian. As shown in Table 10.4, older individuals at the 10th percentile of the distribution of superannuation wealth had zero assets in 2013–14, whilst those at the 90th percentile had superannuation wealth close to $700,000. The older individual at the 90th percentile of the superannuation wealth distribution had fully 34.5 times the wealth of the median older Australian in 2013–14.

Table 10.4: Inequality among older Australian households— superannuation wealth at the 10th, 50th and 90th percentiles for Australians aged 65 and over, 2013–14

	10th percentile	50th percentile	90th percentile	90:50 ratio
All older men	0	$37,032	$768,839	$20.8
All older women	0	$5,586	$610,090	$109.2
All older individuals	0	$20,124	$694,067	$34.5

Source: Authors' estimates from ATO Sample File 2013–14 data on Member Contribution Statements.

Gender equity

The current retirement income and savings system is producing especially poor outcomes for Australian women. Expenditures on superannuation fail the CEDAW test that requires equal distribution. This contributes to a situation where, despite the massive commitment of government resources to superannuation, a significant number of women remain vulnerable to the risks of poverty in old age. As such, current retirement income and savings policy in Australia also falls short of protecting core minimum living standards.

Gender inequity in the current retirement and savings system arises from the (increased) emphasis on the superannuation pillar, the large tax expenditures that support this pillar, and the limited regulation of superannuation contributions and pensions.

Superannuation schemes tie retirement incomes to labour market earnings. As such, they produce larger retirement incomes for men than women, who are, on average, disadvantaged by lower wage rates, lower paid work hours and career interruptions (often brought about by unpaid caring roles). Amongst full-time Australian workers, the gender pay gap favouring men is currently 18.2 per cent; with men, on average, earning $283.20 more per week from their full-time paid work roles than women (ABS 2016). There is also a stark gender divide in both labour force participation rates and work hours. Figure 10.1 presents the labour force participation gap, favouring men, which is close to 10 percentage points. Figure 10.2 illustrates that the female part-time employment rate is five times the male rate. Aspects of the tax-transfer system that produce high effective marginal tax rates on second earners in couple households also contribute to these outcomes, as does the high cost of child care and its limited availability; these issues are discussed in detail elsewhere in this volume, including by Patricia Apps (Chapter 3, this volume; and see Apps 2015) and Guyonne Kalb (Chapter 5, this volume).

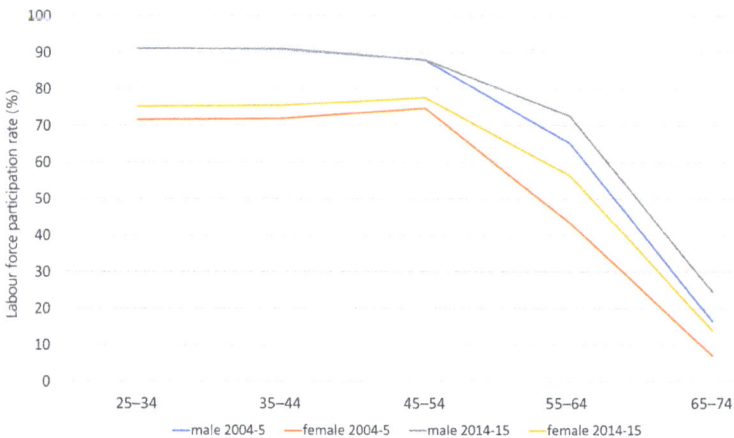

Figure 10.1: Labour force participation rates by gender, trend
Source: ABS (2016).

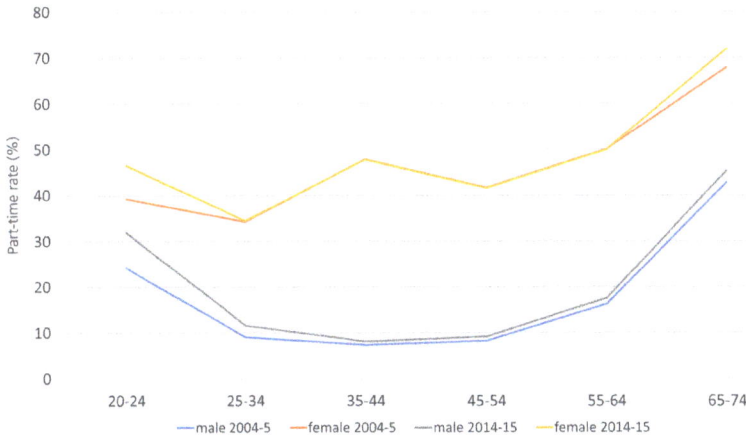

Figure 10.2: Part-time work by gender and age
Source: ABS (2016).

The generosity of the tax expenditures on superannuation, and the limited controls on contributions, magnify the effects of gender differences in paid and unpaid work. The groups most able to benefit from the tax expenditures on superannuation are high-income earners and those with flexible assets that can be moved into the tax-advantaged superannuation system. In 2012–13, 13.2 per cent of the tax concessions for superannuation contributions went to individuals in the top income tax bracket, as shown in Figure 10.3. However, only 1.6 per cent of female taxpayers (and a smaller proportion of all women), as compared to 4.3 per cent of male taxpayers, are in this group. Women, much more than men, are concentrated in lower tax brackets (or pay no income tax due to their non-participation in paid work) and, as such, they receive a relatively small share of the benefits of the increasingly large tax expenditures on superannuation. This gap is illustrated in Figure 10.4.

The consequences of the current policy settings for gender (in)equity in retirement incomes are demonstrated in Phil Gallagher's modelling, as shown in Table 10.2. In the 'base' scenario (where a 12.5 per cent SG rate applies and individuals retire at 65 and then draw down their superannuation assets in accordance with their life expectancy), women's retirement incomes are substantially below men's. At median wage rates, the retirement income achieved by women is less than two-thirds the amount required for a 'comfortable lifestyle', whilst men on median wage rates achieve a retirement income close to 80 per cent of the 'comfortable' level. Gallagher's modelling also demonstrates that women, much more than men, remain vulnerable to the risks of poverty, especially under the scenarios where retirement occurs before age 65 (which is the norm for the large majority of women) and the SG rate remains at 9.5 per cent (which is the current status quo).

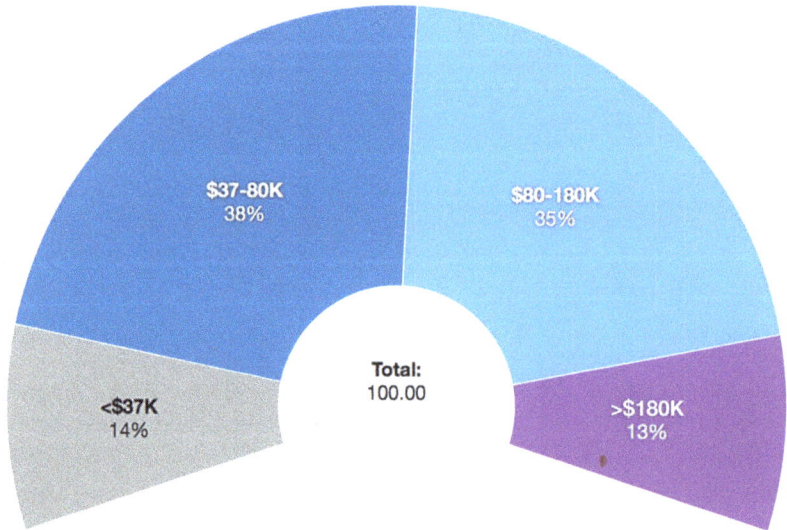

Figure 10.3: Distribution of tax concessions for superannuation contributions across taxable income categories

Source: ATO (2014).

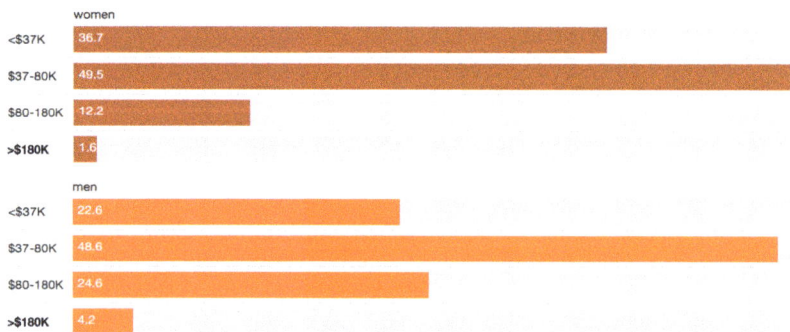

Figure 10.4: Distribution of male and female taxpayers across taxable income categories

Source: ATO (2014).

There is little room for optimism for improvements in gender equity unless the direction of retirement and savings policy changes. In recent years, the upward movement in women's labour force participation rates, full-time employment rates and wage rates has stalled (Austen et al. 2016), reducing prospects for a levelling out in superannuation contributions. There is also a lack of parallel policies such as provisions for SG contributions when on paid parental leave (Broomhill and Sharp 2012, p. 8). As Figure 10.5 shows, the gender gap in contributions emerges in the youngest group, and persists throughout the life course. The overall effect of these gaps and policy settings is to produce consistently lower superannuation account balances for women. Men have more superannuation than women at all ages, but in particular during prime working years 40 to 64, when men have 30 to 50 per cent greater balances than women.

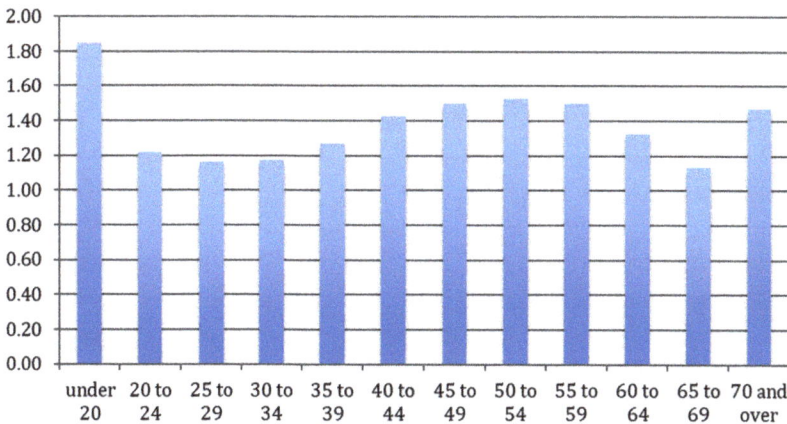

Figure 10.5: Ratio of male to female average superannuation account balances, as measured in member contribution statements

Source: Author's calculations from ATO 2 per cent file data, 2013–14 (ATO 2015).

A report by Feng et al. (2015) adds some important new insights on the sources of these gaps in superannuation account balances. Using administrative data from Mercer Australia, it examined gender differences in super accumulation between 2002–03 and 2011–12 in three age cohorts: individuals born in 1956–58 (age 44–46); 1966–68 (age 34–36); and 1976–78 (aged 24–26). It revealed a number of key gender gaps: attrition rates were higher for women than men in each cohort, reflecting higher rates of departure from paid work; a higher proportion of women than men experienced a reduction in the annual 'employer contribution rate' over the survey period, reflecting reductions in earnings that are associated with, for example, reduced working hours; a relatively high proportion of women missed whole year contributions to their superannuation funds, reflecting, most likely, periods of maternity leave; and, reflecting the influence of women's lower earnings, the super accumulations of women who remained in the fund over the study period were lower than their male counterparts in all but one of the cohorts. The study found that the gender gap in average superannuation balances narrowed over the study period. However, a sizeable gender gap remained in each cohort in 2011–12, and women continued to be over-represented in the lowest contribution groups. Importantly, the position of women in the distribution of individuals—ranked on the basis of their super contributions—worsened between 2002–03 and 2011–12.

Women in couple households

The importance of the large gender gap in retirement income is often downplayed on the grounds that because most women live in couple households they can benefit from their partner's superannuation. This type of argument is deficient on several levels. First, it ignores the substantial risk of widowhood and divorce for older Australian women. At age 65 close to one third of women are not married and by age 75 half of all women are single (Gallagher 2016, chart 4). Thus, the evidence of low superannuation wealth amongst older women that has been outlined in this chapter is directly relevant to the living standards of a large proportion of older Australian women.

Arguments against the importance of the gender gap in retirement income should also be rejected on the basis of their implicit assumption that household resources are pooled and the interests of both partners are taken into account when decisions about these resources are made. In other domains, individual, rather than household, income and wealth are commonly used to assess wellbeing, although account is taken of household size. As Stewart (2011, p. 59) summarises, the Henry Tax Review affirmed the individual tax unit for both efficiency reasons (relating especially to work incentives) and equity reasons, arguing the approach better reflects ability to pay. The review also described the individual tax unit as more stable because 'families change over time, as people partner and separate, and society's conception of what constitutes a couple also changes' (Treasury 2009, Part 2, p. 24).

From an equity perspective, it is vital to focus on individuals' retirement income because maldistribution of the ownership and control of resources within households exposes individuals within the household (more often women than men) to the risks of poor decision-making and inadequate resources. International research by Friedberg and Webb (2006) and Phipps and Woolley (2008) has established the links between the formal ownership of wealth and intra-household processes relating to divestment decisions, and a variety of economic studies have demonstrated the links between men's and women's different life expectancies and household decision-making on consumption and savings in old age (see, for example, Lundberg et al. 2003). Poor decisions about the use of lump sums, the selection of annuity type and housing have been shown to leave women exposed to poor outcomes late in life (Bisdee et al. 2013). These risks are especially important given that older individuals typically cannot respond to poor outcomes by increasing their own involvement in paid work.

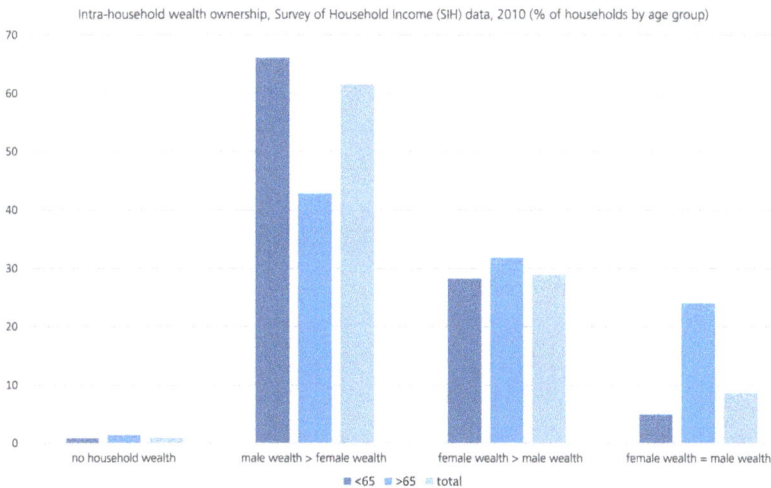

Figure 10.6: Inequality in wealth within couple households, by age
n = 8165 couples age < 65, 2014 couples age 65+.
Source: ABS (2015).

The available evidence on the allocation of resources and decision-making within Australian couple households emphasises the potential significance of these intra-household issues. As shown in Figure 10.6, in the majority (61.5 per cent) of Australian heterosexual couple households, the male partner's (non-housing) wealth exceeds that of the female partner. The same pattern applies to superannuation assets: Figure 10.7 shows that in 52.4 per cent of these households, superannuation assets are greater for the male partner (22.4 per cent of couple households report zero superannuation assets). The size of the gender gaps in superannuation and wealth in couple households is also large. For example, in households where the gap in superannuation assets favours men, the median ratio of the two partners' assets is currently around 330 per cent.

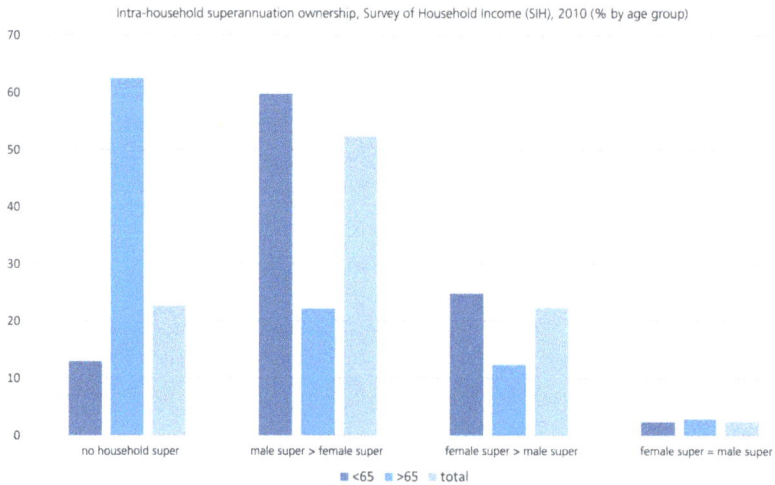

Intra-household superannuation ownership, Survey of Household Income (SIH), 2010 (% by age group)

Figure 10.7: Inequality in superannuation within couple households, by age
n = 8165 couples age < 65, 2014 couples age 65+.
Source: ABS (2015).

Survey data on decision-making control in couple households also indicate that the formal ownership of financial resources matters. Data from the recent Productivity Commission survey on Housing Decision-Making, for example, show that 46 per cent of married men aged 65 and over, as compared to only 20 per cent of married women in the same age group, perceive that they controlled most of their household's financial decisions. The proportion of men reporting control of decision-making was higher (at 51.6 per cent) in the group with superannuation as their key source of income, and lower in the group who relied on the age pension (40.4 per cent). The 16.7 per cent of women with superannuation as their main source of income reported that they made most of the financial decisions in their household. The rate was 20 per cent amongst women that relied on the age pension. One possible explanation is that women with superannuation wealth might be more likely to be married to men with this type of wealth. This evidence is in line with the findings of earlier research projects, using qualitative methods, that have demonstrated that working-age households do not necessarily pool and equally share their resources (see, for example, Edwards 1982), and that the distribution of income from the formal labour market and government transfers has an important bearing on household decision-making processes (Euwals et al. 2004).

Conclusion

This chapter applies a rights-based framework for gender equality based on CEDAW to inform a gender impact analysis of current Australian policy for retirement incomes and savings. The analysis presented in this paper is in contrast to much current public debate on retirement incomes policy, which is overwhelmingly focused on fiscal sustainability. Due to its focus on cost containment criteria, the current debate usually subordinates ends to means and encourages a focus on financial inputs at the expense of the ultimate objectives or outcomes of the retirement incomes system.

The rights-based approach that we have used examines whether budgetary policies are sufficient to provide an adequate retirement income for all Australian women for all the years of their retirement, and whether the policies pass tests of gender equality. CEDAW requires that expenditure be distributed equally with funds being sufficient to meet core minimum standards and revenue raising needs to enable the progressive realisation of the 'full development and advancement of women' (UN 1979, p. 2). In line with gender-responsive budget research, our discussion of adequacy has gone beyond consideration solely of the financial inputs of the retirement incomes' budget allocations to examination of the activities, outputs and outcomes of the policy in order to gauge progress towards the implementation of CEDAW.

Our analysis showed that large financial inputs, valued at 16.2 per cent of federal government–planned expenditures for 2016–17, are associated with government spending and taxation on Australia's three-pillar retirement incomes policy. Spending on the targeted age pension is projected to be similar to the cost of tax expenditures on the superannuation pillars in coming years. These financial inputs into the retirement incomes system deliver a pattern of outputs (namely retirement incomes for individuals) that is characterised by a marked gender distribution. The majority of both men and women aged 65 years and older are highly dependent on either a full or a part age pension; however, women are much more likely to be dependent on the age pension than men. As the two-tiered superannuation system is less than 30 years old, the total cost of the tax expenditures cannot be ascribed directly to the current superannuation of older Australians, though it is clear that their benefits are strongly linked to the pattern of workforce participation and incomes. Women's greater responsibilities for unpaid work, their broken workforce patterns and lower average earnings result in lower superannuation assets and, thus, their share of the substantial benefits from tax expenditures on superannuation is relatively low. For example, in 2013–14, the median superannuation balance of women aged 65 and older was a fraction of men's ($5,586 compared to $37,032) notwithstanding zero superannuation assets of a large percentage of men (37.8 per cent) and women (45.9 per cent).

The government's enacted superannuation objective is devoid of purposes relating to adequacy and equity; it also fails to provide criteria for judging retirement incomes and savings policies. This is likely to reinforce the invisibility of gender issues and gaps in retirement incomes policy rather than shine a light on them and facilitate budgetary and policy changes consistent with gender equality.

However, gleaning outcomes from policy statements at the time of the introduction of the mandatory superannuation scheme, made by then Treasurer Paul Keating, indicates that adequacy, equality and gender equity were initially identified as relevant criteria for evaluation. Against these criteria, we make an assessment of the sufficiency of current retirement incomes policy. First, in terms of adequacy of the age pension, OECD comparisons suggest Australia performs poorly, with a third of age pensioners living below the poverty line. However, the depth of aged poverty in Australia is currently relatively small because of the ameliorating effect of the high rate of home ownership among older Australians. Recent modelling of retirement income outcomes of the SG suggests that even among home owners, except for a few men on high earnings, the majority of Australians will not achieve a 'comfortable' lifestyle in retirement. Second, in terms of equality, our analysis shows that the level of income inequality among older households has been largely unchanged since 1986. Moreover, a very uneven distribution of wealth is being produced with the rising importance of superannuation, making Australia less rather than more egalitarian. For example, older individuals in the 10th percentile of the superannuation distribution had zero assets in 2013–14, compared to an individual at the 90th percentile with superannuation wealth of $694,000.

Finally, in relation to gender equity, Australian women experience particularly poor outcomes from the current retirement incomes and savings policy. Their vulnerability to poverty in old age indicates a failure to protect core minimum living standards, as required by CEDAW. Superannuation ties retirement income to labour market earnings and women's disadvantaged labour market position compared to that of men's means the generous and growing superannuation tax expenditures fail the CEDAW test of equal distribution. Gender inequality outcomes are further indicated with modelling that shows women's retirement incomes substantially below men's and a 'comfortable lifestyle' in retirement much further from reach for women. An examination of different age cohorts shows the gender gaps in superannuation contributions and balances remain large, therefore the gender inequalities in the distribution of superannuation are likely to be sustained for decades. The question of whether retirement incomes spending and taxation is sufficient from a CEDAW perspective also needs to consider the gendered impacts within households. We argue that pooling of household cannot be assumed, and different life expectancies combined with maldistribution of the ownership and control of income and wealth puts older women at risk more than men of poor outcomes later in life.

We conclude that aspects of Australia's retirement incomes policy are in conflict with the government's international human rights commitments required under CEDAW. This should give pause to the current focus on private provision and open up a debate of outcomes as the test of a sound retirement incomes system.

References

ABS (Australian Bureau of Statistics). 2012. *Household Energy Consumption Survey, Australia.* Cat. no. 4670.0. Canberra.

ABS. 2015. *Survey of Income and Housing 2013–14*, Cat. no. 6553.0. Canberra. Accessed May 2, 2016.

ABS. 2016. *Gender Indicators, Australia,* February 2016, Cat. no. 4125.0, Canberra.

Apps, Patricia. 2015. 'The Central Role of a Well-Designed Income Tax in "the Modern Economy"'. *Australian Tax Forum: A Journal of Taxation Policy, Law and Reform* 30(4): 845–863. doi.org/10.2139/ssrn.2662280

ASFA (Australian Superannuation Funds Association). 2013. 'Super system evolution: Achieving consensus through a shared vision, ASFA White Paper—Part 4'. May. Available at: www.superannuation.asn.au/policy/reports

ATO (Australian Taxation Office). 2014. Taxation statistics 2012–13 Individuals. Canberra. Available at: www.ato.gov.au/About-ATO/Research-and-statistics/In-detail/Taxation-statistics/Taxation-statistics-2012-13/

ATO. 2015. Taxation statistics 2013–14 Individuals. Canberra. Available at: www.ato.gov.au/About-ATO/Research-and-statistics/In-detail/Taxation-statistics/Taxation-statistics-2013-14/

Austen, Siobhan, Rhonda Sharp and Helen Hodgson. 2015. 'Gender impact analysis and the taxation of retirement savings in Australia'. *Australian Tax Forum* 30(4): 763–781.

Austen, Siobhan, Rhonda Sharp and Therese Jefferson. 2016. 'Why neither party should ignore gender in this election'. *The Conversation*, May 13 2016. Available at: theconversation.com/why-neither-party-should-ignore-gender-in-this-election-57551

Australian Government. 2016a. *Budget 2016–17 Overview*. Available at: www.budget.gov.au/2016-17/content/glossies/overview/downloads/Budget2016-17-Overview.pdf.

Australian Government. 2016b. *Budget 2016–17: Portfolio Budget Statements 2016–17, Budget Related Paper No. 1.15a, Social Services Portfolio*. Available at: www.dss.gov.au/sites/default/files/documents/05_2016/2016-17_social_services_pbs.pdf

Australian Human Rights Commission. n.d. 'Nature of obligations regarding economic, social and cultural rights, Article 2'. Available at: www.humanrights.gov.au/nature-obligations-regarding-economic-social-and-cultural-rights

Bisdee, Dinah, Tom Daly and Debora Price. 2013. 'Behind Closed Doors: Older Couples and the Gendered Management of Household Money'. *Social Policy and Society* 12(1): 163–174. doi.org/10.1017/S147474641200053X

Bradbury, Bruce and Bina Gubhaju. 2010. *Housing costs and living standards among the elderly.* Occasional Paper 31. Canberra: Australian Government Department of Families, Housing, Community Services and Indigenous Affairs. Available at: www.dss.gov.au/sites/default/files/documents/05_2012/op31.pdf

Broomhill, Ray and Rhonda Sharp. 2012. *Australia's parental leave policy and gender equality: an international comparison.* Australian Workforce Innovation and Social Research Centre: University of Adelaide. Available at: apo.org.au/node/30934

Budlender, Debbie. 2004. *Budgeting to Fulfill International Gender and Human Rights Commitments.* UNIFEM Regional Office for Southern African and Indian Ocean States, Harare.

CEDA (Committee for Economic Development for Australia). 2015. *The super challenge of retirement income policy.* Sydney: CEDA. Available at: www.ceda.com.au/CEDA/media/ResearchCatalogueDocuments/PDFs/27922-CEDATheSuperChallengeofRetirementIncomePolicySept2015FINAL.pdf

Clare, Ross. 2014. 'Spending patterns of older retirees: New ASFA Retirement Standard – September quarter 2014'. ASFA. Available at: www.superannuation.asn.au/policy/reports

Department of Social Services. 2014. 'Income support customers: a statistical overview 2013'. Statistical Paper No. 12. Australian Government Department of Social Services, Canberra. Available at www.dss.gov.au/sites/default/files/documents/01_2015/sp12_accessible_pdf_final.pdf

Edwards, Meredith. 1982. 'Financial Arrangements Made by Husbands and Wives: Findings of a Survey'. *Australia and New Zealand Journal of Sociology* 18(3). doi.org/10.1177/144078338201800303

Elson, Di. 2002. 'Gender Justice, Human Rights and Neoliberal Economic Policies' in M. Molyneux and S. Razavi (eds.) *Gender Justice, Development, and Rights*. Oxford: Oxford University Press. doi. org/10.1093/0199256454.003.0003

Elson, Di. 2006. *Budgeting for Women's Rights, Monitoring Government Budgets for Compliance with CEDAW*. New York: United Nations Development Fund for Women.

Elson, Di and Rhonda Sharp. 2010. 'Gender responsive budgeting and women's poverty'. In Sylvia Chant (ed.), *The International Handbook of Gender and Poverty: Concepts, Research and Policy*, pp. 522–527. Cheltenham: Edward Elgar.

Euwals, Rob, Angelika Eymann and Axel Börsh-Supan. 2004. 'Who Determines Household Savings for Old Age? Evidence from Dutch Panel Data'. *Journal of Economic Psychology* 25(2): 195–211. doi.org/10.1016/S0167-4870(02)00190-3

Feng, Jimmy, Paul Gerrans, Noel Whiteside, Maria Strydom, Carly Moulang, Gordon Clark and Maurizo Fiaschetti. 2015. 'A longitudinal analysis of superannuation outcomes: gender differences'. CSIRO–Monash Working Paper 2015-03, Melbourne.

Friedberg, Leora and Anthony Webb. 2006. *Determinants and Consequences of Bargaining Power in Households*. Chestnut Hill, Massachusetts: Center for Retirement Research at Boston College. doi.org/10.3386/w12367

Gallagher, Phil. 2016. 'Modelling Adequacy for the Broad Retiree Population'. Paper presented to the Committee for Sustainable Retirement Incomes, 6 April. The Australian National University, Canberra.

Keating, Paul. 1991. 'A Retirement Incomes Policy'. Address to the Australian Graduate School of Management, University of New South Wales, Sydney, 25 July.

Korpi, Walter and Joakim Palme. 1998. 'The Paradox of Redistribution and Strategies of Equality: Welfare State Institutions, Inequality and Poverty in the Western Countries'. *American Sociological Review* 63(5): 661–687. doi.org/10.2307/2657333

Lundberg, Shelly, Richard Startza and Steven Stillman. 2003. 'The Retirement-Consumption Puzzle: A Marital Bargaining Approach'. *Journal of Public Economics* 87(5/6): 1199–1218. doi.org/10.1016/S0047-2727(01)00169-4

Morrison, Scott. 2015. Interview with Fran Kelly on *ABC Radio National Breakfast*, 7 October. Available at: www.abc.net.au/radionational/programs/breakfast/federal-treasurer-scott-morr/6832828

Norton, Andy and Di Elson. 2002. *What's Behind the Budget? Politics, Rights and Accountability in the Budget Process*. London: Overseas Development Institute.

OECD (Organisation for Economic Co-operation and Cultural Development). 2015. *Pensions at a Glance*. Paris: OECD. Available at: www.oecd-ilibrary.org/docserver/download/8115201ec028.pdf?expires=1490058094&id=id&accname=guest&checksum=F703874 E99EA62A8C437298236EA931B

Parliament of Australia, House of Representatives. 2016. *Superannuation (Objective) Bill 2016*, Second Reading. The Treasurer, Hon. Scott Morrison, 9 November. Available at: parlinfo.aph.gov.au/parlInfo/search/display/display.w3p;query=Id%3A%22chamber%2Fhansardr%2Fe089c8c3-75b7-4858-80ac-58b4e4c6e749%2F0157%22

Phipps, Shelley A. and Frances Woolley. 2008. 'Control over Money and the Savings Decisions of Canadian Households'. *The Journal of Socio-Economics* 37(2): 592–611. doi.org/10.1016/j.socec.2006.12.042

Pillay, Karrisha, Rashida Manjou and Elroy Paulus. 2002. *Rights, Roles and Resources: An Analysis of Women's Housing Rights—Implications of the Grootboom case*. Cape Town: Women's Budget Initiative.

Productivity Commission. 2015. *Housing Decisions of Older Australians*. Commission Research Paper, Canberra.

Sharp, Rhonda. 2003. *Budgeting for Equity, Gender Budgeting Within a Framework of Performance-Oriented Budgeting*. New York: United Nations Development Fund for Women.

Stewart, Miranda. 2011. 'Gender Equity in Australia's Tax System: A Capabilities Approach'. In Kim Brooks, Asa Gunnarson, Lisa Philipps and Maria Wersig (eds), *Challenging Gender Inequality in Tax Policy Making: Comparative Perspectives*, pp. 53–73. UK: Hart Publishing.

Swoboda, Kai. 2017. 'Superannuation (Objective) Bill 2016'. Parliamentary Library Bills Digest No. 69, 2016–17, 2 March. Canberra: Parliament of Australia. Available at: www.aph.gov.au/Parliamentary_Business/Bills_Legislation/bd/bd1617a/17bd069

Treasury. 2006. *A Plan to Simplify and Streamline Superannuation: Detailed Outline May 2006.* Available at: simplersuper.treasury.gov.au/documents/outline/download/simpler_super.pdf

Treasury. 2009. *Australia's Future Tax System.* Canberra: Australian Treasury. Available at: taxreview.treasury.gov.au/content/Consultation Paper.aspx?doc=html/publications/Papers/Retirement_Income_Consultation_Paper/Chapter_2.htm

Treasury. 2016. *Tax Expenditure Statements 2015.* Available at: static. treasury.gov.au/uploads/sites/1/2017/06/2015_TES.pdf

UN (United Nations). 1979. *Convention on the Elimination of All Forms of Discrimination against Women.* Available at: www.ohchr.org/Documents/ProfessionalInterest/cedaw.pdf

Whiteford, Peter and Kim Bond. 2000. *Trends in the incomes and living standards of older people in Australia.* Department of Family and Community Services, Policy and Research Paper No. 6.

Part IV: Towards gender equality in the tax-transfer system

11

Pathways and processes towards a gender equality policy

Meredith Edwards and Miranda Stewart

All aspects of government action and policy have gender implications. The federal Office for Women has identified three areas of focus for Australian Government policy on gender: (1) women's safety from violence; (2) representation of women, for example on decision-making boards and in politics; and (3) economic empowerment. This volume presents new and important research about gender inequality in Australia's tax-transfer (welfare) system, including theoretical, empirical and policy analysis of this theme. The research in this volume aligns in particular with the goal of women's economic empowerment, which is highlighted by the Office for Women as 'an economic and social priority. It's good for women and their families, their communities, business and the nation's economy' (Office for Women 2016). The Minister for Women, Senator Michaelia Cash, has emphasised policies to support women at the G20 (Cash 2014) and, in particular for parenting and domestic violence, in a statement accompanying the 2017–18 Budget (Cash 2017). However, gender impact remains marginalised in Australia's budget. The most recent Budget Papers (Treasury 2017) do not contain any gender impact analysis of policy. This is in stark contrast to the recent Canadian budget (Government of Canada 2017).

The first part of this volume presents international and comparative principles, context and benchmarks on gender equality by Kathleen Lahey (Chapter 2); a holistic economic approach to gender equality to produce an efficient, equitable and fiscally sustainable tax-transfer system by Patricia Apps (Chapter 3); and a human rights framework that incorporates gender equality as a core element of macro-economic fiscal policy (Hodgson and Sadiq in Chapter 4).

The focus then turns to a policy analysis of unequal effects of current policy on women's economic security. A key element is the engagement of women in paid (market) work. Government policy aims to 'support more Australian women into work, improving their economic security today and to accumulate retirement savings for the future' (Office for Women 2016). To achieve this without further disadvantaging women, government policy must take the gendered issue of care work seriously. The implications for women's paid work of the intersection of government policies over the life course is examined by Guyonne Kalb (Chapter 5), while the inadequate recognition of unpaid or household care work by women in the historical and contemporary Australian welfare state is discussed by Julie Smith (Chapter 6).

Subsequent chapters present novel empirical research addressing the different ways in which men and women balance work and child care time (Huong Dinh and Maria Racionero in Chapter 7); the unequal gender returns to education through earnings and the impact of Australia's higher education financing scheme (Mathias Sinning in Chapter 8); the position of women at the top of the income distribution (Miranda Stewart, Sarah Voitchovsky and Roger Wilkins in Chapter 9); and the implications of retirement and age pension policy for adequacy of women's incomes in old age (Siobhan Austen and Rhonda Sharp in Chapter 10).

In this concluding chapter, we return to the central role of government policy and discuss pathways and processes to achieve a gender equality policy in the future. The chapters in this volume clearly demonstrate the persistence of gender inequality and show the critical role played by government policies, especially tax-transfer policies, in both reproducing and alleviating this gender inequality. The research presented also provides clear directions for policy in Australia's tax-transfer system to achieve women's economic empowerment, thereby contributing to greater wellbeing for all in Australia. The persistence of gender inequalities across a range of public policy areas indicates a continuing need for gender-focused policy processes. We discuss past governmental processes for achieving gender equality and then turn to consider the pathways and processes to achieve gender equality in future government policy. In particular, we consider the question of gender budgeting, including impact analysis and policy formulation through a gender lens.

The ups and downs of gender budgeting in Australia

Gender budgeting is a formalised institutional process that incorporates gender analysis of budget measures and indicators, in government agencies, departments and at Cabinet level, and which may be carried out at various levels of policy formulation, financing and delivery. One widely used definition is:

> [A] gender-based assessment of budgets, incorporating a gender perspective at all levels of the budgetary process and restructuring revenues and expenditures in order to promote gender equality (Council of Europe 2009).

Gender budgeting starts from the proposition that the budget is the central political document that activates government policy by raising revenues and allocating expenditures legislated by the parliament. Within agencies and departments tasked with developing policy and delivering public goods and services, performance budgeting generates a process of tracking policy through to outcomes that can incorporate targets, indicators and measures of achievement on gender equality.

Political action for women's rights has a long history. However, the process of gender budgeting has its origins in Australia during the early 1980s. The circuitous institutional pathways and fortunes of feminist engagement in the Commonwealth bureaucracy, traced by Marian Sawer (1990) are of particular interest to us as the Commonwealth has primary responsibility for broad taxation, social welfare, wages, retirement and higher education policy. During this time, the 'femocrats' (Sawer 1990; Watson 1990; Eisenstein 1996) sought to introduce and embed gender-equal policies; to examine distributional impact and demonstrate where it was unequal in respect of gender; to identify the fiscal cost and extremely high effective marginal tax rates for many women produced by tax-transfer interactions; and to fend off or reduce the impact of policy proposals that would undermine gender equality. They made the case in government that unequal gender and class outcomes were the direct result of tax-transfer policies as well as labour market discrimination and care responsibilities of women. They also showed that government policies could change to support gender equality, address poverty and improve work incentives.

Not surprisingly, the pathway towards achieving gender-equal policy has not been easy and remains challenging and incomplete. The best process is not always easy to identify, and both actions and outcomes have often been marginal or partial. On some indicators, progress has been striking. For example, the aggregate proportion of women in tertiary education is today greater than the proportion of men. Yet, even in this field, the sex-segregation of women and men in fields of tertiary study remains significant and differential outcomes remain. As Sinning shows in Chapter 8, the economic (wage and earnings) return to women for investing in their human capital through tertiary education or technical further study is significantly lower than for men.

Successes or setbacks in gender-equal policy and processes have not always followed a simplistic 'left/right' divide in politics. After activism and government appointments in the early 1970s under the Whitlam Labor Government, the establishment of an office for Women's Affairs in the central Department of Prime Minister and Cabinet (DPMC) occurred in the early years of the Fraser Liberal–National Government. The Women's Affairs office had a say on all Budget submissions, noted by Sawer as one of the most important aspects of its work (Sawer 1990, p. 46). However, in the late 1970s, the Women's Affairs office was demoted to an 'outer' government department, although substantial work continued to be done 'behind the scenes' even in this location.

The Office for Women was reinstated in the central department in 1983 under the Hawke Labor Government and it was during this time, under leadership of Anne Summers, that the Office developed an innovative approach to gender impact analysis to identify and track the effects of policy on women and to recommend directions to improve gender equity. The first Women's Budget Statement was released in 1984, and it was produced in a fairly detailed format until 1996. As has been internationally acknowledged, Australia was a pioneer in this analysis (Sharp and Broomhill 2013). Nevertheless, under the Labor Government of the 1980s and the Liberal–National Party Government of the previous decade, the central economic department of the Treasury resisted engagement with gender equality analysis and never participated directly in the Women's Budget Statement.

The requirement established in 1983 that all Cabinet submissions were to include a statement about impact on women was removed after four years (Sawer 1990, p. 71), even as Australia prepared a National Agenda for Women to the Year 2000 in response to international developments in the United Nations. The late 1980s also saw increasing targeting and means testing of family and child payments for fiscal reasons, undermining the goal of achieving women's workforce participation. The Women's Budget Statement and role of the Office for Women was further demoted in scope and importance under the Howard Liberal–National Government during the mid-1990s. In the early 2000s, it moved the Office for Women out of DPMC and into the Department of Family and Community Services. This major government department was responsible for family payments and social security policy, which had significant implications for women. Some had suggested that this could be perceived as a move of 'so-called women's issues into the mainstream' (Goward 2004), so that gender would be more comprehensively considered in key programs in the public sector.[1] However, it effectively demoted gender equality and did not lead to a fully comprehensive analysis of gender in tax-transfer systems; arguably, the reverse happened, and the Office lost its cross-government coordinating role in the process.

Even under Howard's more socially conservative government, in 2006 Julie Bishop, then Minister Assisting the Prime Minister for Women's Issues, emphasised Australia's commitment to gender equality including budget analysis (Bishop 2006); in that year, the Office for Women released *Women '06: 2006–07 Budget Information*. The Australian Bureau of Statistics (ABS) also in that year conducted and released the results of a major Time Use Survey (TUS) (the largest ever conducted in Australia), which dramatically demonstrated the gender differences in market and household work and care of women and men (ABS 2006). The 2006 TUS provides crucial data for researchers on gender and care. It is relied on in Chapter 7 (Dinh and Racionero) and is referred to in numerous other chapters of this volume (see also Baird et al. 2017). However, this

---

1   On the complexities of gender 'mainstreaming' in Australian Government policy see Walby (2005); Bacchi and Eveline (2010).

survey has not been funded since 2006, and the scheduled survey of 2013 was cancelled, in a broader context of ongoing cuts to funding for data collection and analysis in the ABS and other government agencies.

The Labor governments of 2007 to 2013, including under Australia's first female prime minister Julia Gillard, reinstated a Women's Budget Statement, which did an overview of government policies aimed at women's equality. However, it was relatively superficial and these governments did not bring gender analysis back into the central government agency or reinstate the role of the Office for Women in cabinet processes or as a coordinating agency. More than 30 years after the first Women's Budget Statement was released in 1984, we saw its abandonment in 2014 by the Abbott Liberal–National Government; in the last few years, gender budgeting and gender impact analysis seemed to disappear from Australian Government policy processes, except in the arena of foreign aid, where gender indicators for development still retained a foothold (again under the leadership of Minister Julie Bishop). The Australian Labor Party (ALP) in opposition has continued a tradition of producing a Women's Statement, which is valuable, albeit inevitably restricted to the statement of ALP policy on gender and limited analysis of government policy. Outside government, the most important and comprehensive gender analysis of the budget is carried out by the non-government National Foundation for Australian Women (NFAW), which has since 2014 put a gender lens on the budget *ex post*, with minimal resources (most recently, NFAW 2017).

While gender impact analysis seems to have disappeared from the government agenda, gender remains centrally relevant to much government policy. As discussed in Chapter 1, in the last few years we have seen governments of both stripes introduce and debate major funded policies for paid parental leave, child care policies, income tax rate structures for workers, social welfare and family payments, elder care, pension and retirement policies and disability policy. A central element in these policies is sharing the fiscal cost of care. These policies, which have implications for the wellbeing of the wider population of men, women and children in Australia, have direct and fundamental implications for gender equality.

A tax and transfer reform agenda for gender equality

There is, of course, a diversity of views about how best to achieve gender equality goals and women's economic empowerment, including increased workforce participation and economic security, and what pragmatic policies and priorities are needed. Nonetheless, we identify a clear consensus among our expert contributors on the needed policy direction to achieve gender equality, arising out of the detailed theoretical, policy and empirical analysis in this volume.

1. A progressive income tax

The first recommendation is to maintain and enforce a progressive income tax as an efficient and equitable tool for gender equality. A progressive income tax on individuals with marginal rates that rise as income rises is important for women's equality because women earn less than men. As explained in Apps (Chapter 3), Kalb (Chapter 4) and other chapters, a progressive income tax is both efficient (taxing less responsive higher income earners more highly) and equitable, being based on ability to pay. The tax system operates in the context of gender-unequal workforce outcomes in both wages and hours, and with the lion's share of part-time work done by women. As lower wage or secondary earners in households, women's workforce participation is supported by a progressive income tax, which taxes the lower wage earner at a lower rate.

Feminist advocacy to maintain the progressivity of Australia's personal income tax has a long history and played an important role during the 1980s era of tax reform. The National Women's Tax Summit was convened by the Women's Electoral Lobby (WEL) one week before the famous Tax Summit 1985,[2] which brought together the government, labour and business leaders to debate major tax reform process, influenced by international trends including in the United States and United Kingdom (under Reagan and Thatcher). Described as 'the first national mobilisation of women over an economic issue' (Sawer 1990, p. 93), the Women's Tax Summit included representation from a wide range of women's organisations across all sectors of the community and economy and it

---

2   For a summary and document references, see National Archives of Australia, *Tax reform*, www. naa.gov.au/collection/explore/cabinet/by-year/1984-85/tax-reform.aspx.

resoundingly repudiated 'Option C' (Treasury 1985), which included a tax mix shift from the progressive income tax to a broad-based consumption tax with significantly lower marginal tax rates. In light of recent research into growing inequality across countries and the role of the top tax rate in producing and reinforcing income inequality (Atkinson and Leigh 2007; see discussion in Chapter 9), the retention of a reasonably high top tax rate by Australia has contributed to Australia's relatively equal disposable income distribution.

The progressive income tax is also highly effective at raising revenue in Australia. Women as a class benefit from public expenditure that delivers government services and public goods to all. The question of whether Australia requires more revenue—higher taxes—to fund government in the future remains of central importance in Australian fiscal policy debates. This may require both raising tax rates and broadening the tax base, including income, consumption and wealth taxes, as we see increasing demands on public expenditure for disability, age care and early childhood education, as well as infrastructure. It is worth observing the approach of the Nordic states, which levy both highly progressive income taxes and broad-based consumption taxes to fund their welfare states and also produce the most gender-equal outcomes globally.

2. The individual unit in tax and transfer systems

Second, this volume supports an individual unit as the basis for tax-transfer systems as far as possible but, in particular, where there are caring or dependant responsibilities. We must keep a clear policy focus on women as individuals making decisions, doing care work, bearing tax burdens and receiving benefits in the tax-transfer system and in family, work and care economies. This requires us to pay attention not only to the income tax but also to the design of payments, thresholds and means tests in the welfare system and public policy for child care and families.

The tax-transfer system has a particularly close relationship with women's economic security and empowerment and, specifically, women's workforce participation. Current tax-transfer policies make it rational for one person in a family, almost always a woman, if raising children or with other carer responsibilities, not to work in the market or to work only part-time. This reduces women's chances of remunerative and rewarding work and economic security in the longer term and undermines the government's stated goal of achieving economic independence, wellbeing and lifetime security for women. There is little evidence of a willingness to share time and cost of care between women and men, which would also then share the cost and risks of time taken out of the workforce to do caring and other household work. Recent research indicates that there are significant time, stress and public health implications of the 'extra' time burden of care on top of paid work for women, while still at relatively low incomes (Dinh et al. 2017).

The federal income tax has always had an individual unit in Australia. However, the testing of family and other transfer payments on household or couple income produces a 'quasi-joint' unit especially for women caring for children. At the top end of the income distribution, Chapter 9 (Stewart, Voitchovsky and Wilkins) presents evidence of income splitting in Australia's income tax, producing a 'quasi-joint' unit for high-income families, undermining the individual income tax base. Income splitting produces a lower tax burden for high-income families by using the progressive income tax rate structure, and the benefit has increased as a result of the increase of Australia's tax-free threshold and other rate thresholds in 2012. The use of low-taxed self-managed superannuation funds and discretionary family trusts is widespread and may be combined with the low tax rate applicable to capital gains and other tax planning approaches. As a result, Australia's income tax base is too narrow and a reform to broaden the individual income tax base would be positive for gender equality.

The interaction of the income tax system and the means-tested transfer system has proven to be a major sticking point for gender-equal policy over the last 30 years in Australia. Governments have tightened the means testing of most social welfare payments, to a point where Australia has the most tightly targeted welfare system of any Organisation for Economic Co-operation and Development (OECD) country (Whiteford 2016). The means testing of social welfare benefits on which women rely, at least while they are of working age, would ideally be done on an individual basis; alternatively, relevant benefits supporting the cost of care could be provided universally or with a high income-free area. This would encourage gender equality in workforce participation, with likely long-term benefits for economic growth and taxes. However, it comes at an immediate fiscal cost. The provision of universal benefits is seen as delivering unaffordable 'welfare' to middle-class and upper-income households. The 'iron triangle' (Henry et al. 2009) of means testing family and child care payments, individual income tax rates and an overarching fiscal or expenditure constraint sets gender equality directly against traditional concepts of vertical equity and horizontal equity in tax and welfare design.

The assumption that the household is the correct unit for means testing of transfer payments assumes that income and consumption is shared in the household and that women benefit equally from consumption inside the family. Clearly, some major forms of consumption (such as housing or electricity) can usually be assumed to be shared. However, empirical evidence shows that shared consumption even of food and household goods, and certainly of luxuries or leisure, is not always true (as demonstrated in Edwards 1981). Recent news stories about the lack of sharing of consumption when women stop work to look after children indicate that it cannot be taken for granted (Dunning 2017). Moreover, families, households or relationships are not static, and women's economic security is significantly threatened by separation and divorce. The traditional concept of horizontal equity that treats married couples more favourably than single people on the same income or treats a married or partnered woman as a dependant can no longer apply; in other words, all taxpayers on the same income irrespective of their marital status should be treated equally. Horizontal equity in the tax-transfer system should, however, recognise the cost of care and treat taxpayers with children, or, perhaps, other care responsibilities, differently from those without such responsibilities, as facing greater direct and indirect costs and lower capacity to pay.

3. Public funding for the cost of care

The issue of care remains a 'barbeque stopper' in John Howard's words (quoted in Heron et al. 2017, loc. 4496). A major comparative study shows that Australia today has a family-centred care regime underpinned by significant financial assistance from the state. Parents, in particular mothers, provide most child care, with the assistance especially of grandparents, and daughters (who are often also mothers or grandparents) provide the bulk of care for elders (Heron et al. 2017, loc. 4522). Policies to put more women into the paid workforce for more hours will not achieve gender-equal outcomes unless the cost of care is supported and tax-transfer policies that intersect with labour market programs are adjusted. After more than 30 years of public policy in building child care provision, labour programs and other measures aimed at encouraging women's workforce participation, it is clear that the best chance of success is in providing wide public support for parental leave and child care for women of prime working age (between 20 to 45) and implementing clear policies to share care and connection of children between women and men.

We need to share the fiscal cost and time of care more equally between women and men, and across society via our tax-transfer system, to achieve gender-equal opportunities and outcomes. As discussed by Julie Smith (Chapter 6), it is necessary to acknowledge and support the (unpaid) caring work done mostly by women, ranging from infant care, nutrition by breastfeeding and child rearing through to elder care. We should be encouraging paternal primary care and supporting the value of personal familial care in other situations, of sickness, disability and old age.

It is also important to acknowledge the reality that at present (and perhaps for the foreseeable future) the labour market frequently does not offer attractive choices for women. As Sinning (Chapter 8) shows, women especially those with fewer skills (such as technical certification skills), obtain almost no wage or earnings benefit compared to those who only complete school education; while women doing postgraduate study are no better off, from an earnings perspective, than those who complete a degree. Many women never earn enough to repay their Higher Education Contribution Scheme (HECS) debts for higher education. Current policies are failing to harness this pool of skilled and educated labour for the greater good. It is hardly surprising, in this context, that many women even with further education may prefer to work in the family and raise children or rely on flexible, part-time jobs while also doing caring and other non-market work.

The quality of care, of children and elders, matters to Australians. We also need to take account of the research showing that men and women may make different decisions about balancing child care and work that can impact on both children's and parent's wellbeing (Dinh and Racionero, Chapter 7). A system of paid parental leave is an investment in women's workforce participation and in the current and future health of children and mothers, contributing significantly to the economy as a whole. It may need to be made compulsory for men if the current allocation of care responsibilities is to change. If we do not acknowledge this, current and proposed tax and welfare reforms may not shift fundamental discourses around the family, the market, time and happiness, or may change these in ways that are suitable for the market economy but have unexpected, and still-gendered and oppressive, consequences.

4. Security in retirement

A life course approach to gender equity requires us to examine how women are situated at retirement age. Women are more than 60 per cent of age pensioners and have much less in private retirement savings than men. Siobhan Austen and Rhonda Sharp (Chapter 10) demonstrate that a retirement policy that links security in retirement either solely to waged workforce participation over the working life, or requiring dependence on a male partner for support in old age, is detrimental for gender equality. The issue is also referred to in a number of other chapters in this volume. As noted in the subtitle to the Senate Economic References Committee's *Inquiry into Women's Economic Security in Retirement* (2016), 'a husband is not a retirement plan'. A gender budget analysis reveals the benefits and burdens of the current retirement savings, tax and welfare policy that is skewed towards tax concessions for retirement saving in superannuation.

The importance of policy process: 10 points

In gender policy process and institutions, Australia now lags behind other OECD countries, when once it was in the vanguard. A recent OECD report on gender budgeting describes Australia as having no gender budgeting process planned (OECD 2016, Fig. 1, p. 9). The OECD found that, apart from the occasional specific program and the gender indicators produced by the ABS, Australia does not have a systematic process to assess the impact on women and men of taxing, spending or government programs, either before or after the government enacts legislation, appropriates funds or initiates policy. Indeed, Australia was ranked equal last with Slovakia in terms of gender impact analysis requirements (OECD 2014a, p. 185) and it compares poorly with many Asia-Pacific countries on this issue. In the last decade, the federal government has lost data, capability, networks, analytical capacity and commitment to gender impact analysis. However, we argue that there is significant scope for rebuilding and reformulation of gender capacity in the policy process in Australia. We know from long experience that policy *process* both tactical and strategic is critical (Edwards 2001).

1. Context matters

Tying any policy agenda to the government's current priorities is likely to get it a better hearing. We must be politically pragmatic while being cautious about going backwards in key indicators. The economic agenda is always important—such as a government focus on improving productivity and increasing the workforce participation of women. This is a good topic on which to raise the importance of unpaid work as a substitute in time for paid work and the policy implications of that (see Chapter 3 and Chapter 6, this volume). The tax and social policy agenda of ensuring 'fairness' (committed to by Prime Minister Turnbull) is also a valuable hook. However, the government's concern about fiscal constraint also needs to be taken into account and the continued emphasis on expenditure constraint is ominous for gender equality.

In moving from 'what' to 'who' to influence, currently the Minister for Women is also the Minister Assisting the Prime Minister on the public service as well as being Minister for Employment, which has to be a plus. A key role can be played by the Office for Women, in its newly relocated central position in DPMC, to find the right balance between government and the non-government women's sector and the next steps in the government–NGO–researcher relationship.

2. Clarifying the problem

The problem we want government to confront needs to be clarified, articulated well and then owned by the public and ultimately by policymakers. Only once the issue is identified as a policy problem do people then ask, 'what can we do about it?' You cannot get policy change without this first step in the policy process. In the radical child support reforms of the 1980s, it was relatively easy to articulate the problem— why should taxpayers foot the bill just because parents decide not to live together? By way of contrast, in the case of the National Housing Strategy review in the late 1980s, the focus was on the problem of high financial housing stress for low-income renters, which proved too hard at a time when many citizens were faced with very high interest rates on their mortgage payments.

One area of policy in the tax-transfer area that requires attention to clarify the problem is the high wage elasticities faced by women compared to men. Female employment is very likely to fall if disposable income increases only minimally for market wages that women earn, after costs of working and the effect of the tax-transfer system.

3. The power of data and evidence

It is unrealistic to expect 'evidence-based policy' when policy and politics mix. However, evidence-influenced policy can lead to both good policy and good politics. Having identified the problem, ascertaining what data and evidence can be brought to its analysis is critical. In spite of the current anxiety about 'alternative' facts, in this era of 'big data' and the increasing use and open publication of data sources, we suggest that the climate now is more receptive to the use of evidence in the policy process than it was a few years ago. In this context, we emphasise that disaggregation of data by gender is essential for policy, and to assert that while data is all around us, there is an ongoing problem of a lack of generally available, accessible and affordable data on gender impacts of policy. Part of our argument will be the need for government to be accountable for its stated intended outcomes and international commitments and be more transparent to parliament, to citizens and the broader international community. What gets measured counts. The importance of this issue has been observed by the OECD in noting that, 'The routine availability of gender-specific data sets and statistics would greatly facilitate the evidential basis for the identification of gender equality gaps, design of policy interventions, and the evaluation of impacts' (OECD 2016, p. 3).

The ABS and Office for Women are now highlighting more regularly a range of interesting gender statistics about women in the Gender Indicators; this is to be encouraged and should be expanded in future (ABS 2016). The chapters in this volume demonstrate the creative use of data sources to reveal patterns of gender inequality across a range of different government policies.

One important source, as noted above, is the TUS (ABS 2006). We are concerned about the cancellation of the TUS that was scheduled for 2013. The OECD has recently collated time use data from most member states and some additional countries including China, India and South Africa (OECD 2014b). This reveals more recent surveys in some countries (for example, Canada in 2010 and the United States in 2014). The development and roll-out of a new TUS would contribute to our knowledge about the practices of family and social care within Australian households. This is revealed in time choices about child care by women and men and other family members; how this applies for other kinds of care responsibilities; and decisions about sharing work and care a decade later, so as to design and evaluate policy for contemporary Australian families.

Some kinds of data relevant to analysing taxes and transfers are collected on a household basis, which obscures the treatment of women as individuals in families, including the ABS Household Income and Expenditure Surveys on income and wealth. In contrast, income tax data is collected on an individual basis, and research based on tax aggregate and administrative data has potential to tell us more about the impact of tax systems on women. This resource is the basis for the research by Stewart, Voitchovsky and Wilkins (in Chapter 9) on top incomes of women.

When the environment is receptive, evidence can be powerful both in clarifying a problem and in moving toward a solution. But, again, how the data and evidence is communicated and to which audience matters. Knowledge brokers may be needed to translate to busy policymakers what can otherwise be dense academic research (see Bammer 2010). We have identified some important areas for further policy-related research in this collection. One of these relates to wage and child care elasticities by age, income and education level as well as gender (see various contributors in this volume; and Productivity Commission 2015). Although the previous government established a joint Treasury–Department of Social Services (DSS) working party on tax-transfer system interactions, this task seems to have been sidelined and should be reinvigorated.

4. Value of international comparisons

Our agenda can also be tied to Australia's international commitments— G20, Convention on the Elimination of All Forms of Discrimination Against Women (CEDAW) and Sustainable Development goals. As discussed by Hodgson and Sadiq (Chapter 4) and Lahey (Chapter 2), Australia has international obligations, in particular about workforce participation and children, in the G20 and OECD. The centrality of gender equality including measurement and impact analysis in the United Nations Sustainable Development goals, and the growing interest in gender analysis in countries around the world, provides us with an important lever for activity. There is a role for international comparisons with approaches of other countries more broadly on gender analysis, both for ourselves in this country and as policy leaders internationally. Related is the value of evidence about better practice, especially overseas comparisons. These were particularly valuable in research on possible child support reform (see, for example, Edwards 2001). There is substantial value in comparisons, but in the end it must be recognised that Australia's policy and budget process is highly path dependent.

The concept of gender budgeting is being reinvigorated internationally— in the OECD, International Monetary Fund (IMF) and in recent developments in country governments and non-government activity. In Canada, the federal government included gender analysis in the core budget documentation for the first time in 2017 (Government of Canada 2017), incorporating the gender equality indicators and goals as part of a broader statement of better economic policy and fairness to build a stronger Canadian middle class. Such an approach with a clear gender element would likely resonate in Australia. There has also been significant work by budget analysts such as the UK and Scottish Women's Budget Groups, working within and outside government. Austen and Sharp in Chapter 10 demonstrate the value of a gender impact analysis of retirement policy, examining the policy goal of adequacy of retirement incomes for women. The OECD points to various gender budgeting approaches in different countries including *ex ante* analysis of individual budget measures to identify the impact on gender equality; bringing a gender perspective to performance budgeting of government departments; to resource allocation and in incidence analysis of benefits and burdens. An *ex post* gender impact assessment, or gender baseline analysis or audit of the budget is also applied in some countries (OECD 2016, pp. 7–8).

5. Importance of dialogue

Dialogue is critical, including between policymakers and researchers; between policymakers and those who deliver services; and between policymakers and civil society, researchers and politicians. It is critical for academic researchers to understand the importance of dialogue for getting ideas across—for example, round tables, tailored to issues of concern to the government of the day, rather than just an article, a chapter or a book. The empirical research presented in this book is an important input to public policy. However, busy policymakers are more likely to 'google' to gain information than read what researchers have to say. There is a real conflict here for academic researchers with the incentive structures in universities that emphasise publications in quality journals, but the evidence is very clear on what is needed to best gain research impact and it is not the written word as much as dialogue and exchange of information based on trusted networks that work (e.g. see Nutley et al. 2007; Edwards 2010; Head 2013).

The Office for Women is in an excellent position to reinvigorate its coordinating role across government and with non-government organisations and academics. Through linking research, policy and practice, the Office for Women can lead in developing discussion about potential policies to build women's' capabilities, helping decision-makers meet such challenges. It will be necessary to reintroduce the expertise and training mechanisms for integrating gender analysis across government departments. This calls for combining effective consultation and evidence-based policies from inside government, given especially the inadequacy of funding, resources and access to data of external volunteer organisations such as NFAW.

6. Power of networks and relationships

Who you know and in what context can lead to effective relationships when that is needed across the research, policy and political divides. Networks, relationships and strategic cross-sector collaboration are vital. Engagement with external activists such as the WEL taught the early femocrats the power of women's networks that could later be used to advantage both inside and outside of government. It meant, for example, when dealing with sensitive child support issues, ideas and possible policies could be tested among networks knowing that confidence would be respected. The value of networks and past working relationships was also critical when Bruce Chapman and Meredith Edwards (Keating 1994) advised on policies for the long-term unemployed in the 1990s, having previously worked on developing HECS. A trusting relationship helped to cut the time that was needed to convince those in influential policy positions of desired employment policy options.

7. Strategic cross-sector collaborations

Collaborating to form alliances with others from inside government to the outside and vice versa is now the main game if any complex policy issue is to be resolved. But a strategic approach is needed: about why collaboration is needed, when to do it, with whom and how. It may mean upfront informal bilateral discussions followed by broader collaborations depending on the sensitivity and complexity of the issue. Increasingly as governments, in the interests of short-term politics, avoid good policy and policy processes for the longer term on key concerns of the public (such as housing issues), alliance of non-government players across business, union and relevant not-for-profit organisations may force governments to act.

In terms of the agenda in this volume, there is a place not just for women's groups inside and outside of government (such as the NFAW, National Council of Women in Australia, UN Women, YWCA, the Workplace Gender Equality Agency, female politicians) but also for others such as the Academy of Social Sciences Australia, the Australian Human Rights Commission, the ABS, National Centre for Social and Economic Modelling (NATSEM) at the University of Canberra, and the ANU Tax and Transfer Policy Institute and Centre for Social Research and Methods. Depending on purpose and timing, at a certain stage we could take the collaboration wider; for example, to a parliamentary committee to gain political buy-in or to a Fairfax/*Australian*-type public forum. We might consider forming an independent unit to assess and monitor women's initiatives (such as the Women's Budget Group in the UK).

8. Be politically pragmatic

The scale and targets of gender analysis should be tailored to the political environment. The NFAW in its 2015 Gender Lens on the Budget recommended that '[a]ll budget measures should contain gender equity objectives and indicators and performance measures disaggregated by sex' (NFAW 2015). While not losing sight of this longer-term goal, it is important to go for the possible; to nudge forward to the ideal while ensuring that our incremental steps do not conflict with that ideal. Valuable research papers on gender impact analysis are available, including Sharp and Broomhill (2013), and that is part of our armoury, while the ALP in Opposition has committed to restoring annual Women's Budget Statements if returned to government. Today, we need to start in a more focused manner until we can gather a momentum around why gender impact analysis is such an essential part of developing good policy and delivering good policy outcomes as well as gender equality.

9. Beware of going backwards

We do not need to dwell on the danger of going backwards. Many examples have been given of this in this volume and at the workshop that inspired it. These include shifting from universality to means testing of family allowances and the ongoing challenge of fiscal austerity policies as explained by Kathleen Lahey in Chapter 2; the more than 10-year gap since the last ABS TUS; the improved but still-limited and cost-constrained policies for the financing and length of paid parental leave, child care and early childhood education; and the gender wage gap. History is important but its gains are easily lost in this age of high job turnovers of government personnel. It is valuable to be reminded by Marian Sawer and others about what has been and can be again.

10. Starting point: Institutions to support collaboration

We propose building institutions to support collaboration on gender-equal policy by relevant parties across government, research and non-government spheres. We could contribute to mapping the data gaps if we want to engage in gender budgeting and more broadly gender impact assessments, both *ex ante* and *ex post* in relation to priority policy issues, and to determine the role that various organisational participants might play to assist in meeting those gaps and in the needed gender analysis. A possibility could be establishment of an advisory roundtable coordinated by the Office for Women, including representatives from the key women's organisations and broader organisations identified in Section 7, together with government participants from DPMC, Treasury, ABS, Australian Institute for Health and Welfare, and the Department of Social Services. Informal conversations, first with a few inside the bureaucracy to gauge what is possible and who could most usefully initiate the dialogue, followed by a roundtable using the Chatham House rule to get priorities for action and a commitment to that action.

Conclusion

The goals of good gender analysis of budgets and public policy are also goals of good modern budget governance in general: 'the need for clear, multi-dimensional budgetary impact analyses, and the need for evaluation frameworks that feed directly into the policy and budget cycle' (OECD 2016, p. 4). A gender lens is critical to produce gender-equal policy. The persistent gender inequalities in Australia across the broad policy areas of taxation, welfare, work, education, child care and retirement require an explicit focus on gender in impact analysis and policy design. This requires critical analysis both within and outside government, both *ex ante* and *ex post* budget decisions, building and using data and evidence in policy design and evaluation and including academic and civil society contributions throughout the process.

If it is to be successful, government policy aimed at women's economic empowerment requires data, analysis and clever policy design across all the areas of tax and transfers, wage equity, superannuation and financial literacy, child care and paid parental leave, education, flexible work places and putting women in non-traditional roles (Office for Women 2016). A gender-equal policy will also require governments to pay attention to the work and caring roles of men as well as women, so as to build a flexible approach to work, care and education over the life course of all individuals and their families. More fundamentally, as the nature of work changes and economic security for all becomes an increasing challenge, a policy that supports gender equality over the life course can show the way for a new approach to public and private provision that builds economic empowerment for all.

We need to renew Australia's commitment to best practice with respect to gender impact analysis that comes early in the policy process, not after the fact. A Women's Budget Statement should be included with the budget. This could be comprehensive, covering all spending and taxing and containing detailed modelling about the distributional, social and economic impact of government policy; however, even the earliest such Statements in the 1980s did not achieve this comprehensive goal. A more focused approach seems better for today's times, for example targeting a goal that is a current focus of government policy (such as women's economic empowerment) and analysing all aspects of government taxes, spending and programs to understand the impact on that policy goal; or selecting major indicators on which to focus.

Governments of different political persuasions today appear to recognise the importance of key investments in human capital including child care (but not, yet, a full right to early childhood education); parental leave; equal wage policy; the sharing of public responsibility for disability and elder care; and the need for a secure retirement for women. This is promising, but there is a continued perception that care is a 'women's issue'. This framing of the issue is not merely rhetorical. It is enacted in real fiscal constraints and budgetary limits reflecting the ongoing refusal of the government to share the cost of care through the significant tools at its disposal in the tax-transfer system. This raises questions about the commitment to gender equality, and it also seems to indicate a narrow and short-term view of the fiscal cost of addressing inequality and the broader economic and social benefits of so doing. Re-engaging gender analysis, evaluation and research insights in policy processes will improve outcomes on this issue and others, for women and Australian society as a whole. As indicated in the 10 policy principles and issues set out above, we need to be both visionary and pragmatic; take a systemic view and strategically focus on specific issues to deliver real policy change.

References

ABS (Australian Bureau of Statistics). 2006. *How Australians Use Their Time—2006*. Publication 4153.0. Available at: www.abs.gov.au/ausstats/abs@.nsf/mf/4153.0

ABS. 2016. *Gender Indicators, Australia—August 2016*. Publication 4125.0. Available at: www.abs.gov.au/ausstats/abs@.nsf/mf/4125.0

Atkinson, Tony and Andrew Leigh. 2007. 'The Distribution of Top Incomes in Australia', *Economic Record*, 83(262): 247–261. doi.org/10.1111/j.1475-4932.2007.00412.x

Bacchi, Carol and Joan Eveline (eds). 2010. *Mainstreaming Politics: Gendering practices and feminist theory*. Adelaide: University of Adelaide Press. Available at: www.adelaide.edu.au/press/titles/mainstreaming/Mainstreaming-Ebook-final.pdf

Baird, Marian, Michele Ford and Elizabeth Hill (eds). 2017. *Women, Work and Care in the Asia-pacific*. Routledge: London and New York. Kindle Edition.

Bammer, Gabriele (ed). 2010. *Bridging the 'know-do' gap: knowledge brokering to improve child well-being*. ANU E Press: Canberra.

Bishop, Julie. 2006. 'Gender Budget Analysis: Australia's Commitment to Gender Equality', *The Parliamentarian* 2006/Issue Three, pp. 201–204. Canberra: Commonwealth Parliamentary Association. Available at: www.cpahq.org/cpahq/cpadocs/Australia%20committment%20to%20gender%20equality.pdf

Cash, Michaelia. 2014. *Investing in Gender Equality at the G20 Leaders Summit.* Ministerial Speech, 24 September. Available at: ministers.dpmc.gov.au/cash/2014/investing-gender-equality-g20-leaders-summit

Cash, Michaelia. 2017. *Delivering Opportunities and Support for Australian Women.* Media Release. Available at: ministers.dpmc.gov.au/cash/2017/delivering-opportunities-and-support-australian-women. Media Background Brief. Available at: www.dpmc.gov.au/sites/default/files/files/pmc/Accountability%20and%20reporting%20section/2017-18-budget-delivering-for-australian-women.pdf

Council of Europe. 2009. *Gender budgeting: Practical implementation. Handbook.* Council of Europe, Directorate General of Human Rights and Legal Affairs.

Dinh Huong, Lyndall Strazdins and Jennifer Welsh. 2017. 'Hour-glass ceilings: Work-hour thresholds, gendered health inequities'. *Social Science & Medicine* 176: 42–51. doi.org/10.1016/j.socscimed.2017.01.024

Dunning, Polly. 2017. 'When Having Separate Bank Accounts is the Opposite of Independence'. *Sydney Morning Herald*, 21 March. Available at: www.smh.com.au/lifestyle/life-and-relationships/when-having-separate-bank-accounts-is-the-opposite-of-independence-20170320-gv26o5.html

Edwards, Meredith. 1981. *Financial Arrangements within Families.* Canberra: National Women's Advisory Council.

Edwards, Meredith. 2001. *Social Policy, Public Policy: From problem to practice.* Sydney: Allen & Unwin.

Edwards, Meredith. 2010. 'In Search of Useful Research: Demand and supply challenges for policy makers'. *Public Administration Today*, v. 24 October–December.

Eisenstein, Hester. 1996. *Inside Agitators: Australian Femocrats and the State.* Philadelphia: Temple University Press.

Government of Canada. 2017. 'Equal Opportunity: Budget 2017's Gender Impact Statement'. In *Budget 2017–18.* Available at: www.budget.gc.ca/2017/docs/plan/chap-05-en.html

Goward, Pru. 2004. 'Now everyone can focus on women'. *The Age*, 30 October.

Head, Brian. 2013. *How do government agencies use evidence?* Report for National Board of Health and Welfare, Stockholm, Sweden.

Henry, Ken et al. 2009. *Review of Australia's Future Tax System: Report to the Treasurer.* Australia's Future Tax System Review Panel (the 'Henry Review'). Available at: taxreview.treasury.gov.au

Heron, Alexandra, Rae Cooper and Gabrielle Meagher. 2017. 'Australia: The care challenge'. In Marian Baird, Michele Ford and Elizabeth Hill (eds), *Women, Work and Care in the Asia-Pacific*, pp. 167–181. Routledge: London and New York. Kindle Edition.

Keating, P.J. 1994. *Working Nation: Policies and programs.* White paper on employment and growth, presented 4 May. Canberra: Australian Government Publishing Service.

NFAW (National Foundation for Australian Women). 2015. *A Gender Lens—Budget 2015–16.* NFAW. Available at: www.nfaw.org

NFAW (National Foundation for Australian Women). 2017. *A Gender Lens—Budget 2017–18.* NFAW. Available at: www.nfaw.org/gender-lens-on-the-budget/

Nutley, Sandra, Isabel Walter and Huw T.O. Davies. 2007. *Using Evidence: how research can inform public services.* University of Bristol: Policy Press.

OECD (Organisation for Economic Cooperation and Development). 2014a. *Women, Government and Policy Making in OECD Countries.* Paris: OECD Publishing.

OECD. 2014b. *Balancing Paid Work, Unpaid Work and Leisure.* Available at: www.oecd.org/gender/data/balancingpaidworkunpaidworkandleisure.htm

OECD. 2016. *Gender Budgeting in OECD Countries.* Public Governance and Territorial Development Directorate, 37th Annual Meeting of OECD Senior Budget Officials, Stockholm, 9–10 June.

Office for Women. 2006. *Women '06: 2006–07 Budget Information.* Canberra: Office for Women.

Office for Women. 2016. *Women's Economic Security.* Canberra: Department of the Prime Minister and Cabinet. Available at: www. dpmc.gov.au/office-women/economic-security

Productivity Commission. 2015. *Childcare and Early Childhood Learning Final Report.* Available at: www.pc.gov.au/inquiries/completed/child care#report

Sawer, Marian. 1990. *Sisters in Suits: Women and Public Policy in Australia.* Sydney: Allen & Unwin.

Senate Economic References Committee. 2016. *Inquiry into Women's Economic Security in Retirement.* Canberra: Commonwealth of Australia.

Sharp, Rhonda and Ray Broomhill. 2013. *A Case Study of Gender Responsive Budgeting in Australia.* Research Report: The Commonwealth Secretariat. Available at: www.asiapacificgender.org/ financing-accountability-partnership/case-study-gender-responsive-budgeting-australia

Treasury. 1985. *Reform of the Australian Tax System: Draft White Paper.* Australian Government: Canberra.

Treasury. 2017. *Budget 2017–18.* Australian Government: Canberra. Available at: www.budget.gov.au

Walby, Sylvia. 2005. 'Gender Mainstreaming: Productive Tensions in Theory and Practice'. *Social Politics: International Studies in Gender, State and Society* 12(3): 321–343. doi.org/10.1093/sp/jxi018

Watson, Sophie (ed.). 1990. *Playing the State: Australian Feminist Interventions.* London: Verso.

Whiteford, Peter. 2016. *Should We Be Worried About Zero Net Taxpayers?* TTPI Policy Brief 5/2016. Available at: taxpolicy.crawford. anu.edu.au/publication/9084/should-we-be-worried-about-zero-net-taxpayers

Index

Note: Page numbers in italics indicate information contained in tables, graphics or other illustrative material.

www.ingramcontent.com/pod-product-compliance
Lightning Source LLC
Chambersburg PA
CBHW040149270326
41929CB00032B/3388